TANDY'S MONEY MACHINE

How Charles Tandy Built Radio Shack Into the
World's Largest Electronics Chain

By Irvin Farman

THE MOBIUM PRESS/Chicago 1992

ISBN 0-916371-12-3   92-62631

*To the memory of
Charles David Tandy
who made it all happen*

"He was a man, take him for all in all, I shall not look upon his like again."

—Hamlet

Contents

Acknowledgments

This book could not have been written without the help of a great many people. I am especially grateful to:

John V. Roach, who opened the Tandy archives to my research and challenged me to portray the "real" Charles Tandy, "So that people who didn't know him can learn what he was really like."

Herschel Winn, who helped me navigate many historical and legal reefs and shoals.

Bill Michero, John Wilson, Ken Gregson, Jesse Upchurch, founts of knowledge dating back to the Hinckley-Tandy Leather Company days.

Lew Kornfeld, Bernie Appel and Dave Beckerman, for their Radio Shack lore.

Phil North, for sharing his half-century of memories of Charles Tandy.

Kay Dickson Farman, for her encouragement, support and critical eye.

My thanks also go to the persons listed below for the recollections and insights they so generously provided:

Rachel Barber, Ed Bass, Perry R. Bass, Tony Bernabei, Bill Brooks, Dr. Bobby Brown, William L. Brown, Jim Buxton, Joyce Cantey, H.E. (Eddie) Chiles, Dave Christopher, Bill Collins, William C. Conner, Milton Deutschmann, Pam Buckalew Esquivel, Mary Frank, Bayard H. Friedman, William M. Fuller, Bill Garber, Jenkins Garrett, James S. Garvey, Jack Greenman, Alex Hamilton, Luther Henderson, Leland Hodges, Elton Hyder, Jr., John Justin, Robert E. Keto, Paul Leonard, Bob Leonard, Janet Lesok, Bob Lowdon, Joe W. Lydick, Paul Mason, John McDaniel, W.A. (Tex) Moncrief, Jr., Clif Overcash, Matilda Peeler, J. Roby Penn, Connie Powell, Ann Quinn, Lloyd Redd, Charles Ringler, Billy Roland, Harlan Swain, Joe A. Tilley, Rice M. Tilley, Jr.,

Bill Vance, Hazel Vernon, Eunice West, Delores Whitney, Jim Wright, Elaine Yamagata, and Tadashi Yamagata.

I would also like to express my appreciation to the following individuals who were particularly helpful in many different ways in making this undertaking possible:

Lynne Anderson, Alma Arterburn, Lou Ann Blaylock, Bettye Elliston, Lee Elsesser, Jana Freundlich, Rhonda D. Graves, Pete Griffin, Emily A. Griffith, Lydia H. Hays, Ann Hill, Duane Hughes, Dr. E. Ross Kyger, Jr., Donna E. Levy, and Barbara Salavarria.

Irvin S. Farman
Oct. 1, 1992
Fort Worth, Texas

TANDY'S MONEY MACHINE

Prologue

It was a lovely fall afternoon in New York, the kind of day meant for walking along Park Avenue, enjoying the bright sunshine, the parade of fashionably-dressed women strolling by, and the gentle breeze ruffling the flags in front of the Waldorf-Astoria.

But for the group of men gathered in a smoke-filled suite inside the hotel, there was no time for such frivolous pursuits. That Friday afternoon, November 15, 1963, the seven members of the board of directors of Tandy Corporation were meeting in the suite of their chairman, Charles D. Tandy, and things were getting more than a little strained.

Some seven months earlier, Tandy had made a deal to take over management of Radio Shack Corporation, a Boston-based chain of nine electronic stores that was teetering on the edge of bankruptcy. For a mere $300,000, which represented a subordinated participation in a loan to Radio Shack by the First National Bank of Boston, Tandy secured an option to buy the controlling interest in Radio Shack.

Tandy had gone into the Radio Shack deal with his eyes wide open. He perceived Radio Shack to be a victim of poor management and a promising turnaround opportunity. More importantly, he saw a vehicle to broaden the scope of Tandy Corporation by entering a dynamic, emerging industry with great potential. Consumer electronics, Tandy was convinced, was the wave of the future. Every household in America was a potential Radio Shack customer. This was in stark contrast to Tandy Corporation, whose primary business was leather goods and leathercrafts. Although Tandy Corporation was making money and growing, Charles Tandy knew that leather and leathercrafts, with their limited scope, would never propel him to where his insatiable appetite for achievement, recognition, and reward was driving him.

And, besides, he was getting control of Radio Shack for a pittance.

1

When Tandy initially presented the Radio Shack deal to his fellow board members in early April of 1963, they rubber-stamped their approval, as was their wont, even though some of the directors had misgivings over the venture. Now, at the November meeting at the Waldorf, Tandy was asking the board to authorize a major commitment of resources to reorganize Radio Shack and to begin building a nationwide chain of Radio Shack stores.

Radio Shack had lost $4.5 million the year before. It owed $7 million to a bank and an insurance company and had a negative net worth of $2.5 million. But Charles Tandy was convinced he could turn things around, that he could increase Radio Shack's modest gross margins to the highly profitable levels he attained at Tandy Leather Company by revamping the way Radio Shack did business. Give him a little time, he said, and he would remake Radio Shack into a big winner.

The board members, all long-time associates of Tandy's, had heard that song before. Some of them, like James L. West, the president of Tandy Corporation, whose tenure with the company dated back to its early days as a family-run shoe-findings business, felt that their primary mission was to try to keep a rein on their ebullient board chairman.

Jim West had watched Charles Tandy grow up, had helped teach him the leather business. Now West led the assault on the Radio Shack acquisition as the board meeting convened in Tandy's suite at the Waldorf that November afternoon in 1963.

"Are you crazy?" West asked Tandy.

"Why would you take on this kind of problem, a bankrupt situation, that we don't know anything about, and in Boston, Massachusetts, yet, where we got burned once before? Who needs to bail out a bank and an insurance company?"

Tandy, ever-present cigar in hand, stood stolidly in front of the fireplace in the sitting room of the suite, fighting to keep his emotions under control. His tall, heavy-set presence dominated the room.

Other board members interjected their concerns.

Didn't Tandy realize that in the past year he had acquired Cost Plus, an import store operation, that was going to need large infusions of money? Cost Plus and Radio Shack would be competing for the hard-earned profits generated by the Tandy Leather Company, the corporation's cash cow. Could they afford to build two national retail store chains simultaneously?

But, perhaps most of all, they were worried, they told Tandy, that he was spreading himself too thin by personally trying to run Radio Shack, Tandy Leather Company, and Tandy Corporation all at the same time.

Prior to the board meeting, a majority of the directors had come up with the idea that if Tandy persisted in pushing ahead with Radio Shack, he should relinquish the reins of Tandy Corporation and Tandy Leather Company for a limited period, say a year or two, and devote himself exclusively to his pet project. Their choice of a temporary successor to Tandy as board chairman was Carl C. Welhausen, the head of the Tex Tan Welhausen Division and a corporate vice president and member of the Tandy board.

The chore of presenting the proposal to Tandy was handed to Luther A. Henderson, vice president and treasurer of Tandy Corporation, member of the board, and a close friend of Tandy's since their Sunday School days at Broadway Baptist Church in Fort Worth.

Even though the proposal was not Henderson's idea, nor did he particularly favor the idea, he carried out his mission like a good soldier. He met Tandy for breakfast in his Waldorf suite on the morning of November 15.

All through the bacon and eggs, Henderson worked up his courage, anticipating what Tandy's response would be. Over the final cups of coffee, he could stall no longer.

"The board has asked me to present an idea to you," Henderson began, groping for the right words. "The directors think it would be beneficial if you had more time to give to Radio Shack without worrying about the rest of the company, say for a year or two, until you've had time to put Radio Shack back on its feet..."

He never got to finish what he was trying to say, as Tandy interrupted him with a string of expletives that left no doubt as to how he felt about Henderson's overture.

"What's this crap you're trying to hand me?" Tandy demanded.

"He was so mad, he nearly threw me out of the suite," Henderson recalled. "It placed our entire relationship in jeopardy. Eventually, he calmed down when he realized I was just doing the board's bidding and hadn't been conspiring against him. But he told me in no uncertain terms where the board could go."

When the board meeting convened at 2 o'clock that afternoon, Tandy's combative juices were flowing.

He opened the meeting with the statement, "The Radio Shack acquisition is a good deal for Tandy Corporation."

Then he added, with a sharp glance at Henderson who was seated on a sofa across from the fireplace, "I am perfectly capable of giving Radio Shack the attention it needs and keeping the rest of the company running."

The directors remained unconvinced. Led by Jim West, they voiced their doubts, giving Tandy every indication they were prepared to reject his request for increasing the company's stake in Radio Shack. This, in Tandy's mind, was tantamount to torpedoing the entire deal.

"Now, look, everyone of you has been doing what he has wanted to be doing. One of you has been handling the accounting, and another has been handling this or that," Tandy stated. "At this time, I am making my point clear. We are going to do what I want to do.

"If I don't get an affirmative vote on this, then I will sell every share of stock I own in the corporation and I will, personally, take this on my own hook."

Tandy then strode out of the room.

The board sat there, too stunned to do anything for a few moments, then began considering its options.

Tandy might be bluffing, but the board members were not of a mind to call him and find out.

He was, after all, the corporation's largest stockholder and the dynamic force behind its solid growth. He had led the fight to regain control of the Tandy Leather Company after a brush with disaster only a few years earlier. Tandy Corporation was now a highly profitable going concern, with more than 170 leather and leathercrafts stores in the United States and Canada and sales of more than $20 million.

With most of their individual net worths tied up in Tandy stock, the idea of going it alone without Tandy at the helm was simply not a viable option to the directors.

"There were a few minutes of muddling, fumbling and grumbling," Bill Michero, an eyewitness to the confrontation, related, "and then it was grudgingly decided to give Charles everything he wanted."

Michero, the corporate secretary, was dispatched to escort Tandy back into the room.

Exuding clouds of cigar smoke in his wake, Tandy returned from the corridor outside the suite where he'd been waiting.

Sir Laurence Olivier never made a better entrance.

"Okay, you bastards," he said with a grin as wide as the map of Texas, "now that you know who's running this show, let's go get 'em."

Recalled Henderson, "We owed it to him to support him. So we approved the deal on his terms. And it worked."

That sentence may be one of the classic understatements of all time.

From that November afternoon in 1963 to the day, 15 years later, on November 4, 1978, when he died at the age of 60, Charles Tandy saw his dream of a national chain of Radio Shacks come true.

Where he once had talked of hundreds of stores and $100 million in sales, he lived to see nearly 7,000 Radio Shack outlets across the landscape of America and sales of more than $1 billion.

Today, Tandy Corporation, the company he built virtually from scratch and to which he devoted his life, has grown into a multi-faceted, multi-billion dollar enterprise. Its Radio Shack chain is the largest electronics retailer in the world.

The day after his death, an editorial in the *Fort Worth Star-Telegram* eulogized Charles Tandy as a builder and as a dreamer:

"His is a story of the American dream, of a man rising as high as his desire and his ability and his enterprise will take him.

"Tandy wanted to succeed and he worked long and hard to achieve success. It was a dizzy, roller-coaster trip that paid off in a billion dollar business..."

This is the story of the man and the trip.

Chapter 1
Start on a Shoe String

On a sultry August day in 1925, a bedraggled young man arrived at the Texas & Pacific Passenger Station in Fort Worth after an all-night train ride from Tennessee. He carried his worldly possessions in a cardboard suitcase. In his pants pocket was $1.85, all that remained from the $25 grubstake his father had given him to finance his way to Texas. The young man's name was Charlie Hillard and he had come to Fort Worth because he had a job waiting for him there on a used car lot owned by his mother's nephew, J.B. Jordan.

The 19-year-old Hillard had grown up on his father's farm in Oakfield, Tennessee, and had graduated from high school that summer. His father had offered to send him to Vanderbilt University in Nashville, but Charlie had other ideas.

"Dad," he told his father, "if you'll stake me to $25, I'd like to go to Texas and get a job."

Now, disembarking from the long train ride, suitcase in hand, Hillard began walking north along the sun-baked streets of downtown Fort Worth towards Jordan's used car business at 211 Commerce Street near the Tarrant County Courthouse. Fort Worth was in the midst of an epidemic of oil fever at the time, with fortunes being made and lost daily. Everywhere, there were signs of construction, with new buildings poking their heads skyward. Hillard took in the scene on his long, sweaty walk of some 15 blocks from the depot to Jordan's lot, looking into the shops, restaurants, and bars along his route, observing the people strolling by and ogling the cars rolling past him on the hot-topped streets—sedate sedans, jazzy roadsters, and sporty touring cars.

More than 65 years later, Hillard, by then the owner of one of Fort Worth's most successful automobile dealerships, recalled his walk in the sun and his arrival at Jordan's office.

"There was a guy in there, a slender, well-dressed man in his mid-30s, smoking a cigar. He and Jordan were visiting when I got there, and he listened in on our conversation. After learning that I had just arrived in town to go to work for Jordan, the man asked me where I was going to live. I told him I didn't have the slightest idea. He told me he knew a place that was clean and reasonable. So I got into his car and he drove me to the new YMCA building that had just opened in downtown Fort Worth. He took me inside and told the clerk I needed a room. Then he took $3 out of his pocket and put it down on the counter and said, 'I want to pay this boy's rent for two weeks.' The man was Dave Tandy, Charles Tandy's father."

Dave L. Tandy was a partner in a struggling shoe-findings business located in a seedy end of downtown Fort Worth. That business, the Hinckley-Tandy Leather Company, would become the forerunner of today's Tandy Corporation. The driving force behind its metamorphosis from a two-man operation selling soles and shoelaces to shoe repair shops into a global consumer electronics retailing giant would be Dave Tandy's son, Charles David Tandy.

In 1925, Dave Tandy was 36 years old and had been in the shoe-findings business in Fort Worth since 1919. "Shoe-findings" was the term given to businesses that supplied shoe repair shops with leather soles, rubber and leather heels, shoe laces, shoe polish, and other items. It stemmed from colonial days, when firms called "shoe-finders" provided the supplies for itinerant custom boot and shoemakers.

Dave Tandy and his partner, Norton Hinckley, made a good pair, the feisty, cigar-smoking Tandy, an outgoing, fast-talking extrovert who loved to sell, and the stolid, conservative Hinckley, who knew the merchandise and liked to buy. Standing about 5-8 and never weighing more than 150 pounds, Dave Tandy, in his later years, with his wire-rimmed glasses, bow ties and double-breasted suits, would become a dead-ringer for President Harry Truman.

Early on, Hinckley and Tandy found their respective niches in the business, with Tandy as "Mr. Outside" and Hinckley as "Mr. Inside." The two had become friends while working together in the shoe-findings department of Padgett Brothers, a major Dallas leather house. Hinckley, a Dallas native six years older than Tandy, had worked his way up to manager of the shoe-findings department after a number of years as a traveling salesman calling on shoe repair shops.

Dave Tandy's father, A.N. Tandy, was a successful farmer, shipping his vegetables in crates that featured a big T trademark. Dave Tandy grew up on his father's farm in Brownsville in the Rio Grande Valley, hating the long hours and backbreaking work. He wasted no time leaving the farm after graduating from high school, and eventually wound up in Temple, a central Texas town between Waco and Austin, where he landed a job as a salesman in a shoe store. One day he sold a pair of shoes to a local girl, Carmen McClain. It was love at first sight. They were married in Temple on July 8, 1914.

"How could I help falling in love with Carmen?" Dave recalled in a newspaper interview on their 50th wedding anniversary. "She was the prettiest girl I ever did see."

Dave was earning 20 cents an hour and working a 70-hour week when he got married. There was no income tax. "When the income tax went into effect in 1917, we screamed that the government was robbing us," he often recalled. "The tax was 1 percent."

Dave and Carmen had just returned from their honeymoon in Galveston when disaster struck. The shoe store where he was working went out of business. Times were tough in Temple and job opportunities nonexistent. Dave decided to try his luck in Dallas. There, he learned of an opening for a salesman in the shoe-findings department of Padgett Brothers. Much as he disliked the thought of going on the road, he applied for the job and was hired. His immediate supervisor was Norton Hinckley.

Tandy sold shoe-findings on the road for Padgett until the United States entered World War I in 1917. When his brothers, Cleve and Clyde, were drafted, he responded to his father's call and returned to the family farm as their wartime replacement. He was exempt from military service because by now he was the father of 2-year-old daughter, Margueritte. A second child, a boy, would be born on May 15, 1918, while Dave and Carmen were still living on the family farm in Brownsville. He would be named Charles David.

Dave remained working for his father until his brothers came home from the war. When the Armistice was signed on November 11, 1918, Dave began looking forward to leaving the farm and getting back into the leather business.

His hopes were answered through a fortuitous encounter with Norton Hinckley on a street in Dallas in early 1919. Dave was in Dallas trying to collect some overdue vegetable accounts for his father when he ran into Hinckley. The two hadn't seen each other in nearly two years and had a lot of catching up to do. Over a cup of coffee in a nearby cafe, Tandy told Hinckley about his desire to get back into the leather business and asked about his chances of returning to his job at Padgett Brothers.

Hinckley had another idea. He wanted to go into business for himself. Now he asked Tandy if he'd be interested in joining him. He had been looking into the matter for some time and he believed that Fort Worth was the place to locate. There were no shoe-findings houses there, whereas Dallas already had five or six. Tandy was intrigued.

"How much will it take?" he asked.

"How much have you got?" Hinckley answered.

"I've got $5,000 in the bank," Tandy informed his partner-to-be.

Dave had learned the importance of saving money from his father, who had taught him as a boy to start putting 50 cents a week in the bank. He had followed his father's advice and had, over the years, diligently put away 10 percent of everything he made.

"I'll match your $5,000," Hinckley said. "With $10,000, we'll have enough to get started."

They found an affordable store with a glass front in a one-story brick building at 1607 Houston Street on the lower end of downtown Fort Worth. The shop contained about 2,500 square feet of floor space that included a small office in the rear. In spite of the high hopes of the two fledgling entrepreneurs, the Hinckley-Tandy Leather Company got off to an inauspicious start.

"They had a fire after only six months in business that nearly finished them," Norton Hinckley's son, Douglas N. Hinckley of Dallas, reported. "Starting up the new business was a strain. They were always strapped for cash."

Fort Worth, when Hinckley and Tandy set up shop in 1919, was in the midst of a postwar boom. Already known as a "cowtown" because of the many livestock and meatpacking businesses, Fort Worth was now experiencing another major boost to its economy: oil. In 1911, cowboys on the W.T. Waggoner Ranch near Wichita Falls struck oil while drilling a water well. Fort Worth was the nearest major city to the new oil field, and by 1912 two oil refineries had been built there. In 1917, wildcatters operating out of Fort Worth hit the jackpot with the discovery of a vast new oil field at Ranger. A year later, rich oil deposits were found at Desdemona and Burkburnett.

Fort Worth became a major center of the emerging petroleum industry. Thousands of people jammed into the city. New companies were born daily. By 1919, eight refineries were operating there and producing more than 50,000 barrels of oil per day. The tax value of property in the city more than doubled, surpassing $100 million and the population topped 100,000 for the first time. There were 12 banks in town with total deposits of more than $80 million and a downtown building boom that would continue through the 1920s.

Other factors also contributed to Fort Worth's growth. A major military installation, Camp Bowie, was built in Fort Worth, and became the home of the storied 36th Division that performed so valiantly in France. Three military airfields were located in and around the city. Norton Hinckley and Dave Tandy made the most of the atmosphere. At first they divided up their business responsibilities. Hinckley called on shoe repair shops in Fort Worth and Tandy worked the neighboring cities and towns. As the business grew, they began hiring salesmen and both became full-time managers; Tandy concentrating on sales and Hinckley on buying.

"They were a good pair. They were congenial," Doug Hinckley recalled. "Dave was a talker, always with a cigar in his mouth. Dad was a quiet person."

In 1923, with the business now on a firmer footing, Hinckley-Tandy Leather Company moved to a new location in larger quarters in a three-story, turn-of-the-century building at 1600 Throckmorton Street, at the southwest corner of 15th Street. It was only a block away from the original site and was still in the heart of one of the tougher parts of town, only a few blocks away from an area that had been known as "Hell's Half Acre" during the great cattle drives of the 1870s and '80s. Fort Worth then had been the last stopping-off point on the Chisholm Trail, where cowboys could wet their whistles and enjoy some female companionship before driving their herds of Longhorns across the Red River into Indian Territory on the way to Dodge City and the other Kansas railheads.

"It was tough country," recalled Archie Wayman, who had worked for the Cook Paint & Varnish Company store at 229 West 15th Street in the mid-1920s. "You didn't go down there much after dark. The railroad tracks were right behind us. A guy was running on the street late one night and ran into two policemen. They began running with him. One of the cops said, 'If a tough guy like you is running, we'd better run, too.'"

Throckmorton was a brick street and Hinckley-Tandy was a store front, Wayman remembered. Next door was the Wagner Supply Company, an oil field supply house, and next to it was the Harlow Cone Company, which made ice cream cones. The Cook Paint & Varnish store was located between Throckmorton Street and the Jennings Avenue Viaduct. Burrus Mills was nearby. Across the street was a blacksmith shop, which was still making horseshoes, although most of its business was industrial machinery. On a shelf above the anvil, one of the blacksmiths kept a half-gallon jug of corn whiskey out of which he sipped all day long. His breath was frequently as fiery as his forge. On the opposite corner of 15th and Throckmorton was a salvage store owned by E.C. Dayton.

Wayman remembered Dave Tandy as "the front guy with his cigar, while Hinckley stayed in the back. Hinckley did the buying and Dave did the selling. Dave was always busy on some committee of the Rotary Club or the Chamber of Commerce or the Sales Executives Club. He was nervous, never could sit still, just the opposite of Hinckley. He was a classy little guy, dressed real well, always wore a bow tie."

It didn't take long for the effervescent Tandy to carve out a niche for himself on the local business scene. He joined the Rotary Club of Fort Worth in 1921, became a director and would earn the distinction of having 34 years of perfect attendance. He was a vice president and director of the Fort Worth Chamber of Commerce and led many trade trip delegations across the state extolling the virtues of Fort Worth as a good place in which to do business. He was one of the organizers and the first president of the Fort Worth Sales Executives Club and one of the early promoters of the city as a site for sales meetings and conventions. He served as president of the Manufacturers and Wholesalers Association just before it merged with the Chamber of Commerce in 1927.

In 1924, Dave Tandy chaired a committee that staged a rally for 1,000 traveling salesmen to demonstrate the city's growing manufacturing, wholesaling, retailing, and industrial capabilities. The *Fort Worth Star-Telegram* called him "one of the most wide-awake businessmen of the city, whose interests in Fort Worth are not limited to personal gain."

He also had a prescient eye to the future. In July 1927, he was quoted in the *Star-Telegram*, "Air transportation is still in its infancy, so much so that it is hard to imagine how greatly it can be developed. I wasn't sold on air as a means of practical transportation until recently when I studied it in connection with the proposed mail route to South Texas. I am convinced now that its possibilities are unlimited." On December 19, 1928, Tandy took his first airplane ride, a short hop around Fort Worth in the company of 11 other directors of the Chamber of Commerce.

Hinckley-Tandy opened its first branch store in Beaumont in 1927 in an effort to tap into the growing Gulf Coast market. But by 1932, in the depths of the Depression, the store was closed, never having lived up to expectations. Dave Tandy then offered Jim West, who had joined the company two years earlier as manager of south Texas operations in Houston, the chance to open a new store there. West, who would one day become the president of Tandy Corporation, accepted the challenge.

West had grown up in Corning, Iowa, and had received his early education in a one-room country schoolhouse. After graduating from high school, he enrolled in Grinnell College, a small liberal arts school in Iowa, on a mathematics scholarship.

"I never took a course in math that I didn't get a top grade in," West would later recall, "but I failed to graduate because I ran out of money."

Later, he attended the St. Louis University School of Commerce while working for the Chicago, Burlington & Quincy Railroad, and then went to work for the Fulton Bag and Cotton Company. He was living in St. Louis when Charles A. Lindbergh made aviation history with the first transatlantic solo flight in "The Spirit of St. Louis" in 1927. The entire city turned out to welcome Lindbergh when he made a triumphant return to St. Louis. The Fulton Bag and Cotton Company gave its employees the day off, which West put to good use by answering a help wanted ad by the Seiberling Rubber Company. Seiberling was looking for a sales representative in Fort Worth and West got the job. In Fort Worth, one of the first people West met was Dave Tandy, whose company was the state distributor for Seiberling products.

"I sold rubber heels to Hinckley-Tandy," West was quoted in a newspaper interview shortly before his death. "Goodyear had almost a monopoly on rubber heels, but Seiberling's heels didn't mark floors when you walked on them. With that advantage, Seiberling eventually got half the sales in the state."

In 1930, Tandy hired West and sent him to Houston to oversee Hinckley-Tandy's operations in south Texas.

"Dave knew that I knew how to sell and that I wasn't afraid of hard work," West later recalled. "After all, I'd already been selling him rubber heels."

Eunice West met her future husband in St. Louis while she was going to secretarial school and Jim was attending St. Louis University. She and West were married shortly after he moved to Houston. It was a union that was predestined, she said with a laugh. "My maiden name was East, so we proved the twain could meet."

She recalled how hard Jim worked in those days.

"He managed the store in Houston and also delivered merchandise to customers in the area. He was both on the road and inside. He had to do it all. It was just a very plain store, downtown on Caroline Street. In those days, it was a findings business, and Jim sold leathers for soles and heels and shoelaces and shoe polish. The customers were from all around. They would come in on Sunday and buy from Jim. All of the shoe shops in Houston were customers. Those early days were awful. There was nothing very prosperous about them. It was just a lot of hard work. Jim went to work at 7 o'clock and it was usually 9 or 9:30 when he got home.

"I used to go with him sometimes when he'd go on trips. He'd leave on one day and come back the next, going to Goosecreek and Baytown and those suburban areas and Galveston. We'd stay overnight in Galveston because it was a resort. But a lot of times Jim would be in those shoe shops until late at night. He'd deliver their orders to them. We had a Ford coupe and it'd be full, chock full, of merchandise, and we'd stop at all these individual shoe shops. The owners, of course, worked late because most of them lived in the back of the shop. We'd go in and Jim would stand around sometimes until 10 o'clock because they'd be busy and he'd have to wait until they could see him. He'd stay around to collect because they would pay a little bit at a time on their account."

West was lucky if he could collect anything from his customers in those early 1930s days when a hole in the sole of one's shoe was a symbol of the times. While Al Jolson sang, "Brother, can you spare a dime," there weren't many people around who could spare one. West struggled to keep his store in Houston going.

Back in Fort Worth Dave Tandy and Norton Hinckley, like so many other small businessmen of the time, resorted to some creative measures to keep their struggling enterprise afloat. Tandy told a story of the time the business had two invoices that it couldn't pay. "What we did," he related with a sheepish grin, "was send a check made out to the ABC Company to the XYZ Company, and the XYZ Company check to the ABC Company. It took about two weeks for them to get the checks back, and by then we had enough money to cover them."

Hinckley-Tandy nearly went belly-up in 1937. It bought too much merchandise on credit and lacked funds to pay. Dave Tandy saved the day by going to each of the suppliers, pointing out that if they forced Hinckley-Tandy into bankruptcy, they'd get nothing. But if they would give the firm six to 12 months, they could sell the merchandise and pay their bills. He convinced them that the the merchandise was saleable, that Hinckley-Tandy had just bought more than they could sell right then.

But even when things were at their bleakest, when the stock market was hitting all-time lows and unemployment all-time highs, Dave Tandy, ever the optimist, was making speeches at sales meetings around the state exhorting people to keep their chins up. A news item in the *Star-Telegram* declared: "Selling in spite of the Depression through the use of modern packages will be discussed by Dave L. Tandy, president and sales manager of Hinckley-Tandy Leather Company, at the second annual Southwestern Sales Managers Conference at the Baker Hotel in Dallas. Tandy will outline the evolution of the package from the 'ugly duckling' stage to the present when it is being used to turn sales curves upward."

Dave Tandy also offered a Depression-era marketing tip to the shoe repair industry that was published in a trade journal: "In the present phase of merchandising, we find that psychology is playing a greater part than ever before. The salesman, the advertiser, the manager, all are using more psychology today than ever before. Therefore, we would like to submit to you for your careful study a slight change in the present universally used slogan by the shoe repair shops, namely,—'Shoes Repaired While You Wait.' We believe better psychology would be to use—'Shoes Repaired While You REST,' chang-

ing the word 'wait' to the word 'rest'. People today are living in a
hurry. They do not like to wait for trains, for shoes to be repaired, or
anything. But when they are tired, they might take a suggestion to
REST. Anyway we pass this on to you, and would be glad to know
what you think of the matter."

During the 1930s, Dave Tandy became known as a public speaker
on leather lore. He developed a traveling road show he called the
"Romance in Leather," and he became a sort of Paladin of the lecture
circuit: "Have Speech, Will Travel."

A 1939 story in the *Star-Telegram* told of a talk Tandy made to the
Rotary Club in Brownsville, Texas, at which he displayed 60 pounds of
cow hides and horse hides, plus goat, sheep, lamb, reptile, alligator,
shark, and walrus hides.

In his remarks Tandy informed his fellow Rotarians that their area
had "a wonderful opportunity for a very profitable industry in catching
sharks for commercial purposes, because shark skin cannot be imitated
successfully and is valuable." He also gave an account of what happened to the ostrich after the styles in women's hats changed and ostrich feathers were no longer in vogue.

"It became necessary to find some other use for the ostriches that had
been maintained for their feathers," Tandy reported. "Then someone
discovered that the ostrich, when killed and skinned, furnished a very
fine leather that was very hard to imitate successfully. The birds became so valuable for their leather that in a very short time all of the ostriches in the United States had been used and we began to import
ostrich hides from Australia. A law there prohibits the killing of the ostrich for its skin alone, but it was found that the meat made a very fine
'Wimpy Special.' Now the meat is used there, while the hides are
shipped to the United States."

Hinckley-Tandy's struggle for survival continued until the outbreak
of World War II. The Japanese attack on Pearl Harbor that plunged the
United States into the war had an immediate impact on the
country—and the company. The problem now was not selling the merchandise, but finding the merchandise to sell.

Leather had become vital to the war effort, and the government soon
was taking almost all of the available leather. There was virtually none
left over for civilian use. However, specialty leathers soon began to be

utilized by the armed forces for therapeutic leathercraft programs in military hospitals and in recreation and rehabilitation centers.

Dave Tandy found he could get a priority for providing the armed forces with specialty leathers, which worked very nicely for tooling belts, billfolds, handbags and similar items. As the war progressed, the specialty leather business continued to grow. This was Dave Tandy's bailiwick because it was outside of Norton Hinckley's area of interest and expertise.

For the first time, Tandy began to recognize the potential of leather-crafts for the future of the business. Hinckley, on the other hand, thought leathercrafts was a fad that would die with the end of the war.

Neither recognized it at the time, but the path to a split-up of the company had been charted.

*   *   *

The family that Dave Tandy moved to Fort Worth in 1919 consisted of his wife, Carmen; their two children, Margueritte and Charles; and Carmen's mother, Olive Anne McClain. Another son, Alfred R. (Bill) Tandy was born in Fort Worth on August 19, 1921. Dave soon had Carmen and his mother-in-law selling shoe polish and shoelaces door to door. The family initially lived in a small house at 2240 Alston on the city's non-fashionable south side until the summer of 1929, when it moved into a comfortable, two-story brick home that Tandy built at 1916 Berkeley Court in one of the city's upwardly mobile areas.

Charles Tandy and his sister and brother grew up in a strict Southern Baptist home that was dominated by his mother. "She really made them toe the line," recalled Eunice West. "Dave Tandy just let her take over. He let her do it all, as far as the home and the children were concerned."

Dave Tandy joined the Presbyterian Church after a tent meeting in Temple, but Carmen remained a staunch Southern Baptist and raised the three children in that faith. They attended Broadway Baptist Church, and it was there that Luther Henderson first met Charles Tandy. Charles was 12 and Luther was 10.

"Our mothers were good friends through the church," Henderson recalled. "Charles lived on Berkeley Court and I lived on Park Hill, so we were neighbors and got to be good friends. After we got a little older, we didn't find Sunday School classes too interesting. But we both wound up in the department for high school age people where there were a lot of pretty girls around. We did that for two or three years and thoroughly enjoyed it."

Charles' grandmother, Olive Anne McClain, whom he called "Mother Mac," had grown up in a very strict Baptist tradition. "She was strongly against smoking and drinking, both of which Dave Tandy did, and this was a source of irritation between them that never died out," Luther Henderson said.

According to Henderson, when Charles was about 14 or 15, his grandmother promised him a car if he neither smoked nor drank until he was 21. Charles accepted the challenge and, to the best of Henderson's knowledge, lived up to the agreement.

"His grandmother did give him a car," Henderson said. "I think, though, that by the time Charles was 21 and one week he'd more than made up for all that lost time. That's when he started smoking his cigars that became his trademark."

Charles grew up in a world that was bounded by how far a boy could roller skate or ride a bicycle, another boyhood friend, Phil R. North, remembered. North lived only a few houses away from Tandy when they were growing up.

"Charles and I were the same age. His birthday was May 15 and mine was July 6, so we played together from the time we met," North said. "The games we played were what we and the other neighborhood kids could devise—shinny in the street, kick the tin can, touch football on a vacant lot, baseball where there were two vacant lots together, digging a cave in a vacant lot, building a clubhouse out of abandoned lumber, counting the cars as they came by and seeing who could correctly identify them by make and model year.

"At night during the summer in those days, we didn't have much to do," North related. "We'd sit around outside because there was no air-conditioning. We'd sit on the front sidewalk because it was cooler. We'd sit out there and talk and watch the fireflies. We'd try to catch the fireflies and put them in a bottle. And we'd talk about whether it would be possible to ever make $10,000 a year. Both of us thought it was very unlikely that we'd ever achieve such success, but it was something to dream about. Neither of us had any clear idea of how we could amass this fortune. When you're 10 or 11 years old, the business world seems very far away. It's very vague to you. A boy at that age can imagine being a doctor, or a lawyer, or a professional baseball player. He can have clear aspirations as to what he wants to be at that age, but you don't think about having a business. I didn't know what I was going to do and neither did Charles."

Although North's father was editor of the *Fort Worth Star-Telegram*, the city's dominant newspaper, he and Charles delivered the *Fort Worth Press*, an upstart afternoon paper owned by the Scripps-Howard chain, after school. They also sold the *Saturday Evening Post* and other magazines for additional pocket money.

"Our families were comfortable, in that we had nice homes and a family car," North said. "It wasn't customary to give children vast allowances. I think mine was 25 cents a week and I suspect Charles' was the same or less. And that's when we were in high school."

North recalled that Charles Tandy first displayed his aptitude for salesmanship when he was about 10 years old and attending the Daggett Elementary School on Fort Worth's south side.

"Charles took leather scraps from his father's shoe-findings store and taught the kids how to make quirts and belts out of them. I think he sold two leather strips for a dime. The strips were about a yard long."

Tandy and North also engaged in a joint business venture, operating a punchboard during school recess.

"We charged the kids a nickel or a dime to punch our punchboards. You could win a nickel, a dime, a quarter, 50 cents or a dollar with one punch," North related. "We bought the boards from Herman Brothers Supply for 15 cents, and if we sold the whole board we would net $1.15, less the cost of the board, which gave us a whole dollar profit."

The Depression-era summer of 1936 provided a special set of memories for everyone lucky enough to be living in Fort Worth. It was the summer of Casa Manana, the show business extravaganza mounted by Fort Worth to upstage Dallas which had been chosen as the site of the Texas centennial celebration.

Billy Rose, the pint-sized showman from Broadway, was lured to Fort Worth for the then unheard of fee of $1,000 a day to produce the spectacle that featured a Sally Rand Nude Ranch, a lavish stage show headlined by Paul Whiteman and his Orchestra, bevies of beautiful girls, and spectacular scenery and costumes. Across the state billboards proclaimed, "Dallas for Education. Fort Worth for Entertainment."

For the 18-year-old Charles Tandy and Phil North, Casa Manana provided an idyllic summer of romance and enterprise. "In that Casa Manana show," Phil North remembered, "there was one number that

had 50 chorus girls in it wearing gold cowboy boots. There were 55
chorus girls in all, with five having the night off every night. Charles
and I contracted to regild the five pairs of gold cowboy boots that
weren't in use each night, for $5 a pair. We were 18, and that was as
much money as we'd ever seen. We also got to meet every single one
of the chorus girls."

Slot machines were legal at Casa Manana that summer. Since North
and Tandy had to deliver the regilded boots to the dressing room before
each performance, they had about two hours to kill before they could
pick up the boots of the five girls who would not be performing the following evening.

"So we'd go over to Pioneer Palace, where the slot machines were,"
North recounted. "We'd take a dollar in nickels and dimes with us and
carefully survey the slot machine scene to see which machines were going for 100 percent profit. We'd stand behind old ladies and watch them
put their nickels and dimes in the machines, and then we'd decide
which machine to play that night. We never lost more than a dollar and
we never won more than a dollar because we quit after we won a dollar.
We were never greedy. Then, when the last show was over, we'd pick
up the five pairs of boots and take them home to regild."

Another business venture in which Charles Tandy engaged as a teen-
ager was making ladies' belts. His partner was John Justin, Jr., whose
family bootmaking name is as much a part of Western lore as are Stet-
son and Colt. The Justin Boot Company's brand dates back to the storied days of the old cattle drives, when John Justin's grandfather, H.J.
Justin, began making handmade boots for cowboys in a Chisholm Trail
town called Spanish Fort.

"I first knew Charlie Tandy when my father moved the family boot
business to Fort Worth from Nocona in 1925," John Justin recalled. "I
was 7 years old at the time, the same age as Charles. We kind of grew
up running into each other. Charlie's dad, Dave Tandy, took a very active part in the Sales Executives Club and so did my dad. So I knew
Charlie through that, too. We'd see each other at meetings we'd go to
with our dads. By the time we got to high school, Charlie was very interested in making some money, and so was I. Our fathers were rather
frugal with us, and Charlie kept coming up with ideas for putting a little
more change in our pockets. It was his idea for us to go into the ladies'
belt business together.

"He said to me, 'You've got a lot of scrap leather over at your father's boot factory. Why don't we use it to make belts and sell them to the department stores downtown?'

"At first, I didn't think too much of the idea, but he kept talking about it until I finally agreed. This was when both of us were in high school. I found an old hand-mounted, 16-pound mallet that they used for cutting out dies at the boot factory. And we bought a die. It was kind of an oblong-shaped die with the corners cut off and had four holes, two at each end. I'd bring all this heavy scrap leather home from the boot factory and we'd go out to my garage. I lived on Medford Court in Park Hill, not too far away from where Charlie lived.

"So we'd get in there, in my garage, and we'd start pounding that die with the 16-pound mallet, cutting out belts in the shapes we wanted. We'd place the die on the piece of leather and pound on it. One of us would hit that thing until our arm would just give out. Then the other guy would begin to hit. If you didn't hit the die hard enough with the mallet, it wouldn't cut through the leather, and you'd have to hit it again. Charlie and I sometimes stayed in my garage damn near all night knocking those belts out, particularly when we had orders. He liked to work. We worked nights because we were going to school."

Justin laughed when he recalled the scene.

"When we were grinding out those belts, the sweat just rolled off us. You take that big old 16-pound mallet and beat that die, and you're talking about exercise. We'd just do it until we'd give out."

They used an old burning needle to burn borders around the belts and to decorate them, usually by burning in brands from a book of cattle brands they had acquired. Finally, they got to where they put their own designs on their products, things like backward Ls.

"I think that's one of the ways Charlie got interested in leathercrafts," Justin said.

They sold their belts to department stores and specialty shops and did a pretty thriving business. "We were getting a buck or two apiece and they were selling for around $4 in the stores," Justin remembered. "And, pretty soon, it got to where you'd see a lot of them around town. Women were wearing them as a sort of novelty-type thing, because the belts came without buckles. What we'd do is buy some strip leather and put it through the holes at each end of the belt. You'd just tie the belts in front instead of using a buckle.

"We had a nice little business while it lasted," Justin continued. "The leather was free from scraps we collected at the boot company and the labor was free. We never were able to use scrap leather from Charles' father's business because we needed heavier leather than what Hinckley-Tandy had."

Justin remembered the Hinckley-Tandy Leather Company as a small, struggling business that "did everything in the world" to try to sell leather to his family's boot company.

"But even in those days, my father was buying 100 times more leather than Hinckley-Tandy ever stocked," Justin said. "So there just wasn't any room for the middleman. The boot company was buying direct from the tanneries."

In later years, after Tandy and Justin returned home from sea duty during World War II, they talked about joining forces again, Justin revealed.

"Charlie was fascinated by the boot business, and he would call me periodically about buying the boot company. But I didn't own the company then and there was nothing I could do about it. Then, when I got the boot company, he called me a time or two, but it just never worked out and we just never got together. I probably made a bad mistake. I probably could have made a lot of money if I'd sold the business to Charlie for Tandy stock."

No one in Fort Worth ever dreamed that Tandy would become a "great entrepreneur," Justin said. But it was apparent to those who knew him that the Hinckley-Tandy Leather Company would never satisfy his ambitions or his ego.

"Charles always wanted to get into something big," Justin reported. "He was always looking for something that would match his imagination and his talents. He wanted to sell, to build a retailing empire. Once he got started, there was nothing to stop him."

He would have to wait until after the war to make his start.

Chapter 2
Building a Business in Peace and War

Tandy was already on active duty in the U.S. Navy when the bombs began falling on Pearl Harbor. In the spring of 1941, with the war clouds becoming more ominous, the Navy offered direct commissions to students attending the Harvard Business School. He applied, was accepted, and was commissioned an ensign in the Regular Navy after agreeing to a 6-year commitment.

He was called to active duty although he had not completed the requirements for his MBA. He hoped the business school would award him the degree under the extenuating circumstances, but it was never forthcoming. This colored his opinion of Harvard MBAs forever after. Tandy applied to the Harvard Business School after his graduation from Texas Christian University in 1940, but he was turned down. He was determined to go there, however, even if it meant pulling a few strings. The strings were pulled by his grandmother, Olive Anne McClain, who had grown up in Bonham, Texas, with Speaker of the House Sam Rayburn, one of the most powerful men in Washington.

"Charles' grandmother got Sam Rayburn to write a letter to the Harvard Business School on Charles' behalf," Luther Henderson reported. "That's how he got in."

Charles Tandy's college career started inauspiciously. He flunked out of the prestigious Rice Institute in Houston in his freshman year. Tandy later said that flunking out of Rice was the best thing that ever happened to him because it taught him that he had to study rather than spend all his time chasing coeds. He then enrolled at Texas Christian University in Fort Worth. TCU would remain close to his heart for the rest of his life.

"Charles was always more interested in girls than in academics," Henderson maintained. "Academic subjects never really interested him.

23

He just did enough to get by. It was only after he graduated from TCU that he became interested in preparing himself for a business career."

While at TCU, Tandy worked as a salesman in the ladies' shoe department of Monnig's Department Store in downtown Fort Worth. He initially worked for his father at Hinckley-Tandy Leather Company, but he found selling ladies' shoes far more rewarding. Not only was he was on a commission at Monnig's rather than on the minimal fixed salary his father had paid him, but selling shoes was a great way to meet attractive young women.

"Charles was always a good salesman," Henderson said, "so he had an above-average income for a college student in those days."

Elton M. Hyder, Jr., a prominent Fort Worth attorney and one of Charles' closest friends, remembered Tandy saying, "A man ain't worth a damn unless he's sold ladies' shoes. If you can sell ladies' shoes, you can sell anything."

Tandy was able to put his shoe-selling experience to immediate use when he entered the Harvard Business School, landing a job in the ladies' shoe department of the Jordan Marsh Department Store in Boston.

Reminiscing about his Harvard experience in later years, Tandy described his first year there as one of the hardest of his life, and he frequently recalled the two lonely Christmases he spent on the deserted campus because he couldn't afford to go home for the holidays. "It was horrible," he said.

During Tandy's second year at Harvard, he only took courses that interested him. "I didn't have to worry because they don't wash you out until the end of the year," he told Bill Vance, a former Tandy Leather Company associate. "So I said to myself, 'The hell with their schedule and the courses they want me to take. I'm picking my own courses and I'm picking the ones that fit exactly with what I want to do.'"

Vance called this "one of the smartest things that Charles ever did, because he was able to concentrate on financial subjects taught by people with the best financial minds, and Charles had a mind like a sponge. He just drank it all in."

Phil North added, "Charles enjoyed Harvard. He enjoyed the people there. He got out of it what he wanted. But he never regretted not getting his MBA. What you had in your head or in your heart was what was important. If he had a degree from Oxford or was a don, he'd never tell people. He'd never have worn a Phi Beta Kappa key had he won one. Charles' lack of a diploma from Harvard and flunking out of Rice were merit badges in his book."

Tandy's first assignment with the Navy after being called to active duty was selling war bonds in Hawaii. In 1942, while still an ensign, he sold $1,179,637.50 in war bonds, a record for war bond issuing offices nationwide. He concentrated his sales efforts on civilians holding draft-exempt jobs in Navy shipyards.

It was during his tour of duty in Hawaii that he became aware of the therapeutic and recreational applications of leathercrafts in Navy hospitals. He wrote to Dave Tandy about what he had seen, suggesting that leathercraft might offer an opportunity for the expansion of Hinckley-Tandy's business after the war.

Tandy's next assignment took him to sea as a supply officer on an oil tanker, the *USS Pecos*, in the Pacific. William W. Collins, who had grown up with Tandy in Fort Worth and later became a Radio Shack executive, recalled an experience that took place in heavy seas off the Aleutian Islands shortly after the Battle of Midway.

"Charles was on an oil tanker that came up to the Aleutians to refuel our task force. I was a junior engineering officer on the heavy cruiser, the *Indianapolis*, in charge of one of the diesel fuel connections. The seas were rough and it was a really dangerous situation. These were big ships and they were bobbing up and down. Charles knew I was on the *Indianapolis*, and he knew that I had no way of knowing that he was on the *Pecos*.

"So Tandy got on the bullhorn and called out for everyone to hear, 'All right, Collins, get off your dead ass and hurry up and make that diesel connection.'

"I heard that voice across the roaring seas, and I could see that the captain on the bridge of the *Indianapolis* heard it, too. The hose was still about 20 feet out, and I got word from the captain, 'Collins, I want you to make haste with that diesel connection. You heard that supply officer over there on the tanker saying things are going too slow.' I answered, 'Yes, captain, sir.'

"Then I looked over at the tanker and I recognized Tandy. He was doubled over laughing. He thought that was the funniest thing, because I'd gotten my ass eaten out by the captain of my ship. That happened right off Kiska, and there were a lot of German submarines around, and we needed the fuel."

Collins added a postscript to the Aleutian incident.

"Just after I joined Radio Shack, I was working in the store in downtown Dallas to learn the business. Charles came over to the store one evening. I didn't even know he was there. We were busy, it being Christmas time, and we were selling these little bullhorns. Charles went over to a corner of the store, got one of the bullhorns out and said, 'All right, Collins, get off your butt and hurry up and make that sale.' I'll tell you, he thought that was funny as hell, too."

After a tour of sea duty, Tandy was one of about 100 officers accepted to attend the Naval Accounting School at Harvard. Luther Henderson, a naval officer then stationed in the Aleutian Islands, also applied for the Accounting School assignment and was accepted.

"You can imagine our mutual surprise when we ran into each other on the Harvard campus," Henderson said. "We immediately signed up to room together." As it turned out, they became roommates, but not in the Harvard dormitory to which they were assigned.

"Charles knew a family in Boston, the Meyers, who were in the leather tanning business and had done business with Hinckley-Tandy," Henderson recounted. "So Charles called Mr. Meyers, and when he learned that Charles was stationed at Harvard, he invited him to live at his home and bring a friend. So Charles and I moved into the Meyers' home. We went to school from 9 to 4 and the rest of the time we were on our own. The Meyers really made us a part of their family, introduced us to lots of people. Since there was a shortage of men, we got invited to lots of parties, met lots of pretty girls. After that, we went to separate duty stations and didn't see each other again until after the war was over. Charles stayed in the Navy for about a year after the war ended because of his six-year Regular Navy commitment. He spent the year in the States working primarily on disposal of war surplus equipment."

Tandy chafed under that extra year of active duty while his peers were getting started on their postwar careers. When he got out in 1947, he was a man in a hurry. The war had taken six years out of his life and he had a lot of catching up to do.

He came back from the war with a wife, the former Gwendolyn Purdy Johnston, an attractive, vivacious, and wealthy widow. She and Charles had been married in Seattle on October 25, 1945, after a whirlwind courtship. He was 27 and she was 41 and the mother of an 18-

year-old daughter and a 15-year-old son. Gwen had been widowed eight years earlier when her husband, Sherwood Johnston, was killed in a plane crash. Johnston was the scion of a wealthy family with extensive holdings in Mexico, including a sugar plantation and sugar refineries in Los Mochos, among other interests. The family maintained estates in Burlingame, California, near San Francisco, and Rye, New York, plus homes in Cuernavaca and Mexico City.

Charles and Gwen met while he was stationed in San Francisco. They were introduced by Gwen's daughter, Connie, a freshman at Stanford University and a volunteer driver for the Red Cross assigned to the Navy. She met Charles when he was escorting a group of admirals in a staff car driven by Connie. One of the staff car's tires suffered a blowout. Taking advantage of the privileges of rank, the admirals watched while the young woman got out of the car to change the tire. Charles, who was then a lieutenant, offered his assistance even though it meant soiling his sparkling Navy whites. Connie was so grateful, she invited the chivalrous young officer to her home in Burlingame, where he met Gwen.

Hazel Vernon of Fort Worth, who was living in the Bay Area at the time with her Navy husband and was a close friend of Gwen Johnston's, remembered when Charles came to call for the first time.

"It was a Sunday afternoon at Gwen's beautiful home in Burlingame. We had just finished lunch at the Burlingame Country Club and had come back to the house to have a swim when Charles arrived. He was smoking a cigar at least a foot long and I could hear him talking up a storm to a group of young ladies. He was really something. I wondered, who is that brash young man?"

Mrs. Vernon asked Tandy what he was going to do after the war, and he said, "I'm going back to Fort Worth and put my family's business on the map. I'm going to make us all millionaires, my father, my brother, and my sister."

Gwen and Charles began dating and were married shortly after Tandy was transferred to Seattle in October of 1945. Mrs. Vernon, who later moved to Fort Worth where she became a successful realtor, acted as a "baby-sitter" for Connie and her brother, Sherwood, while Gwen was in Seattle for the nuptials.

When Gwen and Charles arrived in Fort Worth in 1947 following his separation from the service, they set up light housekeeping in a small apartment without air-conditioning and other amenities near the TCU campus. The experience provided Gwen with a severe case of culture shock. Not only had her lifestyle changed drastically, but her adjustment wasn't helped at all by the 12 to 14-hour days Charles began putting in at the Hinckley-Tandy Leather Company.

"Hours didn't mean a thing to Charles," Eunice West said. "He worked from early morning until, a lot of times, 9 or 10 o'clock at night. Charles would stay down there after they closed the store. I know Gwen would get so provoked. She'd call me and ask, 'Is Jim home yet?' And I'd say, 'No.' And she'd say, 'I wonder where they are?' and I'd say, 'They're down there someplace.'"

Bill Collins remembered the day Gwen and Charles arrived in Fort Worth upon his return from the service. "They drove up to my house in a Duesenberg roadster that Gwen owned and there was this big dog standing up in the back seat. It was like something out of *The Great Gatsby*." Harlan Swain, who began working for the Hinckley-Tandy Leather Company in 1942, found that Tandy lost no time making his presence felt upon his return to work.

"After Charles came back into the business, life became pretty much hell for everybody, so to speak. I thought he was real hard in those days. That was before I got to know him for what he really was, which was a warm, big-hearted, totally unselfish person. But he didn't come across that way at first. He was very impatient. But he could see exactly where the future lay. At the beginning, when he couldn't get people to see what he saw, it was very, very frustrating for him. He was hard, tough, demanding, and profane."

Swain recalled an incident in which he felt he was victimized by Tandy's apparent lack of sensitivity to other people's feelings. It happened shortly after Charles' arrival on the scene and was something Swain said he never forgot. A great-uncle of his had died and he had asked Dave Tandy for time off to attend the funeral because the great-uncle had been especially close to Swain's mother.

"Charles found out about it and was furious," Swain reported. "He didn't think I should have taken off to attend a funeral for a great-uncle. He said to me, 'I had a chicken once that died and I didn't take time off from work.' In retrospect, I can hardly believe that he really said that, but it has subconsciously stayed with me over all these years. I know

now, and I got to believe later, that he really wasn't that insensitive. But, I guess, that was the one thing above all others that doomed me to a life of intimidation at the hands of Charles Tandy."

Swain paused for a moment as if composing his thoughts, then added, "You know, Winston Churchill once said, 'Never have so many owed so much to so few.' Well, I'd say about Charles Tandy, 'never has anybody accomplished so much with so little.' By that I mean he took ordinary people like myself, people with humble backgrounds and not much education, and by dint of his tremendous energy and determination, flogged us into doing more than we thought we could do. I'm absolutely convinced that there is no one that could have done what he did with the people that he did it with. Not that he picked dumb people. I don't mean that. I mean that he picked ordinary people, and by the unselfish remuneration plans that he devised and by the judicious use of the cat-o'-nine-tails, he accomplished miracles."

Swain recalled how in later years Tandy accompanied him and other employees to the Fort Worth National Bank, "hat in hand, so to speak, so that we could borrow money to invest in our stores and to buy Tandy stock, and a lot of us became millionaires because of that. It's unbelievable that it could happen. But it happened because of Charles Tandy. To build an empire as he did, it was just phenomenal."

Swain began working as a stock boy at Hinckley-Tandy Leather Company in September of 1942, right after high school graduation, at a starting wage of 30 cents an hour. He had learned about the Hinckley-Tandy job opening at the Texas Employment Commission Office in downtown Fort Worth and had been instructed to talk to a Mr. D. L. Tandy.

He recalled his meeting with Dave Tandy.

"He was very animated, very energetic, and had a cigar in his mouth. He talked with me for a while, then excused himself and went over and got Mr. Hinckley. He and Mr. Hinckley conferred and then Mr. Tandy came back and told me I was hired."

Hinckley-Tandy's business was still shoe findings, supplying shoe repairmen with all of their needs, including the machinery they utilized.

"Of course at that time, shoe repairing was a pretty big thing, much more so than it is today," Swain said. "People got their shoes repaired and kept them until they wore them out. Hinckley-Tandy had three salesmen working out of Fort Worth, covering west Texas, east Texas, north Texas, and southern Oklahoma. We also did some mail order business. The shoe repairmen would mail in their orders for their fill-in needs in-between calls by the salesmen, but generally you had to call on the shoe repair men personally to maintain their business; not only to retain their business, but to see that they paid. There were three kinds of customers: those that would and could pay their bills, those who would pay but couldn't, and those who could pay but wouldn't. The effect was the same with each of the latter two. You didn't get your money. But our company had good credit, paid its bills, and was always properly financed to conduct the kind of business it was doing."

All new employees started out on the packing table, packing merchandise for shipment, Swain said. "Then, after you accumulated knowledge of the merchandise, you got to be an order filler, the guy who went around with a clipboard filling orders. Then there were the shipping clerks who, after the orders were filled and packed, had to know which truck lines went where, and whether the package should go by truck or railway express or parcel post.

"Mr. Hinckley was strictly a shoe findings man," Swain continued. "He was in charge of buying and inventory control for everything except what we called the upper leathers, which were mostly calfskin and kangaroo skins from which the upper parts of boots and shoes were made. The customers for upper leathers were custom bootmakers and shoemakers. Mr. Tandy handled that phase of the business. But he was principally an outside man, a salesman, an outgoing, extroverted fellow. He also handled the advertising and the merchandising for the whole business."

The Hinckley and Tandy division of labor apparently worked, Swain decided. "They got along pretty well, although, on occasions, you could hear their voices raised. Mr. Hinckley was a quiet man. He never had much to do with directing the employees. Mr. Tandy did all that sort of thing, and with all of his nervous energy he could keep things stirred up. Mr. Hinckley represented a sort of quiet, stabilizing influence."

After Charles Tandy's return from the Navy, Hinckley-Tandy began a modest expansion program, opening new stores in Amarillo, Dallas, and Albuquerque, which necessitated hiring some part-time help. One of those applying for a job was Bill Michero, a newly-returned Navy veteran, who needed to augment his GI Bill stipend while he finished work toward his degree in business at TCU.

"It was in December of 1947," Michero recalled. "I spotted a 3-by-5 card tacked on the wall of the business school that invited part-time job applicants. So I drove my 1932 Reo to this place in the seedy end of downtown near the wino district at 15th and Throckmorton Streets, where I eventually found the headquarters of the Hinckley-Tandy Leather Company.

"The building was a typical, crummy pre-World War I structure, sort of oblong-shaped, four floors, including a basement. The back of it and the freight doors faced on Lancaster. Two blocks east was the Richelieu Grill, which had been down there for years since the advent of the railroad. The freight elevator had this giant, 6-foot diameter wheel that was pulled by rope, and if you overloaded it the brake failed and everything would go to the basement. It was a pretty primitive environment."

Michero was interviewed first by Charles Tandy, then by Dave Tandy before they hired him at $1.10 an hour, which was 10 or 15 cents above the minimum wage at the time. Michero began working in January of 1948 filling orders in the warehouse, helping in the shipping department, wrapping packages, and servicing mail order customers.

"By the time I got there," Michero related, "a good part of the sales were coming from customers who were not shoe repair people, but people who were doing other things. Some advertising pieces were being done and some modest little homemade mailing pieces were being produced and aimed at this new market for leather. Dave Tandy created these little advertising and mailing pieces on his kitchen table."

Another Navy veteran, Bill Vance, who spent the war as a medic on a small water tanker in the South Pacific, had also returned home and enrolled in the TCU School of Business. He had just gotten married and had mentioned to one of his professors that he was looking for a job. The professor referred him to the Hinckley-Tandy Leather Company.

"The building it's in looks like it's about to cave in," the professor told Vance, "but there's a young man there who impresses me no end. I think, if he can get some help, he can do something with the business. His name is Charles Tandy. You ought to go and talk to him."

A few days later, on a Saturday afternoon, Vance drove downtown to answer a Burroughs Business Machine Company want ad only to discover the office was closed. Getting back into his car, he began driving south. At the corner of 15th and Throckmorton Streets, he saw a sign that said, "Hinckley-Tandy Leather Company" on an "old, yellow stucco building," and he remembered his conversation with the professor. Parking his car in front of the building, Vance went inside to be greeted by a less than inviting setting.

"I'm not kidding," he avowed, "I actually walked through some cobwebs going in. I walked up two or three little steps and came to a little wall at the back of the room. Then I turned left and that put me in the office. Just a couple of lights were on. At least it was pretty dim in there. I couldn't see anybody and I couldn't hear anybody. But the door was open and I said to myself, 'There's gotta be someone here.' So I walked in and then I saw two big feet sticking out from under a desk and I figured there had to be a body somewhere under those feet. So I said, 'Hello.' The feet kind of rustled and then I saw a big guy about 6 feet 2 and 200 pounds pushing himself out from underneath the desk, looking up at me with a big smile on his face and saying, 'Hi, what can I do for you?'"

That was Bill Vance's introduction to Charles Tandy.

Vance told Tandy he was looking for a job and Tandy said, "Come in and let's talk." He explained that he'd been lying on the floor plugging in a new IBM electric typewriter. "I want to see what it can do," he added.

"We began talking," Vance said, "and then Charles asked me if I minded working on Sunday. By this time it was 4 o'clock on Saturday afternoon. I answered, 'I don't like to work on Sunday. I worked on Sunday when I worked in a restaurant. But if the ox is in the ditch, I'm more than happy to get him out.'"

Tandy replied, "Well, we've got a big ox in the ditch. How about 7 o'clock tomorrow morning?"

The job was installing fixtures Tandy had bought from a friend who made knockdown furniture and fixtures. The fixtures were cheaply made and didn't fit very well, but Tandy wanted them installed to make racks for a shipment of western belts that had just arrived. Vance and Tandy finished the job about 7 o'clock Sunday night. Then Vance brought up the subject of permanent employment.

"Charles said they really didn't have a spot open, but would I be willing to work for $25 a week to find out if I fitted in somewhere? I told him I would if I could start in the bookkeeping department. When he asked me why the bookkeeping department, I told him that was the best place to learn the business. He nodded his head and said, 'I guess that makes sense.' He told me to report for work the following morning for a week's tryout."

The head bookkeeper, Bush Jones, wasn't particularly happy to see Vance, informing him that there was really nothing for him to do. But after a while Jones reappeared and said, "Here's a statement from the Albuquerque bank that's wrong. I don't know what's wrong with it, but you find out." Vance discovered that the bank had made a $10 error in its favor. The next day the young woman who did the invoices called in sick, so Vance sat down at her desk and did the billing. Then he got his big break. The man who did the pricing became ill and was hospitalized in the Veterans Administration Hospital in Dallas. It was his job to check the catalog when the orders came in and price all the orders. Vance was assigned that task.

"Dave Tandy began warming up to me when I began pricing," Vance said. "He gave me half a day to see how I was doing and checked up on me. Since he did the buying of the upper leathers, he was familiar with the upper leather prices. When he didn't find any mistakes in my pricing he went back to his desk. I worked that way all week without being told whether I'd been hired permanently or not."

On Friday night near quitting time Vance approached Charles, who told him, "Let's go see Dad." They found Dave Tandy in a receptive mood. "I guess so," he said when Charles asked him if Vance was hired. "What I didn't know," Vance added, "is that Dave had just found out his pricer was going to be laid up in the hospital for three months."

The relationship between Dave and Charles Tandy was frequently stormy. Both had a propensity to giving vent to their feelings and didn't mind being overheard. "They'd yell at each other, but they also really liked each other. It was that kind of a fun ball game. Everybody used to yell at each other," Michero reported.

But there was also a lot of mutual respect.

Charles Tandy often said that he learned more about business from his father than he ever did at the Harvard Business School.

"My dad probably taught me the biggest part of the most important things I know," he once told Vance. "He always taught me in a simple way that was easy to understand," and he gave as an illustration the time his father permitted him to buy shoe dye for the first time.

"He gave me an amount of money to spend and told me I was on my own. There were about 25 or so colors available, so I divided them up equally and bought 10 bottles of everything. When the shoe dye arrived, we quickly sold out of two or three of the most popular colors. But I had no money left to replace them. I asked my dad where I'd gone wrong."

"'Charles,' Dad said, 'I've never considered myself an expert inventory man, but I have learned this over the years. When you look at that dye and you find out what you're selling, you'll find that you sell about 20 bottles of white to every bottle of purple. Now, if you're gonna run out of a color, which one would you rather run out of?' Then dad asked, 'How many sales would you miss if you were out of purple for a month?' I told him, 'Maybe none.' Then he asked me, 'How many sales would you lose if you were out of white for a month?' I never forgot that conversation. To this day, when I'm thinking about inventory, I always ask myself if I have enough white dye or too much purple?'"

By early 1948, Hinckley-Tandy had stores in Dallas, Amarillo, Albuquerque, and Houston, in addition to Fort Worth, and a small catalog business.

Vance and Charles Tandy used to drink coffee together at 10 o'clock every morning at the Texas & Pacific Passenger Depot across Lancaster Avenue from the Hinckley-Tandy offices. They always talked business. "Charles wasn't interested in gossip or sports," Vance said. "We'd spend about 15 minutes talking and Charles was always full of ideas. Charles always wanted to set sales goals, but they really weren't goals. They were more like hopes. Our annual sales then were about $750,000. Charles would say, 'I hope that sometime we can build it up to $5 million.'"

Vance was the 14th person hired by Hinckley-Tandy in Fort Worth. The work was hard, Vance recalled, but it had one redeeming feature. It was steady. No one ever was let go.

"Dave and Charles didn't like to fire anybody," Vance explained. "The only person they ever fired, they caught him stealing one Sunday when they came down to do some extra work. They didn't have any choice. Then they went home and moped about it. Charles' mother told me, 'Dave can't fire anyone and neither can Charles. They bark but they don't bite.'"

There was also a special feeling about the place, Bill Michero remembered. "I started out with the company at 23," he explained. "I knew it was a small organization, but we were doing a little more business each month. The ambience and atmosphere were crappy, and I knew that all of my classmates were making the same money that I was with a lot less effort, but it was fun to be there even though I was working my fanny to a frazzle. Perhaps it was Charles and Dave and the other guys, but you had the feeling you were a part of a team that was building something. In a short while I had seen the evolution out of the staid shoe-findings business into a new, interesting direction. Sure there were those who didn't find it all that great. They went on to work somewhere else. It was a self-screening environment."

* * *

Hinckley-Tandy's leathercraft business, begun as a wartime sideline, began to expand after Charles Tandy's return.

"There were a lot of servicemen coming back home wounded and incapacitated in varying degrees and they were placed in Veterans hospitals for treatment and rehabilitation," Harlan Swain reported. "The occupational therapists, looking for things to help them occupy their time and get back some of their confidence, found that working with leather had a great deal of therapeutic value." In addition, leathercraft provided an opportunity for people to augment their incomes because the finished products possessed genuine value.

"Dave Tandy initially recognized the possibilities of leathercraft, but the aggressive pursuit of it as a business came from Charles," Michero asserted. "Dave had 30 years in the business and knew the merchandise. Charles didn't know the merchandise that well, but he was keenly aware of what was happening in the marketplace, and he was convinced that a large, untapped market existed for leathercrafts. So the combination worked out pretty well. Charles and Dave admired each other very much, and Dave deferred to Charles when he kept insisting the future of the business lay in leathercrafts and not in shoe findings."

Luther Henderson recalled, "When Charles returned from the Navy, he didn't take a line job in the family business. He was a general all-around person. He was trying to find a way to make the business grow. He thought in terms of having a little better, a little bigger, a little nicer place for people to go to have their shoes repaired. He thought very seriously about this and was trying to find locations and things like that. But he never actually tried it. The next phase of the story is that he did begin to get interested in the leathercraft side of the business and he realized the difference in the amount of gross profit it was contributing in relation to the sales volume. The shoe-findings business was so competitive, with pretty tight gross margins and a lot of expenses. It operated on a gross margin of 25 percent, while the leathercrafts gross margins were at the virtually unheard of rate of 38 percent to 39 percent."

The split-up of Hinckley-Tandy was inevitable. Norton Hinckley, a dyed-in-the-wool shoe-findings man, saw no future in leathercrafts. Charles Tandy wanted the company to spend all of its resources in building up leathercrafts. Norton felt that Charles was an opinionated, pushy young man whose talk about creating a nationwide chain of leathercrafts stores was a pipe dream.

Dave Tandy was "a reluctant recruit" to the leathercrafts side of the business, Henderson opined. "I think if he'd been given a free vote, he'd probably have voted against the split-up with Hinckley. But because Charles did have this enthusiasm, and the fact that Charles could marshal some pretty good arguments, Dave agreed to the proposition."

Charles Tandy held firmly to his beliefs, as he explained in a talk at Brigham Young University in 1973. "After I had been in my father's business for about a year-and-a-half, doing my best in research and study, I came to the conclusion that the only thing that looked as if it was worthwhile was leathercraft," he revealed. "This was doing about $300,000 a year in sales at that time. Shoe repair supplies were running, maybe, a million dollars. We were making a living and that was all. I knew from observing other types of businesses around the world that there had to be a better way. There had to be more opportunities. I had studied enough to know that there was another way, and that we had to find it."

The beginning of the parting of the ways came at a special meeting of the board of directors of the Hinckley-Tandy Leather Company in the company offices at 1600 Throckmorton Street on May 31, 1949. Norton Hinckley and Dave Tandy were present as the firm's directors and stockholders. Also in attendance were Douglas N. Hinckley, Charles D. Tandy, and James L. West. Norton Hinckley, acting as chairman, announced that the purpose of the meeting was to consider "a feasible plan of departmentalized operations."

Dave Tandy, acting as secretary, reported that the company was operating a wholesale, retail and mail order business with two distinct classes of merchandise: shoe findings and upper leathers. "Under the system of operation presently used," Tandy stated, "it cannot be determined the amount of profit made from each class of business." He cited an example from the operating results of the year ended May 31, 1949, compared to the previous year's operations. "Sales of $535,362 in the prior year provided a net profit of $21,959, while sales of $578,798 in the year just ended produced a loss of $1,012. It cannot be determined from the present method of operations which class of business produced profits or losses. For this reason, it is necessary that the business be departmentalized."

The minutes of the meeting declared, "After much discussion, it was resolved that the business shall be divided into two departments, one department to be described as the shoe-findings department, the other to be described as the upper leather department, effective for the fiscal year beginning June 1, 1949, and ending May 31, 1950. The net assets of the company shall be divided between the two departments in a manner sufficient to meet the requirements of the plan, and each department shall maintain a complete set of books and shall account for all business transactions of every kind and character, shall render monthly operating statements and shall maintain separate bank accounts."

Norton and Douglas Hinckley were named operators and managers of the shoe-findings department, which would occupy three floors of the building at a rental of $225 per month. As an incentive, it was stipulated they would receive, in addition to their salaries, a bonus equal to 25 percent of the net profits of their department after income taxes were prorated.

Dave and Charles Tandy were named operators and managers of the upper leather department, which would occupy two floors of the building at a rental of $150 per month. They, too, received an incentive bonus of 25 percent of their net profits after taxes.

Bill Michero recalled the separation. "We physically separated the inventories of the upper leather and the shoe-findings departments. The upper leather department later became our leather business. We split the building and we allocated the people. There were about 13 of us working there. There were about 45,000 square feet in the building, roughly 15,000 on each of the three floors. So the physical separation was made, and this group of employees stayed with the shoe-findings business and this group stayed with the upper leathers."

The separation agreement lasted for nearly a year, but it soon became apparent that a divorce was inevitable as the two entities drew farther apart. The official end of Hinckley-Tandy Leather Company came on

March 31, 1950, when a final settlement was consummated. Dave Tandy agreed to pay Norton Hinckley $155,848, half in cash and half in promissory notes, for the Hinckley-Tandy operations in Fort Worth, Houston, Amarillo, and Albuquerque. The notes totaling $78,588 were secured by a lien on property owned by Dave Tandy in Fort Worth, and were payable in three annual installments of $26,196, due April 1, 1951 through April 1, 1953.

Hinckley retained the Dallas shoe-findings operation, for which he agreed to pay Dave and Charles Tandy $14,918. He was joined in the business by his son, Douglas Hinckley. Norton Hinckley maintained his home in Fort Worth after the split, and commuted to Dallas by car. He died in Fort Worth on October 14, 1964, at the age of 83.

The Tandy Leather Company was established on May 31, 1950, with about a dozen investors, with Charles and Dave Tandy holding the majority ownership. Other original investors included Bill Tandy, Jim West, Bill Michero, Bill Vance, and Harlan Swain.

The Tandy Leather Company took over the premises at 1600 Throckmorton. It would remain there until 1952, when it moved 13 blocks north to a new location at 2nd and Throckmorton streets, an area of downtown Fort Worth that would 26 years later become a part of the Tandy Center.

A new era was about to unfold, with Charles Tandy firmly in the driver's seat.

Chapter 3
Tandy Leather Company Spreads Its Wings

The move of the Tandy Leather Company to 2nd and Throckmorton Streets satisfied the growing company's need for larger quarters, but it also was a manifestation of Charles Tandy's longing to improve the firm's public image and establish his own.

Dave Tandy, despite his involvement in the Chamber of Commerce, Sales Executives Club, and Rotary, had never been granted entry into the Fort Worth power structure dominated by the big downtown banks, utilities, law firms, oil companies, and monied families. So to Charles the trek uptown to a location across the street from Leonards Department Store, the city's dominant retailing force, represented an upwardly mobile step, something akin to a family moving across town to the "right" side of the tracks.

The new home of Tandy Leather Company was a post World War I four-story brick building with a glass storefront at street level that stood stoically on a 50-foot corner lot amid more imposing structures. The Leonards Department Store complex sprawled catty-corner across a full city block from the Tandy Leather site.

On the first floor of the rented premises occupied by the Tandy Leather Company was a leather and leathercrafts store, behind which was the mail order department. Unfortunately this arrangement meant that order fillers were constantly elbowing their way past the customers to get to the merchandise on display. The street floor was concrete, but the three floors above were of wood that had become impregnated with oil over the years. A freight elevator large enough to accommodate a good-sized truck served the building.

The offices were located on the second floor and were wide open, devoid of partitions, as they had been at the Hinckley-Tandy Leather Company, but now several four-foot planters graced the premises.

Everyone, however, was still within easy shouting distance of everyone else, and there was still no privacy for anyone. Lined up against the back wall were the desks belonging to Charles Tandy, Dave Tandy and Jim West.

"You could hear every telephone conversation, every argument," recalled Rachel Barber, who began working there in June of 1952. "Charles, his father and Mr. West rarely spoke in quiet voices. They really enjoyed a good argument with a great deal of shouting. They'd be at each other's throats, criticizing each other. Then, at the stroke of 12, they'd say, 'Hey, it's time to go to lunch,' and all smiling they'd go out together. They picked each other's brains openly. There were no secrets, no intrigue. Everybody knew what was going on. It was wide open. I loved it."

Miss Barber, who would later become director of corporate and shareholder relations for Tandy Corporation, was working for the Justin Boot Company in advertising, print materials, and communications in 1952, when a friend advised her that Tandy Leather Company was looking for someone with experience in advertising and direct mail.

She remembered walking through the retail store on the way to her first meeting with Charles Tandy and being impressed that it was "crammed with merchandise" and "full of customers." Tandy offered her a job, but she wasn't sure she wanted to take it. After that, nearly every Friday evening, when the store stayed open until 9 o'clock, she would drop by and chat with Charles, who was already obsessed with his dream of building a nationwide chain of leathercraft stores. Tandy finally persuaded her to leave her better paying job at Justin and join Tandy Leather at a starting salary of $250 a month.

"We had a subsidiary called Cardat Leather Goods Company, which sold finished manufactured leather goods—belts, billfolds, handbags, watchbands primarily," she recalled. "Charles had split the merchandising into two parts and he gave me the billfolds and watchbands to ride herd on and a man named Don Frazier had the belts and handbags. We had catalogs and we sold through retailers and jobbers. We contracted for the manufacturing and we did the designing, the projections, the buying, the advertising and the shipping. This was all on the second floor. Even the shipping room was on the second floor. They were also shipping to all of the Tandy Leather Company stores from the second and third floors, and, eventually, they had to have more room. So they put the shipping and warehousing for Cardat up on the fourth floor and moved accounting to the third floor. They moved me up to the fourth floor which had no air-conditioning. It had 24 windows and some big fans, but it really got hot up there."

The heat, however, didn't deter Tandy from coming up to the fourth floor for the daily grillings and harangues she suffered at his hands. "He would come by asking questions and lecturing and preaching to me. With the hours we were keeping, from 7 a.m. to 7 p.m., I was beginning to get a little weary. And one night, I went up to him and asked him, 'Why do you pick on me?' And he answered, 'If I didn't think you had it in you, I wouldn't even bother with you.'

"When he picked on me, it was always about merchandising. He taught you by asking questions. He asked you questions and when you answered, he piggy-backed on your answer. 'Why is that?' Pretty soon you were admitting that you could quadruple sales. He suggested I could increase sales by zeroing in on wealthy people in town by coming up with special designs. He taught me how to figure costs, what my profit should be, what I should charge. He spent hours giving me suggestions and explanations and making me think. He gave me a fantastic education. He could be real mean to people, but he was teaching them constantly. I appreciated that he didn't care whether you were a woman. He treated men and women exactly alike. All he cared about was for you to produce. His only concern was sales and profits. You got a P&L every month and that's all that counted."

One of Charles Tandy's first moves after the formation of the Tandy Leather Company was to open two retail stores specializing exclusively in leathercraft. The pilot stores were located in El Paso and San Antonio where the company was already enjoying a good mail order business. It was Charles' idea that wherever there were 1,000 catalog customers a store could be operated profitably. Bill Healy was named manager of the El Paso store and Barney Barnett manager of the San Antonio store.

The stores sold to individuals and institutions, "anybody that was doing leather work," Bill Michero said. "There were an awful lot of things you could make for much less than they would cost you at a retail store, particularly ladies' handbags. So lots of people were getting into it."

The two new stores exceeded even Charles' optimistic forecasts, racking up a whopping 100 percent return on investment in their first year of operation and bolstering Tandy's conviction that his formula for developing a leathercraft chain store operation was sound.

A major factor in the success of the program was the company catalog. The first one, published in 1950, contained only eight pages. Robert R. Lowdon, then a young printing salesman for the Stafford-Lowdon Printing Company in Fort Worth, remembered that the first Tandy Leather Company catalogs were printed on a multilith press that was really too small to do the job.

"We had the only web press in this part of Texas, so I finally convinced Dave Tandy to give us the business. This was in the early 1950s, and by then the number of catalogs they were printing had grown to 30,000 and the number of pages to 32. So this represented a big order for me."

Problems arose immediately, however. To hold down costs, Dave Tandy made liberal use of illustrations from competitors' catalogs as artwork for his catalog, Lowdon learned.

"If he needed a picture of a mallet, he'd cut it out of a competitor's catalog. And if he needed a $17.50 price, he'd go through the catalog until he found one. "Then he'd paste four or five of those things down on a sheet of paper to make a catalog page. But he always used only one drop of rubber cement. 'I don't want to waste any cement,' he said. Well, the first catalog we printed, after he put the pages together using one drop of cement, the cement didn't hold. By the time I got back to the office, some of the items had shifted around. The $17.50 price tag had shifted down to a pair of scissors costing $4.50, and the $4.50 price tag had shifted to something else more expensive. So when the catalogs came off the press, we had a lot of wrong prices."

To keep Tandy's goodwill, Lowdon offered to publish a correction sheet at Stafford-Lowdon's expense. Corrections were printed on both sides of an 8½-by-11-inch sheet of paper that was inserted inside the catalog. "We did this rather than having to print the whole 30,000 catalogs over," Lowdon related. "The funny thing is that Mr. Tandy got some prices on that wrong, too. Charles really got a kick out of that. He said, 'We're gonna have to put out a correction sheet for the correction sheet.'"

These catalogs and other direct mail items were not slick, but when sent to the right people, they triggered sales. Mailing lists were developed by placing small ads in the back of *Popular Science* magazine and by enclosing ads in shipments.

"Compared to the catalogs you see today, their first catalogs were not outstanding," Luther Henderson said. "But they were a big factor in the success of the business because the catalog was the only place where people interested in leathercraft could find a source for the different supplies they needed to make something out of leather. Prisons became big catalog customers for this reason."

The new stores that were opened in the early 1950s were located near prisons that were buying leathercraft materials from Tandy Leather Company for their rehabilitation and recreation programs. Leathercraft not only gave the prisoners something to do in their spare time, it provided them with extra income from the sale of their finished products to other prisoners. "Those first stores," Henderson added, "were sort of outposts of the mail order business. The stores did mail order as well as retail, and in those early years mail order was half or more of the total sales volume."

In 1952, with the mail order business growing rapidly and the number of stores mounting, the need for a centralized accounting system became acute.

"Charles had taken accounting courses and had a reasonable knowledge of bookkeeping and accounting," Henderson noted. "I had majored in it and was a CPA. In addition, my family owned the Chickasaw Lumber Company which operated a number of branches. I had grown up in the business and was familiar with the problems of branch store reporting and accounting. So Charles asked me if I'd give him a hand."

Henderson began coming into the office after finishing his day's work at the family lumber yard.

"I tried to set up a better accounting system for Charles and supervised its operation," Henderson recounted. "That's when I first began to get familiar with the numbers in his business and saw that the profit potential appeared to be considerably greater in leathercrafts than in selling two-by-fours. Everybody and his brother can sell two-by-fours at a very tight margin. Nobody was selling leathercraft. So that's how I got started with Charles."

Tandy Leather Company was now operating eight stores, including new outlets in Beaumont, Salt Lake City and Charlotte. The Charlotte store, which served prisons in North Carolina and Georgia marked the firm's first venture east of the Mississippi. All of the stores were company-owned and separately incorporated to take advantage of the federal income tax regulation then in effect that exempted the first $25,000 of a corporation's earnings. Each store manager had a 25 percent interest in the venture.

Charles Tandy would tell his prospective store managers, "If you want to manage a store, you won't get much in salary. But I'll guarantee you 25 percent of the profits if you invest 25 percent of the cost of the initial inventory."

Harlan Swain, who became manager of the Tandy Leather store in Fort Worth in 1952, said Tandy was convinced that his investment/ compensation plan would form the basis for building a national chain of leathercrafts stores. Tandy believed his program would not only motivate his store managers but would raise some needed capital as well.

"If a guy has his own money tied up in a store," Charles told Swain, "he's going to work a lot of extra hours, not for you, not for the company, but for himself. Why? Because it's his own money that's at risk. And he knows that if he loses it, it's gone for good."

When it turned out that few, if any, of the aspiring store managers had the funds to put up the initial 25 percent investment, Tandy cosigned the notes for the store managers at the Fort Worth National Bank. The average loan was for about $2,500.

"This worked very well," Swain said. "Now Charles could really hammer on you, not about what you were doing for the company but what you were doing for yourself."

Tandy offered all employees an opportunity to invest in the new stores. Rachel Barber remembered that to open a new store usually required about $10,000. "Charles would go around the office and collect $1,000 here and a $1,000 there. If you didn't have the money, and most of us didn't, he'd co-sign a note for you at the bank."

When he opened the first two leathercraft stores, Tandy worked out a formula where they operated with 10 percent less gross profit than he was sure his competitors were realizing, Harlan Swain said.

"He figured he could regain 5 percent of that by representing tanneries, but to represent tanneries he had to have a top salesman out selling. That's why he convinced his father to bring Jim West to Fort Worth from Houston. West would be paid $500 per month, but would have to sell at least enough leather to pay his salary and his traveling expenses. By doing this, however, he would be keeping the tanneries happy, and Charles would be getting the 5 percent edge he was seeking. That gave Charles some margin to play with. The last thing he put down on his original profit and loss pro forma statements was salary. That was the one thing he felt he could control. You could beat the salaries Charles paid on almost every block in town."

Swain had opened a Tandy Leather store in Dallas in early 1951 and was the first manager of the Charlotte store when it opened in November of 1951. He had borrowed the $3,000 for his 25 percent interest in the Charlotte store, with Charles Tandy guaranteeing the note at the Fort Worth National Bank.

"The store managers selected the store sites in those days," Swain said. "What we looked for was a well-known street. It didn't have to be a 100 percent retail location. Generally, we were looking for a street that was just off the main street, a street that was known, not only to everybody in the city itself, but to the whole trade territory. If people knew the street, we knew they could find the store. That's the way we looked for locations. In San Francisco, where I opened a store in 1953, we located our store on Mission Street. Everybody in the Bay Area knows where Mission Street is. In Dallas, we located on Pacific Street in the heart of the downtown area."

Kenneth L. Gregson, a former store manager who later became chairman of the board and chief executive officer of Tandycrafts, Inc., recalled Charles Tandy's instructions on finding store sites.

"We want a store in this town. Find a street in town that everybody knows, and then keep on walking on that street until you come to where we can afford the rent. When you rent the building, here's 10 bucks and a bag of nails, and you put the store together. And what petty cash you have left over is what you open the store on."

In Beverly Hills, the Tandy Leather Company store was located on Wilshire Boulevard. But, said Gregson, "It wasn't down where people think of when they think of Wilshire Boulevard. It was out where we could afford the rent."

In St. Louis, Gregson opened three leather stores on Olive Street. "Everybody in St. Louis and everybody coming in from southern Illinois and northern and southern Missouri knows where Olive Street is," he explained. "Sure, they might have to go west a long way on Olive Street, but sooner or later they were going to run into one of our stores."

In the fall of 1952, Bill Vance, who had just gotten back from two years of recall duty in the Korean War, was getting ready to take over management of the Tandy Leather advertising department, when the manager of the retail store at 2nd and Throckmorton became ill. Charles asked Vance to take over as store manager. Vance recounted how Tandy's constant nagging motivated him to break a store sales record.

"Charles was the kind of guy who was always looking over your sales and asking, 'Is this the best you can do?'" Vance said. "I think he did that about my third or fourth day as a store manager. I hadn't even had time to find out what kind of sales we had done. A week or two later, Charles again came down to the store and he asked me again, 'Is this the best you can do?' I said, 'No, that's not the best I can do.'

"This was probably about September 1, and I was so steamed up that I told him that before the year was over, I'd have at least one $30,000 sales month. Charles said, 'There's no need to be silly about this. You're not going to be able to do $30,000.' Up to then our highest month had been about $16,000 in the previous December. But I said, 'My figure still goes, $30,000.' Charles said, 'Okay, I'll hold you to it.' After he left, I asked myself how in the devil I was gonna do it? But we went to work, and in November our sales went to $26,000 and in December we did $31,000 and something."

Tandy Leather's business at that time, Vance revealed, wasn't nearly as advanced as it eventually became. "We were selling a few kits, but mostly it was hides, tools and instruction books, and cutout pieces. And we had only two or three instruction books. We still were learning how to sell leathercraft."

But the system was working. The ads were getting results, the inquiries were coming in, and new stores were being opened. The cycle was self-perpetuating: One of the criteria for selecting store locations was the number of inquiries received from the immediate area.

But Charles Tandy was now looking for other ways to grow, and in October of 1952 he found a likely candidate in American Handicrafts Company, a firm based in East Orange, New Jersey, that would have the distinction of becoming Tandy Leather Company's first acquisition.

"This was the first big deal Charles and I worked on together," Luther Henderson recalled. "American Handicrafts was primarily a mail order business that had two retail stores. Charles saw an affinity between Tandy Leather and a catalog business selling a full line of crafts and leathercrafts. The fact that American Handicrafts was about to go bankrupt was an asset rather than a liability as far as Charles was concerned.

He thought he could make it profitable." Charles Tandy, Luther Henderson and Bill Michero flew up to New Jersey to negotiate the purchase. The owner wanted too high a price, in their estimation, and negotiations were about to break down.

"Charles and I sat around that night and decided what we thought we could pay," Henderson recounted. "So I wrote out a proposal on a sheet of yellow paper. The next day Charles took it down to this guy and told him, 'Here are the terms I'm willing to pay for your business. Take it or leave it.' The guy sputtered and fumed, but his back was really against the wall. So he took it. It was a fairly complicated deal because there were a lot of debts involved. We didn't pay the guy very much, about $90,000 in cash, and we absorbed all the liabilities. But his equity didn't amount to very much as a result of the debts he owed."

Bill Michero was tapped by Tandy to return to New Jersey to liquidate the excess inventory and run the American Handicrafts operation. Michero by now had gained considerable managerial experience in a variety of jobs that had included a stint as credit manager of the Tandy Leather operation after the Hinckley-Tandy split-up. His initial assignment had paired him with Jim West to effect the winding down of the accounts receivable.

"If you can," Michero said, "try to envision the quality of the accounts receivable of a small, independent shoe repair shop—cobblers that Jim West had been selling to all these years. Our task was to clean up the receivables. But Jim's task also was to unload a lot of inventory that needed to be unloaded. You've got a conflict right there. He's got to move all this inventory, but I also want to collect for it. So that was my first introduction to Jim West and it was not a pleasant one. I was a wet-nosed kid and he was a veteran. It was tough going. I remember one account in San Antonio, where we took a horse as payment in lieu of cash."

That was his first introduction, Michero added, to Charles Tandy's virtuosity in setting two people to competitive tasks in order to get a tough job done.

In the fall of 1952, Michero and his young family migrated east to take over his American Handicrafts duties, moving into a new apartment complex in Irvington, New Jersey, a suburb of Newark.

"American Handicrafts had been in business about 20 years, right through the Depression," Michero recalled. "It was primarily a mail order business with schools, hospitals, youth groups and church groups, camps and that sort of thing all over the country. It had a general handicrafts line that included sculpture, work with clay and pottery, artwork, art supplies, and a range of crafts. About 25 percent of its sales was in leathercraft, which was our meat. So it seemed like a decent thing to add to our enterprise, one that appeared to be buildable. It also was our launching pad for our introducing Tandy Leather stores in the Northeast. That was one of my collateral tasks. I got five of them opened in the nearly two years that I was up there." The American Handicrafts warehouse was on Harrison Avenue in East Orange, and one of the company's two retail stores was located across the street. The other store was on 41st Street off 5th Avenue across the street from the New York Public Library in mid-town Manhattan. Initially, the company offices were located in the warehouse, but in 1953 Michero moved the warehouse and the offices to Hoboken.

In 1954, after Michero had been recalled to Fort Worth, American Handicrafts began opening additional stores across the country, conforming to the Tandy Leather Company policy. "They were little shops," Michero said, "about 1,500 to 2,000 square feet. As a result of that program, we did eventually peak out at about $35 million in sales. We ran that business for 30 years," he continued, "but we never were able to get it singing like a good violin should. Profitability was uncertain. One year you'd make a nice profit; but the next year, because of the inventory you had to eat, the profit would disappear. And as we opened new stores, the catalog and mail order business subsided."

The American Handicrafts acquisition did result in bringing to Fort Worth the Tandy Leather Company's first woman executive, Mary Frank. Miss Frank had been serving as American Handicrafts' advertising manager in East Orange at the time of its acquisition by Tandy. Shortly thereafter she was offered the opportunity of moving to Fort Worth to become the advertising manager of Tandy Leather Company. She accepted with some trepidation, having never been to Texas and envisioning Fort Worth as a frontier outpost. Her first glimpse of the Tandy Leather Company offices at 2nd and Throckmorton reinforced her doubts.

"It was in the middle of the night and I had just driven in from East Orange," she reported. "It was the first time I'd ever been in Texas. The streets were deserted. I pulled up in front of this building and I said to myself, 'My God, what have I come to?'"

In her new position Miss Frank found herself having to deal on a daily basis with Dave Tandy, who was then still overseeing advertising and merchandising. "The ads we were running were little 2-inch ads in magazines selling little baby mocassins for 50 cents," she recounted. "They were darling. The inquiries would come in from the ads and we'd fill the orders. We advertised in magazines like *Work Basket, Ladies Home Journal,* and *Good Housekeeping.* This was before you could buy ads by specific geographic areas and we'd have 50 to 100 little ads running at a time. We ran little ads because that's all we could afford. Mr. Tandy had a simple coding system for his ads that enabled him to know immediately which ads pulled and which ones didn't. Magazine salesmen would call on him and he had all the answers. Here was this little guy in his mid-60s, still sharp as a tack. He'd say, 'Your magazine is no good for us.'"

Years later, Jim West would nostalgically recall the ads in a speech at a Newcomen Society of North America dinner honoring Tandy Corporation at the Fort Worth Club on October 29, 1968.

"Among our first successful ads in 1951 was a 2-inch ad selling baby mocs for 50 cents a pair," West recounted. "This was a do-it-yourself kit cut from white lambskin. When completed, it became an infant's bootsie. Orders poured in. This item sold 3 million pairs in the next five years and was the first of several thousand unique leather do-it-yourself kits. From book marks to full size saddles, these kits formed the solid base of the new company and made the word leathercraft synonymous with Tandy across the country. By 1952, sales were $2.9 million."

Miss Frank, who served as director of corporate relations for Tandy Corporation during the 1960s and '70s, recalled those early days at 2nd and Throckmorton.

She remembered one incident in which Jim West demonstrated a three-legged chair with a leather seat they called "The Little Buckaroo" to Charles and Dave Tandy. "Mr. West was lying flat on the floor with his head in the little chair, and Charles and D. L. were standing there laughing while I took a picture of it. There was a wonderful spirit in that big, old barnlike office. There was no politicking. It was open. We worked hard and we had a good time."

Charles Tandy even then was demonstrating his "vision and charisma," she said. "He had dreams. He was always teaching by asking questions. 'What were sales last week?' 'What was the percentage of gain?' 'What did you spend on such-and-such last week?' 'What did that cost you?' And you had to know the answers. If you didn't and you said, 'I'm not sure,' he'd take the time to give you a lesson. You never knew when he was going to come by.

"You had to have the numbers at your fingertips. One time he came by and asked me something and I gave him an answer and he said, 'That's not right.' I said, 'It is right. I'll bet you.' He loved to bet, but never a lot. I said, 'I'll bet you a nickel,' and it turned out I was right. When he gave me the nickel, I scotch-taped it to the wall, and every time he came by my desk he looked at that nickel until he finally won it back."

Tandy never came into the office in a bad mood, she related. "He was always full of energy. You could feel it. He always walked fast, and it seemed in those days that he always wore the same suit, just like that lawyer on TV, Matlock, always the same suit, the jacket never buttoned, a neutral-colored suit that was always rumpled. And there was always a cigar in his hand. His hair was very black." She also recalled the many "knockdown, drag-out fights" that she had with him over the years.

"I was in his office one day when we got into a heated argument, a real battle. He read the riot act to me and I lost my temper. I pounded my fist on his desk and he pounded the desk right back. I remember how much larger his fist was than mine. He hit the desk so hard, papers and things flew off onto the floor. I stalked out of his office, figuring my career was over. This was on a Friday afternoon. On Monday morning, I came to work and began to clean out my desk. Charles leaned over the railing from the second floor, where his office was, and said, 'Miss Frank, why do we have to fight like a pair of Boxer puppies?' We talked it over and he gave me a raise. He never held a grudge. Rachel Barber and I called him, 'Uncle Dudley.' We never went to him with personal problems, but if you had a family problem and you needed help, Charles would be right there."

She began buying stock in Tandy Leather Company upon her arrival in Fort Worth, Miss Frank disclosed. "Dave L. Tandy loaned several of us $1,000 to buy stock because we didn't have any money. I was making all of $300 a month. Mr. Tandy made us the offer and we took him up on it. I paid him back over a couple of years. From that point on every bonus check I received went for stock. Charles was always urging us to buy stock. I used my bonus checks to pay back the loans I took out to buy the stock. First it was $5,000, then $10,000. I never got to see a bonus check in those days."

She would later discover that she had this in common with most of her colleagues. Over the ensuing years, it would become almost a ritual for Tandy managers to succumb to Charles Tandy's exhortations and exchange their annual bonus checks for company stock. A great many of them would become millionaires as a result.

Chapter 4
High Hopes Turn to Frustration

There was a deep paradox about Tandy's willingness to stake every-thing on a business that catered exclusively to leisure time activity, something that he found unappealing. He was convinced that there was a great and growing market for leathercrafts just waiting for him to tap and that by catering to it, he could fashion Tandy Leather Company into a vehicle for gratifying his lofty ambitions.

"What to do with extra time is a problem that hits everyone of us sooner or later," he told Harold Monroe, a business writer for the *Fort Worth Star-Telegram*. "We've researched the problem. Handicrafts can be completely time- and mind-consuming. This is an immense business and people are spending more and more money on it."

In addition, there were all those millions of people who did nothing more than sit aimlessly in front of their television sets all day long. If only a small percentage of them could be motivated into working with their hands and minds, the payoff could be staggering.

"How about yourself?" Monroe wanted to know.

"I'm too busy to have a hobby," Tandy replied.

Hobbies were for customers, not for him. Making wallets and belts out of leather were fine for other people, but he had no time for idle pastimes. His job was creating hobbies for others.

"People respond to the idea of accomplishment after they are shown the way," he contended. "This is particularly true when such accom-plishment can be a source of pleasure and even extra money for those interested in capitalizing on their creative abilities. We've got to show them how to do it."

That he was succeeding was manifested in an article about him in *The New York Times*, in which the writer said that "handicrafts was be-coming synonymous with Tandycrafts."

This was a heady time for Charles Tandy. He was seeing his optimistic growth forecasts for his company being realized and surpassed. Even Dave Tandy and Jim West had to concede that he was outperforming their expectations.

Dave Tandy was now in his 60s and beginning to slow down. More and more, he was content to let Charles run the show under a loose leash that he occasionally still found it necessary to yank. But there was no doubt around the company who was now in the driver's seat. One of those who got the message was Bill Tandy, who had returned from combat duty as a B-26 pilot in Europe and joined the family business after the war.

"This car has only one driver's seat, and I'm sitting in it," Charles told Bill upon his return home.

Three years younger than Charles, Bill Tandy was even larger in stature, had an ego that matched his older brother's, was equally ambitious, and had a competitive streak just as wide. Finding it difficult to accept being in Charles' shadow, he decided to strike out on his own in 1950 and moved to Tulsa, where he started his own leather business modeled after the Tandy Leather Company.

"I always believed that Dave Tandy used to tell Charles that he'd never be the businessman that Bill was," Ken Gregson opined. "I believe Dave helped Bill become successful and that he held that up to Charles. Charles spent his lifetime wanting Dave to pat him on the back, but Dave wouldn't do it. He knew that not patting Charles on the back would make Charles drive that much harder. And that was probably the reason Charles very rarely patted anyone on the back. There was a lot of conflict between the two boys."

Dave Tandy, who was devoted to both of his sons, found it difficult being caught in the middle after Bill started his leather company. But although he tried to remain neutral, he would occasionally give Bill a helping hand by sneaking copies of the Tandy Leather mailing list to him. Charles would learn of it and mumble and grumble.

A week after Lloyd Redd, who was managing a Tandy Leather store in Omaha, sent in the names and addresses of a group of Farm Bureau women to be added to the mailing list, all of the women on the list received catalogs from Bill Tandy's leather store in Tulsa, Redd reported. He complained to Jim West.

"Blood is thicker than water," West replied dryly.

The sibling rivalry carried over into competition for store managers. John Wilson was teaching vocational leatherwork at Highlands University in Las Vegas, New Mexico, when Charles Tandy talked to him about joining Tandy Leather Company. When Wilson came down to Fort Worth for further discussion, he found that Charles had been called out of town on an emergency. At the Tandy Leather offices, Wilson met Bill Tandy, who was in town on one of his frequent visits.

"Dave Tandy must have told Bill what I was in town for, because he began recruiting me to go to work for him," Wilson said. "He talked to me all one day and half of the next day, and I flew with him to Tulsa in his plane on my way back to New Mexico. I didn't know it at the time it happened, but I found out later that Bill and Charles flipped a coin to see who was going to hire me. Bill won and I went to work for him in his Denver store on August 26, 1951. I remained with Bill until he merged his business with Tandy Leather Company in 1955."

The competition between the Tandy brothers was equally intense out in the field. Ken Gregson, who was managing a store for Bill Tandy in St. Louis, told of his rivalry with Delbert Harrell, the manager of the Tandy Leather Company store in Kansas City. "We spent a lot of time trying to steal customers from one another. When the two companies merged, it took us two years to bury the hatchet," Gregson said.

Wilson, Gregson, and Redd shared evocative memories of the Charles Tandy of that era.

"The first time I met Charles was when he came out to Highlands University where I was teaching," Wilson recalled. "He walked into the shop and I heard him say, 'Where's Wilson?' in a big, loud voice. Then I saw this big, brash guy. I didn't know who he was, but my first impression was that he was an obnoxious son of a bitch. Gwen was with him and he insisted that they take my wife and me to lunch. I called my wife and she said she couldn't go unless we took the baby with us. The baby was maybe a month or so old. So we picked up my wife and baby and went to lunch. By the time he left, I'd changed my mind about him. He was the kind of guy who was convincing because everything that he told you he was going to do came true."

Gregson added, "He always dreamed big. Back in the leather days, when we got together, sometimes with him sitting on a desk and swinging his legs and some of us sitting on the floor because we didn't have enough chairs to go around, we'd sit and dream. He was the leader. He'd tell us what we were gonna do, where the sales were gonna go. He was setting the pace, pointing the direction, and we were following him because we believed in him. Some people called him a bear, said he'll tear you to pieces. My thought was that the only thing he'd ever done was try to make better men out of us. Any time he came down on you with both feet, he did it to make a point, to help you learn from your mistake. If you took it the wrong way, he could seem unmerciful. But I always felt that when he took me apart, laid my guts out on the table, he always ended up sewing me back, turning me around, and pointing me in the right direction."

Redd recalled, "Before I joined Tandy Leather Company in the fall of 1952 as a store manager-trainee in Fort Worth, I talked with Charles for about an hour on the phone. He had the ability to paint a beautiful picture. He told me they were going to open leathercraft stores all over the country and that Harlan Swain, one of their store managers in North Carolina, was going to make $10,000 that year. That sounded pretty good to me. Charles was already a dominating person, both physically and mentally. He had the ability to really inspire you, to make you dream, to make you believe that he was going to do everything that he said he would."

Redd remembered one occasion when Charles pounded his fist on the table and said, "I intend to be the head of a $15 million corporation some day." Well, it wasn't long before that was $50 million, then $100 million, then $500 million and, finally, $1 billion. But every goal that he set, he achieved ahead of time, and then he couldn't understand why it took him so long to get there. He was very impatient. He could be exasperating. He would domineer and browbeat you to the point where you did everything you could to prove to him that you weren't as stupid as he said you were. But the other side of the coin was that he didn't have a selfish bone in his body. He dreamed big, but he made it possible for everyone who worked for him to get a piece of the action. He loved to put you on some kind of a formula and pay you a bonus based on that formula."

Redd had served a three-month apprenticeship in what had then been the Tandy Leather Company warehouse at 2nd and Throckmorton at a salary of 90 cents an hour before shipping out to open the Omaha store. His training, he reported, left something to be desired. "All I did was work like a dog in the warehouse. They didn't tell me anything about running a store. I didn't know how to do C.O.D.s, or anything."

At that time, Tandy Leather Company had a policy of issuing a credit memo on refunds up to $5. The credit memo could then be used as payment on the next order or converted into cash. Just before he left for

Omaha, Redd was confronted by Dave Tandy, who pulled a $10 bill out of his pocket and asked, "If a customer sends you this $10 bill in the mail and you ship him $5 worth of merchandise, what are you going to do with the other $5?"

"I'd bill the customer for the $5 worth of merchandise and give him a credit memo for $5," Redd replied.

The answer appeared to upset Dave, who said, "No, no," and began shouting at Jim West, "West, West, we're sending these guys out of here and they don't know what they're doing."

West hurried to the scene, closely followed by Charles Tandy, and a shouting match ensued among the three, with Redd a bemused and befuddled bystander. Finally, Charles turned to Redd.

"Here's the way to do it. First, you take the money," and he took the $10 bill out of Dave Tandy's hand and put it in his pocket. "Then you ship the merchandise and then you write a credit memo. You got it?"

Charles then strode off, Dave's $10 bill still in his pocket.

Dave turned to Redd and told him, "I want you boys to know what you're doing when you're out on your own. Now, at least, you know how to handle a credit memo. It cost me 10 bucks, but it was worth it."

Like all of the other new store managers, Redd borrowed the $2,500 that represented his 25 percent interest in the new venture. Just prior to his leaving for Omaha, Redd accompanied Charles Tandy to the Fort Worth National Bank, where Tandy co-signed his note.

His salary was $250 a month, but he was guaranteed 25 percent of the store's net profit. "That kind of arrangement made it possible for Charles to stick people out in the boondocks without much supervision, because they had the incentive to make it work," Redd said. "They had the incentive, not only to make sales, but to watch everything else, because a fourth of all they made was theirs to keep."

By 1954, Tandy Leather Company had established itself as the nation's leader in packaging and distributing pre-cut, pre-punched, unassembled leather kits and as a major distributor of other handicraft materials through its 67 retail stores, including six American Handicrafts outlets, in 36 states and the Territory of Hawaii. The company catalog was now a 68-page product that was mailed to 1,000,000 customers. Four factories were churning out "U-Do-It" kits for making leather handicrafts items such as shoes, handbags, and belts. Sales reached $8 million and earnings had grown to $580,000. Distribution center for the far-ranging enterprise was the central warehouse that had been opened on Fort Worth's north side in 1954. There, materials were received from all over the country and the kits assembled and packaged for shipment.

But, as the company grew and profits mounted, a nagging problem began tempering the euphoria of the employee-shareholders who now numbered more than 100. It was a problem not at all uncommon in a closely-held enterprise. But, in this case, it was magnified by the fact that the shareholders owned varying amounts of stock in 67 different corporations. This was because each of the 67 stores was a separate corporate entity. Bill Michero, for example, had accumulated minor interests in 30 stores. Most of the shareholders had one thing in common—the stock they owned was highly leveraged because they all had borrowed the money to buy the shares.

Some years later, Charles Tandy described the situation that faced the company at the time. "We got into a mess with ownership," he reported. "Anybody who wanted to sell his stock didn't know what price to ask for it."

The situation became increasingly worrisome after Dave Tandy suffered a severe heart attack in 1954. Bill Vance recalled, "At one point, we thought he was gone. And, if he was gone, the company was gone, because of the inheritance taxes. We didn't have any cash. Everything was in merchandise, equipment, things of that sort. This really scared Charles a great deal."

Vance was managing the Tandy Leather store in Chicago when Tandy dropped in for a visit. The two sat up most of the night talking at an all-night beanery in the Loop. "We talked about how close we had come to losing everything we had worked for, that we'd have had to liquidate the company to pay the inheritance taxes on Dave's estate," Vance related. "That's when Charles told me that one way to solve the problem was for us to get a listing on a stock exchange."

Bill Michero delineated the dilemma facing the shareholders. "Dave Tandy's death or imminent retirement illustrated the spot most of us would eventually find ourselves in. What was the value of the stock he held in Tandy Leather? How do you evaluate it without arguments? How do you deal with estates and people's wills? We knew we would all ultimately have that same problem. We needed to bundle up our assorted ownerships, large and small, into a vehicle to provide liquidity."

There were two solutions available, Michero added. "One was to take the company public. Well, first of all, the company wasn't large enough for that and the leather business was a dead horse in the stock market for a potential public offering. So Charles began looking for a connection that would give us the same result in terms of liquidity and give us a market for our stock. The decision he made was either to buy a company with a New York Stock Exchange listing or sell Tandy Leather Company to a New York Stock Exchange-listed firm which would issue us its shares in exchange for our Tandy Leather stock."

Starting in 1954, Luther Henderson related, "Charles began making trips to New York to get acquainted with the financial community up there, and started looking for companies to buy or sell. We were not big enough to buy anything very big. But Charles was a great one to play all the angles he could, taxwise. And he soon recognized that if he could make a deal with some company that had a substantial tax loss on its books, there'd be more money left over for the Tandy Leather shareholders than any other vehicle he could create."

Tandy found the vehicle he was seeking in the American Hide and Leather Company of Boston, an old-line New England firm that had fallen on hard times.

He heard about American Hide and Leather from sources on Wall Street. He began talking with leather contacts in Boston who steered him to the First National Bank of Boston, a major American Hide and Leather creditor. The bank was energetically seeking a knight in shining armor to take over the failing firm and get the bank off the hook on its loan.

The First National Bank, acting as a matchmaker, set up a meeting between Charles Tandy and Stanley M. Rowland, president of American Hide and Leather, in early 1955. While it was hardly a case of love at first sight, the two suitors were immediately intrigued by the fact that each party had certain irresistible charms.

American Hide and Leather was virtually a corporate shell, its total operations consisting of two obsolete, money-losing tanneries in the Boston area. While the company was not in formal bankruptcy, it was, in effect, insolvent, its assets insufficient to pay its liabilities. Sales had dropped from $17 million to $9 million over the past four years and it had lost over $700,000 the year before. The company had been founded in 1899, when the leather business was one of the nation's major industries. Now, it was on its last legs. But it had one asset that Charles Tandy coveted—a listing on the New York Stock Exchange that dated back to 1935.

To Stanley Rowland, looking for a way of keeping his company afloat, a marriage with the profitable Tandy Leather Company represented his last best hope for survival. It now became a question of working out the terms of the marriage contract. The negotiations with American Hide and Leather went on for about six months.

"Rowland wanted to make a deal, but he didn't know how to go about doing it," Luther Henderson recounted. "Charles knew what he wanted, but he also was very cognizant of the fact that American Hide had no cash and no credit. So he had to work something out that would overcome that obstacle. We finally came up with the deal we wanted and they agreed to do it. The tax laws were different then from what they are now, and we were able to structure a magnificent deal in which nobody could lose."

Before the deal could be consummated, however, the consent of all of the Tandy Leather Company shareholders had to be secured. This was no simple task.

"From 1950 to 1955, one of Charles Tandy's jobs had been to allocate shares in the new stores," Henderson explained. "His usual practice had been to take 50 percent for himself and Dave Tandy, give 25 percent to the store manager, and distribute rights to the remaining 25 percent among other members of the organization. Charles decided how much of each deal he was going to let various people have. For example, Charlotte was considered a very good store and Charles allowed me to have 15 percent of it, which was out of the kindness of his heart, probably because I was a newcomer to the organization.

"By the time of our deal with American Hide and Leather, we had about 110 shareholders with varying interests in corporations all over the country. In addition, we had brought in Bill Tandy's 12 stores in anticipation of the merger. Now we had to get every one of the stockholders to consent to the American Hide and Leather deal. It was a very difficult job. It's very hard to get any group of 110 people to agree on anything unanimously.

"Charles and Jim West and I divided up the country into three parts and each of us took a third and went out and visited with each individual store manager to get him to sign up. We didn't dare assemble them all in one place and try to sell them all at one time. So we decided to divide and conquer. We eventually got everybody. But, for a while, there were two or three who held out. The lawyers we were dealing with in New York didn't think we could swing it, but we told them we'd deliver and we did."

Under the terms of the agreement which Charles Tandy hammered out with Stanley Rowland, Tandy Leather Company was acquired by American Hide and Leather Company for nothing down and $2.3 million in noninterest-bearing notes. American Hide and Leather also obligated itself to make contingent payments to the Tandy group based on Tandy Leather's own earnings for a 10-year period. The key part of the agreement, however, was the granting of options by American Hide and Leather Company to Tandy Leather Company shareholders to buy 500,000 shares of American Hide and Leather stock over a 4-year period at a price of $4 per share.

The $2.3 million in notes was to be repaid in fixed quarterly payments equal to 40 percent of Tandy Leather's consolidated net earnings before federal income taxes. American Hide and Leather also was required to make further payments on the notes equal to all amounts it received from the sale of shares of its common stock upon exercise of the options by Tandy shareholders. The agreement stipulated that a portion of the options would come due quarterly, and that any options not exercised would be forfeited. The option price of $4 per share was the estimated fair market value of American Hide and Leather stock as of September 30, 1955.

The contingent payments were based on a percentage of Tandy Leather's consolidated net earnings before federal income taxes over a 10-year period. The payments would amount to 50 percent of Tandy Leather's net earnings for the 4-year and 9-month period ending June 30, 1960; 31 percent for the fiscal year ending June 30, 1961; 25 percent for the 4-year period ending June 30, 1965, and 6¼ percent for the year ending June 30, 1966.

"American Hide and Leather Company acquired Tandy Leather Company on a payout basis," Luther Henderson elaborated. "We got a fixed payment of $2.3 million for our tangible assets at book value, plus a contingent payment based on the Tandy Leather earnings after the acquisition was completed. It was a 10-year deal under which we basically would get half of the profits we generated for the first five years and one-fourth of our profits for the next four years."

Bill Michero added, "We literally sold the company for cash that the buyers didn't have. They bought us with our own earnings that we shipped up to Boston and they then sent back to us."

The options to purchase 500,000 shares of American Hide and Leather stock, however, provided Charles Tandy with the stock exchange listing he was seeking.

"The phrase used on Wall Street was a 'back door' listing," Michero noted. "They were a shell of a company that had little or no operations, and we exchanged stock with them. Suddenly, we were a publicly-held enterprise with a ready market for our stock at a price that was quoted in the newspapers every day. It was a stock swap. We swapped our closely-held stock for the stock of a company with a listing on the New York Stock Exchange. The nature of the exchange was through the option to buy the 500,000 shares of American Hide and Leather stock at $4 a share."

Alexander Hamilton, a partner in the New York City law firm of Burke & Burke, which represented American Hide and Leather Company, has remained convinced that Charles Tandy hoped to gain control of American Hide and Leather through the exercise of the options.

"He was a brash young Texan, very ambitious, very sure of himself, very bright, with a mind like a computer," Hamilton said while being interviewed in his office overlooking Park Avenue. "I remember being amazed at his ability to toss out numbers and figure out ratios in his head in jig time."

Tandy's game plan, according to Hamilton, was for American Hide and Leather to liquidate its tanneries and use the money to pay down its obligations. "Then, hopefully, with Tandy Leather Company making money, that would provide a new direction in manufacturing rather than tanning for the parent company."

Jesse Upchurch, who married Gwen Tandy's daughter, Connie, and later became a Tandy director and a major stockholder, recalled that he had "serious reservations" about the method Tandy chose to get a New York Stock Exchange listing. Upchurch was especially concerned that American Hide & Leather was generating losses greater than the profits of the Tandy Leather Company. "However," Upchurch added, "Charles was convinced he could stop the American Hide and Leather losses and generate a strong cash flow for aggressive expansion of the very profitable Tandy group."

Bill Michero didn't believe it was initially Tandy's intent to acquire control of American Hide and Leather. "If the Rowland management had done some successful investing and some successful enterprising, very likely Charles would have been content to let that management remain in control," Michero opined. "But early on it was obvious that the management was not doing things right." Stanley Rowland had described American Hide and Leather's rationale for making the deal in a letter to company employees, dated October 18, 1955.

"As you know, American Hide and Leather Company has lost money for several years," Rowland wrote. "Under our present tax laws, such losses can be used to offset earnings at any time during the five years following the year in which the loss occurred. The effect of this procedure is to eliminate federal taxes on future earnings as long as the total amount of the earnings during the five-year period does not exceed the amount of the accumulated loss.

"By purchasing the Tandy Leather Company, their earnings become a part of the earnings of American Hide and Leather Company and thus will not be taxed. If the Tandy Company continued to operate as a separate company, a large part of their earnings would be paid out in taxes. Since it is advantageous for the Tandy Company to become a part of a company with a stock listed on the Stock Exchange, we were able to arrange with them to pay for their company on an installment basis out of their own earnings—utilizing that part of their earnings which would otherwise have been paid out as taxes. The American Hide and Leather Company has not used any of its own capital to complete this transaction. It is an unusual transaction, but one that is advantageous to both companies," the letter concluded.

Rowland later described the deal this way: "We bought this cow with its own milk."

With the signing of the agreement, effective October 1, 1955, Tandy Leather Company became Tandy Industries, Inc., a wholly-owned subsidiary of American Hide and Leather Company. Charles Tandy retained the title of president of Tandy Industries, Inc., and he, Jim West, and Luther Henderson became members of the American Hide and Leather board of directors.

The term leveraged buyout was never mentioned in connection with the deal, but the fact was that Charles Tandy had engineered a classic LBO years before it became a Wall Street staple.

The marriage of convenience began to flounder even before the honeymoon was over.

The three Texans, who represented a minority on the 7-member board, immediately began pushing for the divestiture of the two money-losing tanneries.

"We used all our influence to convince them that the tanning business didn't have much of a future, and we finally succeeded," Henderson said. "But it took some time." It also resulted in some strained feelings among the old line board members who resented the Texans' blunt approach in telling them how to run the business.

But the main cause of friction on the board occurred as a result of the Tandy group's negative reaction to the aggressive acquisition program on which the American Hide and Leather Company management now embarked.

"They began looking for other businesses to buy," Henderson related. "They found these sorry businesses to buy, and Charles, Jim and I couldn't stop them."

Three companies were snapped up in a three-month period between July 1 and October 1, 1956. The first acquisition was Musgrove Petroleum Corporation, Inc., of Wichita, Kansas, an oil and gas drilling and producing firm with operations in Kansas and Oklahoma. Next came Shain & Company, Inc., of Boston, a converter and distributor of fabrics and meshes to the shoe industry. The third company to join the fold was Dunbar Kapple Inc. of Geneva, Illinois. Dunbar Kapple had been organized in 1942 to produce military aircraft components. After the war, it began making auto trailers and farm trailers under contract with Sears Roebuck. With the advent of the Korean War, it had returned to manufacturing aircraft components, primarily flexible stainless steel hose and ducting for jet engines.

The American Hide and Leather name was no longer considered reflective of the enterprise, and on December 1, 1956, the name was changed to General American Industries, Inc. James H. Dunbar, Jr.,

President of Dunbar Kapple, and Pierce C. Musgrove, President of Musgrove Petroleum, were elected to the board of directors, replacing Jim West and Luther Henderson.

"We weren't enthusiastic about it," Henderson said. "But Charles accepted it."

It was Jesse Upchurch's contention, however, that Rowland and Dunbar induced Tandy to agree to West and Henderson leaving the board in exchange for his being named board chairman of General American Industries. "But they never had any intention of permitting him to run the company," Upchurch added. Tandy, indeed, was later elected board chairman, but his tenure of office was short-lived.

With the departure of Henderson and West from the board, Tandy's voice was the only one left to question company policies that were being routinely rubber-stamped by the other directors. Tandy was concerned, not only about the dubious quality of the companies that had been acquired, but by the fact that the Musgrove and Dunbar Kapple acquisitions had been made through an exchange of stock. A total of 196,820 shares was issued in the Musgrove purchase and 294,342 shares in the Dunbar Kapple deal. Tandy viewed this as a serious dilution of his group's equity in the corporation.

"Charles felt that they were giving away too much stock to make these deals, and that the companies they were buying were simply not contributing to the total picture," Henderson said. "The Musgrove Oil acquisition was the biggest mistake. If Stanley Rowland and his people had known more about the oil business, they'd never had made the deal. Dunbar Kapple got so many shares that Charles saw Jim Dunbar as a potential rival for running the company. As far as he was concerned, the Dunbar Kapple acquisition was what sunk the ship."

One acquisition that did carry Charles Tandy's imprimatur was the purchase by General American Industries, on December 31, 1956, of Tex Tan of Yoakum for cash and notes amounting to approximately $1 million. Tex Tan, based in Yoakum in south Texas, manufactured and sold a complete line of Western leather goods such as saddles, riding equipment, gun cases, wallets, boots, moccasins, and hundreds of other items to retail outlets across the country. It was a good complement to the Tandy Industries operations, Charles believed. Begun in 1919 as a small tannery, the company had moved into the production of leather consumer goods in 1929 after Carl C. Welhausen became Tex Tan's general manager.

Relations between the Tandy group and the General American management in Boston continued to deteriorate. The frustration and anger in Fort Worth mounted as it became all too apparent that of the five divisions that made up the parent company, only Tex Tan and Tandy Industries were profitable.

Charles Tandy's fury boiled over as he saw the hard-earned Tandy and Tex Tan profits being used to plug the losses of the other divisions rather than being utilized to expand the profitable Texas-based operations. It was maddening to see profits generated in Fort Worth and Yoakum being dissipated on drilling dry holes in Kansas and Oklahoma.

"Most of us were exercising our options on General American stock, as they fell due, and we had built up a pretty sizable position in it," Bill Michero noted. "So we weren't happy over the way things were going." General American stock was selling at around $3 to $3.50 during this period, which meant the Tandy group was exercising its options at a price above market value. It took about two years for the situation to become really unbearable. We faced the problem of what we could do about it? And it all boiled down to a simple question. Who was going to run the company?"

Tandy Industries sales and earnings were continuing to grow, with net income before taxes exceeding the $1 million mark for the first time in the fiscal year ended June 30, 1957. As the earnings poured in, they were utilized to amortize the $2.3 million in fixed payment notes held by the Tandy group and to finance the exercise of the stock options as they fell due each quarter.

At the General American Industries annual meeting held in Flemington, New Jersey, on November 13, 1957, Charles Tandy was elected chairman of the board, succeeding Claude Douthit, Sr., who had died earlier that year after having served as board chairman for nearly three decades. This was essentially an honorary title. Stanley Rowland, who was re-elected president and treasurer, continued as chief executive officer. However, the Tandy group was granted another board member with the election of John B. Collier, Jr., president of the Fort Worth Poultry and Egg Company, as a director.

The bickering at board meetings between Tandy and the other directors now began to get highly emotional. Alex Hamilton recalled the tension and controversy as the in-fighting became increasingly volatile.

"It became clear that Jim Dunbar of Dunbar Kapple wanted to be the big cheese and that Pierce Musgrove of Musgrove Petroleum did, too. And so did Charles Tandy. Each one of the three thought that the other two should go and that he should be the boss. They were really bad-mouthing each other at board meetings."

Stanley Rowland, seeing his power base eroding, had made the decision to ally himself with Dunbar in order to keep his job as president, apparently convinced that Dunbar would emerge on top in the internal power struggle. During this period, Charles Tandy had made it a point to keep up his contacts at the First National Bank of Boston, which was still a major General American Industries creditor. Now, totally frustrated, Tandy asked Luther Henderson to prepare a report for submission to the bank that summed up the situation from the Tandy group's point of view.

Henderson's report stated unequivocally that there was no way for General American to be profitable under its current mode of operation. In summary, the report stated, the more business the company did, the more money it would lose.

"The report was written," Henderson said, "both for own internal purposes and to present an orderly review of the situation to the proper people at the bank. Charles didn't send a copy to Stanley Rowland because the report did not contain anything that Rowland had not heard from him before."

The report, which was handed to Mort Jennings, the loan officer handling the General American account at the First National Bank of Boston, eventually found its way into the hands of Stanley Rowland and Jim Dunbar. To them, Tandy's going to the bank behind their backs was an act of treason. They viewed the move as a declaration of war and they decided they would fire the first shot. They held their fire until the board of directors meeting that followed the General American Industries annual meeting in Flemington, New Jersey, on November 12, 1958. The General American annual meetings were traditionally held in Flemington, a sleepy town that had achieved worldwide renown as the site of the trial of Bruno Richard Hauptmann for the kidnapping of Charles Augustus Lindbergh, Jr., in 1932. One of the principals in that trial was Norman Schwarzkopf, the head of the New Jersey State Police, whose son, General H. Norman Schwarzkopf, would one day become a national hero as the commander of the United States armed forces in the Desert Shield and Desert Storm operations in the Persian

Gulf. Flemington, located in an isolated section of rural New Jersey, was favored by the General American management as the site of the annual meeting because it was difficult to get to, and that meant fewer irate shareholders with which to contend.

The meeting of the General American board took place in New York City on the morning of November 13, 1958, and was highlighted by the election of Jim Dunbar as chairman of the board succeeding Charles Tandy, who was elected president. Immediately after the meeting adjourned, Dunbar confronted Tandy and notified him that he was being terminated as president of the corporation and would be replaced by Stanley Rowland.

"Your ploy with the bank backfired," Dunbar told Tandy.

Dunbar, however, was reluctant to go the final step of firing Tandy from his position as president of Tandy Industries, General American Industries' most profitable subsidiary.

"Go back to Texas and keep on running the leather business," Dunbar directed Tandy.

It was the lowest moment of Charles Tandy's life.

As he later told Boston banker William L. Brown, "I thought I'd lost the family jewels."

Charles and Gwen visited Bill Collins and his wife in San Miguel, Mexico, shortly after Charles' ouster as board chairman. "He was really sweating out what was happening. He was very close to losing control of Tandy Leather Company and he was very worried, very concerned," Collins said.

He was also ready to go to war.

"It was now obvious," Jesse Upchurch related, "what had to be done to regain control of the Tandy Leather group's assets."

Charles Tandy returned to Fort Worth with fire in his eyes. He had left Boston without voicing any threats to the General American management because he figured there was nothing to be gained from alerting them about what he planned to do. Now he called his people together and told them to get ready for the battle of their lives.

As he talked of the proxy fight he planned to launch, his animation grew. Smoke seemed to be coming out of his ears, as well as from the cigar on which he was furiously puffing. He pounded a hamlike fist on his desk.

"I'm gonna beat those bastards," he proclaimed, "if it's the last thing I do."

The contest would mean that every member of the Tandy group would be asked to lay everything he or she owned or could borrow on the line in one giant crapshoot.

"But I promise you this," Tandy trumpeted, clenched fist upraised and hammering the air, "when we win, and win is what we're gonna do, you won't be sorry. We're gonna take back this company and I'm gonna make you all rich."

Chapter 5
Saving the Family Jewels

It was now Charles Tandy's hand to play, and as he looked over the cards he was holding, he found an ace in the hole—the nearly 250,000 shares of General American Industries stock on which the Tandy group still held options at $4 per share.

As of June 30, 1958, the end of the fiscal year, the Tandy group had exercised options on 256,260 shares, approximately half of the 500,000-share option it had received as part of the merger agreement with American Hide & Leather Company in October 1955. The fixed payment notes totaling $2.3 million held by the Tandy group had been fully retired, and contingent payments of $1,440,886 had been paid to the former Tandy stockholders, all out of Tandy Industries' earnings.

Now, in the waning days of 1958, as Charles huddled with Luther Henderson, Jim West, and Jesse Upchurch to plot the strategy for gaining control of the company, it was readily apparent that the first priority was to exercise the options on the remaining 243,740 shares. This would give the Tandy group approximately one-third of the General American outstanding stock, a sizable position of strength from which to deal. It was Tandy's hope that he could avoid an expensive proxy battle by convincing Stanley Rowland and Jim Dunbar that he held the winning hand.

"When we decided to fight them, we knew we had to be able to win an election to control the board," Luther Henderson revealed. "With our options, we had about 30 percent of the stock in our group. So we didn't have to acquire too much additional stock to be dangerous."

One of the Tandy group's major assets was Jesse Upchurch, who had married Gwen Tandy's daughter, Connie, in 1951. Upchurch had begun accumulating American Hide and Leather preferred stock immediately after its merger with Tandy Leather Company.

"I bought a tremendous amount of American Hide 6% cumulative preferred stock which nobody else seemed to be interested in," Upchurch reported. "Since the company had ceased paying dividends, nobody thought the preferred stock would ever be worth anything. I was buying the stuff for 50 cents on the dollar. Later, I traded it all in for 5% income debentures, plus warrants to buy Tandy stock at $7 a share for five years and at $9 a share for two additional years. Those warrants turned out to be very valuable. But you could have picked them up at one time for as low as 75 cents."

Upchurch eventually would become Tandy Corporation's largest individual shareholder, owning more than 2 million shares. By the time he exercised his warrants to buy Tandy stock at $9, the stock was selling at more than $100 per share. When it appeared in early 1959 that a proxy fight was inevitable, Connie and Jesse Upchurch promised Tandy that he could count on their financial support in acquiring any major blocks of stock that might become available. In addition, Gwen Tandy told Charles that her checkbook was open to him when and if he needed it.

In the spring of 1959, Tandy engaged the services of George Bemas, a New York attorney, to advise him on proxy fighting strategy. One of Bemas' recommendations was that Tandy retain Georgeson and Company, a leading Wall Street proxy solicitation firm. Tandy flew to New York for a meeting with the Georgeson principals who informed him they would require a retainer fee of $375,000 to take on the project.

"There was no way Charles could raise that kind of immediate cash," Upchurch reported. "So Gwen Tandy wrote a check for $375,000 from her personal funds and handed it to Charles."

Buoyed by this backing, Tandy now threw himself into the effort to wring every last ounce of financial support from his coterie of former Tandy Leather Company stockholders. Resorting to the same tactics that had worked so effectively in 1955 to gain their approval of the sale of Tandy Leather Company to American Hide and Leather, Charles divided the country up into three segments and once again hit the road with Luther Henderson and Jim West.

"They formed a team," John Wilson recalled. "Charles went in one direction, Luther Henderson went in another direction, and Jim West in still another."

Wilson, who was managing a Tandy Leather store in Denver, was in the store early one morning when the phone rang. Luther Henderson was on the line.

"I need to talk with you privately," he told Wilson.

"Where are you?"

"I'm in the hotel right behind the store. Why don't you come over and have a cup of coffee with me?"

A few minutes later, Wilson was seated across from Henderson in a booth in the hotel coffee shop. "What we'd like you to do," Henderson said, "is go over to your bank and borrow all the money you can."

In recalling the incident, Wilson declared, "Now remember, this was Luther Henderson talking, not Charles. I would have preferred that it was Charles, but I knew that Luther was his agent. So I said, 'Okay, I'll do it.'"

Later that morning, Wilson went to see his banker to find out how much he could borrow, and was shocked when the bank agreed to lend him $11,000.

"They loaned it to me on the spot, on my signature. Of course, the fact that we were doing business with the bank helped. With the money, I bought General American stock, so that Charles would have the paper when it came down to a vote," Wilson said. "That's exactly what every other store manager did."

Lloyd Redd, then the manager of a Tandy Leather store in Omaha, was standing at the cash register, having just completed a sale, when Charles Tandy walked in, cigar in hand, a big grin on his face.

"If you're wondering what I'm doing in Omaha," Tandy declared, "I'm here to do you a favor. I'm gonna make you rich." He then steered Redd to the back of store where his small office was located.

"Charles then made his pitch about how each of us had to go into hock to buy up all the General American stock we could lay our hands on," Redd recounted. "He showed me his own financial statement that revealed his entire net worth was tied up in General American stock, making the point that he was putting everything he had into buying stock because he had total faith in what he was doing."

"What I want you to do is go to your bank and borrow $18,000," Tandy told Redd.

"That was a large sum to me," Redd acknowledged. "I didn't figure I could borrow that much money. But the thought went through my mind, 'I'll go to the bank and ask for the loan, and after they've turned me down, at least I can tell Charles that I tried.'"

Redd went to the Omaha National Bank, where he was informed he could borrow $4,000 on his assets.

"What about the other $14,000?" he asked. The banker told him that the bank would lend him that sum on his signature.

"So I had an $18,000 loan," Redd said. "Charles didn't have to co-sign the note. I did it on my own, but I did it because Charles was saying, 'Do it.' I took that $18,000 and bought General American stock at $4 a share."

Bill Vance was enrolled in a nine-month middle management program at the Harvard Business School when the battle for control of General American Industries erupted.

"Charles had sent me up to Harvard to take the course and then come back and help him decide whether or not to send other of our young men up there," Vance reported. "While I was at Cambridge, I had gotten to know Stanley Rowland. He'd invited me to come by and visit him in his office so he could show me the company operation and we'd had lunch and dinner a few times. Then, one day, Stanley asked me to come out to his office. We talked about what I might do in the company, what my future might be, and I sensed that something was wrong. I didn't know about the proxy fight that was coming up, but I got the distinct impression that Stanley Rowland wanted to get rid of Charles. Charles was aggressive. He wanted to go one way and Stanley wanted to go another. It was like two bulls meeting head on."

Rowland now asked Vance, "Could you go the full course that I've laid out?"

Vance replied, "I don't know, Stanley. I'm not sure I understand the full implications. But I can tell you this. If it's what I suspect, that I'd have to turn my back on Charles Tandy, I'd rather leave the company first. Tandy Industries has become my home, the Tandy people have become my family." Then Vance added, "I've been trying to think of any of the original Tandy people who'd turn their backs on Charles, and I can't think of a single one. It'd be like turning your back on a brother." That was the last time Bill Vance saw Stanley Rowland.

Vance recalled what now ensued.

"Not only did Charles and Jim West, and Luther Henderson spend a lot of time on the road, they also spent a lot of time on the telephone.

They had private and small-group meetings with store managers. It was just before I left Harvard and came back to Fort Worth that all this traveling took place. We all realized there was a real danger of losing the company."

To Vance's knowledge, not a single store manager failed to go along with what Tandy, Henderson, and West asked them to do. "Every one of us agreed to hock himself to the neck," he declared.

Vance told of going to the Fort Worth National Bank with another Tandy Industries employee. "You weren't supposed to borrow money to buy stock," he noted. "That's illegal. The loan officer knew what we were there for. He told us, 'If you're here to borrow money to buy stock, I can't lend it to you.' We told him we had some other things in mind that we needed the money for. When he asked us what we had to put up for collateral, we told him we had some stock we could put up. He asked us, 'When can you let me have the stock?' We told him, 'In a few days.' And he said, 'Okay.'"

The Tandy group now received a major boost that couldn't have come at a more fortuitous time. Pierce Musgrove, who had become disenchanted with the internal strife, offered his shares in General American Industries for sale so that he could buy back his oil company with the proceeds. Musgrove and his associates had received nearly 200,000 shares of stock when Musgrove Petroleum Corporation had been acquired in July 1956.

"When Charles talked to Musgrove about siding with us in the proxy fight," Jesse Upchurch related, "Musgrove responded, 'Jesus, Charles, I didn't come into this to get into this kind of fight. I just want to get out and get back into the oil business again on my own.'"

The Tandy group now faced the problem of coming up with more than $1 million, to buy the critically-needed Musgrove shares. Connie and Jesse Upchurch again rode to the rescue.

"By now," Upchurch reported, "Charles had just about run out of cash and had used up all of his credit at the banks. So my wife and I advised him that we would personally take the entire block of Mr. Musgrove's shares."

This satisfied Musgrove, who agreed to vote his shares with the Tandy group upon the assurance that he would be able to reacquire ownership of Musgrove Petroleum as soon as the new management assumed control.

There was still one major hurdle to clear—a significant block of stock, close to 300,000 shares, held in The Netherlands by foreign investors and controlled in Amsterdam by Baron Cornelis Johannes Schimmelpenninck van der Oije. Baron Schimmelpenninck had acquired the stock over a period of several years, acting as a broker for a group of investors. With a nip-and-tuck election looming, the foreign-owned shares represented the balance of power.

In the late summer of 1959, with the November annual meeting drawing closer, Charles Tandy learned to his dismay that Baron Schimmelpenninck was leaning toward voting his shares with management. A distraught Tandy immediately hopped a plane to New York for a conference with Coleman Burke, a prominent Wall Street lawyer and a partner in Burke & Burke, legal counsel to General American Industries, Inc. Burke was a former director of General American Industries, and he and Tandy had become good friends while serving together on the General American board. Burke had become impressed with Tandy's business acumen and the strong earnings performance of Tandy Industries. He had sided with Tandy on a number of occasions at board meetings. He had privately told Tandy that he believed a change in management would be beneficial to the future of the company. He now gave Tandy a sympathetic ear as they met in his office.

"Rowland thinks he has the baron's vote sewed up," Tandy told Burke. "I know the baron thinks a lot of you and has followed your advice before. Would you go to Amsterdam and talk to him? If you can't get him to vote with us, at least try to get him to remain neutral. If he remains neutral, we can't lose."

Burke, who remained a close friend and advisor to Charles Tandy over the years, flew to Amsterdam several days later and outlined the situation to Baron Schimmelpenninck. Before returning to New York, he extracted a pledge from the baron that he would remain neutral in the dispute.

Jesse Upchurch recalled a visit he and Charles Tandy had with Baron Schimmelpenninck several years later.

"It was in 1963 or '64," Upchurch said. "We'd been skiing in Switzerland, Charles and Gwen and Connie and I, and we went to Amsterdam to meet the baron who was then the head of the Amsterdam Stock Exchange and also the European Exchange Association. We talked about the proxy fight and the baron told us he looked at his records and said to himself, 'Wait a minute. All the rest of the General American companies are losing money. Only the Tandy group is making money.' So he threw his blessing to the Tandy group by remaining neutral."

The baron remained a Tandy shareholder until his death in 1982. The Tandy shares he controlled continue to be managed by his investment firm in Amsterdam.

With the large block of foreign shares neutralized, the Tandy group now had a lock on the ultimate outcome, holding a clear majority of the shares that would be voted.

"Management never did read the signals right," Luther Henderson observed. "By the time Stanley Rowland finally got the message, it was too late. But he wouldn't capitulate and it turned into a real head-butting situation."

Neither side, however, had actually engaged in the formal solicitation of proxies, although the Tandy forces had filed all of the necessary papers with the Securities and Exchange Commission and had completed all of the other needed arrangements. But after the baron's decision to remain neutral, the necessity for a proxy fight was precluded.

As the drama reached its climax, one bit of Tandy histrionics remained to be staged.

On a brisk mid-September afternoon, a car pulled up in front of an old, red brick, malodorous building in Lowell, Massachusetts, that once had been the home of an American Hide and Leather Company tannery. A tall, husky man in a rumpled suit alighted and strode purposefully through the entrance, flicking the ashes from the cigar he clutched in his right hand. He entered a large room that had been converted into an office area and swaggered up to the receptionist seated behind a desk.

"I'm Charles Tandy from Fort Worth, Texas," he drawled. "I'm here to see Stanley Rowland."

Rowland had only recently begun officing in the old tannery, although the company's executive offices were still officially located at 17 East Street in downtown Boston.

"I'll let Mr. Rowland know you're here," the receptionist told Tandy.

"That won't be necessary," Tandy said. "I'll tell him myself."

He swung past the receptionist's desk toward a nearby office and strode in.

Rowland couldn't have been any more shocked had he looked up and seen Paul Revere standing there, lantern in hand.

For a moment, there was dead silence as the two antagonists stared at each other.

Tandy's voice then broke the silence.

"Stand up."

Automatically, Rowland responded to the order. He stood up.

Tandy now insouciantly sauntered around the desk behind which Rowland stood and sat down in Rowland's chair.

"This is my chair now," Tandy said, savoring each word. "I'm in and you're out. I've got the tickets."

As he described the scene, from an account related to him by Charles Tandy, Bill Brown, the Boston banker, chuckled and added, "That was Charlie Tandy. He was the most fascinating guy I ever met. There'll never be another like him."

Several days later, Coleman Burke sat down with Stanley Rowland and Jim Dunbar in Boston to inform them officially that the game was over. Charles Tandy held the winning hand.

"You guys are going to get licked," Burke said, mincing no words, "and you'd be much better off to make peace with Mr. Tandy."

The peace treaty that was negotiated included giving the Tandy group five seats on the 9-member board and electing Charles Tandy board chairman and chief executive officer. It also authorized a cash payment of $1,000,000 in full settlement of the contingent payments due the Tandy group through July 30, 1966. As of June 30, 1959, contingent payments totaling $2,108,481 had already been paid out of Tandy Industries' earnings.

The five Tandy representatives who were subsequently elected to the board at the annual meeting were John B. Collier, Jr., president of Fort Worth Poultry & Egg Company; Luther A. Henderson, Charles D. Tandy, Carl C. Welhausen and James L. West. The other four directors named were James H. Dunbar, Jr., Alfred H. Hauser, vice president of the Chemical Bank New York Trust Company; Joseph S. Nye, a partner in Nye & Whitehead, New York City, an investment advisory firm, and Stanley M. Rowland. Charles Tandy was the largest individual stockholder on the board with 116,550 shares.

The annual meeting, which was held on Thursday afternoon, November 12, 1959, in Flemington, New Jersey, was called to order by James H. Dunbar, Jr., chairman of the board, promptly at 2 P.M. Alex Hamilton served as the secretary of the meeting. Inspectors of election were Edwin K. Large, Sr., and Edwin K. Large, Jr.

The inspectors of election reported that the holders of 10,898 shares of six percent cumulative preferred stock were present or represented at the meeting out of 14,509 shares issued and outstanding and that 1,371,143 shares of common stock were present or represented out of a total of 1,667,705 shares. Alex Hamilton now rose to place into nomination the candidates for election to the board of directors.

Charles Tandy, seated in a front row seat in the small meeting room which was actually a part of the law offices of Edwin K. Large, Jr., listened expectantly as Judge Large announced the results of the vote. It was a moment he would forever savor.

"Mr. Chairman," Judge Large intoned, "each nominee for director has received a total of 1,382,041 votes, represented by 10,898 shares of preferred stock and 1,371,143 shares of common stock."

"I declare the nominees duly elected," Dunbar declared.

After a brief flirtation with disaster, the family business was back in Charles Tandy's hands.

The takeover of General American Industries by the Tandy forces had actually begun a month earlier, when Charles dispatched Bill Michero and Billy R. Roland, to Boston. Roland, who had joined the Tandy Leather Company in June 1954 after earning a degree in accounting from Texas Christian University, had started out as $300-a-month accounting supervisor reporting to Luther Henderson. By October 1959, when he was ordered to Boston, he had moved up to the number two slot in the accounting department behind Henderson.

He and Michero set up camp in the General American Industries' offices across from the South Street Station in a warehouse district in downtown Boston. "The revolution was over," Michero said, "and Bill and I went up there to take charge of the corporate office, Bill as the accounting brains and I as everything else."

They found a husband-and-wife team in the office, Alice and Lawrence Carboney. Carboney held the title of assistant secretary and assistant treasurer and handled all of the bookkeeping and treasury functions, while his wife was in charge of stockholder relations.

"Stanley Rowland still held the title of president, but he was on the way out," Roland said. "That's why Charles sent Bill and me up there. We learned the operations as quickly as possible and Bill took over some of Alice's functions, the stockholder relations bit and all that, and I took over all the accounting that Larry Carboney was doing for all the various companies. He had consolidated all of the accounting for the

various subsidiary companies, so I had to brush up on my consolidations of accounting. I'd been doing it for some time in Fort Worth, but
nothing on as large a scale as they were doing in Boston. Dunbar Kapple was losing a lot of money, and Jim Dunbar was still chairman of the
board of the corporation. But I knew that he was on his way out, too."

The first item on Charles Tandy's agenda after he assumed control
was to move the General American headquarters to Fort Worth. But
when he told Coleman Burke and several New York stockbrokers of his
plans, they cautioned him to hold his horses, at least for a while.

"The financial people that Charles talked to told him that if he moved
the company immediately from Boston to Fort Worth, General American would become the laughingstock of Wall Street," Jesse Upchurch
recalled.

To assuage the fears of his financial advisors, Tandy made an interim
move in December 1959, transferring the General American headquarters to New York City at 357 Park Avenue, across from the Commodore Hotel and adjacent to Grand Central Station. Michero and Roland
set up shop in the imposing skyscraper that overlooked New York's
most prestigious thoroughfare and shared a suite at the Commodore.
Recalling that period, Roland spoke nostalgically of how he and Michero patronized the seafood restaurant in Grand Central Station nearly every day to enjoy a bowl of its famed clam chowder at lunch. Their
duties found them working closely with representatives of the Chemical
Bank and Chase Manhattan Bank, which were involved in the financial
affairs of the company. They also spent considerable time developing
Wall Street contacts, which Charles Tandy then followed up.

"Charles kept real close tabs on us," Roland reported. "He'd pop in a
couple of times a week. We never knew when he was coming. We
might still be in our office at 7 o'clock at night, when he would come
in and we'd begin talking. He wanted us to fill him in on what we were
doing and he'd bring us up to date on what was going on in Fort Worth.
But he always had new things to throw at us. We'd keep talking till 9
or 10 o'clock, and then Charles would finally say, 'Let's get something
to eat.' And we'd go to a restaurant down in Greenwich Village, and at
3 o'clock in the morning we'd still be sitting there talking. Bill and I
would get up at 7 o'clock the next morning to go to the office, but
Charles might not show up until 11 or 12. But that's the way he was."

After the move of the General American corporate headquarters to
New York, Tandy lost no time in getting rid of the companies that had

been acquired by the previous management. "He felt they weren't ever going to contribute a heck of a lot to the organization," Luther Henderson said.

The dismantling process began with Musgrove Petroleum Corporation in line with the agreement Tandy had made with Pierce Musgrove. The Musgrove Petroleum assets were sold to Pierce Musgrove and his associates on December 28, 1959, for $1,250,000, of which $1 million was paid in cash and the balance in secured, interest-bearing, 3-year installment notes. Involved in the sale were 210 oil wells, located mostly in Kansas, producing 20,000 net barrels of oil per month and approximately 100,000 acres of undeveloped leases.

Shain and Company was put on the block on March 30, 1960. Its assets were sold to Fred G. Folts and associates for $350,000. "Shain's highly specialized operations, vulnerability to changes in footwear styling, and limited accretion of earnings in cash did not permit it to develop the potential expected of it as a division of General American Industries," Tandy said in announcing the sale.

The final divestiture took place on April 19, 1960, when the assets of Dunbar Kapple, Inc. were sold to the D-K Manufacturing Company of Chicago for $1 million in cash. As part of the deal, General American also bought back 143,376 shares of General American stock held by former Dunbar Kapple stockholders at a cost of $681,036, or approximately $4.75 per share.

Commenting on the sale of the three subsidiaries in a letter to shareholders, Tandy stated:

"While the losses incurred in the disposal of three operating units will considerably affect earnings this year, it must be noted that these moves are part of a program which, by June 30, 1960, will have eliminated the divisions of less stability while retaining well-seasoned operating units with substantial profit records, a strong balance sheet, greatly reduced indebtedness, a simplified corporate structure, reduced administrative expense, and a cash position permitting the consideration of sound acquisitions or expansion programs.

"Tandy Industries, with its chain of 109 company-owned stores serving the educational and recreational markets throughout the U.S. and Canada, continues its scheduling of new outlets. The Tex Tan division, through its growing sales organization, is enjoying a good reception of recently-installed techniques in the marketing of its fine leather accessory and saddlery lines."

Having rid himself of the albatrosses around his neck, Tandy proceeded to satisfy his long-held desire to move the corporate headquarters to Fort Worth. The site that he selected was at 1001 Foch Street, in a warehouse district on the city's near west side close to West 7th Street, a major thoroughfare. The move took place in the latter part of May, 1960.

Bill Roland described the new headquarters. "It was a pretty good-sized office," he said. "Charles Tandy sat at one end and Dave Tandy at the other end, facing each other. The American Handicrafts warehouse backed up to where they sat."

Stories in the Fort Worth newspapers on May 20, 1960, announced the move and quoted Charles Tandy as stating that the relocation placed the General American headquarters closer to its two subsidiaries, Tandy Industries of Fort Worth and Tex Tan of Yoakum.

On the same day, May 20, the *Wall Street Journal* carried a short item reporting the resignation of Stanley M. Rowland as president and director of General American Industries, Inc. Four days later, on May 24, the Journal reported that Rowland had sold 5,690 shares of General American Industries stock, decreasing his holdings to 400 shares.

As the 1960 fiscal year came to an end on June 30, Tandy was faced with reporting some bad news. The disposal of the three money-losing divisions created a net loss of $366,151, which, in turn, produced an overall net loss of $267,689, or 17 cents per share, for fiscal 1960. This compared to a net profit of $1,174,483, or 68 cents per share, in fiscal 1959. Sales also had fallen sharply, from $24 million in 1959 to $20 million in 1960.

On the positive side, Tandy informed shareholders, "The earning power of the remaining divisions is substantial. It is anticipated that the Company will report regular profits and maintain a strengthened financial position in the future." He also reported that the Tandy Leather Division planned to open two new retail stores during the first quarter of the 1961 fiscal year in Rockford, Illinois, and Syracuse, New York, and that a second New York City store would open in early December of 1960 on the Avenue of the Americas between 43rd and 44th Streets. The new store in mid-town Manhattan, Tandy said, would feature a broad stock of merchandise from each division of the company and enjoy the largest foot-traffic of any store in the system. The three new openings would bring the total number of Tandy Leather retail outlets to 119, including six in Canada.

On June 24, 1960, Charles D. Tandy was given the additional title of president of General American Industries, Inc., and on July 18, 1960, the election of James L. West as president of the Tandy Leather Company was announced. West was beginning his fourth decade of service with the company.

A year had now elapsed since the Tandy forces had gained the upper hand in the battle for control of General American Industries. Now, with the annual meeting coming up on November 10, 1960, in Flemington, New Jersey, Charles Tandy immersed himself in the pleasure of preparing for the final act of the drama, the eradication of the one remaining symbol of the entire abhorrent episode.

There were two items on the annual meeting agenda. The first was the election of directors. Management submitted a seven-man slate that included incumbents John B. Collier, Luther Henderson, Charles Tandy, Carl Welhausen, Jim West, and Alfred H. Hauser, plus a new nominee, Lawrence E. Dempsey of Chicago, executive vice president of Price Brothers, Inc., manufacturers of display and directional signs. Dempsey, a former vice president of Dunbar Kapple, was the holder of 60,627 shares of General American Industries stock. On a motion from the floor, the seven nominees were duly elected.

The second item on the agenda was the one Tandy had been awaiting with great anticipation. It reached the floor shortly after 3 p.m. as a motion was made to change the name of General American Industries, Inc., to Tandy Corporation. The primary reason for the name change, shareholders were informed, was to "capitalize on and identify with the many Tandy stores throughout the country."

Once again, it fell to Judge Edwin K. Large, Sr., serving as an inspector of elections with his son, Edwin, Jr., to announce the results.

"Mr. Chairman," he intoned, "on the motion, there are 1,147,095 votes in favor and 18,570 votes opposed. The motion carries."

The final tie to the American Hide and Leather episode had been cut. The old Tandy Leather group had its name back, a fitting crown for the victory it had achieved a year earlier.

On Monday morning, November 14, 1960, a long, black limousine braked to a stop outside the New York Stock Exchange Building on Wall Street and an exuberant Charles Tandy bounded out. A few minutes later, he stood on the floor of the exchange and watched the first trade of Tandy Corporation stock clear the tape at a price of $4 per share under the symbol, "TAN."

The lad who once had sold strips of leather to his schoolmates for a dime was now one of a handful of people, living or dead, to have a stock with his name listed on the Big Board.

Chapter 6
"He Could Sell Iceboxes to Eskimos"

Charles Tandy had gambled and won. He had his company back, plus the coveted listing on the New York Stock Exchange that almost cost him the family business. Now he faced the task of convincing the Doubting Thomases on Wall Street that the company bearing his name was a sound investment. What good was a stock exchange listing when the stock was languishing at $4 a share?

"After we got control of the company, the stock didn't do anything for a long time," Lloyd Redd, then a Tandy Leather store manager in Omaha, recalled. "It made me pretty nervous because I had all of my assets in Tandy stock."

Redd recalled a book, *"The Richest Man in Babylon,"* whose chief character believed in investing 10 percent of everything he earned. "Charles believed in that," Redd said. "He preached it. He practically forced us to invest in company stock. He wanted us to have as much of an equity in the company as we possibly could."

Around bonus time every year, Redd said, "Charles would come up with another idea for us to buy stock at a little bit better than the market price. And once you got the stock, you didn't dare sell it because of the pressure he put on you to be a stockholder."

Other longtime employees echoed a similar refrain.

Billy Roland, who made his first stock investment in 1955 with $1,000 he borrowed from Dave Tandy at 6 percent interest, remembered how worried he was over how he was going to repay the loan on his $325-a-month salary.

"Charles always wanted you to buy stock," Roland said. "The more stock in employees' hands, the better. That was always his philosophy. Charles especially wanted his key executives to own as much stock as possible and he initiated a program on his own where he backed them personally to get loans at the bank. He wanted them to be 'socked up to the hilt.' That was his expression. He talked to the bankers to get the arrangements for the loans made."

John Wilson recalled how Tandy applied pressure on his store managers to buy stock with their year-end bonuses. "At bonus meetings, when it came time to distribute the bonus checks, Charles would always let it be known that you had an opportunity to buy some stock," Wilson said. "I'll never forget the time I was getting ready to leave Denver to go to a bonus meeting in Albuquerque, and my wife said to me, 'Please don't spend all your bonus money on stock because we need a new divan.' And we did. I mean the one we had was really ragged. I said, 'Well, I won't make any promises, but I'll sure try.'

"I was operating the largest sales volume store in Denver at the time and Charles called on me first to come up and pick up my check or sign up right there for stock. You can guess what happened. He wasn't about to let me off the hook and set a bad precedent for the others. So I signed up for stock. There were, maybe, 15 or 20 store managers at that bonus meeting and I don't think there was a one of them that turned Charles down. They each laid on the line every penny of their bonus money, and let me tell you when you're working for $250 or $300 a month that was a big step. The average bonus in those days was $3,000, $4,000 or, maybe, as high as $6,000. We bought the stock at, maybe, $4 a share. There have been eight or nine stock splits since that time."

When Wilson returned home without his bonus check, he received a less than cordial greeting from his wife. Her attitude softened, however, as Tandy stock began to soar and split. "She and I laugh about it now and we talk about it frequently," Wilson said. "We both were born in poverty. Her family was on relief during the Depression. My family was never on relief, but we were plenty hard up. We never dreamed what would happen, that we would wind up with stock worth 10 to 12 million dollars."

Wilson recalled that he received 200 shares of Tandy stock at the meeting in Albuquerque for coming in second in a regional sales contest. First prize, which was won by Dean Lawrence, another store manager, was a new compact car. "That was one time when coming in second best was better than winning," Wilson said. "The car was probably worth 2 or 3 thousand dollars and the 200 shares of stock was worth $800. Now those 200 shares are worth about $1 million."

One of the first indications that Wall Street was beginning to recognize Tandy Corporation's potential was a report issued by Standard & Poor's Corporation on November 25, 1960, recommending Tandy stock as a speculative investment. The report aroused an immediate reaction from Charles Tandy.

"At last some of those dumb bastards (Tandy's favorite word for securities analysts) have finally figured out what we're doing and where we're going."

Standard & Poor's noted that Tandy Corporation was the country's largest manufacturer-distributor of leathercraft kits and leather specialty items, selling about half of its output by mail order to some 300,000 customers, with the remainder of its sales coming from its chain of some 118 retail stores located in 42 states, the District of Columbia and Canada. Although the company's sales and earnings had been adversely affected by the divestiture of three subsidiaries, the disposition of the unprofitable entities placed Tandy in a position to realize a satisfactory profit in fiscal 1961, the report said. It concluded, "Long-term, the increase in leisure time and the growth of both the younger and older segments of the population are constructive factors in the outlook for sales of hobby materials. The issue offers some speculative possibilities."

Tandy Leather customers were schools, prisons, hospitals, sanitariums, "everybody who was a shut-in," Lloyd Redd said. "The school business was the thrust of it, because you not only got the business that you sold the schools, but you got the students who learned how to do it. Mail order was our big business. We put out two catalogs a year and a sales flyer every 45 days." The other Tandy division, Tex Tan, was a leading producer of ready-made leather merchandise, including a large line of high-style leather fashion goods such as belts, wallets, key cases and saddlery. One big selling item was a patented billfold for people who carried a large number of credit cards.

"Put your trust in a worthwhile leisure time activity for Americans and you're pretty sure to make money," Tandy was quoted in a story that moved across the United Press International news wires early in 1961. "The catch in Mr. Tandy's advice," the story went on to say, "is that word 'worthwhile.' Lots of wise businessmen are aware that Americans have huge amounts of money to spend on leisure activities and keep dreaming up schemes to make a fast buck out of it." To this comment, Tandy retorted, "You must avoid fads like the hula hoop or something that's too expensive for most folks if you're going to build a solid, growing business."

* * *

In 1961, convinced that growth was the name of the game, Tandy embarked on an acquisition program. Cleveland Crafts, Inc., of Cleveland, Ohio, a distributor of handicraft and educational supplies with stores in Cleveland, Los Angeles, Nashville, and New York City, was acquired in May, and Corral Sportswear of Ardmore, Oklahoma, a manufacturer of leather sport and western clothing, was added to the fold later that month.

Over the next six months, four additional acquisitions were completed—Merribee Embroidery Company of New York City; the Electronic Crafts Division of Swieco, Inc., of Fort Worth; the Plexon Corporation of Greenville, South Carolina; and Toys for Men, Ltd., of Honolulu, Hawaii. To facilitate the expansion program, the board had authorized the redemption and retirement of the remaining 9,269 shares of 6 percent cumulative convertible preferred stock at $55 a share, effective January 31, 1961. This freed more than 48,000 shares of common stock, previously reserved for conversion of the preferred stock, for use in future acquisitions. The company also began buying its own stock in the open market in moderate amounts, with the shares being earmarked for acquisitions.

Jim West recalled that it was during this period that Charles Tandy's merchandising talent really began to assert itself, as he utilized resources within the various divisions to develop new products for the other divisions. In a talk at a Newcomen Society dinner, West reminisced about a saddle kit the Tex Tan group developed for the Tandy Leather Company.

"I believe this item was one of the first full-size, high-quality saddles ever developed in kit form. The publicity received on this one item more than matched the development cost. Among the first customers for the saddle kit was a YMCA summer ranch in Texas. The boys made the saddles and used them at the ranch. They learned first hand about craftsmanship and quality and relived some of the romance of the old West while making saddles. Average age of the boys was 15. At the same time, American Handicrafts was busy developing new kits and markets for tile, and introduced a new liquid plastic called Clear Cast."

Tandy had been demonstrating his merchandising touch to his hired hands ever since his return from the Navy.

"He was some merchant," said John Wilson with a touch of awe in his voice. "He could sell Eskimos iceboxes. He could sell anything and he taught his people how to sell. He also was the greatest motivator I ever met."

Wilson, who managed a Tandy Leather store in Denver before moving to Fort Worth in 1961 to become western regional manager, recalled an incident that demonstrated Tandy's motivational prowess.

"I'd gotten carried away buying inventory for the Denver store and didn't have any money left in the bank. When the weekly paychecks arrived from Fort Worth on Saturday morning, there was a note attached to mine. It said, 'These checks will be good only if x number of dollars in cash are deposited in the bank on Saturday night. Otherwise, don't bother cashing them Monday morning.' Now there was an incentive to rack up some sales on Saturday."

Wilson remembered one of Tandy's favorite exhortations, "If you've got a lemon, make lemonade out of it. Make a sale out of it." And he told the story of how he once followed this sales tip to move a large quantity of pliable goatskins in the late 1950s. He had acquired the skins from John Ellis, who was then the manager of the Tandy Leather store in Los Angeles.

"John had access to a lot of smaller tanneries out there and had bought a lot of this beautiful leather. He had really loaded up on the stuff at 10 cents a foot. It was really beautiful stuff. The skins were real pliable. You could make jackets out of it, almost anything you wanted. I was out there on vacation and, of course, I always visited stores wherever I was. And John asked me if I wanted to buy some of the skins from him, and I jumped at the chance. So I had him ship the skins to me in Denver.

"I put three or four bundles of these skins out on a special table we kept for special deals, and put up a big sign, '39 cents a foot.' Maybe we sold two or three skins a day. This went on for a couple of weeks and I couldn't understand it. It was such a great buy. Then I thought back to what Charles Tandy had taught me one time, 'You've got to make the public think it's scarce.' So I took all the bundles back to the back of the store and brought out half a bundle and put up a sign that said, '69 cents a foot while they last.' We sold all of the skins we had in two weeks. Unbelievable."

Working for Charles Tandy wasn't all sweetness and light, however, Wilson emphasized. "He could be real rough on you. He could give you a lambasting up one side and down the other, but before he left the room, you wanted to hug his neck. He'd say to you, 'You dumb so-and-so, I can't believe you're that dumb, Wilson.' You'd look at him kind of funny and he'd get a twinkle in his eye and come over and put his hand on your shoulder, and by the time that he left, you were walking on air."

Wilson smiled as he relived old memories.

"He was very strong on inventory control, and he would deliberately pick on someone he knew he could pick on to make a good example. I was one of them. He knew I wouldn't get too mad or walk away. He liked to tell people the story of how I once screwed up on my craft tool inventory. I had purchased way too many craft tools, and he came to Denver. I knew I had too much inventory because we were working a real slim inventory. You needed to turn your inventory. I turned mine 18 times in one year. But you couldn't do that if you had all your money tied up in craft tools. I had a big rack of them. I'll never forget this. I just knew I was gonna get fired.

"Charles walked in and said, 'Hello,' and the usual greetings, and he kept edging toward that craft tool rack. I already knew I'd made a helluva mistake. He walked over there and he said, 'Looks like you got a pretty heavy inventory.' Real calm. Now this is the way he handled things. He wouldn't jump right on a guy's back when he knew that the guy knew that he was guilty. 'It looks like you've got a pretty hefty inventory there,' he said.

'Yessir.'

'Well, I think you ought to send most of those back to the warehouse, don't you?'

'Yessir.'

"That's all that was said about it. And he liked to tell that story at store manager meetings with me in the audience. But that's the kind of guy he was. It wouldn't take him two minutes to tell what you were over-inventoried in. He taught us how to turn our inventory. When I think back, everything was really so simple. Everything we stocked came out of the warehouse. Why order six months of cowhide?"

The thing that impressed Lloyd Redd the most about Charles Tandy was that he forced his people to think big. "He set goals and he moved heaven and earth to get those goals achieved on time or ahead of time. And, then, if you achieved the goals he'd made you set, he'd say, 'Why in hell did you set it so low?' You never satisfied him. It was his way of making us all do our best. He could come in and fire you up to really achieve. He had a real knack for that. Another knack he had was the ability to look at a profit-and-loss statement and spot a weakness in it just like a neon sign. He'd do that before he came into your office. Then he'd ask you leading questions. Every time he opened his mouth, it was a question. And he knew the answers to the questions before he asked them. He'd make you look like you weren't on the ball and then he'd get after you. And you'd want to prove to him that you weren't that dumb."

Tandy's toughness on his managers was legendary, and they often compared notes among themselves. Redd recalled Charles striding into his office right after he became a Tandy Leather regional manager in Fort Worth and picking up a national sales report that showed the store in Little Rock, Arkansas, had had a sales loss that week. Tandy slammed shut the door and demanded, "What in the hell is Mr. Simmons doing, liquidating the business in Little Rock?" Then he told Redd, "My job is to inspire you guys, and I've failed. When are you guys going to get your head out of your ass and get to work?"

The tirade went on from 9 o'clock in the morning until about 2:30 in the afternoon, Redd related. "Before he got out of there, we'd covered government sales, school sales, every avenue that you could possibly get some leathercraft business out of. He gave me tons of ideas. That's what he was really doing, and you can bet your bottom dollar that I pursued all of those ideas to try to find out where I could get more business. That's the way he did it. That was his way of motivating people."

Redd remembered another incident when Tandy Leather had experienced a dip in sales and Tandy called in all of the company's top executives for an early morning meeting. Tandy looked around the room, where Harlan Swain, John Wilson, Redd, and several others were seated. He was puffing furiously on his cigar, and he barked, "How much money is represented in this room?" Then he went around the room, making each man state, in front of his peers, how much money he thought he was going to get paid that year in salary and bonus.

After everyone had given his forecast, Tandy growled, "You're all wrong. For the kind of money I'm paying you bastards, I can expect what? How long does it take the New York Yankees to jerk the pitcher when they're losing the ball game? Do they wait until the ball game's lost before they take the pitcher out? You guys are liquidating the business." He went on and on.

"We were there all day," Redd reported, "with him browbeating us all the way. But, in the process, he covered every conceivable angle and brought up things that none of us had thought about that we could pursue and, maybe, get some business out of."

One of the things that has remained strongly in Bill Vance's memory, however, is that Tandy would come down hardest on his managers when their sales and profits were up rather than when they were down. "If you had a 60 to 70 percent increase in sales and your profits were up 30 to 40 percent or whatever, you just knew you were going to be seeing Charles very quickly and that he was going to be all over you," Vance recounted.

"Damn, is that the best you can do?" Tandy would demand.

The store manager would reply, "Charles, 60 percent ain't bad."

"That's nothing, that's peanuts," Tandy would retort. "If you can do 60 percent, why can't you get 100 percent out of it?" Tandy would then begin throwing out ideas on what the manager could do to increase his sales and profits.

"This was one of his keys," Vance said. "He knew that he knew how to think. Now he tried to teach you how to think. He'd ask you a question about your expenses or your sales forecasts, and you'd give him an answer, and he'd say, 'Is that your best guess?' Then he'd proceed to inform you that you didn't know what you were talking about. That's when he would really push you hard; but when he got through, he'd start telling you how 'You can do this' and 'You can do that.' 'You've already done this, so you can sure do that.' 'We've already agreed you can do this, so just go out and do that.'

"First, he ripped you up. Then he put you back together again and got you optimistic. So when he left, you weren't thinking so much about the scolding you got, you were thinking about how you were going to climb this mountain. And, oftentimes, when he was getting ready to leave, why he'd wrap his arm around your shoulder and punch your other shoulder with his big fist and say, 'Go get 'em, tiger.'

"But if you were really having trouble, when your sales were down about 20 or 30 percent and you'd been working your heart out, as most of us did, Charles never scolded you. He never scolded me or anyone I was around when things were tough. And I heard him talk to a lot of people over the years. Mostly, he was trying to help you figure out what was wrong. He would start a series of questions, 'What if you did this?' 'What if you did that?' and he'd get you to thinking. Before he got through, you would have a direction to take that promised better results. Until you got those results, Charles didn't do anything but try to help you. He was like a rock to lean on."

In June of 1961, Charles Tandy was the subject of a personality sketch in a *Sales Management Magazine* series titled, "Dynamarketers." The article took note of Tandy's "unique claim to fame, that in a period when everybody is expanding his business, Tandy made money by contracting his business. By selling off profitless divisions, Tandy began to make money again." Publication of the article coincided with the Tandy stock hitting a high of $10 a share. The favorable comments continued with the publication, on October 19, 1961, of a bullish report by Shearson, Hammill & Company that said Tandy's "transition from a not-too-successful, 'catch-all' industrial company into an aggressive enterprise with a strongly-entrenched position in the educational, hobby and leisure time markets is now reaching the pay-off stage." The report noted that Tandy would soon open its first Tandy Craft Mart in Fort Worth, which would incorporate a variety of small hobby shops in one large retail center on a leased department basis. "This move could open up entirely new markets for the company," the report added.

The mart idea was the outgrowth of Charles Tandy's belief that the do-it-yourself movement had gained sufficient momentum to support a new merchandising concept. He was convinced, he told Jim West and Luther Henderson, that "mom and pop" specialty shops engaged in the sale of hobby-type merchandise, such as rockhounds, gourmet foods, ceramics and other related businesses, could operate under one roof and become a sort of family shopping center for hobbyists of every age.

The first Tandy Craft and Hobby Mart opened with appropriate hoopla in a new two-story, 18,000-square foot building at 2727 West 7th Street on November 1, 1961. Present at the opening ceremonies was Charles Tandy's former partner in the ladies' belt business, John Justin, then the mayor of Fort Worth. Billed as "America's first one-stop leisure time shopping center," the mart contained 35 different shops representing more than 50 crafts and hobbies selling more than 50,000 craft and hobby items, all under one roof. In addition, on the mezzanine level, was space for the Tandy corporate headquarters.

The shops offered everything from A to Z—artificial flower making to a Zip 'N Trim Shop. There was an aquarium and pet store, a record store and a joke store, a stamp and coin shop and a Sit 'N Knit shop, even a gourmet food emporium. Anchor tenants were Tandy Leather and American Handicrafts stores. There was also a portent of the future, a hobby electronics store called Electronic Crafts that sold do-it-yourself kits for making stereo hi-fi systems.

Jack Gordon, columnist for the *Fort Worth Press*, reported: "Crowds at the new Tandy Hobby and Craft Mart are fascinated by the battery-powered toy bartender at Jack Mayfield's The Joker. The foot-high figure from Japan shakes up a martini, pours it, drinks it, smacks its lips, and then turns red in the face. A bad olive, perhaps?"

Tony Slaughter, a columnist in the rival *Star-Telegram*, reported: "A lot of monkey business has been going on around this town in the last three weeks. That's when Freeland's Pet Shop opened in the new Tandy Hobby and Craft Mart on W. 7th. The shop seemingly has been keeping the South African banana boats busy hauling in squirrel and Capuchin monkeys to meet the demand for the 6-month-old jungle inhabitants. Maybe people bought them for Christmas presents. Anyhow, Fort Worth people in the last three weeks have bought more than 150 monkeys."

More than 20,000 visitors thronged through the mart during its initial week of operation. As part of the opening promotion, Tandy offered to redeem food wrappers, labels and bottle caps from Fort Worth-made products. More than 200,000 bottle caps from soft drinks bottled in Fort Worth were collected during the opening month. For every 10 bottle caps turned in, Tandy applied one cent, with a maximum of $1, on a merchandise certificate.

As 1961 wound down, the resurgent Tandy stock hit another high of 11⅜ on December 20 before closing at 11, a gain of $1 per share on the day. The 10 percent one-day jump captured the attention of *The New York Times*, which carried an item about it the next morning.

"Several reports about the company were in circulation," the *Times* said. "One spoke of the success of the first of a chain of 'hobby centers' opened in Fort Worth a month or so ago. Others are being opened on a leased-department basis in other stores. This news, however, was somewhat old, and the market appeared to get its main drive from two rumors. The first one spoke of an imminent acquisition. One Wall

Street house said it had asked the company about this and had been told that nothing was imminent. The second rumor had the Boy Scouts of America 'signed up to distribute Tandy's handicraft kits.' This was denied by the director of the National Supply Service Division of the Boy Scouts of America and by the administrative assistant to the Chief Scout Executive."

Not that Tandy was averse to having Boy Scouts or any other organized group hustle his products, as two prominent Fort Worth businessmen, John Roby Penn and Joe W. Lydick, attested. Penn enjoyed telling the story of how he and Lydick asked Tandy to sponsor a Junior Achievement company.

"Charles had never heard of Junior Achievement, which was getting started in Fort Worth," Penn said. "After we explained how it worked, he asked if they could make things out of leather. When we told him they could, he really got fired up and asked, 'If I gave them all the leather, could they all make leather?' Before we were through talking, he was envisioning making it a statewide deal. He was ready to call Carl Reistle, the president of the Humble Oil Company, who was then the volunteer head of Junior Achievement in Texas."

Penn laughed. "Charles could see how every kid in Texas would grow up doing leathercraft. 'You guys have a nice idea. Now I'll take it over.' That's how his mind worked. We had to tell him that we couldn't turn over Junior Achievement to him."

Tandy Corporation did, however, become a Junior Achievement sponsor and has continued its support of the program since that time.

The Tandy Craft and Hobby Mart had one flaw, as it turned out, a lack of adequate parking space. Business was so good that gigantic traffic jams became a daily occurrence on West 7th Street. A quick move was dictated, and on April 12, 1962, the mart re-opened at a new location beneath a bowling alley at 1515 South University Drive, with double the floor space of the West 7th Street site and greatly increased parking facilities. In addition to crafts and hobbies, the new mart also contained an Italian restaurant, a Mexican restaurant, and a sandwich bar.

At the opening of the new mart, an enthusiastic Tandy declared: "When we opened the Tandy Craft and Hobby Mart on West 7th street, it was an experiment in retailing, grouping craft, hobby, and related specialty shops under one roof to provide a leisure time city for residents of North Texas. Frankly, we were not certain, at the outset, of the public response the mart would receive. It's certainly gratifying that after only four months of operation we've had to move into quarters twice as large as the original mart, with many times more parking."

The Tandy Mart was a dream Charles long had harbored "to put all those companies in one pot," Jim Buxton said. "After they moved underneath the bowling alley on University Drive, it just went hog wild. It looked so promising that Charles began looking around in Houston and Dallas for a second mart, and I began looking in San Antonio." Buxton was then a Tandy Leather district manager in San Antonio and also manager of Tandy Leather and American Handicrafts stores there.

The second Tandy Mart opened in Dallas on the first two floors and basement of the Praetorian Building in the downtown area in November of 1962.

"Charles then came down to San Antonio and rented a 43,000 square foot building for a third mart," Buxton reported. "At that time, the corporation was doing about $17 million in sales overall. I think my leather store in San Antonio had done about $160,000 or so that year and American Handicrafts about $50,000 or $60,000, and here Charles rents 43,000 square feet. Neither Luther Henderson nor Jim West would sign the lease. Charles said to me, 'You keep two airplane tickets handy. If this doesn't work, we're gonna have to go to Mexico. You'd better get your butt out and try to rent space to some other businesses.'"

The San Antonio mart, called Tandy's Wonderland, opened in the Wonderland Shopping Mall in September 1963. It featured a huge sign out front that simply said, "Tandy's." The sign, 14 feet long and 50 feet high, immediately became a local landmark because it was located on the dead center of one of the approaches to the San Antonio municipal airport, about 2½ miles from the runway. Airline pilots would come into the mart and tell Buxton, "We saw your sign and here we are."

* * *

Things were on a definite upswing as the fiscal year ended on June 30, 1962, with healthy increases in both sales and earnings. Net income of $980,000, or 63 cents per share, represented a 36 percent gain over the previous year. Sales had risen 11 percent to $17.7 million. There were now 140 company-owned retail and mail-order stores in 110 cities in the U.S. and Canada, including a new Tandy Crafts store at Fifth Avenue and 36th Street in New York City. Reporting on the opening of the new outlet in mid-town Manhattan, Charles Tandy said, "Some of the stores opened during the past year have been placed in 100 percent retail locations as opposed to the semi-wholesale type of store location normally leased by the company. The outstanding example of this new type of location is the Tandy Crafts store opened in June on Fifth Avenue at 36th Street in New York City. The Fifth Avenue store features the merchandise of four separate divisions of the company and the sales trends being experienced there may presage future stores of a similar type and location."

In early September of 1962, Tandy Corporation shareholders were notified of a recapitalization plan for the company that Shearson, Hammill & Company called "unusual, imaginative, and constructive." Under the proposal, which was subject to shareholder approval at the annual meeting in November, stockholders were given the opportunity to exchange part or all of their shares for 6½ percent debentures with a face value of $7 for each share tendered, plus warrants permitting the holder to buy 49 common shares for each 100 shares surrendered at a price of $7.50 per share between January 1, 1965 and December 31, 1967, or at $9 per share between January 1, 1968 and December 31, 1969. The offer was subject to tender of a minimum of 300,000 shares and a maximum of 500,000 shares.

Commenting on the proposal, Shearson, Hammill stated, "The plan proposed by Tandy's directors will give stockholders the opportunity, by means of the interest on the debentures, to obtain some income on their investment while at the same time enabling them to maintain a stake in the long term growth of the company through the warrants. The company has not paid any cash dividends on its common stock since 1959. On the other hand, the recapitalization proposal is designed to reduce the number of outstanding shares and to increase the leverage on the remaining equity, thus, in effect, adding to per share earnings."

The Dow-Jones newswire quoted Charles Tandy as asserting that the company had devised the exchange to reduce the number of common shares outstanding and to provide stockholders income on their investments. "During the 1950s, Tandy's predecessor company, General American Industries, Inc., issued more than 1,000,000 shares for three acquisitions," Tandy explained. "These acquisitions were later sold, creating the tax loss that benefited recent earnings and leaving an unworkable number of outstanding shares. In addition, Tandy Corporation has no plans to begin paying a dividend, but debenture holders will receive interest payments and warrants to buy common shares later."

Shareholders at the annual meeting on November 8, 1962, approved the proposal, which required the tendering of at least 300,000 shares of stock by January 2, 1963.

On December 12, Corporate Secretary Bill Michero reported that 240,112 shares of Tandy common stock had been turned in to be exchanged for debentures and warrants, and that none of the shares tendered had come from company officers or directors. "This assures the success of the offer," he declared.

However, on December 31, Tandy announced it was extending the deadline for the exchange to January 30 from the original date of January 2. Michero reported that 285,000 shares had been surrendered through December 27, exclusive of participation by directors. He added that the extension would not alter the January 15 commencement date of interest on the debentures and that issuance of warrants and debentures would begin January 15.

In all, 500,123 shares of common stock were surrendered by shareholders, reducing the number of shares outstanding from 1,561,061 to 1,060,938. A total of $3.5 million of 6½ percent debentures due in 1978, plus warrants to purchase 245,000 shares of common stock, was issued in exchange for the common shares tendered.

Recalling the event, Bill Michero pointed out that the debenture and warrant offerings were a response by management to "louder and louder clamor from the stockholders for some kind of recognition of their interests. It was done to satisfy and placate those shareholders who were weary of seeing no dividend and the price of the stock flat in the market, who wanted something for their money. And with the passage of time and the development of earnings of the company, those warrants, which were traded separately, took on a greater and greater value."

With the completion of the exchange, the company was now positioned for sharply increased earnings per share, plus sales growth from existing operations and further acquisitions. But in the office of the president and CEO there was a curious absence of euphoria. People began to speculate on what was bothering the boss.

Luther Henderson described what had begun to temper Charles Tandy's enthusiasm and normal joie de vivre.

"Here he was, in control of a New York Stock Exchange-listed company, with a beautiful little business in the leathercrafts stores which were laying golden eggs quite regularly, but only of a certain size. He began to recognize that there was a definite limit to the size of the leathercraft business. It was hard for Charles to accept this. He hated to accept the fact that the last 20 stores we had opened were doing only 75 percent of the volume of the old stores. We had some open and frank discussion about this. But you could always show Charles the numbers, and if the numbers proved the point, he wouldn't argue. That's one of the great abilities that the guy had. In spite of being such a strong-minded person with such strong ideas, he would always listen. And if he was wrong, he'd admit it and change course. His pride was not so great that he'd do things his way, come hell or high water. In my opinion, that's one of the prime distinctions that made him a really great businessman.

"But, anyway, recognizing that the company's horizons needed to be expanded, he consented to let me attend the Harvard Business School Advanced Mangement Program in 1960 to tune me into the bigger picture and sharpen me up in preparation for a major acquisition program. After I got back from Harvard in 1961, my real job was to go out and look for companies to buy. We made a number of acquisitions, but no large ones. We bought two or three companies related to the leather business and a couple of companies related to the leathercraft business, but there just weren't very many to buy."

Bill Roland recalled how Tandy and Jim West were constantly looking for something that would fit the Tandy business. "Jim and I would go to New York and we'd walk the streets looking for something that we could get into that fit with the leather business," Roland said. "Jim would stop at every little store and go in and talk to people. He saw knives in a store window and thought, 'Maybe this is something we can sell in our leather stores?' Jim loved to walk the streets.

"What Charles wanted was merchandise that he could put into a nationwide store operation. He knew retailing and he understood buying power concepts of concentration of goods and then dispersing them through the store system. He was looking for merchandise that would really sell." Henderson added, "Two or three times we approached companies equal or larger than us and we were pretty thoroughly snubbed. I guess nobody had really looked carefully at our financial statement. We were turning out really successful profits."

Unsuccessful in his efforts to find what he was looking for in the leather and leathercrafts fields, Henderson began to look around at other enterprises, other industries.

"Why limit ourselves," he said to Tandy.

Tandy agreed.

Unbeknownst to either Henderson or Tandy, a development was taking place on the West Coast that would provide them with just the vehicle they were seeking.

Chapter 7
"Luther, I Don't Understand This Business"

Lincoln Bartlett had a problem. The former J.C. Penney executive was managing Amthor and Company, an import firm in San Francisco, and he was up to his ears in rattan furniture. He had to figure out a way to move it or eat it.

Amthor and Company was a small wholesale house that dealt primarily in rice cloth wallpaper and rattan furniture brought in from the Orient and sold to retailers in the Bay Area. It was a modest operation, with a net worth of around $150,000, that had been started by a San Francisco resident named Jack Amthor who was married to the daughter of a wealthy coffee-growing family in El Salvador. Through his wife, Amthor had access to capital in El Salvador, and that was how he had managed to form his own company in the mid-1950s and had hired Bartlett to run it.

Like most small businesses, Amthor relied on bank credit to get itself through its seasonal needs. It had been doing this for several years without encountering any problems. By any measure, the company was doing reasonably well without setting the woods on fire. Then, in 1958, a problem arose. As sometimes happens to even the best-run companies, management got carried away in stocking up on rattan furniture in anticipation of a big spring selling season. Rattan, at that time, was considered a spring and summer merchandise item. As it turned out, sales failed to match expectations, and when the spring selling season came to an end, Bartlett found himself with a big inventory of rattan furniture. He also had a note of around $200,000 coming due at the bank which he was going to be unable to meet. So he and Amthor went to see their banker.

"We want to carry over our loan," they asked.

"No way," the banker told them. "We expect this line to be liquidated on schedule and for you to continue to be in a seasonal operation, as you have in the past."

Bartlett contacted his customers and offered them a 25 percent discount to buy the rattan furniture. Much to his dismay, his customers turned him down.

"We don't need any more rattan," they informed him. "We've already bought all we need to carry us through to next year."

Bartlett was between the proverbial rock and the hard place. He needed to liquidate his inventory in order to pay off the bank, and he didn't know how to go about doing it. He mulled over the problem and finally approached Amthor with a last-ditch idea.

"Let's have a sale," he suggested. "If we can't sell it to our retail customers, let's by-pass them and see if we can sell the stuff directly to the public."

By now, Amthor was willing to try anything. He gave Bartlett his blessing. Bartlett rented an old warehouse on Taylor Street between the end of the cable car route and Fisherman's Wharf. He moved his surplus rattan furniture inventory into it, cut the prices from the regular retail price (they were still above his cost), and ran ads in the San Francisco newspapers, "Big Bargain, Rattan Furniture."

To Bartlett's and Amthor's amazement, the public descended on the warehouse and took all of the furniture away. In two weeks, they had solved their inventory problem.

Now Bartlett and Amthor saw an opportunity. The public seemed to like this kind of merchandising. Why deal with a middle man when they could deal directly with the consumer? In the early fall of 1958, they went around to each of their regular customers in the Bay Area and picked up their odd lots of furniture and other merchandise at bargain prices. They installed the entire haul in their store near Fisherman's Wharf and again advertised "Big Bargains" in the San Francisco dailies. Again, the customers came in droves. By the end of the Christmas selling season, they were down to bare walls once more.

Bartlett came to the conclusion that there was a market for a lot more imported merchandise than he had ever dreamed existed. So, he began sending buyers to the Far East to acquire larger quantities of furniture, decorator furnishings, housewares, even gourmet foods, and bring them in for sale in the converted warehouse. The enterprise, now a wholly retail operation, needed only one more thing to make the transformation complete, a new name; so, in 1959, Cost Plus Imports, Inc., was born.

For the next three years the business prospered and grew, and the Cost Plus Imports store near Fisherman's Wharf became a San Francisco shopping landmark. But by 1962, it had outgrown the ability of Jack Amthor to finance its continued growth. Complicating matters further was the fact that El Salvador, the source of Amthor's funds, was going through another of its recurring revolutions. So Amthor was unable to get any money out of the country at a time when Cost Plus badly needed a fresh infusion of working capital. Amthor couldn't go to his banker because the company had already used up its line of credit. There was only one way to go, Amthor decided. Go public.

He began making the rounds of Bay Area brokerage firms, and finally struck a deal with a San Francisco house to take Cost Plus public. Under the agreement, the broker promised to sell $300,000 worth of newly-issued Cost Plus stock on a "best efforts" basis. Amthor, being relatively naive financially, didn't realize that this was just a promise to try to sell the stock and that there was no guarantee the offering would be successful. He did a rather rash thing. As soon as the underwriting agreement was signed, Amthor permitted Bartlett to begin spending the anticipated proceeds in the Orient stocking up for the upcoming Christmas season. The reason for the hurry was to accommodate the long lead time between ordering and delivery of merchandise. Neither Amthor nor Bartlett wanted to be caught short.

The stock offering was set for the spring of 1962. Unfortunately, the stock market took a tumble just as the Cost Plus offering hit the street. Despite his "best efforts," the broker could not move the stock; the offering was withdrawn during the summer. Amthor and Bartlett were really behind a financial eight ball. They had all this merchandise on order, which was supposed to be shipped in September so that it could arrive in San Francisco in time for the Christmas selling season. They were obligated to pay for the merchandise when it hit port. Under normal operations, an importer signs a 90-day note with his bank to finance the shipment. The bank advances the money and the overseas supplier gets paid. Unfortunately, Cost Plus had already used up all of its bank credit.

Fortunately, Luther Henderson entered the picture.

"Back in Fort Worth," he related, "we had seen copies of the Cost Plus 'Red Herring' prospectus offering this stock for sale. It was impossible for us to visualize what kind of business this was. It sounded crazy and we didn't know much about it. But in August 1962, Charles and Gwen were going to San Francisco on a vacation, primarily because Gwen used to live there. Charles didn't have much to do in San Francisco, businesswise. We didn't have much Tandy Leather business out there. And I knew he didn't like to go on strictly social vacations."

So Henderson gave Tandy a copy of the Cost Plus prospectus and said, "Charles, since you're going to be out in San Francisco, why don't you go call on these people?"

That's exactly what Tandy did. When he walked into the 15,000-square foot store, huge by Tandy Leather Company standards, his mouth fell open. He saw all this merchandise on the shelves and filling the interior of the store, but what impressed him the most was that there were seven cash registers and long lines of customers at each one. He watched the scene with increasing interest, as the lines of eager buyers never seemed to diminish.

Tandy then proceeded upstairs to the second floor, where the Cost Plus offices were located, and introduced himself. He was, of course, warmly received. As Henderson put it, "Here was this big, rich Texan with his big cigar. They were immediately interested in getting acquainted and talking seriously."

That night, as Henderson was enjoying dinner, the phone rang. It was Tandy calling from San Francisco. "Luther," he boomed, "get out here right away. This is the damnedest thing I've ever seen. I want somebody else's eyes to look at it."

Henderson flew to San Francisco the next day, arriving in the late afternoon. He and Tandy immediately headed for Fisherman's Wharf. For Henderson, it was love at first sight.

"I fell in love with the business then and there," he reported. "The merchandise was very similar to Pier 1's today, but a little cruder, with a lot less finesse than we later developed. But they had a big store. What's so remarkable about this is that in renting this old building in San Francisco, they had stumbled into the very best location in the United States for this kind of store. They were doing $7 million or $8 million of volume out of this one store. I think the biggest Tandy Leather company store at that time might have hit $200,000.

"It was just the perfect location and continues to be. You've got San Francisco as a magnet for tourists. They love to ride the cable car and there are thousands of people walking by your front door every day. And every day there's a new group of people going by. The Cost Plus people were smart enough to recognize what a great location they had, so they began to buy up and lease adjacent property. Soon they had a full city block and, undoubtedly, the biggest volume store in its field in the country."

With Tandy and Henderson entranced over the prospect, and the Cost Plus principals anxious to make a deal that would get them off the hook with their suppliers, serious discussions got under way that same evening. To Tandy, Cost Plus represented a retailing concept that appeared to dovetail beautifully with his newly-opened Tandy Marts. Another incentive was the fact that it would take only a small amount of cash to bail Cost Plus out of its financial bind. The deal that was eventually hammered out gave both entities what they were seeking.

"What we did," Henderson reported, "was loan them the $300,000 that they expected to get from the public offering of their stock. In return, we got stock options to buy three-eighths of their company at its then book value."

The agreement, which was completed in September of 1962, provided for the issuance of transferrable warrants to Tandy Corporation for the purchase of 150,000 shares of Cost Plus, Inc., common stock at $2 per share, exercisable to February 1, 1968. This gave Tandy a period of more than five years to decide whether or not to exercise the option. The agreement also granted Tandy Corporation the right to establish its own national chain of Tandy-owned Cost Plus stores across the United States, operating them under the Cost Plus name.

"They didn't have the capital to open new stores," Henderson pointed out. "We did. So we got the right to open up additional import stores, for which they would supply the merchandise at cost, plus a 7 percent handling charge."

Tandy quickly opened three Cost Plus stores in California and Texas. The first one was opened in San Mateo, California, down the peninsula from San Francisco, before the ink was hardly dry on the agreement, and the two others were opened in the Tandy Marts in Fort Worth and Dallas just before Thanksgiving Day in time for the Christmas shopping season.

"The people in San Francisco thought we were crazy when we told them we were going to open the stores in Dallas and Fort Worth," Henderson chuckled. "They said, 'The people down in Texas aren't going to appreciate this merchandise.'"

In opening the new stores, Tandy was not only getting a quick start on building a new chain store system to augment the ones it already had in operation, it was also relieving Cost Plus of the excess inventory it had acquired and couldn't digest.

"So we were a big help to them," Henderson said. He recalled the day the San Mateo store opened in the fall of 1962. "Total sales were around $3,000, while a good day in a Tandy Leather Company store at the time was $400 to $500. Charles' mouth really fell open when he realized the amount of volume we'd gotten out of this first store."

During 1963, stores were opened in Richmond, San Leandro and San Jose, California, and in San Antonio and Houston, bringing the number of Tandy-owned Cost Plus retail outlets to eight and adding about $1.5 million to the company's sales volume. The agreement seemed to be working and all signs pointed to an eventual formal marriage between the two entities. But before the two lovers marched to the altar, they discovered that their relationship was not as idyllic as it had originally seemed.

"We found out fairly quickly," Henderson said, "that the Cost Plus buying techniques were suitable only for their one big store that could sell almost anything because it had such tremendous traffic. But the little stores that we were opening didn't have that kind of traffic. So things that they were successful with, we wouldn't be. They also didn't have to pay too much attention to quantity, because, again, they had such a fast turnover in their store at Fisherman's Wharf. They could digest stuff that, for us, was indigestible. So it was not a completely satisfactory relationship."

In 1964, the Tandy group opened its first stores in the rapidly-growing Los Angeles market and increased the number of outlets in Texas, but it was now apparent to Henderson and Tandy that a divorce from Cost Plus was inevitable. Their solution was to sever the connection and go it alone.

"We decided our best bet was to make our operation independent," Henderson explained, "so at the beginning of 1965, we gave them notice. We had to give them 12 months' notice under our agreement, but now we began to do our own buying, purchasing directly from foreign sources. We also had to change the name, and that's when we came up with Pier 1 Imports."

Over the next year, Pier 1, with Henderson as general manager, more than doubled its sales. It was now importing and retailing a worldwide selection of household items, decorator novelties and furniture at low prices made possible by direct purchasing from foreign sources. A new store that had been opened in Phoenix in August 1965 had brought the number of outlets in the Pier 1 chain to 15, all located on the Pacific Coast and in the Southwest.

But problems persisted.

"Pier 1 was a business that was anxious to expand, but was a cash-eater," Henderson explained. "It was consuming cash because it wasn't making any money. It had great potential, of course. Another problem was that we were experiencing difficulties at Pier 1 trying to duplicate the management style, techniques and controls utilized so successfully in the leathercrafts business by Charles Tandy. In the import store business, those techniques and controls were only about 75 percent effective. The other 25 percent didn't work because the business was just different, primarily due to the long lead times. We had to buy merchandise so far ahead."

The situation came to a head in 1965 with an inventory surplus crisis, for which Tandy blamed Henderson. Henderson, in turn, held Tandy equally culpable.

"Charles, in those days, was not given to a lot of advance planning," Henderson contended. "I'm not demeaning him, but that's simply the way it was. So I couldn't go to him at the start of the year and say, 'Charles, we would like to open up three stores, four stores or six stores this year.' I knew that we could open up some stores. I didn't know where we could open them because it depended on finding satisfactory locations, and they were very hard to find for import stores which need a lot of cheap space.

"So I misread Charles' mind, if you want to call it that, or his plans. Anyway, I bought too much merchandise for Pier 1 in 1965. Now we were faced with a similar situation that Cost Plus had had in 1962; that is, we had a lot of stuff coming in and we didn't have enough outlets to turn it. We could see a glut coming."

In anticipation of the oversupply, Henderson had cut off all buying by June. Tandy, however, did not become fully aware of the seriousness of the problem until August. By then, the rapidly-growing inventory was totally out of line with sales expectations. A furious Tandy called Henderson on the carpet.

"Charles really chewed me out about it," Henderson recalled. "It was my fault and I didn't deny it. But that sort of disillusioned him about the import store business."

For his part, Henderson was not unduly concerned about the excessive inventory. He felt that what he had ordered was good merchandise. "We had just bought too much of it," he acknowledged, "and we were just going to own part of it, more than we needed, for quite a bit longer than we liked." He tried to explain this to an obdurate Tandy.

"I know we can clean this up," Henderson avowed.

Tandy remained unconvinced.

"We're gonna have to get rid of it," he snapped. "We're gonna have a giant liquidation sale."

Tandy now gave Henderson a direct order: "I want you to take out full page ads in the newspapers in all of the cities where you have stores, and I want you to throw the cost book away. Forget what you paid for the stuff. I want you to price it to sell."

Henderson took him at his word.

"I remember one item we had at the time," he recounted. "It was a simple rattan chair. We'd paid about $2.25 for this chair. We customarily sold it for $3.49 and we would occasionally 'special' it for $2.99. We had a lot of these chairs. Charles had said, 'I want you to get rid of them.' So we priced them at $1.99 at the liquidation sale.

"This was November of 1965," Henderson continued. "The sale was a total flop. We got about a 20 percent to 25 percent increase in sales volume. That's all we got out of it. And the reason it flopped, it's simple when you step back and see it now, was that the public didn't know what a bargain it was being offered. We were literally giving the stuff away, but the public didn't realize it. It also could be that they feared the merchandise couldn't be any good because it was priced so cheap."

At any rate, in Henderson's opinion, the liquidation sale fiasco "sort of completed Charles' disillusionment with the import store business."

Coupled with that, Henderson asserted, was the fact that Tandy "was facing the considerable capital restraints of having the Tandy Leather Company laying golden eggs while its two hungry pups, Pier 1 and Radio Shack, which he had acquired by then, were eating them up. Charles recognized that he had these two vehicles, each of which could suck up a lot of money."

Tandy engaged in a protracted period of soul-searching. Then he summoned Henderson to his office. Tandy's desk, Henderson noted as he entered the room, was covered as usual with sales reports from around the country. Tandy, however, seemed unusually subdued. He was about to admit defeat, and he didn't relish the experience.

"Luther," Tandy said, "I don't understand this business. I've decided to get rid of these import stores, and I'm going to give you the first chance to buy them. I'll sell them to you at book value."

Recalling the moment, Henderson said: "I kind of gulped because, of course, I knew we had almost broken even in the prior fiscal year. I knew we were going to lose money in the fiscal year we were currently in because of the huge gross profit kick that we had had to take following the liquidation sale that Charles had ordered. But the more I thought about it, the more I liked it. So I approached the other people who were working with me in the import store division. Most of them, of course, were transfers from the Tandy Leather Company, and they all seemed willing to go along."

Henderson and his associates now pooled their resources.

"We needed to raise $1.8 million to buy Pier 1," Henderson reported. "We raised $500,000 among ourselves, which was to be the capital stock of the new company. We were going to get another $500,000 from the Federal Small Business Investment Corporation and borrow $800,000 from the Fort Worth National Bank secured by my personal guarantee. That's how we were going to finance it."

Henderson and Tandy shook hands on the deal in December of 1965 and were shooting for a closing by the end of January 1966, when a complication developed.

"As we got closer to completing the deal, the SBIC began to put the squeeze on us on the terms for lending us the half-million dollars they had promised to lend us back in November," Henderson said. "They kept raising the ante and the terms got more and more onerous. It finally got to the point where they were getting themselves into a preferred position. If the venture was successful, they would have control of it. If it was unsuccessful, they would get paid off ahead of everybody else."

Henderson went to Tandy with his problem.

"I'm sorry, but I can't proceed with the deal," he informed Tandy. "The terms that the SBIC wants are unreasonable."

Tandy nodded his head in agreement as Henderson outlined the details of the SBIC terms.

"I guess this means we're just going to have to kill the deal," Henderson said ruefully.

Tandy looked at his long-time friend and associate through a cloud of cigar smoke.

"Let me think about it," he said.

The next day Tandy summoned Henderson to his office. He had figured out a way to raise the $500,000 that Henderson needed and, at the same time, remove the SBIC from the picture.

"I'll make this deal with you," he told Henderson. "Tandy Corporation will take $500,000 worth of Pier 1 preferred stock, which, with the $500,000 you've already raised from your own group, will provide the $1 million of equity you need in order to get the $800,000 bank loan."

Then Tandy quickly added two provisos.

"I want your handshake that you will retire this preferred stock as quickly as you can. And I want the preferred stock to be convertible. I want it to be convertible on a scale where I receive more stock the longer you wait to pay me off."

Recalling that moment, Henderson said feelingly, "This preferred stock could not be redeemable on its face or the bank wouldn't have loaned us the money. So Charles and I had nothing but a handshake agreement that I would endeavor to pay him off as quickly as we could. It was a very nice gesture on his part. He could afford to do it, of course. Tandy Corporation had plenty of money, but Charles had better uses for it than loaning it to a company that was just going out on its own. I always appreciated that, because without that bit of financing I doubt if we could have made the deal."

The agreement that Henderson and Tandy finally shook hands on, after some additional dickering back and forth, stipulated that Tandy Corporation would receive 10 shares of Pier 1 common stock for each share of preferred stock it held, if the preferred stock were converted immediately. Tandy would receive 20 shares of common stock if the conversion took place within a year, and 50 shares if the preferred stock was converted after one year.

So the deal was struck. The Fort Worth National Bank loaned Henderson the $800,000. He now had the $1.8 million he needed to take Pier 1 off Tandy's hands. The sale was completed on February 10, 1966. Henderson resigned as vice president and treasurer of Tandy Corporation to become the president and chief executive officer of Pier 1 Imports, Inc.

"Now we got real busy," he confided. "We were very strongly motivated. We cleaned the business up. We got rid of the excess inventory. We paid off the bank before the next year was up. I adopted a short fiscal year. You see, we completed the deal in February. So I adopted a March 31 fiscal year for the company, so that I could get that loss behind us, and that was the last time the business lost money. We bought back all of the preferred stock from Tandy in less than three years."

Tandy was delighted when the final shares of preferred stock were converted, Henderson said. "And, of course, for the next umpteen years after that his standard query every time we saw each other was, 'Why didn't you bastards do this good a job of running the company when you worked for me?' I never could tell him, but what I really wanted to say to him was, 'Because you wouldn't leave us alone,' which was the real answer."

Henderson took Pier 1 public in 1969 and then sold it to Fuqua Industries for $35 million in December 1979, receiving a management contract and a large stock option as part of the deal. He continued to serve as Pier 1 president and CEO until his retirement in 1983. By then Pier 1 was owned by Intermark Corp., which had bought a controlling interest in Fuqua Industries the year before.

"After I bought Pier 1, Charles and I continued to see each other quite frequently," Henderson recalled, "and I asked him to join our board. He was always a very active board member. He was really good. He always had lots of ideas. Frequently he would not agree with the policy that I thought was right for the company, and we'd talk about it at the board meetings. He'd express his reservations, and when you hold a discussion like that before a group of intelligent people, it frequently causes you to modify your course of action. But he would never vote against it if that's what I wanted to do."

The Pier 1 board meetings were held in Henderson's office on the third floor of the building which served as the company headquarters. There was no elevator, which caused a problem after Tandy suffered a heart attack in October of 1968.

"After Charles had his heart attack, we fixed up a conference room down on the first floor because he couldn't climb those two flights of stairs, and we didn't want him to," Henderson said. "We were always very close," he added, "and he used to tell me, and I think he meant it, that I was a lot more like a brother to him than his brother Bill was. He and Bill didn't get along too well. They kind of sparked. I remember that Bill was very skittish about getting into bed with Charles in 1955 on the American Hide & Leather deal. His attitude was, 'I may get a lot of money out of this but I don't want to work for you.' Charles didn't want him to work for the company, either. Bill had some good stores, but he wasn't in Charles' league as far as business acumen, drive and determination are concerned."

Charles was "undoubtedly" a genius in motivation and a genius in merchandising, Henderson said of his old friend and mentor, but he had some weaknesses, too.

"He didn't take the time to realize that there were subtle differences between the kind of retail chain that Pier 1 was and the kind he was used to running," Henderson opined. "If he'd given us a little more room, we'd have probably remained with him. We could have been a very successful division of Tandy Corporation."

Chapter 8
A Bargain Basement Buy in Boston

Even before the initial deal was struck with Cost Plus Imports in 1962, Charles Tandy had become interested in electronics as a possible avenue for enhancing the growth of Tandy Corporation. In the early 1960s, he had made a pass at Lafayette Electronics of New York City, then the largest operator of electronics stores in the country.

"We were completely rebuffed," Luther Henderson said of the effort. "Lafayette had about 25 stores at the time, and here was this little upstart wanting to buy them."

Tandy approached Allied Electronics in Chicago and again received the cold shoulder treatment. The second turndown caused him to conclude that if he wanted to get into the consumer electronics business, he would have to do it on his own. The opening of the Tandy Mart in Fort Worth in December of 1961 provided him with the vehicle he was seeking. Tandy convinced Charles C. Gumm, the owner of a small electronics retail business on Fort Worth's east side, to open an electronics crafts store in the Tandy Mart. Two months later, Tandy bought the store from Gumm and shortly thereafter opened similar stores in Dallas and Houston under the Electronics Crafts name.

"The stores sold electronics supplies very close in nature to what the old Radio Shack stores sold," Luther Henderson said. "The Electronics Crafts stores were not failures exactly, but neither were they very successful. Charles, however, continued to have an interest in this field because he saw the potential in it."

Bill Michero observed, "I don't think Charles would have had any interest in Radio Shack if it hadn't been for our entry into the do-it-yourself electronics business by buying out Charley Gumm. This gave him a year or more of fumbling with it and deciding he liked it."

The stores sold electronics kits, wire, alligator clips, soldering equipment, and doodads, which Michero referred to as "electronics findings," a nostalgic reference to the old Hinckley-Tandy "shoe findings" days.

"We were marching to the wrong drummer entirely in our initial efforts with those 'electronics findings' stores," Michero stated, "but that was the precursor of our interest in the electronics business."

While Tandy was getting his feet wet in the consumer electronics business in Texas, a series of events was transpiring in Boston involving his old banker friend, Bill Brown. More than a quarter-of-a-century later, Brown, who retired as chairman of the board of the First National Bank of Boston in 1989, recalled the circumstances that led to Tandy's return to Beantown in search of another deal.

"In the fall of 1962," Brown began, "I was a vice president in the Commercial Loan Department of the bank when I received a call from John Toulman, the First National's senior lending officer, asking me to come to his office. When I got there, he handed me a manila folder containing a thick file. 'I want you to take over this account,' Toulman said. 'We're in real trouble on this one. We've got a big loan that's gone sour. We've had to cut off their credit. I want you to see what you can do with it.'"

The company Toulman was talking about was Radio Shack.

It had been founded in 1921 by Theodore Deutschmann as a one-store retail and mail order firm selling radio and electronic components to ham radio operators and electronics buffs. Deutschmann, who had emigrated from London to Boston with his parents in 1890 at the age of 3, had gotten interested in radio after serving as a foreign representative for several German telephone groups. The budding enterprise was given its name by William Halligan, a former amateur radio operator and an early employee of Deutschmann's, who later founded the Hallicrafter Corporation.

The name Radio Shack was derived from maritime lore dating back to Marconi's invention of the radio at the turn of the century, when the wireless equipment installed aboard ships plying the Seven Seas was housed in a wooden structure above the bridge that was called the "radio shack." The ship's radio operator was an officer who was called "Sparks." Halligan convinced Deutschmann that Radio Shack was an appropriate name for a venture whose initial customers were primarily "Sparks" and "radio hams."

The first Radio Shack store was located on Brattle Street in downtown Boston only a block away from the scene of the Boston Massacre and adjacent to the Brattle Tavern, where General George Washington held meetings with his staff during the Revolutionary War. By the end of 1962, the enterprise had grown to nine retail stores and a mail order business offering electronics products from around the world, with annual sales of about $14 million. The stores were located in Boston, Braintree and Saugus, Massachusetts; Stamford, West Hartford and New Haven, Connecticut; Cranston, Rhode Island; and Syracuse, New York.

In the late 1920s, the small company had taken a brief fling at marketing completed radios, and by the late 1940s had become a leading distributor of electronic parts and equipment to do-it-yourselfers and to industry. It had issued its first catalog in the early 1940s. In 1947, it moved somewhat away from its traditional field of regular electronics into the then new field of high-fidelity components and had opened what it called "the nation's first Audio Comparator Showroom." The distinctive feature of the Audio Comparator was a switching console that provided immediate "aural" comparisons between speakers, amplifiers, turntables and cartridges.

The company had begun marketing its early products under the "Realistic" private label in 1954. Its first products were an FM tuner retailing at $39.95, an AM tuner at $29.95, and a matching 10-watt amplifier with built-in preamplifier at $29.95. A 1956 issue of *High Fidelity* magazine reported it had tested the Realistic FM tuner and had found it to have "sensitivity surprisingly close to that of tuners which sell for three or four times its cost." Radio Shack had begun importing merchandise from Japan in the mid-1950s, and in 1961 had opened an engineering office in Tokyo.

In 1961, the company which was now headed by Milton Deutschmann, brother of the founder, reported a net loss before income taxes of $836,358 on net sales of $16,711,833, after having realized a net profit of $445,804 on sales of $12,583,546 in the previous year. Milton Deutschmann attributed the loss to "severe operating difficulties as a result of the expansion of our main plant" and to "additional costs in other phases of our expansion program." In the annual report, Deutschmann listed several "major achievements" during the year, one of which was the "successful" introduction of revolving credit.

As it turned out, Deutschmann would later acknowledge in a telephone interview from his home in Wellesley, Massachusetts, the introduction of revolving credit proved to be a major factor in Radio Shack's financial collapse.

"Our experiment with extension of credit got us into trouble," Deutschmann said candidly. "We knew how to merchandise, but we didn't know anything about credit. It was a perfect plan on paper, but the execution was pitiful. We simply didn't know how to collect our money."

By the time Bill Brown was called into John Toulman's office and given the assignment of finding a buyer for Radio Shack, the company was losing $200,000 a month. And, in addition to its $5 million note at the First National Bank of Boston, it also owed $2 million to State Mutual Life Insurance Company of Worcester, Massachusetts.

Toulman didn't have to emphasize to Brown the problem the bank faced with the imminent Radio Shack default. "In those days, in the early 1960s," Brown explained, "the bank didn't take losses. Write-offs hadn't started yet at our bank and at all other banks. So this would have been a disaster. And we were looking at a situation where the bank would probably lose 75 cents on the dollar if we liquidated Radio Shack because most of its assets were inventory—and inventory doesn't go through a fire sale very well."

It was a grim Brown who returned to his office after his session with Toulman to begin pondering his options. Brown, fortunately, was somewhat familiar with Radio Shack because one of his former classmates at the Harvard Business School, Tim Quillan, had been Milton Deutschmann's number two man at one time. Now he took out a yellow pad and began making a list of possible buyers.

Several potential candidates immediately came to Brown's mind, including Allied Radio in Chicago and Lafayette Electronics in New York City. Brown got on the phone to set up appointments to meet with the heads of the prospects on his list. No one was interested in taking over an almost defunct, debt-encumbered operation. In addition, after talking with the Allied Radio people in Chicago, Brown became convinced they were in the same precarious condition as Radio Shack, but didn't know it.

"Now I was really worried about what the hell I was going to do," he said. "I kept thinking about it, because this was my big chance to impress the big boss. Finally, I thought of Charlie Tandy."

Brown knew that Tandy was interested in getting into the electronics business. They had talked about it after Tandy had gained control of General American Industries.

"Charles knew he had to get into some other lines of business, and Radio Shack was right down his alley," Brown recollected. "So I had suggested then that he talk to Milton Deutschmann. They talked. But nothing came out of that conversation. So I was reluctant to call Tandy again on the same deal."

Brown sat around for a couple of days agonizing over his predicament. He knew Toulman would be calling him to ask for an update on the Radio Shack situation. Finally, seeing no other alternative, he put in a call to Tandy in Fort Worth, only to learn that Charles and Gwen had just left on a trip to Mexico and were not expected back for at least a week.

"I thought it over," Brown continued, "and the next day I called Charles' office again and asked if they would give me a number where he could be reached. They said they couldn't do that. So I told them it was extremely important and asked if they'd call Charles and tell him that I was trying to reach him. The next day he called me and asked what he could do for me. I said, 'You told me once you would like to own Radio Shack. Now's your chance.'"

Tandy's response was, "Oh, no. No way."

Brown persisted, "Why don't you come to Boston and talk about it?"

"I don't want to waste my time."

"Why would you be wasting your time?"

"It's Deutschmann. It's impossible to make a deal with him. All he wants to talk about is how much money he's going to spend on advertising, and what he's going to do to expand the company."

Brown's tone hardened. "It's different this time. The State Mutual Life Insurance Company in Worcester has a big loan to Radio Shack, and Dick Russom at State Mutual is my close personal friend. He and I have talked this over and we've agreed to work together to help you make a deal with Deutschmann."

"All right," Tandy said, "I'll be there tomorrow."

As soon as he hung up the phone, Brown dialed the office of Francis Hooks Burr, a senior partner in the Boston law firm of Ropes & Grey and a director of Radio Shack. He had served as treasurer of Harvard University, board chairman of Massachusetts General Hospital, and as a director of American Airlines and a number of other major corporations. How and why Burr ever became a member of the Radio Shack board was beyond Brown's knowledge. "Maybe," he guessed, "it was because one of the junior partners asked him to go on the board after it became a client. Anyway, he was on the board and he had a reputation to protect."

When Brown got Burr on the line, he told him about Tandy's scheduled visit to Boston the next day to talk about buying Radio Shack, and asked if the meeting could be held in Burr's office.

"I'm going to need your help in getting Milton Deutschmann to at least meet with us and talk with us and find out what can be accomplished," Brown informed Burr. Then he added, "Hooks, you're a director of Radio Shack and I don't think you want to be a director of a bankrupt company."

Burr's reply was a brisk, "I'll have Deutschmann in my office tomorrow morning at 9 o'clock."

After talking to Brown, Tandy asked Jesse Upchurch's travel agency in Mexico City, Percival Tours, to make the arrangements for him to get to Boston that night and reserve him a room at the Ritz-Carlton Hotel. He and Gwen had been visiting the Upchurches at their home in the Mexican capital. Tandy was able to catch a flight that got him to Boston in the early evening.

Shortly before 9 o'clock the next morning, March 27, 1963, a cab picked Tandy up at the Ritz-Carlton and deposited him at the First National Bank Building, then located at 67 Milk Street in the financial district. He and Brown had a quick cup of coffee, then walked across the street to Burr's office about half a block away.

"We walked into Burr's office about 9:30," Brown recalled. "Deutschmann was already there. We sat down and I told them that, under the right circumstances, Charles would be interested in buying Radio Shack. At this point, Deutschmann took over the floor, and for most of the next two hours did most of the talking.

"And Tandy was right," Brown continued. "Deutschmann didn't accept the fact that Radio Shack was really in trouble. He sounded like everything was really golden, that they were just in a little over their heads, that all they had to do was spend some more money on advertising, spend some money up front, and they could get this thing rolling again. He said they had opened two huge stores, one in Hartford, Connecticut, and the other in Braintree, Massachusetts, in the past two years and that this had impacted their earnings; but they were now positioned to cash in on these and other capital outlays."

Brown had seen Tandy fidgeting in his chair, pulling impatiently on his cigar and expelling clouds of smoke for the past hour. The meeting was not going the way he had planned. Then, at about 11:30, Tandy suddenly rose to his feet and, without saying a word, began walking towards the door.

"Where are you going?" Brown demanded.

"I'm going back to Mexico," Tandy said.

"Just a minute," Brown said. "I'll go out with you," and he motioned to Burr to follow him. "Burr came to the outer office, where Charles and I were standing," Brown recollected. "I took him down the hall away from Tandy and I said, 'Hooks, you'd better talk to this guy.' Then I told him about all the work that I'd done and I said, 'There just isn't another buyer around.'" Brown paused in his narrative to offer an aside, "Things then weren't like they are today, where people will buy anything."

At any rate, Burr got the message. "Let me talk to Deutschmann," he told Brown, "and you bring Tandy back here after lunch."

Brown returned to the outer office and invited Tandy to join him for lunch. He escorted Tandy back across the street to 67 Milk Street, and the two went up to the tastefully-appointed First of Boston's dining room. It was a large open room, not yet crowded at that pre-noon hour. A captain escorted them to a table with a breathtaking view of the historic harbor where history's most famous tea party took place.

After they were seated, Tandy told Brown, "I'm happy to have lunch with you, but I want you to know that I'm leaving immediately afterwards. I can catch a plane this afternoon that'll get me back to Mexico City tonight. My wife's still down there."

"No, you're not," Brown responded. "You're going to make a deal with Deutschmann."

"You can't make a deal with that guy," Tandy retorted.

"Yes you can," Brown insisted. Then he looked at Tandy searchingly and asked, "What kind of a deal would you be willing to make?"

Tandy began sputtering, as he tried to articulate what he had in mind, and Brown stopped him and said, "Just a minute," and handed Tandy a menu which was lying on the table. "The menu was thick like a cardboard and it served as both a menu and a place mat," Brown remembered, "and I turned it over and I said, 'Write down your deal. What'll you do? What'll you pay? What are your terms?'"

Tandy said, "All right, okay," and he pulled a pen from his inside coat pocket and began writing. Several minutes later he handed the menu back to Brown.

"Basically," Brown said, "he wrote down three provisions for making the deal. The first was that he would take over management immediately and with full authority. Second, he would hire one of the Big Eight auditing firms to conduct an audit. And third, he would pay book value as of June 30, 1963, the end of the Radio Shack fiscal year."

Brown looked at Tandy's proposal and said, "Hell, you want the business for nothing, don't you?"

"What do you mean?" Tandy replied innocently.

"You know damn well what I mean," Brown shot back. "You know as well as I do that they're not going to have any net worth when you finish the audit."

Tandy grinned and conceded, "Yeah, you're probably right."

"Well," Brown stipulated, "there's going to be a fourth provision if we're going to have an understanding. You're going to have to put some money in there that's at risk."

"I'll put money in if it's needed," Tandy countered.

"No," Brown was adamant, "that's not going to be the agreement. You're going to agree with me that you're going to put in at least half a million dollars."

Brown chuckled softly as he recalled the scene in the swank dining room that was now beginning to fill up with bankers and their guests.

"We did a little negotiating and settled at $300,000. So we had a verbal agreement that if he took over Radio Shack, he'd have $300,000 in the pot ahead of us," Brown said. "Then we went back down across the street."

Tandy presented his terms to Deutschmann, who was now receptive.

"He was perfectly happy with the terms because he figured he was going to get a lot of money after the audit and get out of his problem at the same time," Brown said. "Deutschmann simply couldn't believe how broke his company really was. So they signed the deal."

Brown had one final memory of that history-making meeting.

"As we went back across the street, Charles said he was heading back to Texas and would be back very soon to take over Radio Shack. He said, 'I'll see you,' and I said, 'Just a minute, where's your check?'

"Charlie said, 'What are you talking about?' And I said, 'I want a check for $300,000.' So he stood outside on the street and wrote out the check to Radio Shack for $300,000 and I took the check back to the bank with me."

On March 28, 1963, a special meeting of the board of directors of Tandy Corporation was hastily convened at the company's main offices on West 7th Street in Fort Worth. A quorum was barely present represented by Charles Tandy, John B. Collier, Jr., Luther Henderson and Jim West. Absent were the three other members of the seven-man board, Lawrence Dempsey, Alfred Hauser and Carl Welhausen.

Tandy called the meeting to order and presented a description of the operations and financial condition of Radio Shack and a summary of the agreement he had struck with Deutschmann. The minutes of the meeting gave the following details:

"A description was given of the proposed plan, under the terms of which Tandy Corporation would be granted options to acquire controlling interest in Radio Shack Corporation and would be granted immediate control and operating management of that company. There followed a lengthy discussion of the proposed plan, after which, upon motion by Mr. Henderson, seconded by Mr. Collier, and unanimously approved, it was resolved that the president be authorized to enter into an agreement with Radio Shack Corporation and with certain of its original stockholders and take any action he deems necessary or desirable to implement and carry out the intent of such agreements."

The agreement granted Tandy Corporation an option to acquire 237,687 shares of Radio Shack common stock from the company, plus an additional 355,881 common shares from the Deutschmann family, at a price equal to the per share book value of Radio Shack at June 30, 1963, as determined by Price Waterhouse & Company. The option would expire June 30, 1964, but would be extended to December 31, 1964, if Tandy had by June 30, 1964, purchased at least 49 percent of the shares offered by the Deutschmann family and had made a written offer to purchase the remaining shares.

So, for the $300,000 advanced to Radio Shack, for which Tandy Corporation was granted a subordinated participation in the loan agreement with the First National Bank of Boston, plus the payment of $5,000 to secure the options, Charles Tandy now held in his hands the right to acquire, at book value, a 62 percent ownership of Radio Shack.

"As Charles expected," Bill Brown said, "the Price Waterhouse audit came up with a very large negative net worth, which made the book value zero. So, except for the $300,000, he took over Radio Shack for nothing. But there's no doubt that Radio Shack would have folded if Tandy hadn't stepped in."

Luther Henderson added, "The Radio Shack management was very reluctant to give up control of the business. The bank, of course, had a lot of leverage. But for a total risk of only $300,000, Tandy got effective working control of a business with around $14 million worth of sales volume and assets of between $8 million and $9 million. That's all Tandy had at risk. The company was not liable for anything but $300,000 if we didn't succeed in making it work."

Tandy had his go-ahead, but it had been granted with considerable misgivings on the part of his board. The directors still held a healthy skepticism about the Radio Shack venture and they made it clear that they were reserving judgment on any additional commitments of company resources.

Jesse Upchurch believed that the board members' doubts stemmed to a great extent from their less-than-happy recollections of Charles' prior escapade with a company domiciled in Boston.

"After the fiasco with American Hide & Leather, Jim West and some of the others simply didn't want anything to do with any of those Eastern companies," Upchurch said.

He recalled how just a short time before the Radio Shack agreement was okayed, Tandy had brought another proposal before the board for its approval.

"Charles had hammered out a deal with Hoffritz Cutlery, the people who have all these shops at all the airports, but the directors said, 'No way.' They didn't want to get into a deal with another Eastern company."

Eunice West recalled the strong reservations Jim West had about getting involved with Radio Shack.

"In the beginning, he tried to talk Charles out of it," she said. "Then, as time went by, he saw that this was a good thing after all."

The ball was now squarely in Charles Tandy's court as he faced the formidable challenge of turning Radio Shack around and defying the conventional wisdom of the time that there was no money to be made in consumer electronics.

"If Charles Tandy had read the papers and listened to the analysts, he would never have gotten into consumer electronics," said John V.

Roach, who became chairman of Tandy Corporation in 1982. "But Tandy was looking at electronics as a retailer, rather than as an electronics manufacturer. It was a case of one man seeing what no one else saw. The success of Radio Shack is a measure of Charles Tandy's genius as a merchant."

Tandy later would say that the main thing that attracted him to Radio Shack was the fact that "it did have business, it did have a quantity of customers. The only problem was, it was spending more money than it was taking in. So all I had to do was change that."

He didn't waste any time getting started.

What Milton Moskowitz, a prominent business writer, later called "the most spectacular retail expansion under one name since the explosion of the A&P grocery chain in the early part of the century" was about to be launched.

Chapter 9
The Crusade is Launched

Whenever he stayed in Boston, Charles Tandy favored the Ritz-Carlton Hotel. So it was in a suite in that elegant hostelry that Tandy ensconced himself on Sunday night, March 31, 1963.

Bright and early the next morning, Monday, April 1, found Tandy in Bill Brown's office at the First National Bank. He had a busy day ahead of him, including a meeting at the Ritz-Carlton that evening at which he was going to introduce himself to his new employees.

Brown questioned his visitor right off the bat.

"Who are you going to bring in to run Radio Shack?"

"Nobody."

Brown couldn't believe what he was hearing.

"What do you mean, 'nobody?'"

"I mean that I'm not going to get anybody. I'm going to run it myself."

"You mean you're going to move up here to Boston?"

"No," Tandy told Brown, "I'll come up here on weekends."

Brown's stomach began to churn. He thought, "Oh, Jesus Christmas, with all of the problems Radio Shack has..." But it quickly became obvious that Tandy had been doing his homework. Brown began to feel better as Tandy outlined his program.

"He knew exactly what he wanted to do with Radio Shack," Brown said. "First of all," Tandy told him, "I'm going to cut out all mail order. You can't sell these kinds of products by mail order. People will buy a recorder and pull the wires off and ship it back. I'm cutting out credit. So it's no mail order, no credit, all cash, and we're going to buy most of our merchandise in Japan."

"What about having a lead line?" Brown wanted to know.

Tandy answered, "I'll make my own."

Tandy continued, "We're going to liquidate our big stores and we're going to open lots of small stores, little holes in the wall. I'm going to rent them. So, if one location doesn't work out, I'm not stuck for a hell of a lot. We're gonna open lots of locations. The customers are gonna come in. They're gonna look at the merchandise. They're gonna pay cash and they're gonna walk out. And a sale is a sale."

Then Tandy added, "I'm gonna fire all the chiefs and promote the Indians."

Among the Indians that Tandy was talking about promoting were Bernie Appel, Dave Beckerman, and Lew Kornfeld.

A balding, heavy-set man with an infectious smile and an accent that is as Boston as a can of baked beans, Appel had joined Radio Shack as a $125-a-week buyer in August of 1959. He was named president of Radio Shack in 1984, but remained a buyer at heart, happiest when discovering and introducing a hot new product. A native Bostonian, Appel began working at the age of 10 throwing a newspaper route and delivering groceries. "I never had a penny in my pocket," he recalled, "Whatever I made, I gave to my folks."

After graduating from high school, Appel worked for a catalog discount house and attended Boston University at night, but he didn't get along with his boss. "We didn't agree on how the business should be run," Appel reminisced. "I believed we ought to do our thing with a fairly heavy push to profits. He believed in picking out every odd and end and trying to make every last sale, whether we made money on it or not."

So in May of 1959, Appel went to the Snelling & Snelling employment agency looking for a job and was referred to Radio Shack. He was interviewed by Lew Kornfeld in the Radio Shack offices then located at 730 Commonwealth Avenue, across the street from Boston University. Radio Shack had opened its third store in downtown Boston on Commonwealth Avenue the year before, in a three-story concrete building, in which a very successful Radio Shack store still operates.

"The first floor was the store, the second floor were offices, and in the basement was the mail order warehouse," Appel recalled. "Lew had an office on the second floor. He was then the vice president of advertising."

Although his initial interview didn't result in a job offer, Appel was interested enough to begin dropping in on Kornfeld several times a week after getting off work. Kornfeld seemed to enjoy chatting with the eager young job seeker. They would talk about the catalog business and merchandise.

"Lew would hold up a wristwatch and ask me, 'What do you think this is worth?' And I'd tell him. Once he showed me a Schick shaver, one of their big promotional items at the time, and he said, 'What do you think of this electric razor?'

"I was an honest, blunt kid, and I said, 'It's a piece of junk.'

"But we've sold hundreds of them."

"So now you've got a whole bunch of people who bought something cheap and maybe are mad at you," Appel retorted.

"Right after that, Lew hired me as a buyer," Appel related. "He said they could always make a store manager out of me if I didn't pan out as a buyer. He hired me as a buyer of non-catalog merchandise—pots and pans and things like that." A staff memo from Kornfeld announcing Appel's hiring said that he would be buying sporting goods, housewares, toys and games, books, watches and clocks, and phonograph accessories. Appel kept the memo in a file that he claimed contained every memo Kornfeld ever sent him over the years they worked together.

Appel was still a buyer when Charles Tandy appeared on the scene.

"I'll never forget the day I first heard about Charles Tandy," Appel related. "It was April 1, 1963, April Fool's Day, and we all got a call that afternoon saying that we had a meeting that night at the Ritz-Carlton. And we all went into one of the junior ballrooms of the hotel, and that's where we met Charles Tandy."

Appel was in the new Hartford store unpacking cartons and barrels when the summons to the meeting at the Ritz-Carlton arrived. He had had no forewarning of what was about to happen.

"Milton Deutschmann never told us the status of the business," he reported. "No one would tell us anything. No one knew what our sales were. The merchandising staff, the buyers, didn't know we were going broke. This was kept a big secret. We knew we had a new president, Norman Krim. We knew there were new people in management, but we never knew why. We knew we were a little slow paying our bills. It was a little of a screwball situation."

Appel walked into the meeting room at the Ritz-Carlton that evening to find a group of some 30 or 40 Radio Shack people in the room.

"Charles Tandy was there with C.O. Buckalew of the Tandy Corporation's accounting department," Appel related. "Buck was carrying a big stack of P&Ls." This was Appel's introduction to the profit and loss statement, which he soon discovered was as inerrant to Charles Tandy as the Bible is to a fundamentalist Baptist.

Tandy came right to the point as he opened the meeting.

"I'm Charles Tandy from Fort Worth, Texas," he told the assemblage. "I now own Radio Shack."

Tandy's message was upbeat, Appel said. "He told us that we were going to be in the basic electronics business, that we were strong in electronics. He told us he had talked to Allied and Lafayette. He had talked to everybody, and he thought there was a bright future in electronics, that we would open a lot of stores."

Then Tandy began asking questions about the profit and loss statements Buckalew was holding.

"What happened in 'this and this' store?"

"What was the gross margin?"

"How much does the store manager make?"

To each question, Buckalew flipped open a P&L and gave Tandy the answer. "I can never forget Buckalew standing there with the P&Ls, turning those pages," Appel said.

Lewis F. Kornfeld attended the meeting that night in his capacity as Radio Shack's vice president of merchandising and advertising. Kornfeld joined Radio Shack in 1948 as advertising manager and later became president of Radio Shack and then executive vice president and vice chairman and director of Tandy Corporation. He retired in 1981, but continued as a member of the board of directors.

Kornfeld, a trim, articulate man who has written books on advertising and marketing, first met Milton Deutschmann in 1947, when he was interviewed for a job. Kornfeld's father was a stockbroker and Deutschmann was one of his customers.

"My father told me that Deutschmann was looking for an advertising manager, so I went to see him," Kornfeld recalled. "I probably would have gone to work for them in 1947, but I had my mind set on a salary of $5,000 a year. That was a lot of money then. I was fresh out of the Marine Corps and temporarily was ad manager of a little company in the direct selling shoe business, the Coats Shoe Company. But I hadn't been there long enough to be meaningful and I was not making $5,000 a year. I had in mind that specific number, and I was not going to settle for anything less. So Deutschmann didn't hire me."

A year later, Kornfeld walked into the Radio Shack store on Washington Street in downtown Boston to buy a hi-fi system. "Radio Shack had only one store then," Kornfeld recalled. "On the corner was a sporting goods store called Ivar Johnson, world famous for shotguns and bicycles. That old store is history now. Radio Shack owned a five-story building, about 100-feet wide, with the store on the street level."

While looking at hi-fi systems, Kornfeld discovered that Deutschmann had not yet hired an advertising manager. They talked again and this time Deutschmann agreed to meet Kornfeld's $5,000 figure. In September of 1948, he went to work.

"The first year I was there," Kornfeld recalled, "the sales of the company were about $1 million. About a third of that was what we called industrial. It was selling via salesmen and telephone to commercial outlets like Raytheon and General Electric. A small amount of the sales that year, about 10 or 15 percent, was mail order. The rest was retail at the one store, at 167 Washington Street."

Kornfeld traced the onset of Radio Shack's financial difficulties back to 1958, when the company moved its headquarters from Washington Street to 730 Commonwealth Avenue. By that time, as the vice president for merchandising and advertising, he was in charge of all the buying.

Shortly before the move, Deutschmann had retained the services of Cresap, McCormick and Padgett of Chicago, one of the nation's largest consulting firms.

"The reason we hired them," Kornfeld said, "was that our biggest rival then, Allied Radio Corporation of Chicago, had hired them to engineer their move. So they came in with all of their prestige and experience and their list of high-powered customers, and they engineered our move and set up our new warehouse. Our old warehouse was on three upper stories and a basement on Washington Street, and it was a mess. So the move was okay in itself. But, if you're not careful with consultants, they will grab anything that's loose and they'll even loosen some stuff that isn't loose. They convinced the management that sales would skyrocket merely on the basis of all this improvement."

By 1958, Kornfeld continued, Radio Shack had developed a fairly substantial mail order business. Now Cresap, McCormick and Padgett recommended the doubling and quadrupling of all purchase orders. "It was a fantastically stupid move," Kornfeld contended. "We now were getting in two times to four times the number of, say, broadcast microphones, which we carried mostly in industrial. And there's no way you're going to double or quadruple your sales on those. It was a hell of a mess. That was problem number one."

Problem number two, Kornfeld felt, was a misunderstanding on the part of Deutschmann and his cohorts as to what their gross margin was.

"For example," Kornfeld pointed out, "we estimated that we had a going-in gross margin of 40 percent. And, of course, we knew we had that. But after that, there is a need to break out your gross margin in terms of the actual sales of items. And if you're selling a lot of marked-down stuff, that is going to lower your gross margin. Going-in margin has to be reduced by all of the realities, whatever they are, be they markdowns, returns, etc. Additionally, you have to know your costs. It turned out in not very far hindsight, that our management did not understand the mechanics of gross margins. How much it cost to do business versus how many bucks you had in receipts. If you take the former from the latter, you either have a margin or you don't. And our maintained margin was probably on the order of 28 to 32 percent. But if management does its arithmetic on a 40 percent basis, it's heading for real trouble. In other words, they didn't know all their costs."

Then there was the problem with mail order returns, a large problem that continued to grow larger as the volume grew.

"In the 1930s, '40s and '50s," Kornfeld explained, "electronics tended to be heavy and fragile. And when the mail order returns would come in, either because the customer didn't want the shipment and sent it back or it didn't work or because it was collected for nonpayment, the returned stock would usually arrive in poor shape and wind up in stacks. This meant that even if it arrived in reasonably good shape, it was going to be smashed in the interim. And we had quite a few acres of returns in our warehouse, all of which, of course, reduced our gross margin." That was problem number three.

The company's credit business also was in trouble as a result of its inability to collect on its shipments. "You have to add all of their other problems to the fact that they didn't know how to get their money from the sales they made," Kornfeld agreed. "But their problems were a lot more complicated than not knowing how to make people pay their bills."

They also were grossly overstaffed, he claimed.

"Cresap, McCormick and Padgett, the consultants, had put in a table of organization. They had all these boxes. But you don't fill them in until you have a need for the additional personnel. But Deutschmann and his people filled them in."

Kornfeld gave his recollection of the historic April 1 meeting.

"Actually, what happened, Charles had a little dinner for key employees and Mr. Deutschmann at the Ritz-Carlton in a private dining room on the restaurant floor. I don't think there could have been more than 20 people there. I can't remember too much of what he said, but I do recall I was in a state of shock. Prior to that evening, it was already known to a few of us that we were going to be sold to Tandy. I already had a few catalogs of Tandy Leather Company. There were two speeches that night. One by Milton Deutschmann of farewell and one by Charles of hello. I guess, like all new owners, he didn't threaten to rattle the cages. But it was implicit that the cages would be rattled."

David Beckerman, who was then reporting to Kornfeld as advertising manager, also was present at the Ritz-Carlton that night. Beckerman had joined Radio Shack as advertising manger in 1956 and later became senior vice president and general manager of the Eastern Division and then vice president of marketing services. He was hired after Lewis Kornfeld was promoted from advertising manager to vice president for merchandising and advertising. Beckerman had been managing the advertising department of a firm in Maryland when he heard from a manufacturer's representative about the Radio Shack vacancy, so he flew up to Boston for an interview with Deutschmann and Kornfeld and got the job. The advertising department at the time consisted of two other employees, a copywriter and an artist.

Beckerman recalled the company headquarters on Washington Street.

"It was in a four or five-story brick building, with roughly 6,000 to 7,000 square feet per floor, in downtown Boston not far from Filene's and Jordan Marsh. The main floor was parts and ham equipment, with a parts counter across the back. There was no stereo or audio on that floor. The audio was sold out of a room on the second floor, which was up a single, large staircase. Right behind the audio showroom, we had our offices. On the floor above that we had some warehousing and repair and industrial electronics. The building was across the street from Jurgen Park in an area that was later reconstructed as part of a federal complex. It was taken over by the city in 1965 and is no longer standing."

Beckerman negotiated the building's sale in 1965 and secured a better price from the city because of a sign on the structure that had become a civic landmark. The modernistic neon sign on an enameled background had been designed by a well-known local artist named Keppish as a symbol of the electronic age, Beckerman recalled. "I was able to get $200,000 more for the building than the city offered." The building was the only one in the nine-store Radio Shack chain that wasn't leased.

Beckerman first met Charles Tandy in 1962, when Tandy was looking at a company named Brecks of Boston, a mail order firm that imported tulip bulbs from Holland. "Radio Shack also was interested in buying Brecks and that's when I met Tandy," Beckerman said. "Brecks was eventually bought by a Boston mail order firm, but I remember a conversation in which Tandy said he was interested in getting into the electronics business. He knew that Radio Shack was having problems, and he might have been fishing around, because he was curious as to what we thought the problems were."

Beckerman recognized that Radio Shack's financial problems stemmed from the fact it was running on an assumed gross margin that was higher than its realized gross margin. "It was simply a matter of assuming gross margins that weren't there and spending money as if they were."

In addition, the Radio Shack mail order business was generating a tremendous amount of damaged goods. "All of those goods were funneled back, and we didn't have the kind of repair staff to refurbish the goods and return them to the inventory," Beckerman said. "So a large segment of the inventory consisted of goods that were essentially nonsaleable. This amounted to real dollars."

Radio Shack was losing money in the mail order business. Beckerman continued, "Radio Shack was carrying its own revolving credit paper, and on a no-money-down basis. We were able to sell a lot of goods across the country. But when you're sitting in California and you owe money to a company based in Boston, and your local credit is due, you pay your local credit first. So we issued a lot of bad credit, probably $6 million or $7 million worth, and our assumed gross margin didn't include these bad credits."

Inventories were badly out of balance, Beckerman contended. "Some departments were turning as slowly as once every two years, while others were turning six times a year. The balance of inventory was very, very poor. We also had too many stockkeeping units. We were incapable of controlling the number of stockkeeping units."

Beckerman's recollection of the April 1 meeting at the Ritz-Carlton was that there weren't more than a dozen Radio Shack executives present.

"Charles told us he was taking over the company and that Radio Shack would undergo significant changes. He said what he was going to be doing for the first few days was talk individually to each of us and then make his decision as to the direction that the company would have to go. He told us he knew the hobby business through Tandy Leather and American Handicrafts and that he was familiar with store operations and the mail order business, having done both, but that he didn't know too much about the industrial electronics business."

Tandy closed his remarks that night with the reassuring statement, "There's no reason for productive people to feel threatened by the change in ownership."

Charles Tandy's own version of what transpired that evening was contained in one sentence in the speech he made in April 1973 at Brigham Young University.

"The night before, we had a good dinner and I introduced myself to my new associates and I said, 'Tomorrow morning there'll be a new ball game.'"

Lew Kornfeld recalled being asked by Milton Deutschmann as they were leaving the Ritz-Carlton that night, "What do you think of Charles Tandy?"

"He looks like a smart, hardworking man who's in a hell of a hurry and running scared," Kornfeld replied.

"But did you see that red face and the hair in the middle of his forehead that comes to a triangular peak? I think, by God, he's part Indian," Deutschmann persisted. "And there's something else. I think he's going to take this company into Chapter 11 and run."

"Gee," Kornfeld said, "I don't see it that way at all, and if he wants me to stay around, I probably will."

Tandy wanted to hit the ground running, so he convened a meeting of the Radio Shack board of directors early the next morning, April 2.

Someone believing in omens could have interpreted what happened at the meeting as a less than auspicious harbinger for the new regime.

One of the Radio Shack board members present that Tuesday morning was George Cullinane, a former vice president of merchandising and advertising for a major mail order company in Chicago, who had for the past few years been a consultant to Radio Shack on mail order strategy. Cullinane suffered from a disease of the pituitary gland that caused a deformation of his face.

"He wasn't the prettiest guy in the world, but he was a brilliant mail order mathematician and marketing man," Beckerman said. "Right after the meeting began, Cullinane suffered a heart attack. He sat down at the board table with his pipe, had the heart attack, and died. They really hadn't even gotten started on the board meeting, except for exchanging banalities about the differences in the weather between Boston and Fort Worth."

The board meeting was aborted. A shaken Tandy attempted to salvage the rest of the day by proceeding with another scheduled meeting with ten Radio Shack department heads and store managers. The session was held in Milton Deutschmann's dingy old office, which Tandy had taken over as his own.

Lew Kornfeld, who was present, recalled Tandy holding a small piece of Ritz-Carlton stationery, about 6 inches by 9 inches, on which he had written a list of names in his left-handed scrawl.

"This," Tandy said, squinting over his half-lens glasses, "is the only memo you are ever going to get from me. These are the names of the people that I'm keeping in management. You're my team." And he read off the names of the ten men in the room and their job assignments.

"I was to continue as vice president of merchandising and advertising," Kornfeld said. Tandy now addressed himself individually to the chosen ten, beginning with Kornfeld.

"Now, as far as merchandising and advertising are concerned, I want you to reduce your staff by half."

"Which half?" Kornfeld asked.

"I don't care," Tandy shot back. "But don't fire anybody. Offer them all jobs as store managers."

"Which stores?" Kornfeld wanted to know.

"Don't worry about the stores," Tandy responded. "You find me the store managers and I'll keep them occupied until we open the stores, because, by God, we're gonna open stores."

Kornfeld's recollection of the number of stores Tandy was talking about was vague. "I know he wanted to put stores where our customers were, which made good sense. You don't want to put stores where there are no customers. And we knew where our customers were because that's where the mail orders came from. But, I thought at first that we had a goal of 30 stores for the first year, which meant that we would open either 21 more or 30 more, and it wasn't important which number was accurate."

Recalling the meeting, Kornfeld reflected on the way Tandy was perceived by the ten men he had selected as his teammates.

"Tandy," Kornfeld said, "had eyes that reflected or mirrored or exhibited no fear and absolute confidence. You felt that basically he was going to do what he said. And if it didn't happen that instant, nevertheless it would actually happen. So Tandy doled out these ten jobs and then he said, 'I'm going to tell you this as bosses. One out of every ten employees is a crook.'"

As the ten men in the room looked at each other speculatively, counting the number of people which added up to ten, Tandy added, "I want that crooked son of a bitch out of here when we find him, and we will find him, believe me."

Kornfeld paused for effect. "Well, to make a long story short," he continued, "one of the ten turned out to be a crook. This bore out Charles's basic rule of thumb, if it wasn't in inventory or in the bank, it was stolen."

Among those to whom Tandy offered a store manager's job, Kornfeld disclosed, was Radio Shack's President, Norman Krim.

"He offered Krim a job managing a store, not one of our nine existing stores, but one of hundreds of new stores that, at the time, existed only in Charles' mind," Kornfeld said.

"A store! Where?" Krim asked, deeply offended.

"Well, how about Philadelphia," Tandy said.

"No, thanks," Krim replied.

"So, you see," Kornfeld continued, "Krim wasn't fired. He was offered a real job, but turned it down and quit. As Tandy said on his first day in Boston, 'I want everyone here to stay on, but at the job I want him to have.' Nobody was to be laid off. They'd have to quit of their own free will."

The strategy that Charles Tandy devised for restructuring Radio Shack into a profit-making machine and developing it into a national chain was born primarily from his experience with the Tandy Leather Company, Kornfeld expounded.

"His theory was to have lots of small stores and a limited number of stockkeeping units. They are called SKUs, and at that time we had somewhere between 15,000 and 30,000 SKUs depending on the industrials and all that other stuff. And it was Charles' plan to go out of mail order, maybe not instantly. But it was within the next year or two that I stopped putting mail order coupons in the catalog."

It was Tandy's idea, Kornfeld continued, to lower the number of stockkeeping units to 2,400 units. "This was probably the number he had in his other businesses," Kornfeld guessed, "or it might have been a multiple predicated upon the fact that our electronic stores did more volume per annum per square foot per employee than his leather stores did. But it was very obvious that the smaller number of SKUs would make it easier for everyone to understand the business, particularly the customers."

Tandy aspired to go to a total private label operation, and he also wanted to begin manufacturing some of his own merchandise, Kornfeld declared.

"I already loved private label and I was dying to get into manufacturing," Kornfeld continued, "so he and I were on the same wavelength. I actually had started us in private label in 1954 with phonographs that I had made by others for our brands. After 1955, when I first went to the Orient, we had quite a few items. And while the number of SKUs was not large, the number of dollars was."

By 1963, Kornfeld estimated, Radio Shack's private label business amounted to about 15 percent of its total sales of some $14 million.

Tandy's first act after acquiring control of Radio Shack was to carry out his threat to get rid of the chiefs and promote the Indians.

"He got rid of that whole echelon of top management and kept the merchandisers and advertisers," Dave Beckerman related. "He retained Lew Kornfeld and me and Dick O'Brien, who was in charge of mail order, and all of the store managers, and got rid of all of the levels above that. He made Lew the senior officer and made me the second senior officer as general manager of Radio Shack. I was in charge of the stores and the warehouses."

Beckerman recalled, "The first time I heard Tandy express his dreams of what he wanted to do with Radio Shack was shortly after that. The first thing he did was hold a store managers meeting. That was the first time he expressed publicly his plans for opening up hundreds of small retail stores. He had expressed that privately to Dick O'Brien and to myself, and had instructed us to let people go whose expertise could not be translated into store operations. If someone showed the potential of becoming a store manager, we tried to keep him in some job and then moved him out to a store as fast as possible."

When Tandy spoke of his plans to open hundreds of stores, it sounded "a little far-fetched," Beckerman said. "There was no electronics operation in existence at the time that had that many stores. But he had the feeling that if he could put in 250 Tandy Leather stores, he could certainly put in that many Radio Shack stores. So it wasn't a wild number to him."

Bernie Appel's recollection of the first days after the Tandy takeover was that they were marked by turmoil and lots of meetings.

"He had to decide whom he trusted and whom he didn't," Appel revealed. "One of the people he didn't trust was the vice president of retail sales, who tried to get political. Charles didn't like political people. He wanted to hear it like it was. He didn't want stones thrown around management. He thought that the way to run a business was with everybody above board and trying to get along with everybody else. He was a very ethical person. He never lied to any of us. He told us what he honestly believed. He had incredible integrity."

But during the period immediately after the takover, Appel and the other Radio Shack employees had some doubts about their new boss.

"Here was this young, brash guy from Texas, with a big cigar in his mouth, who had no knowledge of the consumer electronics business. He didn't know what electronics was all about. And here he was telling us that he was going to show us how to run our business, teach us how to make money, show us how to open a lot of stores. We thought it was wild. We thought he was full of bull. How could you blame us? He was talking about 500 stores. We thought that was crazy. He said we could do it in the next few years. Who could believe that when all we had at the time was a handful of stores."

Over the course of the next two weeks, Tandy laid out "a very diligent program with a lot of hard work," Appel reported. "He didn't believe in writing memos. He told us what he wanted. He went away one weekend and came back with a whole reorganization plan for the company scribbled on the inside of an American Airlines ticket. He came in and said, 'Gentlemen, you're going to need so many buyers, so many store managers, so many of this and so many of that. You're going to carry this many products. These lines will be thrown out.' He came in with a whole program of where we were going, what our direction was going to be, how many stores we were going to open."

Appel recalled one of Tandy's early ideas that backfired on him and was promptly changed.

"Charles came up with a plan that everybody that wanted to stay in their current position would have to take a 10 percent pay cut. Everybody who would be willing to work in their current position, knowing that they would eventually become a store manager, would not have to take a pay cut. Well, for one full day there was a lot of confusion. I personally decided to remain a buyer. I didn't want to become a store manager. But I would have left if I would have had to take a cut in pay. But by the end of the day, the pay cut was rescinded."

Appel, as it turned out, was one of the few people who received a pay raise after Tandy took over Radio Shack. The reason, he said, was that he had had a prior agreement with Lew Kornfeld about the pay hike.

"So I got the raise because it was promised to me," Appel said. "Charles screamed bloody murder when he heard about it. 'Why would you give him a raise? Nobody else is getting one!'

"Lew Kornfeld and Dave Beckerman explained to Charles that I was a professional and that if the company wanted to maximize my talents, it had to live up to that commitment. We were only talking about $5,000 a year. But from that day on, Charles Tandy called me 'The Professional.' That was how he rubbed it in."

Tandy's basic program for Radio Shack, Appel said, had six major elements:

• Get out of things that were not electronic.
• Cut down the mail order business.
• Open stores in zip codes where Radio Shack already was strong.
• Make it easier for the customers to shop.
• Cut down the stockkeeping units.
• Advertise like hell.

"Soon after, he also came to realize that brand name, with other people's brands, was not a way to go," Appel added.

Appel remained convinced that Tandy had a misconception about what Radio Shack really was when he made the deal to acquire control of the operation.

"I think he believed we were really and truly a hobby house, selling small parts to hobbyists. And that's what he wanted. He then came to realize that we happened to have some real strength in radios, in hi-fi, tape recorders, phonographs and whatever the products of the day were. We were selling finished end equipment, rather than parts and pieces, and that surprised Charles. But that didn't cause him to lose a beat, because when he realized it, saw our strength in it, he said, 'Okay, this is the business we're in. They can both get along. But, in order to do it, you need more gross margin in your end equipment, and you can't get it in brand name. You've got to go private label.'"

A week after Tandy's takeover of Radio Shack, the phone rang in Bill Brown's office at the First National bank of Boston. Tandy was on the line. He had just flown into town after a weekend in Fort Worth.

"Come on out to Radio Shack," Tandy told the banker. "I want you to see something."

When Brown arrived, Tandy escorted him into the warehouse, where boxes of merchandise were stacked to the ceiling. Tandy began showing Brown the dates that were stenciled on the crates.

"There were all these boxes with out-of-date years stamped on them," Brown recalled. "Charles said, 'These things have model years, just like automobiles. All this out-of-date inventory has to go.' So he put all that obsolete merchandise in a tent on Commonwealth Avenue and had a huge sale."

Dave Beckerman remembered that first tent sale.

"It was on the parking lot right alongside our store at 730 Commonwealth Avenue. Things were marked down substantially—40 percent, 50 percent, 60 percent off. We ran big newspaper ads and we generated very large volumes and an awful lot of cash, which we needed, because we had very little cash flow."

No one buying that obsolete merchandise under a canvas top that spring day in Boston in 1963 could have possibly foreseen what would evolve from that humble beginning.

The first step had been taken.

Chapter 10
Confrontation at the Waldorf

Charles Tandy's recollections of the eventful first days following his takeover of Radio Shack, when he found himself spending more time in a Boston hotel room than he did in his apartment in Fort Worth, are contained in a videotape of a talk he made to a group of students at the Massachusetts Institute of Technology in Cambridge, Massachusetts, in April, 1978.

The presentation was vintage Tandy, rambling, off-the-cuff, down-to-earth, with a variety of pungent and insightful asides, and refreshingly devoid of academic pretension.

"I was never a very good student," he informed the group in his opening remarks, "but I was a damn good salesman. And I've discovered since I entered that field, and I entered it young, that it is probably one of the most important things in the business development of the United States."

At the time he took over Radio Shack, Tandy told his audience of aspiring scientists and engineers, Norman Krim, an engineer, was serving as president.

"He'd been put in as sort of an interim president by, I guess, a combination of banks and directors and so forth, because the company had been undergoing some bad times and they thought they needed a new head," Tandy related. "Here's a company that was supposed to be electronics, so let's hire an engineer. Well, Mr. Krim was very qualified as an engineer, very qualifed as a business executive, but he'd never sold anything. I was sort of the last resort. They couldn't find anybody else, so they called on me in Texas. They knew I didn't know anything about electronics, and I still don't today. And I don't intend to. I don't have to know how to run a sewing machine in order to know how to sell one.

That's for somebody else. The same way, it's often been said, 'Whiskey's made for selling, not for drinking.'

"There has been a revolution in engineering and design, things learned in a school like this," Tandy conceded, "but what's made them possible are the distribution systems that have been developed. The one thing that attracted me to Radio Shack was that it did have business. They did have a quantity of customers. Now, I've heard it said ever since I took over Radio Shack that we lack a name brand, a national brand. Well, in studying the process, I looked and said, 'What is a name brand?'

"I found out, in rethinking it in my own mind, if I bought something from a merchant, I expected the merchant to stand behind it. When I bought something from Jordan Marsh, I knew they would stand behind it. Incidentally, when I was going to Harvard Business School, I worked at Jordan Marsh, and they have an impeccable reputation of satisfaction and fair play, fair trade and customer satisfaction. I don't think anybody comes close to being second in this marketplace. They earned that reputation. They expect it of their salespeople, they expect it of their merchandise, they expect it of everything. So I said, 'What is a name?' Here's Radio Shack. The public comes to it. They come to it by the thousands. The only problem is, and it is very simple, they're spending more than they're taking in. So all we gotta do is change that.

"Our first approach was to analyze what it is we were selling, whom we were serving, and study that as quickly as possible. I'd spent some time on this prior to coming into this field, because I had wanted to be in the electronics do-it-yourself field. So I had a pretty good idea already to whom we were going to be selling, what we were going to be selling, and what was left were just the details of the supply system.

"Well, at that time, Radio Shack had a catalog of some 500 pages. I wish I'd brought one of the old catalogs with me so you could see what it looked like, because not only did they have hi-fi and speakers, wire tape, and ham radio gear, there were tires and go-carts, and there were musical instruments and Polaroid cameras and shavers. I got dizzy looking at all of the different kinds of things that we were supposed to be. And I said, 'Now, what really and truly does a Radio Shack customer expect to find?' You can sell anything, even bananas, if you put them in the store. But is this the place people go to buy bananas? So I tried to create the image of what I saw as a Radio Shack. Hopefully, it would be what our customers would see as a Radio Shack.

"Keep in mind," Tandy told his now rapt audience, "this company was losing a couple of hundred thousand dollars a month. And they didn't send for me to let me experiment around and lose another two, three, four million dollars. The First National Bank and the State Mutual Life of Worcester were the big bankers, the big bankrollers in this company. Well, I came to the hard conclusion, because the new catalog had to be done, that the peripheral items had to go. As you know in your own life, there are certain courses you do well at and there are certain other courses you don't do well in. Well, life out here is the same way. You can be a jack of all trades and a master of none, as you've heard for years.

"We wanted Radio Shack to be a specialist, not to be everything to everybody. That's the reason you don't find television in our stores. That's the reason you don't find records. You don't find a lot of things in a Radio Shack store. We have manufacturers come to us and say, 'You should have this.' Well, maybe we should and maybe we shouldn't. Our first criterion today is can we make a profit? And if we see we can't make a profit, who needs it? Let them go buy their bagels or their pretzels somewhere else.

"So we took that catalog of 500 and some odd pages, and I sat the merchandise department down and I said, 'Look, here's basically where we want to be. We want to be a specialist in electronics, specializing in the do-it-yourself field, the guy that's gonna put up his own antenna, the guy that's gonna repair his own telephone, the guy that's gonna fix his own hi-fi. We want those pieces and parts. We're not gonna be a big research house. At that time, they had an industrial division that had 25,000 to 35,000 different parts in it. I said, 'We're gonna reduce this down to a minimum number of items that we can specialize in. We want to analyze every item, how many of them we've bought in the last year. And, in the meantime, while you merchandise department people get hold of that, we want to come down to not over 2,500 stockkeeping units.'"

Tandy asked, "I don't know how many of you have ever been to a Radio Shack store. Is there anybody here who hasn't?" Satisfying himself that no one in the room fell into that shameful category, he detailed how, when he had taken over Radio Shack, ham radio operators had been able to go to a Radio Shack store and buy $1,500 Collins transceivers. "Are there any hams in this room?" he asked. One arm shot up. "We got one, I see," Tandy acknowledged. "Well, the transmitters they use, they can talk to Russia, they can talk to South America. They have no limitation on the kind of power they can use. But, when they want to buy a new piece of equipment, they want to trade in an old piece. Well, I'm not in the second-hand equipment business. And we weren't going to be in it. But that's what they were doing.

"The number of hams in the United States today may be half a million," Tandy noted. "The number of CB radio users in the United States is, like, 20 million. So the market potential is where? Now the hams are going to spend a lot more money individually, but the ham doesn't buy very often. Once he buys it, he keeps it, so that you don't get that repeat factor. But a man who's got a CB rig, when he changes cars he's gonna buy another one. At the outset, we left the ham goods in and we left some of the marine things in. We left a variety of parts in. But we started in on the details of how you actually control a business."

His first two priorities after taking over control of Radio Shack, Tandy disclosed, were getting the right kind of merchandise on the shelves and upgrading the gross margins. "Merchandise is where you start," he asserted. "Now we had to select the merchandise out and we had to change the gross margins. Now, what they were paying for the merchandise and what they were getting for it came to a 26 percent gross margin. Do you all understand 26 percent gross margin? It costs you a dollar, you put 33 percent onto it, and you've got a 25 percent gross margin. We always figure gross margin from the sales price down, not from what you paid out. Some people say, 'You've got a 100 percent gross margin.' There's no way in the world to have a 100 percent gross margin unless you use mirrors. A 50 percent gross margin is when you buy it for a dollar and sell it for two dollars. And that's the way you want to run things in the business world.

"All right, how were we going to go about changing that gross margin? Well, it's so simple when I tell it to you that you're going to want to ask the question, 'Why didn't they do it before? Why didn't they think of it before?' Well, keep in mind the important name was Radio Shack. Keep in mind we were going to stand behind that product. Keep in mind that we were going to make it good if it wasn't right. We were going to check the quality before it went out. And we were going to spend the money to advertise it. We were not going to use RCA's name, and then pay them for the product and pay them for their advertising when they were selling everybody else.

"We took one item at a time. And we traced down that product, because there is always somebody else that's manufacturing that product somewhere that doesn't have to pay for all that advertising that Proctor & Gamble, Standard Brands Food, or some other company puts on that product. We went to the Orient. We went to Europe. We went all over the United States looking for an item at a time. We knew what the specs were, and what we wanted was a product that would work and work adequately, that would be a fair trade of that customer's dollar for our piece of merchandise. We reduced our cost of merchandise. We didn't raise our prices. That's the easiest way to go broke. You know, change the price of your coffee from 25 cents to 50 cents. The public is not stupid. And so many people think that they are. They are not. We wouldn't have the 21 million customers at Radio Shack, the 21 million families that come back and come back and come back, if they hadn't already known something about values, if they hadn't already checked us out. You can't fool the people. You can't just take a hi-fi machine and say, 'That's $200 and now it's $400.' No way. People are not fools. They want to compare quality. They want to compare value. And that's what you've got to give them. Let me give you an example. I'll give you a little cute one. This was a trick to show my merchandisers how to think.

"Do you know what a receiving tube is?" he asked. "Anybody here know what a receiving tube is? Well, when radios first came out, they all had one big tube in the back and five little tubes. They called them an AC-DC package. They were in all the kitchen radios. They were all over the place. When a tube went out on you, you had to replace it or get a repair man to fix it. Tubes were a very easy product to sell. Radio Shack carried General Electric, they carried RCA, they carried Westinghouse, and they carried a couple of other brands. I said, 'Hell, we don't need all those brands.'

"Raytheon was sitting here in Cambridge," Tandy continued. "Now, remember, I don't know nothin' about electronics. I only know about business. I'm just a businessman and I've got a common-sense head on my shoulders. RCA would come along in the summertime and say, 'If you'll buy big cases of these tubes, we'll give you six months to pay for them. We'll give you a lot of free merchandise.' And I'm sitting there thinking, 'There's not a lot of profit in those tubes. How can they afford to do that?' So I called up each one of the suppliers, General

Electric, RCA, even went out to see RCA out in Harrison, New Jersey, wanting to know if they'd private label for me.

"I asked them all, 'If we throw out all the other manufacturers and give you all our business, what's the best deal you'll give us on buying tubes from you?' They all came back with the same price. All except Raytheon, because Raytheon wasn't on our shelf, you see. And that's one of the first things you need to do. Find a guy that's not getting any of your business, and he's a little more anxious to talk to you. So Raytheon came over with flip charts and so forth, and I said, 'Teach me about the tube business. I don't know anything about it. But I've just got the feeling that there are some things I ought to know about it, being president of my company.'

"They came over and they said they would private label for us. And, with that, they were out from under the fair trade laws. They could give us a private label and save us 10 to 12 percent. Well, 10 to 12 percent on a million dollars, you know, gentlemen, is more than $100,000, and I don't find that money easy to come by even today. And they kept turning the charts and they said, 'Now, we have OEM prices and we have distributor prices and, then, we have OTM prices.' Now that was one I hadn't heard of. I'd heard of the original equipment manufacturers. You know, if Zenith's gonna buy a bunch of tubes, they're gonna get a special deal. But OTM?

"So I asked the Raytheon guy, 'What's OTM?'

"'Other tube manufacturers.'

"'What do you mean?'

"And he said, 'Well, we're the only company that makes an OT-4, which is a tube used in an automobile radio, and we make them for RCA and Westinghouse and everybody else.'"

Tandy whistled.

"Now I'm really learning," he confided. "I mean, it don't pay to be smart. It pays to be dumb, to just ask questions. And he says, 'Yeah, we've got different prices when we trade tubes between ourselves. None of us make them all.'

"And I said, 'How much difference is there in those prices? Do I have to become a tube manufacturer?'

"And he said, 'I can't give you that OTM price because you aren't a tube manufacturer, but we've got still another one.'

"And I said, 'What's that?'

"And he said, 'Imported tubes. We are completely familiar with and we're involved with the importation of tubes from all over the world.'

"'All over the world?'

"'Yeah, Spain, Portugal, South America, Japan...'

"And I said, 'Well, what about the quality?'

"And he said, 'We'll guarantee the quality right on the table.'

"'How about the price?'

"'Fifty percent cheaper.'

"Did you hear that?" Tandy queried his audience, his voice rising in disbelief. "Fifty percent cheaper. I asked, 'Do you put my name on 'em?'

"'All right.'"

There was a pause as Tandy let the magnitude of what he had just described sink in.

"So we shook hands on it," he continued. "Now I called in my merchandising staff. We only had three or four people at that time, and I outlined the deal to them. I said, 'Gentlemen, this sounds pretty good. What do you think we ought to do?'

"'Oh, boy, we ought to take those tubes and just cut the hell out of the prices and sell a lot of them.'

"I said, 'Oh, no, oh, no, that's not what we're gonna do. I'll put the problem to you the other way. How are we gonna get more for these tubes than RCA gets for their tubes when it costs us half as much?'

"Well, I might have hit them on the head with a baseball bat, as far they were concerned. It never occurred to them for one moment that you can get more for a piece of merchandise that costs you half as much. Anybody got an idea what we did?"

There were a few scattered responses to the question, all of them wide of the mark.

"I'll tell you what we did," Tandy said. "We gave a lifetime guarantee on the tubes. If any one ever broke, we gave you a new one. And we guaranteed we'd give you a new one. And we still do that. Unfortunately, the tube business is going down the drain because we don't use tubes any more. But this was an object lesson, and I give it to you because it's an important lesson. People would rather have you guarantee something and make it good than they would have it work.

"I've had men come in with the five tubes out of an AC-DC radio set and throw them all away, never test one of them, and say, 'I want your new, guaranteed tubes.'"

Tandy permitted himself an ear-to-ear grin.

"Well, I had a little advantage there," he admitted, "because I had some information about those tubes. It seems that the average set of those tubes had been in existence about seven years. The first failures started about the end of the third year. So, if I had to replace one tube, the chances were that it would last three more years. And if there were any other failures, it'd be in the other tubes because the new tube was stronger. So the customer was going to have to come back with the other tubes, and I'd have the chance to get him then.

"Here's what we promised, 'Our tubes will last as long as your radio set or we will replace them free.' Now, in our stores, we still had the RCA tubes when we put the new ones in. And we were charging 10 cents a tube more for the new tubes. The store managers were on a percentage of the profits. What do you think the store manager did when a guy came in to buy a tube? Which one do you think he sold him? The RCA tube or the lifetime guaranteed tube? Which one would you have sold if you were going to make twice as much money?

"It improved my merchandisers without a question of a doubt," Tandy summed up. "Those men on the floor found out that the name Radio Shack was stronger than the RCA name, and they'd always leaned on the RCA name. And that was all I was trying to prove to these guys that, number one, the place of business where the customer is being served is the most important place for you to give service, to give quality, and your own name is that much more important. When I hear of a nationally-branded name, and I know that we do $1 billion a year, I'm like Texaco. We've got that star everywhere. And I don't care what other brand out there you call a national brand. Baby, we've got more business than they've got. And what makes a national brand? You not only can buy Radio Shack merchandise in the United States, but in 40 other countries, all over Canada, England, Belgium, Holland, Germany, France, even five electronics stores in Tokyo. That's what makes a national brand.

"I was playing games with those tubes," Tandy conceded. "I was trying to teach my men that you don't have to sell merchandise for what you paid for it, that you can make a reasonable profit. Then, when you do your pricing, people will believe you. I had to show them that we knew how to sell merchandise. It took time to do it. It took time to train them. It took time to get the men together. But this is the kind of thinking that went on in the building of a merchandising team.

"Who taught me how to do these things? Well, I had a wonderful dad, but he'd gone for years on the old theory that you need brand names, that you set prices the way everybody else does. Not at Radio Shack. We've got our own ideas, our own merchandise."

There was one business he decided he didn't want to be in, Tandy admitted. "You'll never see a repair truck running around Boston with the name Radio Shack on it," he averred. "Anything that doesn't work right, you come to the Radio Shack where you got it. Bring it back with you. Everything's portable. Why? It costs a ton, an arm and a leg, to send a repairman to your house. That's the reason our merchandise comes in components. Unplug them, bring the speaker in, bring the other parts in. Bang. You can't send a repairman to somebody's house for under $15 or $20. And who's gonna pay for it? You're gonna pay for it. And I don't want to charge you for that. Take it to somebody else, because I don't make any money doing that. And, secondly, you get mad.

"This way, you come in. We look you in the eye. We've got our 90-some repair stations across the country. We give you that service. And if it's not working just right, we don't try to fix a sick transistor radio. We give you a new one and throw the other one in the second-hand box. You can't afford to repair it, not with the cost of labor and repair today, again keeping in mind what we faced at the outset, that we wanted to take in more than we put out. I'm trying to draw this all together in a picture for you," Tandy continued, "because you have to conceive in the business world where you fit, who you are and what you're qualified to do. Then you use the common sense behind it, because there has to be a spread, there has to be a difference, between what you take in and what you put out. We say on everything we do, 'How do we save on this? How do we save on that?'"

* * *

In an interview published in *The New York Times* on July 28, 1963, Charles Tandy told the reporter, Clare M. Reckert, of a disappointment he experienced when he was 15 years old while he was selling ladies' shoes. He thought he would be paid a weekly salary plus commission. Instead he got only a commission.

Before making a long-term commitment, he insisted on a "pre-marriage trial arrangement" for a term of at least six months, and he made this a proviso in both the Cost Plus and Radio Shack deals. At the time the article appeared, Tandy's trial marriage with Radio Shack was well into its fourth month. He was spending the better part of each week in Boston, flying home for the weekend and returning Sunday night. In Boston, he operated out of Milton Deutschmann's former office above the Commonwealth Avenue store, directing the activities of a steady stream of Radio Shack underlings who trooped in to receive their orders for the day.

From the office, Tandy's voice could be heard reverberating through the premises, exhorting people to "get their heads out" and to "shape up or ship out."

From the outset, it was apparent that the "hotshot from Texas," as he was derisively known, had a job on his hands convincing the Boston cadre that he knew what he was doing. After all, what did the leather merchant know about the electronics business?

"Most of all, the people in Boston couldn't believe it was possible to get the kind of numbers that Charles wanted," Luther Henderson said. "They had been operating on a 26 percent gross margin and Charles was insisting that was much too low. He got a lot of resistance on that. 'You can't do that.' 'The public won't buy this.' Radio Shack also had a credit business that had to be stopped."

"It was obvious to Charles from the start," Bill Michero said, "that a number of top management decisions had been made in the past that had just killed, had just gutted Radio Shack as a business. Credit was a real back-breaker, but they had also wandered off into toys and auto supplies and all kinds of things. So there were some obvious curative measures that had to be taken. It was a matter of eliminating the non-electronic goods, cleaning and curing the credit practices, simplifying the product line, and installing a more focused advertising and marketing effort."

According to Henderson, Radio Shack's most obvious weakness was its inventory. "It was not only large, but there was also a poor selection of merchandise. It required a huge reduction in merchandise, and this meant that the Radio Shack people had to learn to live with a much smaller level of merchandise than they were used to living with. The old management had gotten used to the First National Bank of Boston giving them all the money they needed, so they had never had to be careful in the use of money."

Reducing the number of stockkeeping units became Tandy's number one priority, David Beckerman said. "We did it in a most simplistic fashion," he reported, "based on the theory that 80 percent of your sales comes out of 20 percent of your inventory. We took our first pass at Radio Shack's inventory and Tandy said, 'Let's identify the 20 percent that represents 80 percent of the sales.' Having done that, we were now down to 10,000 items, which he felt was still too many. So we made another sweep on the same 80-20 basis and we wound up with 2,500 units. That left us with 40,000 items that had to be discontinued. To get rid of them, we held a series of tent sales to generate cash out of them. You might say that this really depreciated Radio Shack's inventory, but in essence Radio Shack's inventory really depreciated itself by lack of turn, not by anything that Tandy did to it. All that Tandy did was recognize that the inventory didn't have the value in it to begin with. So he got rid of it."

The key to attaining the higher gross margins Tandy was demanding lay in the Orient, Henderson said. "Charles had become familiar with buying in the Far East because of our import store business, and he quickly recognized that he was going to have to emphasize overseas merchandise with Radio Shack instead of letting it be ancillary to the brand names. Radio Shack, at that time, had brand names. That was another thing he got a lot of resistance on. His people would tell him, 'We've got to have Fisher's name. We've got to have Gatewood and all of the other brand names.' Charles felt, and he was proven right, that the public didn't really know all the brand names.

"Charles said, 'A customer coming in off the street is coming into a Radio Shack to buy, and so I want to promote Radio Shack's brands.' And this was one of the big changes he made in their operations. Realistic products were already being imported from Japan through A&A Trading Company. It was only later that Tandy began making his own products. But, initially, Charles looked to the Orient to try to find the cheapest source of merchandise for Radio Shack."

In Lewis Kornfeld's recollection, it was Tandy's idea to buy merchandise anywhere that the price and quality were right. "It just happened that the Orient was the oyster we'd already opened," Kornfeld declared, "and it had a lot of pearls in it."

In his book, *To Catch A Mouse*, the title of which was derived from a Charles Tandy saying, "If you want to catch a mouse, you've got to make a noise like a cheese," Kornfeld said he found a singular lack of high-tech merchandise in Japan on his initial merchandise-hunting junket in 1955. "There were no transistor radios, no real hi-fi. The only recorder I saw was a knock-off of an Ampex unit called Jampex. I did visit one television set manufacturer named Yao, where I was told that not many Japanese could afford to buy TV sets because of their aversion to owing money. This company agreed to clone our hitherto American-made 10-watt audio amplifier at a landed cost of about 33 percent under what we were paying our Midwest supplier, and it became the first Radio Shack 'Realistic' electronic product made overseas."

Kornfeld also brought with him, on his 1955 buying expedition, an all-transistor pocket radio made in the United States that he wanted to have copied. But the radio that had cost him $50 in Boston proved uncopiable in Japan due to a lack of transistors and know-how. "When we finally had radios made there for our Realistic line, we sent American transistors to Japan in American shoe boxes," Kornfeld reported.

But there were some other things that Kornfeld found in abundance in Japan, among which were "skillful, dedicated workers and manufacturers eager to export and anxious to manufacture to our specifications and under our brand names." The manufacturers, Kornfeld added, were undeterred by the comparatively small Radio Shack order quantities, "which had been laughed at by most of the domestic and European vendors we had previously approached."

Kornfeld recalled that Charles Tandy arrived on the scene "gung ho on private label." He could hardly wait for Radio Shack to close out the national brands. Previous management had sought to carry enough stock to satisfy anyone who walked in off the street, but Charles Tandy's position was, "We have only what we have, our own brands, and we'll try like hell to sell you something."

Bill Brown questioned the strategy. In his characteristically bravado manner, Tandy told him, "I'm gonna sell so much merchandise, I'll make my own brand name."

So the course was charted.

Inventories were reduced, the product line pared, profit margins hiked, private labels installed, new stores opened, the credit business dissolved, and a start made on the eventual elimination of the mail order operations.

"When Tandy was formulating his operating program, he called in every executive and asked us things like, 'What do you think we need to do?' 'What's wrong with what we're now doing?'" Dave Beckerman recalled. "In my conversations with him, I was not protective of the mail order business, in which I had the most expertise, because I knew it was doomed. I knew it was unprofitable. To be protective of it was to be suicidal, if not immediately, then later on. My analysis of it was that the mail order business was not good for Radio Shack. The retail business was good for Radio Shack, but not the way we'd been running it. And Charles quickly concluded that the mail order business was generating poor returns and that the cost of operating it was onerous."

Meanwhile, Radio Shack was running out of cash.

Faced with the problem of keeping the patient alive while his mouth-to-mouth resuscitation was being applied, Tandy once again turned to his banker friend in Boston, Bill Brown.

"I need half a million dollars to tide me over," Tandy told Brown.

"I'll lend it to you provided you put another $100,000 into Radio Shack," Brown responded.

The deal was consummated on May 25, 1963.

In return for advancing the $100,000 in the form of a loan to Radio Shack, Tandy Corporation received the exclusive right to sell products under the Radio Shack name west of the Mississippi River, an area where Radio Shack had mail order sales at the time of some $4 million annually. Under the terms of the agreement, Radio Shack was required to furnish merchandise to Tandy at prices approved by the First National Bank of Boston.

In a news release announcing the franchise agreement, Tandy reported it would open four Tandy electronics stores within 60 days in Texas' four largest cities, Houston, Dallas, San Antonio and Fort Worth, "to supply the 'do-it-yourself hobbyist' with electronics equipment." The Wall Street Journal quoted a Tandy spokesman as saying, "This will be Tandy's major entry into the radio and hi-fi hobby market."

The announcement left Wall Street singularly unimpressed. Tandy stock, which had sold at a high of 11¼ only a few months before, sank to a depressingly low 5⅞ by early June. On June 10, 1963, Shearson, Hammill & Company carried a report on Tandy that declared: "There seems to be no apparent reason to account for the current weakness in this stock other than the fact that with its thin market, any sizeable selling activity is likely to have a disproportionately depressing effect on the price. In addition, the company's third quarter report, which was published at the end of April, was somewhat disappointing. Even though 9-month per share earnings advanced to 57 cents per share from 54 cents in the comparable year earlier period, this gain was due entirely to a recapitalization effected during the third quarter which reduced the number of shares outstanding from 1,566,661 shares to 1,060,938 shares." (The 500,123 shares were exchanged for $3.5 million of 6½ percent debentures due January 1, 1978.)

The Shearson report continued: "However, we understand that the fourth quarter should be quite good. Both sales and earnings are believed to have shown good gains in April and May and with a large portion of the expenses which depressed third quarter earnings out of the way, profits for the full fiscal year ending June 30, 1963, are likely to amount to around 70 cents per share or even slightly better. This would compare with 63 cents per share reported last year on the larger number of shares outstanding." (Tandy's actual fiscal 1963 earnings turned out to be 67 cents per share.)

"It is also worth mentioning," the Shearson commentary added, "that Tandy has an option to buy the controlling interest in Radio Shack Corp., an important distributor of electronic parts and hi-fi components. This New England-based company was facing financial difficulties when Charles D. Tandy assumed its management last April, but is now making progress and could be in the black by the end of the 1963 calendar year. The decision whether or not to exercise the option for the Radio Shack interest will be made after the end of both companies' fiscal year on June 30."

This was the challenge that Tandy faced.

On September 13, 1963, he transported his entire board of directors to Boston for a special meeting, where he secured approval for the conversion of the original $300,000 loan to Radio Shack into 300,000 shares of Radio Shack stock and for the exercise of options to acquire 359,000 shares of Radio Shack common stock from the Deutschmann family and 240,000 shares from Radio Shack Corporation. This gave Tandy control of Radio Shack.

In addition, the board approved an option for Tandy to acquire an additional 1,000,000 shares of Radio Shack common stock at a price of $1 per share over a period of five years, with the proviso that any funds paid by Tandy to Radio Shack from the exercise of the option be used to reduce Radio Shack's bank loans.

On November 12, Tandy convened a special meeting of Radio Shack shareholders in Boston, at which formal approval was given to the financial reorganization of the company. Shareholders also elected a slate of Tandy-backed candidates to the Radio Shack board. The new directors were Charles Tandy, Luther Henderson, Carl Welhausen, Jim West, Hooks Burr, Alfred H. Hauser, and Richard Barth, a Boston attorney. Burr was the only holdover from the previous board.

As part of the reorganization plan approved by the Radio Shack shareholders, State Mutual Life Assurance Company exchanged its $2 million senior note for 100,000 shares of Radio Shack senior convertible participating preferred stock, which was convertible into common stock on the basis of five shares of common for each share of preferred. State Mutual also agreed to purchase for $300,000 a new issue of 30,000 shares of Radio Shack junior participating convertible preferred stock, which was convertible into ten shares of common stock for each share of junior preferred. State Mutual also was granted an option to sell the 100,000 shares of senior preferred stock and the 30,000 shares of junior preferred stock to Tandy for $500,000 in cash or Tandy stock or a combination of both.

The stage was set for a classic confrontation between Charles Tandy and his board on the afternoon of November 15, 1963, in Tandy's suite at the Waldorf-Astoria Hotel in New York.

Tandy needed board action ratifying the Radio Shack reorganization plan and the option agreement with State Mutual Life Assurance Company. He placed both items on the agenda of the board meeting that followed the day after the annual meeting. Although he was aware of the board's concerns over the Radio Shack venture, he was totally unprepared for the near revolt that erupted at the board meeting.

Luther Henderson reviewed where they stood just before the fateful meeting.

"We had now gotten the Cost Plus import store group going, which was capable of using up a lot of money. We had Charles personally and directly involved in Radio Shack which also needed money. We had the Tex Tan Welhausen operations down at Yoakum, American Handicrafts Company and Tandy Leather Company. In effect, Charles was running the Tandy Leather Company, Radio Shack and the general corporation all at the same time.

"By this time, we had also gotten acquainted with the internal operations of Radio Shack and realized it was going to require a tremendous amount of work to get it straightened out and earning the kind of profits we wanted. And Charles had expressed his determination to personally run the Radio Shack Division, as I was then running the import store division and Carl Welhausen the Tex Tan Welhausen operation.

"During this period, a concern had developed among all of the other directors as to whether Charles was overextending himself to take on this commitment to personally run Radio Shack, plus the rest of the company which was not in bad shape but needed leadership. So several of the directors came up with the idea that, for a limited period, one or two years, that Carl Welhausen become the president of the corporation and that Charles be the president of the Radio Shack Division. Charles wouldn't exactly be under Mr. Welhausen, but Charles' attention would be wholly on Radio Shack.

"This idea was presented to Charles by me on the day of the board meeting in New York. This was not particularly my idea, but I was asked to be the spokesman for the other directors. I got elected, I would guess, because I was Charles' oldest friend on the board. Needless to say, Charles didn't like the idea and let me know how he felt in very blunt terms. He was very upset, so much so that I felt our entire relationship was in real jeopardy."

Henderson, who epitomizes the words, "laid back," and is the embodiment of understated candor, shook his head and smiled ruefully as he recalled Tandy's reaction to his proposal.

Bill Michero, who was present in Tandy's suite at the Waldorf in his capacity as corporate secretary, remembered that the annual meeting in Flemington, New Jersey, the day before had been "perfunctory", and that afterwards all of the directors, except for Tandy, got together for dinner at a steak house on Third Avenue in mid-town Manhattan.

"The Radio Shack thing got a lot of discussion that night, most of it negative," Michero said. "So, at the board meeting the next day, when it came up that this was going to call for 'x' dollars and it was going to call for all of Charles' time, that's when the fireworks began."

The motive of the board, Michero insisted, "was that it just didn't want Charles to get lost or to wander off, because things still needed to be done at the Tandy organization. That was the primary objection.

There might have been a couple of abstainers on the board, or a couple of guys who would keep their mouths shut, but the general mood of the board was negative, against it."

Charles Tandy, as chairman, opened the board meeting with a report that, "In accordance with the terms of the option agreements with certain individuals, a total of 355,881 common shares of Radio Shack Corp. were delivered to the company on November 8, 1963. These shares represent 50.15% of the common stock outstanding, and due to the evaluation formula contained in the option agreements, no consideration was payable by the company for the shares."

Tandy called for board approval of the option agreement with State Mutual Life Assurance Company, under which 130,000 shares of Radio Shack preferred stock would be acquired at a price of $500,000, payable in cash or stock, or a combination of both. This led to a heated discussion over the merits of the Radio Shack acquisition and of Tandy's resolve to run Radio Shack, Tandy Leather Company, and Tandy Corporation simultaneously. It now became apparent to everyone in the room that a do-or-die point had been reached.

"It was a very dramatic moment," Michero recalled. "I remember quite distinctly at that point that Charles was leaning against the mantle of the fireplace in the suite, and he made it very clear that if the board did not approve of his further pursuit of Radio Shack, he would resign from the board and take the deal on personally. Then he exited the room."

Tandy's dramatic departure stunned the board. The tension in the hotel suite was like that agonizing moment in a "sudden death" football game when the ball is placed on the turf for a winning field goal attempt, or the heart-palpitating moment in a murder trial when the foreman of the jury rises to announce the verdict.

The directors followed Tandy out of the room with their eyes. Then the reality of what was happening took hold. This was not a group accustomed to internecine warfare or to standing up to Tandy.

The board backed off.

"It took a few minutes of muddling and fumbling and grumbling," Michero said, "but there was no longer any doubt that Charles was going to get everything he wanted."

"We all realized," Henderson concurred, "that the company's being carried to this point was largely on the momentum of Charles' own personal drive and strengths and that he was the largest shareholder in the company by a large margin. The feeling was that if he thought that he could do it, we owed it to him to support him. So we approved the deal on his terms."

The minutes of the historic meeting, written by Michero, simply stated, "Following a discussion of the Radio Shack reorganization and the plans of management for the operation of Radio Shack, and upon motion by Mr. Henderson, seconded by Mr. Dempsey, and unanimously approved, it was

> "RESOLVED: That the actions of the officers of the company in entering an agreement with State Mutual Life Assurance Company of America which, among other things, provides State Mutual the option to sell to Tandy Corporation all of the 100,000 shares of Senior Convertible Participating Preferred and all of the 30,000 shares of Junior Convertible Participating Preferred of Radio Shack Corporation held by State Mutual for a consideration of $500,000 in cash or Tandy Corporation common stock, or a combination of both, be and hereby are confirmed and ratified.

"There followed a discussion of the operating affairs of Radio Shack Corporation and of the program of its management to achieve satisfactory profitability and expansion objectives.

"There being no further business to come before the meeting, and on motion duly made, seconded, and carried, the meeting was adjourned at 4:30 p.m."

Tandy had gotten his mandate. He could now proceed with chasing his dream.

Chapter 11
A Vision of 1,000 Radio Shacks

Even before securing his grudging go-ahead from his board of directors, Tandy began opening new Radio Shack stores. The first additions were in New England, where they could be easily served from the Boston warehouse. These were merely the opening trickle of what would become a flood.

In his initial meeting with his new team after taking over the Radio Shack reins, Tandy had asserted, "We're going to put stores wherever the mail orders are coming from." The Radio Shack mailing list was to be the key to the first stage of the expansion effort.

"Charles recognized that our mail orders by themselves were generating poor business, but he simultaneously realized that in our mailing list we had the tool to tell us where to open new stores," Dave Beckerman said.

"He studied the mailing list and came up with a breakdown by state and then a breakdown by city as to where our customers were, and that's where we put in our first retail stores. Our expansion was concentrated initially in the New England area because we could service that region easily from our Boston warehouse. But we also quickly opened stores in California, in the San Francisco and Los Angeles areas, and in Texas, where we had good clusters of customers."

The first new outlets in Texas were located in Fort Worth, Dallas, Houston, San Antonio, and Waco; in New England in Brookline, Cambridge, Framingham, Lowell, Springfield, and Worcester, Massachusetts; Manchester, New Hampshire; East Providence, Rhode Island; and Portland, Maine; and in California in Bakersfield, Downey, La Mesa, Long Beach, and San Leandro. These were swiftly followed by new store openings in New York City, Chicago, Philadelphia, Cincinnati, St. Paul, Seattle, and Arlington, Virginia. In addition, five electronics supply stores operated by Tandy in California and Texas were sold to Radio Shack in March 1964 and eight unprofitable Tandy Leather Company stores were converted into Radio Shacks.

"I gave the Tandy Leather store managers a 30-minute course in how to sell electronics and turned them loose," Tandy quipped.

To those on the scene at the time, the start of the store expansion program appeared to be more of a "seat of the pants" proposition than a meticulously thought out undertaking. "The first plan was for 30 stores," Lew Kornfeld recalled. "The plan was also a little slapdash," he added. "I can remember Tandy sending Dave Beckerman out west from Boston to open stores in places like Cincinnati and Louisville without much thought as to the supply lines. But the second or third wave of thinking was that in order to take on an area, you had to have enough stores to support a warehouse; or, vice versa, have a warehouse to support the stores.

"I can't remember the exact order of openings, but I know we had a giant leap to California, and we soon discovered that the lack of a warehouse, the lack of fast replenishment of stock, and the cost of advertising were way out of line when you had only a few stores. If you have one store in San Francisco, it costs you 100 percent to advertise. If you have 10 stores, it only costs each store 10 percent. So that became part of the strategy. Eventually, the thinking was crystallized as to how many stores we could have per head of population, regardless of the age, color or sex of the people living there."

Between June 30, 1963 and June 30, 1964, Radio Shack opened or acquired 27 stores, bringing the total number of outlets to 37 at the 1964 fiscal year-end.

"The stores that we opened were 2,500 square feet," Bernie Appel reported, "just about the same size as they are today. We're just paying higher rents today. We didn't go into the higher-class malls in those days. In the beginning, we made some mistakes going into low-rent, out-of-the-way places. When we were parts and pieces people, that's where you had to be. But when Charles realized we could sell end equipment, he adapted very rapidly. He played everything strictly by the numbers."

Appel said that Tandy was far ahead of his time in anticipating the explosive growth of consumer electronics and that he backed up this belief by opening stores when the business was still losing money.

"If we go back and look at the consumer electronics industry in the early 1960s," Appel pointed out, "there was none. It was a nothing business. We grew with the industry as the predominant supplier of components and accessories, and at the same time did a reasonably good job on inventory, on finished hi-fi, radios, and tape recorders. It was Charles' genius that enabled him to see the potential in consumer electronics, even though it's the thing he's given the least credit for. He recognized that the consumer electronics business was absolutely the future business of this nation. He saw things before anyone else realized them. Keep in mind that before he came to Radio Shack, he had visited all of the electronics specialists. When he tried to buy Allied and Lafayette, they laughed at him. They told him he was crazy. But once the ball started to roll, nobody could catch us.

"Charles knew that the leather business was limited to a small percentage of the population doing leathercrafts," Appel said, "and somehow he just knew that consumer electronics would become a big, big business. Initially, he recognized the hobbyist parts and pieces of the electronics business more than he did the finished equipment, as we know it today; but he was quick to seize on that, too, when it became apparent that that was where the bucks were.

"What we have to realize is what has happened to the electronics industry since Charles got into it. Factory sales in 1963, the year Tandy bought Radio Shack, were only $2.6 billion. He saw it at the very, very beginning. In 1990, consumer electronics was a $34 billion industry. Charles had the vision to see that coming."

One of Tandy's first priorities after taking over the Radio Shack helm was to tackle the problem of the $7 million in revolving credit that the previous management had accumulated under its policy of selling mail order merchandise for nothing down and monthly payments as low as $5. To salvage what he could of the credit disaster, he put hundreds of collection agencies and law firms to work.

"Of the $7 million that was on the books at that time," he later recalled, "we collected all but about $2½ million, but at a tremendous cost."

Another priority was to clamp a lid on Radio Shack's free-spending proclivities. For this assignment, he dipped into the ranks of his longtime associates and plucked Bill Vance out of an executive position with American Handicrafts.

"My job was to control the money, sign all the checks," Vance recalled. "Charles said to me, 'Don't allow a nickel to be spent without your okay. If there's anything those guys up there in Boston don't know, it's anything about money. They don't have any idea how to create a buck, earn a buck, or save a buck. That's where their problem is.'"

"How much authority do I have over this money?" Vance asked.

"Absolute," Tandy replied.

"Does that include you? You're not going to come in and tell me to spend money on this and that?"

"That's right," Tandy agreed, "but I would like to have the privilege, if I think we ought to do something, to sit down and discuss it with you."

"I understand that," Vance came back. "I just want to make sure you're not going to come in and tell me we're going to buy this or we're going to buy that. If you want this money controlled, I'll control it."

There was a great deal of room for belt-tightening at Radio Shack headquarters.

"The boys up in Boston were pretty free with the company money," he disclosed. "After I looked it over, I told Charles that I was going to cut this out and that out and that there were going to be some complaints up there among some of the people he considered important."

Tandy's response was, "They're not important unless they learn how to use money. Go ahead and do what you have to do."

For 13 months, while on this special assignment, Vance controlled the Radio Shack purse strings.

"I cut some general things," he reported. "They did things like once a week or every two weeks, they'd have an executive group that would go out to one of the nice restaurants in Boston and they'd have themselves some drinks and a nice dinner. Supposedly it was a business meeting. Those meals would run from $350 to $450. I didn't know they were doing that until I got the first bill. So I sent it back and told them the company doesn't accept this as a legitimate business expense. And I told them, 'If you want to meet, meet in your offices. We can't spend money this way. We don't have it to spend. We're not being tight-fisted, it's a matter of making what money we have go round."

Some months after starting his duties, Charles asked Vance, "Based upon what we've done with Tandy Leather, what would your guess be as to the number of Radio Shack stores we can put in across the country?"

Vance guessed, "Maybe 200 or 300 stores and, ultimately, maybe 500."

Tandy pondered that, then wondered aloud, "Do you think we can put in at least 50 profitable stores?"

Vance answered, "I certainly think so. But we've got to learn how to sell. We have to run some bigger ads."

The small, 2-by-4-inch newspaper ads Radio Shack was running, Vance said, weren't paying for themselves. "We didn't seem to pull enough business from our newspaper ads, at least the size ads we could afford. I did a 2,000-customer survey to see what I could find out about customer habits. We got a 22 percent reply. At the time, seven or eight percent was considered good. The survey showed that the thing that seemed to be our best possibility for pulling in more people was to run bigger ads, a full page or even a half page. Obviously, there were millions of people interested in electronics and, obviously, electronics was going to keep on growing and get better all the time. But how do you survive in the meantime? It seemed to me our survey said, 'Go ahead and run larger ads in the paper and develop a good catalog.'"

Tandy didn't have to be convinced about the necessity for spending advertising dollars. He and Lew Kornfeld had come to a quick agreement on that subject right after Charles' arrival in Boston. Kornfeld recalled the conversation:

"Lew, how much do you think our ad budget ought to be?"

"Six percent of sales is what I think."

"I can live with that."

Kornfeld, who would see Radio Shack's ad budget soar to $140 million in 1981, the year he retired, retained fond memories of Tandy's commitment to advertising. "He was holding court one day with a group of Radio Shack executives. Everyone was complaining about soft sales. 'The business is out there,' Tandy said, glaring at the assemblage. 'Let's up the ad budget.'"

Another early decision Tandy made was to continue two Radio Shack publications, the catalog and the monthly flyer, but to discontinue mailing them to purchased lists of names. Soon after that, he ordered the discontinuance of mail order solicitations.

"The paradox," Kornfeld pointed out, "was that Radio Shack increased its mailings at the same time it stopped doing business by mail.

But first and by far the most important thing we did when we opened the new stores and brought in the customers was that we captured their vital statistics on our sales slips. This gave us access to customers who *might*, who *could*, and who absolutely and trackably *did* become repeaters. When Radio Shack made its store personnel keenly aware of the importance of each customer's curriculum vitae, the names of their recent customers really started pouring into our computer center in Boston, and the advertising people really started pouring out the mail."

Tandy credited the "massive use of advertising" as a major factor in Radio Shack's success.

"At the time I took over Radio Shack," he recalled in a talk at the Massachusetts Institute of Technology in 1978, "they were spending about five or six percent on advertising. Now, in a $10 million business, you can see that's about half a million dollars. This year, Radio Shack's expenditure for advertising will be in excess of $90 million. If you say it real fast, it doesn't hurt. But every piece of it has been measured. We measure what a television commercial brings us. We measure what a newspaper ad does. We'll follow a system and a habit if one works. Every year, in August, you'll find us with a big, massive display of TV antennas. We start manufacturing in January, getting ready for a sale in September, the last of August."

Tandy paused, then asked, "Why antennas? Why TV antennas in August, the first of September? Anybody got an idea? Well, you hit it. The men like to see a good football game. (Chuckle.) And we've got to get there a little ahead of the time, don't we? So we've got to give you a good price and a good reason to get up there on that roof to fix that antenna. So why does that work? Common sense. That's all it adds up to. And we've been doing that for five years. You'd think somebody else would follow us. You'd have thought somebody would have copied Radio Shack. I was afraid that they would for the first five or six years, and I was running like hell."

He was, indeed, running like hell during the period he was commuting regularly between Fort Worth and Boston.

"He was a hard worker," Dave Beckerman attested. "When he was in Boston, he stayed at the Ritz-Carlton or the Sheraton, and we'd pick him up for breakfast in the morning. He took over Deutschmann's old office. It was a large office with a conference table. I'd usually pick him up. He often had a guy with him from Fort Worth, a Harvard Business School graduate named Gerald Rolph, who was brought in to handle the collection of the revolving credit money and to dissolve the revolving credit unit."

The hard work and the new programs began paying dividends in increased recognition on Wall Street.

On March 17, 1964, Boenning & Co., a New York brokerage house, published an in-depth report on Tandy Corporation, describing it as "the nation's largest manufacturer and retailer of a diversified line of handicraft supplies, educational, do-it-yourself and occupational therapy products, with 179 retail stores in 43 states and Canada, plus a mail order business." The report then added:

> The recent sharp increase in the price of Radio Shack Corp. common stock from ¾ to 1½ wasn't reflected in the price of the common stock of Tandy Corp., which holds as its principal investment 893,568 shares (71 percent) of Radio Shack common at a cost of $305,000. This complete lack of recognition leads us to believe even more strongly that Tandy common is an undervalued situation. The last time Tandy Corp. was written up was in early 1962. At that time, the company was to earn about 60 cents (with the benefit of a tax loss) and the stock sold as high as 11⅞. Now the company is estimated to earn 75 cents to 85 cents in the year ending June 30, 1964, and the stock sells at 6½. In the meantime, a potentially explosive investment, Radio Shack, has been added to the company's assets.

> The company has decreased its capitalization and increased potential dilution by issuing warrants and leaving the convertible American Hide & Leather 5% Income Debentures outstanding. It is also true that there is no current dividend on the common stock. These are the two major negative factors in the Tandy picture.

> Now let's look at the plus factors.

> 1. Sales of Tandy Corp. have continued to grow quite rapidly. So has the number of stores. The expense of rapid store expansion has penalized earnings. Experiments in types of stores, locations, etc. have been undertaken. Some were successful and, naturally, some areas unsuccessful and costly. The period of rapid store expansion and experimentation appears over. The time to reap the benefits has arrived. In the first six months, operating income was up 20.6 percent, commensurate to the sales increase of 20 percent.

This is the first indication of increased profitability in the past two years. Sales during that period rose, but profits lagged well behind because of expansion and experimentation costs.

2. When Charles Tandy undertook the reorganization of Radio Shack in April 1963, Radio Shack had 9 stores. Today there are 23 stores in the chain. When Radio Shack was taken over, there was complete chaos. A seemingly impossible task of reorganizing the company was laid out. The concept of the business was analyzed with regard to margins, turnover of inventory and costs. As a result, drastic changes in inventory control were installed. The give away of the no-money-down-revolving-charge-plan was changed to a policy of down payments. Unrelated lines were liquidated. Inventories were reduced by almost $2,000,000. Gross margins were analyzed and unprofitable lines eliminated. As a result, a gross margin of 31 percent, based on actual physical inventories, was indicated in the six-month report for the period ended December 31, 1963. Sales were off, but a profit from operations was indicated. This was offset by unusual charge-offs for revolving credit and interest. A financial reorganization was effected which gives Radio Shack $4,500,000 long-term credit at very reasonable rates, plus an additional line of $1,000,000 for seasonal needs. This financial structure should be adequate for near-term needs.

3. The low price-earnings ratio of 8½ times on a growth company is unusual, I believe. Our guess is that Tandy is still relatively unknown, even though listed on the New York Stock Exchange, and certainly not recognized as a growth company. In going from obscurity to recognition, price-earnings ratios change. This could account for more immediate price appreciation than earnings increases. In the case of Tandy Corp. common, there appears to be plenty of room for both.

4. Standard & Poor's recent stock report on Tandy points out the substantial dilution prospects. This would scare one away if one couldn't see an even greater offsetting factor that doesn't even show in the income account, i.e., Tandy's investment in Radio Shack. Each share of Tandy has approximately .83 of a share of Radio Shack behind it. Radio Shack, at 1½, amounts to $1.25 per share of Tandy.

5. Tandy Corp. sales have increased from $15 million in 1961 to an estimated $23 million this year. Earnings have increased from 46 cents (mostly non-taxable) to an estimated 75 cents to 85 cents for this year ended June 30, 1964. The price of Tandy common stock was 6⅝ back in 1961. Today it is 6½! The price-earnings ratio is, among other things, dependent upon confidence in management's ability to make profits with fair consistency and the quality and amount of promotion given their stock. There has been an almost complete absence of promotional work done on this stock in the past nine months. This is partly due to top management's preoccupation with the reorganization of Radio Shack. Another factor was possible financing hanging over Radio Shack and the reluctance of management to make statements which might snarl the underwriting procedure. With the Radio Shack picture stabilized, the proposed financing indefinitely postponed and current results of the main Tandy Leather Division increasing satisfactorily, along with the profitable Tex Tan Division, we expect seeing this 'hands-off' policy reevaluated.

6. Over the past 1½ years of seeming inactivity in the common stock of Tandy Corp., the stock has built an interesting point-and-figure pattern on the one-half point chart. The reading of the chart indicates an upside objective of $16.

As bullish as the Boenning & Co. report appeared, there was no immediate impact. Three months later, when nine-month earnings of 63 cents per share on sales of $18.3 million were reported, Tandy stock was still languishing at around $7 per share.

The stock was trading at 6¾ on June 10, 1964, when Shearson, Hammill, another New York brokerage house, labeled it an "attractive low-priced speculation." The report added, "Radio Shack's operations have been turned around sharply and have been in the black since the early part of 1964. For fiscal 1964, Radio Shack will just about break even, compared with a loss of $4.2 million in fiscal 1963."

The report concluded: "The recent market performance of Tandy's common stock has been unexciting to say the least, and the shares have stayed in their present narrow trading range for well over a year, even though the company's per share earnings have continued to improve slowly but steadily. Currently selling at around 9 times estimated fiscal

1964 results of 75 cents per share on sales of $24 million and at less than 8 times our projection of fiscal 1965 earnings of around 90 cents a share on sales in the area of $27 million, Tandy appears to have a good deal of speculative attraction, based on our expectation that the company's growth is likely to be recognized by the market before too long."

As it turned out, Tandy's actual fiscal 1964 earnings of 89 cents substantially surpassed the optimistic Shearson, Hammill forecast of 75 cents and represented an increase of 33 percent over the prior year's 67 cents. Sales rose 17 percent to $23.8 million.

Tandy proclaimed the 1964 results in an advertisement on the business page of the *Fort Worth Star-Telegram* under a headline that announced: "Fourth Consecutive Growth Year Recorded by Tandy Corporation."

Apparently Charles was no longer averse to touting his stock.

Tandy Leather again had been the largest contributor to corporate earnings in fiscal 1964. With its 115 company-owned retail and mail order stores and a mail order customer list that included 30,000 institutions and 250,000 individuals, it was the fount from which all blessings flowed. By comparison, Radio Shack had experienced a net loss of $323,238 in its 1964 fiscal year.

"Let's face it," Lew Kornfeld said candidly, "Radio Shack was the dregs. Tandy Leather was the cash cow. When I would come to Fort Worth from Boston, I could actually feel the hostility of people who saw Radio Shack draining off corporate profits."

Phil North, who by this time was a large Tandy Corporation stockholder and confidante of Charles Tandy's, remembered Jim West complaining over how Radio Shack was eating up the profits generated by Tandy Leather Company.

"He'd take me aside at every possible moment and say, 'Phil, Radio Shack is eating our money. It's a money-eater. I'll tell you, Phil, you and I will not live to see the day that Radio Shack will make a nickel.' He'd shake his finger under my nose and say, 'Mark my words, Phil, this thing is just going to eat us all to death.' He always viewed Radio Shack with a great deal of skepticism, even after it turned the corner. I think that even after he recognized that Radio Shack was going to become a great success, it was part of his character to say it would never amount to anything."

Recalling that era, Eunice West said, "Of course, you have to keep in mind that Jim started out in the leather business, and it was always his first love. But, you know, you have to prosper and go along. So after Charles got into Radio Shack, Jim went along with it even though he had opposed it at first. But they were a good pair together. Charles was the dreamer and Jim was the fulfiller."

After Dave Tandy's retirement as president of Tandy Leather Company in 1956, Jim West took over sole responsibility for trying to keep a rein on Charles' high-flying aspirations.

"Charles always wanted to do big things, and Mr. Dave worried about that," Mrs. West related. "You know, just before Mr. Dave died in 1966, Jim and I visited him in All Saints Hospital. Just before we left, Mr. Dave took Jim's hand and he said, 'Now, West, you must try to control Charles. You know he'll go wild. I want you to control him. You always helped me do it. Now you'll have to do it by yourself.'

"Jim and Charles were like father and son," Mrs. West went on. "And Jim was good with Charles. He could control him most of the time, but it wasn't easy. They had tremendous arguments. You'd think they never were going to speak to one another again. Then, when it was all over with, why, they'd shake hands and just laugh and be the best of friends. They could throw it off."

She laughed as she recalled an incident that took place late one night in the Tandy headquarters on West 7th Street.

"Charles wanted to make a deal of some kind and Jim didn't want him to do it. Jim had a tremendous temper. He'd get so angry. But he'd say what he wanted and then it was all over with. This night, several of the men were still there, including John Wilson, and they said that Jim kept arguing with Charles, and Jim finally said, 'Look, you're going to listen to me or else...' And he pushed Charles up against the wall and began shaking him, beating his head against the wall. Charles just looked at him, and when Jim turned loose of him, Charles just slumped down. Jim had made a believer out of him. After it was over, they were the best of friends again. Jim came home that night and never said a word to me about it. I heard it from the fellows. They said it was very funny, in a way, because Charles was so much bigger than Jim. And here was Jim just shaking him like he was a doll. Charles just put up with it."

John Wilson disputed the contention that there were hard feelings towards the Radio Shack group on the part of the old-timers in Fort Worth.

"We had no resentment over the fact that Tandy Leather was financing the early days of Radio Shack," Wilson asserted. "We knew that if we were going to become a nationally-recognized corporation, we damn sure weren't going to do it in leathercraft. All of us were substantial shareholders in Tandy Corporation. It was to our advantage in the long run to make Radio Shack go. Charles went into Radio Shack because he knew the potential of Tandy Leather was limited and that in order to become really big he had to find another vehicle. The way we were running Tandy Leather was actually the proper way. We were making money every year. It had a tremendous return on investment and on equity. But the growth was really limited.

"We ran many surveys that showed that only 2 or 3 percent of the people were interested in doing leathercraft. That obviously was not a situation you wanted to hitch up to to get anywhere in the corporate world. I recall having many conversations with Charles where he said we needed to find another vehicle. We would have discussions on where we were going to take Tandy Leather. We would have meetings on how big a gain we were going to have this year and next year. I hadn't been in Fort Worth too long, when at one of the meetings I talked about 10 and 20 percent gains, and Charles shook his head and said, 'John, that's not in the cards. We've got to get into something that's got some real growth potential'. We'd been having 2 or 3 percent gains."

Jim West's opposition to the Radio Shack venture was beginning to abate as the 1964 fiscal year ended, although he continued to express concerns about the financing of the Radio Shack expansion program. He was frequently heard muttering in Charles' earshot about the folly of "robbing Peter to pay Paul."

Tandy would usually pretend he hadn't heard him. Other times, he'd look up and grin and give West the Churchillian "V for Victory" sign. Sometimes, he'd merely raise his middle finger.

Nevertheless, in September of 1964, Tandy showed his affection and esteem for his long time mentor by naming West to succeed him as president of Tandy Corporation, with Tandy assuming the title of chairman of the board. West, who had been serving as president of the

Tandy Leather Company Division, was succeeded in that position by Harlan Swain. John Wilson was named a Tandy Leather Company vice president.

Tandy stock was now beginning to move. On October 20, it hit a 52-week high of 10½, and a financial wire service messaged its clients, "Tandy is another low-priced recommendation of not too many weeks ago that broke through on increased volume yesterday and reached a new high. Here we see the trend to near 12, and as it nears that figure, we would then consider accepting short term gains."

At the same time, Vanden Broeck Lieber, a New York Stock Exchange firm, advised its clients that Tandy, "at some 9 times prospective earnings," appeared to be "an attractive speculative commitment in an interesting corporate rehabilitation situation."

On November 30, 1964, Tandy moved to reduce indebtedness and stabilize the shareholder dilution factor represented by its 5 percent convertible subordinate non-cumulative income debentures due October 1, 1975, by calling the debentures. This resulted in the issuance of 96,325 shares of common stock at the conversion rate of one share of stock for each $10 principal amount of debentures. The redemption was funded through the sale of $1.1 million of 5 percent senior convertible notes due in 1975 to State Mutual Life Assurance Company of Worcester, Massachusetts. At the same time, Tandy secured further financing for his Radio Shack expansion program by negotiating long-term loan agreements totaling $3 million with State Mutual Life and the First National Bank of Boston.

Also in late November 1964, Tandy exchanged 96,000 shares of its common stock for 130,000 shares of Radio Shack senior and junior convertible preferred stock held by State Mutual Life. The preferred stock would later be converted into 800,000 shares of Radio Shack common stock, increasing Tandy's ownership in Radio Shack to 85 percent.

The dilution caused by the issuance of the 192,325 shares had little immediate effect on Tandy earnings, which nearly doubled from 53 cents per share to $1.04 per share for the first six months of the 1965 fiscal year which ended on December 31, 1964. First half sales also rose sharply from $12.6 million to $22.7 million.

"The excellent earnings increase of the past six months is the result of a 50 percent gain in profits of our Tandy divisions, plus a large earnings contribution from the recently-consolidated subsidiary, Radio Shack Corporation," Jim West crowed in a news release. "Sales continue strong in all divisions, and plans call for further expansion of the retailing divisions during the coming months."

On the strength of the improved earnings performance, Tandy stock had reached a new high of 13 at the end of the 1964 calendar year and was flirting with 14 when the company was invited to make a presentation before the New York Society of Security Analysts on February 16, 1965. The invitation had arrived while Charles was in London looking over marketing opportunities for Tandy products in England, but he cut short his European junket to avail himself of the opportunity of telling the Tandy story to this influential audience.

In his opening remarks, Charles admitted he had been waging an uphill battle in attempting to get across the real nature of the company. He pointed out, "It was only recently that one of the large and widely respected financial publications finally moved Tandy Corporation from a listing in the same category with Swift & Co. and Armour & Co. and placed us in the 'Retailing, Miscellaneous' category. And, a few years back," he continued, "Tandy's correspondent at the New York Stock Exchange was a specialist in the petroleum industry."

Tandy then asked for a show of hands of all the parents in the audience whose youngsters had ever attended a YMCA, YMHA, or Boy Scout camp or a similar youth program. A considerable number of hands shot up. "Thank you," he said. "If your youngster ever brought home a woven pot-holder, a pair of moccasins, or any other handicraft item which he personally made or put together, the chances are the materials for the project came from one of our divisions."

He drew a laugh when he added, "I believe it was comedian Phil Foster who once remarked, 'I spent $500 to send my son to summer camp and all I have to show for it is a little round ash tray!' Well, the materials used to make that ash tray probably came from our company."

Tandy drew some whistles from his audience when he said his goal was to triple sales and net income during the next five years. "When I speak of tripling our current sales and earnings per share during the next five years," he asserted, "I must hasten to point out that we have accomplished approximately that during the past five years."

One reason for his optimism, he declared, was Radio Shack.

"Having personally brought Radio Shack into Tandy Corporation, and having personally directed its operations for the past 21 months, I know Radio Shack's growth potential is greater than any of our other divisions. Its merchandise lines have a more universal market than the products of any of our other divisions. We are shooting for the opening of about 25 new Radio Shack stores during the next six months, and we have been carrying enlarged payrolls and overheads in preparation for this.

"This is the time of year I like us to get set for fall. I don't like to wait until September to decide where to open stores. We've been opening stores in California, the Pacific Northwest, and heavily in the Southwest. We've got 43 stores now, with the new store opening costs being paid for out of current earnings. I honestly believe," he added, "that the country could support 1,000 Radio Shack stores."

His statement was greeted by amused looks from some of the members of the audience. The very idea of a chain of 1,000 electronics stores sounded like another tall tale from Texas.

Little did they know....

Chapter 12
"When Are We Gonna Get Some Damn Stores Open?"

Opening Radio Shack stores from scratch in brand new locales around the country took a lot of chutzpah. Chutzpah is a Yiddish colloquialism for audacity and brass, which describes the very essence of Charles Tandy. Opening stores also took a lot of cash, which he had in less plentiful amounts.

Most of all, opening stores required qualified people to run them, a commodity that Tandy lacked to an even greater extent than money.

"It was a bit difficult to staff a company like Radio Shack that started with only nine stores," he recalled. "So I had to take people from the leathercraft division. In 1965, I had to take eight to ten of its best men and move them over to help me in Radio Shack."

"The essence of the national expansion came from the old Tandy Leather group," Bill Michero said. "That was a very important factor, that we did have people, some really seasoned guys. We took them out of our old Tandy Leather Company and assigned them the task of opening new Radio Shack stores around the country."

The recruitment of the Tandy Leather operatives was carried out in a hush-hush scenario that could have come out of the pages of a spy novel. Ken Gregson, then a Tandy Leather Company district manager in St. Louis, was one of the people mysteriously summoned to Fort Worth.

"I'll never forget," Gregson recalled, "it was 1965, in the spring of the year. The call I received just told me to come to Fort Worth for a meeting on such and such a date. When I arrived, I found there was a group of about 12 of us, all Tandy Leather district managers, all staying at the same hotel where reservations had been made for us. You would have thought we all had the Black Plague. There was nobody to talk to. Our friends in the company were all out of town or couldn't be reached.

We'd call and get the information they weren't there. The wife would answer the phone and say he wasn't there. We were isolated from everybody in the company. A lot of crazy things went around in our minds as to what was going on."

The next morning, after an early breakfast at their hotel, Gregson and his Tandy Leather cohorts gathered in the conference room on the second floor of the Tandy Corporation headquarters on West 7th Street. Gregson described the scene.

"We were all sitting around the table, waiting for something to happen, when Charles and Jim West walked into the room. Jim then locked the door and gave the key to Charles. Charles put the key in his pocket, and he and Jim walked up to the head of the table and took their seats."

Jim West rose to his feet.

His opening words were, "I want you all to know that at one time I was called to Fort Worth from Houston, and when I walked into the room I was told that I was fired."

He looked around the room and said, "You're all fired."

Tandy stood up and explained that the men in the room were being asked to leave their jobs with Tandy Leather Company to help him build a national chain of Radio Shack stores.

"He explained to us what we were headed for, what he wanted to build," Gregson said. "He told us that he wanted to expand the operation and that he was getting a lot of static from the eastern people because they didn't believe he was going to be able to expand like he said he wanted to. He told us that when he told them he wanted to have 100 stores, they laughed at him. His statement to us was, 'I want some boys that are going to go out and put these stores together.'"

In addition, Tandy reminded the men in the conference room, "You gentlemen are invested heavily in this corporation. The money that we've put into this thing has already gone down the sewer. We have to make this thing fly, because if we don't make it fly we're going to lose what we've got. There's a future here. The potential is here. It's what we make of it. We can make this great. And this is what I want to do. This is the thing of the future. Or we can let it fall on its face. You boys are invested in the company. And if we don't make this fly, what you've got is gone. So let's get on with it."

Tandy laid down the ground rules for the rest of the meeting.

"First, I'm gonna outline what we're gonna do. Then you're gonna make your decision whether you're gonna do it or not. But, by God, you're gonna make the decision here and now. You're not going to call your wife or your sweetheart or your mother or your father or your banker or your lawyer. You wear the pants in the family. You make the decision, and after you've made it, we'll unlock the door. Now, if you decide that you don't want to do this, you go right on back to where you've been, and God love you. Go right ahead with the job you've been doing. But those who are gonna stay and do this with me are gonna sit in this room and we're gonna start working out a program."

The program was challenging. Each man who decided to participate would become the manager of a new Radio Shack store, which would be operated as a joint venture in which the store manager owned 50 percent and the company 50 percent. Each store manager would have to put up $17,000, which would pay for the store's initial inventory. The company would back the lease, with each manager responsible for his own payroll.

"Each of us was going to have go on the hook personally for the money," Gregson said. "No one had that kind of cash."

It was a dramatic moment, as each of the 12 men in the room caucused with his conscience. There was no one to call on for guidance. A few closed their eyes, apparently seeking a word of advice from a higher authority. Tandy finally called a halt to the soul-searching and began making the rounds of the table asking for individual commitments. When it was over, eight men remained seated at the conference table. The other four stood to be let out of the room when the door was unlocked. No one faulted them for making the decision they did, but their lack of faith would cost them dearly in bonuses over the years.

The question remains: Why did the eight stay?

"It was our belief in him, I guess," Gregson ventured. "I know that I had started with his brother Bill. Bill could have called me in anytime in his lifetime and said, 'I need you,' and I would have said, 'where' or 'when,' and I'd have gone. It was the same thing with Charles and his father. They had instilled pride in me. They gave me mountains to climb, but they made me feel that they believed I was capable of it. And I wasn't about to let them down. As I said, my job was to prove them right. So if they felt I was capable of doing a job, I didn't dare not accomplish it for them. I can't put it into words, but I know it was a feeling."

The eight men who cast their lot with Radio Shack began a marathon session that lasted until the early hours of the following morning.

"We were given a choice of where we wanted to be," Gregson said. I chose to go back to St. Louis, Marvin Cash stayed in Houston, Dean Lawrence stayed in Seattle, Randy Capp went to Denver. Then there was Jim Millang up in Minneapolis, Jack Labar in Pittsburgh, Leroy Pratt in Norfolk, and Ken Stallings in Atlanta."

Two other former Tandy Leather managers also were part of the program that Tandy had laid out. Bill Nugent was already managing the first Radio Shack store in Fort Worth. And Jim Buxton was already operating a store in San Antonio for Radio Shack.

The ten Tandy Leather Company alumni didn't realize it at the time, but they were to become a part of Radio Shack folklore as "The 10 Disciples," the trailblazers of a store opening program that would make merchandising history.

"We were the beachhead breakers," Gregson said, "not the troops that came in afterwards. We went out and found the locations, we negotiated the leases, then sent the leases down and had them signed. We found the employees, found the managers, and trained them. We physically opened the stores, down to cleaning the glass, scrubbing the floor, waxing it, cleaning the showcases, and being there when the truck delivered the furniture. In the first stores, when the truck delivered the furniture, the merchandise came off the truck along with it. So you had to check it in, line the store out, see that the pegboard was hung and hang the merchandise. In the first stores, under the lease agreements, we had to do part of the work ourselves. Some of us actually did the carpentry work or found a carpenter to do what needed to be done.

"Other companies had people that found the location, signed the lease, found the employees and trained them, installed the fixtures and merchandise, and set up the advertising. When you looked at what they were doing, you said, 'God, no wonder we're getting there. We've got one guy doing what other people need 10 guys to do.' But we were salesmen first of all. We'd grown up in the stores. We'd grown up dealing with people. We'd grown up learning how to arrange our store, learning how to put the thing together. Any ideas that could funnel down, we used. We literally opened the stores single-handedly."

Things, of course, changed as Radio Shack began to grow.

"As we got bigger, we had our own people designing the stores," Gregson said. "You do that when you get bigger. But when you don't have any stores to run, you do it all yourself. Today, when you're given a full larder to start with, you don't have time to do all those things. We used to laugh, those of us who came up through the battle fire. We grew up through the thick and the thin. But that was the way we built the operation."

Gregson and the other disciples had a common problem as they started their store-opening odyssey. They all had to start from scratch in building an identity for Radio Shack.

"The name Radio Shack meant nothing in St. Louis when I opened my first store in the Houseland Shopping Center in 1965," Gregson recounted. The new store actually was the second Radio Shack outlet in St. Louis. The first was a converted Walter Ashe Radio Company store at 1125 Pine Street in the downtown area that had been bought by Radio Shack a few months before. The store, which catered primarily to ham radio operators and also had a large industrial business, had a totally different atmosphere from the new Radio Shack outlets. For one thing, it was located in an old four-story building that at one time had been a parking garage.

"The basic Radio Shack inventory that we began selling in St. Louis as we opened stores was parts and pieces," Gregson recalled. "We sold to the tinkerer, the guy who was building his own things. But we were also selling stereo and hi-fi equipment and receivers and some communications equipment to the CB buffs. Charles saw the electronics end of the business coming, stereo and hi-fi, so we were building our business based on that. This was a departure from the traditional Radio Shack approach in Boston. Charles foresaw the company's future in Radio Shack, that electronics was coming of age, that it was going to be a byword, a part of our everyday life, a necessity, just as radio had become, and that the development was going to be continuous. He had the foresight to see that there was a marketplace out there that would touch every person and every home."

None of the former Tandy Leather district managers knew anything about electronics, Gregson emphasized. But they did know how to sell. He recalled his first day in a Radio Shack store.

"I had a customer who asked for a 10K pot. I didn't have any idea what he wanted. So I grinned sort of sheepishly and said, 'Mister, I know what I use a pot for. What do you want a pot for?' He laughed and I laughed. Then he said, 'You're new.' I said, 'You bet your bucket.' He said, 'Come over here, I want to show you something.' He led me over to the board and pointed and said, 'This is a 10K pot.' I said, 'That's a potentiometer. Why didn't you just ask for a potentiometer?' He answered, 'Because we call them pots.' I sold him about $60 worth of merchandise.

"He became a fantastic customer. And every time I opened a store in the St. Louis area, and I opened about 16 of them, every time at the grand opening, he would walk into that store and announce to me, 'Gregson, this is your lesson for today.' Then he would walk me over to the board and show me something and tell me what it was."

Gregson chuckled. "One day I was a skin merchant, the next day I was an electronics expert. I knew we had technicians who repaired merchandise, who knew why and how they worked. We had buyers who knew what to buy. My job was not to be the technician or the buyer, but to be the salesman, to turn that merchandise into cash. When a customer brought in a record player that didn't work, the technician would try to fix it with a screwdriver and then say, 'I can't help you.' That wasn't being a salesman. I didn't need technicians on the sales floor. I'd stop the customer at the door and say, 'Let me see if I can help you.'

"Then I'd try to turn on the record player and say, 'You're right, it doesn't work. But I've got one right here that does and makes yours seem like washing clothes on a river bank with rocks. Why do you want this old relic when, at this price, I can give you this piece of equipment and we'll take care of it. It's our merchandise and we stand behind it.' Sales. That's what my world was and that's what Charles was always pushing me to do."

Radio Shack was also developing a new kind of customer because of what it was doing in St. Louis and other marketplaces across the country, Gregson pointed out.

"I was opening new stores in the major shopping centers and malls and strip centers, but we were noticing a new trend. People were coming to the strip centers and malls and into our stores in family groups in the evening after supper. We were selling component stereo equipment which, in our mind, was the coming thing. That's what we were really working on. So we were developing a basically new business with a new customer base."

The people coming into the new stores also were being exposed to Radio Shack merchandise for the first time. Gregson recalled their initial reactions.

"People would come in and ask, 'Do you have any name brands?'

"We'd say, 'Like what? We have Realistic.'

"They'd say, 'Oh, no, we mean Sony or Magnavox or General Electric or Emerson.'

"And we'd say, 'Well, we have Realistic and it's a worldwide brand. We have stores all over the world, and this is our own merchandise. We back up our merchandise and we believe in our merchandise.' What we were doing was selling what we had. We had a good price. We sold from price. And we sold from the fact that we were servicing what we were selling. We were backing it up. And we had our lifetime tubes."

Gregson smiled as he remembered those lifetime tubes.

"Tubes were still a prevalent item in radios at that time. We sold a lot of tubes. We had two testers in the stores. We'd tell the customers to bring their tubes in and test them. Then we'd sell them our Realistic lifetime-guaranteed tube. The first step was to convince the customer that we meant lifetime. We had a lot of leery customers to start with.

"They'd bring a tube back and we'd replace it, and they'd ask, 'What are you gonna do with that tube, resell it?'

"We'd laugh and say, 'No.'

"I kept a hammer under the counter and I'd say, 'Can I have the box that that tube I just sold you came in?' They'd give me the box and I'd put the old tube in the box and lay it on the counter. Then I'd hand them the hammer and say, 'Would you please smash that old tube for me.'

"That kind of led them to believe that we were serious about what we were saying, plus the fact that when they smashed the tube there were four or five other customers looking at what this guy was doing, and then they had to come over and find out. So it was a process we were using as a sales tool."

Over the next three years, the nationwide expansion program gathered steam. Gregson's territory expanded to include Kansas, Iowa, and Nebraska, as well as Missouri, and he opened 42 stores in the four-state area. "We initially bypassed the big cities like New York and Chicago," Gregson said. "Chicago was dominated by Allied Electronics and New York by Lafayette Electronics. We couldn't afford to march on the big cities yet."

But for some of the newly-minted store managers, the initial going was rugged.

"There were a few of us who had our heads above water, who were getting the job done, who were opening quite a few stores," Gregson reported. "But we were on the hook for quite a bit of money at the bank and we were going to have to go back to the bank and get more money. And there were some who were drowning, who were in over their heads. So, a year later, we had a meeting with Charles and we converted to a company-owned operation under which we all became district managers and were paid a salary plus a bonus off the operations of the stores."

Under the new plan, Gregson and the other store managers were guaranteed a salary of $7,200 a year, plus a bonus of 50 percent of the store profits.

This was a period in which Tandy was driving his store-opening crews relentlessly.

Gregson recalled sitting in a room with Tandy in Fort Worth. "There was one guy on one side of me who had opened nine stores and a fellow sitting on the other side of me who had opened seven stores, and I had opened 36 stores in 28 months. Charles was chewing on me about not getting any stores opened. I could feel the people on both sides of me squirming. He was really letting me have it. I finally said, 'Charles, don't you realize how many stores I've gotten open?'

"He said, 'Yes, I do. Hell, you've gotten 36 stores open.'

"And I said, 'What do you want?'

"And he said, 'Gregson, we both know you could open 36 stores. They're open. Couldn't you open 38?'

"I looked at him and said, 'Yeah, I guess I could have worked a couple of more Sundays and did a few other things and gotten 38 open.'

"And he said, 'That's all I'm asking. When are we going to get some damn stores open?' And he began to grin."

As for the guys on either side of him, Gregson went on, "They were in hell. They were really suffering, because they knew when Charles was finished with me what he was going to say to them. But after he finished with me with a grin on his face, he changed the subject to something else and he never said anything to the other two guys. However, I would guarantee you that in the next 60 days they did a lot of scrounging and opened up some stores. He used a lot of us to get through to other people. I know that he chewed on me to get through to other people without having to tear them up. When he rode me, I knew he was trying to make a better man out of me. But I also knew he was really riding the individual next to me. I guess he figured I could take it better than the next guy."

Many a time at meetings, Gregson said, Tandy chewed on him without letup for 45 minutes or more. "But I knew down inside that he was also getting his message across to a lot of other people in the room. So I sold the same way," Gregson said. "We all sold the same way. We might have a customer in front of us at the counter that we were selling, but we were selling loud enough for the other people in the store to hear. That's how we got their attention. And that's what Charles was doing. He was selling. He was selling every minute of the day. You asked what our feelings about him were? It was a feeling inside us. We'd paid our dues. We had our seat on that 747. We didn't know where it was gonna go, but we knew we were going to be on it. We were gonna stay on it, and we were gonna see where it landed. A number of us did just that..."

Jim Buxton, one of the 10 Disciples, was in the midst of planning the opening of the giant Tandy Mart in San Antonio in early 1963, when he was summoned to Fort Worth for a meeting with the boss. Buxton had begun his career with Tandy Leather Company in Amarillo in 1955 and had been managing a leather store in San Antonio since 1962.

"Charles was asking me about the status of the San Antonio mart and was also talking about putting in another mart in Dallas," Buxton recalled, "and then out of the blue, he said to me, 'Buxton, do you know anything about radio?'

"I said, 'Well, I know how to turn one on.'

"And he said, 'Well, there's something happening up in Boston that I'm involved in. The bank that brought us American Hide has a company in trouble and they want me to come up and take a look at it. You go down to San Antonio and build your thing, and I'll look into this radio thing.'"

The San Antonio mart, called Tandy's Wonderland, opened in September of 1963 and contained Tandy Leather, American Handicrafts, Merribee Embroidery, and Cost Plus Imports retail outlets, plus a restaurant, beauty parlor and barber shop. It also contained a location for a Radio Shack store that opened a few weeks later. The store, under Buxton's management, would become the first Radio Shack outside of Boston to do over $1 million in annual sales.

Rachel Barber remembered that some of the most successful Radio Shack managers had come from the Tandy Leather Company ranks. "They knew the system, they knew how to sell, they knew the formula, they knew about daily reports, they knew about turnover. Everything that didn't fit our formula didn't work out too well," she expounded.

She also recalled the skepticism that greeted Tandy's grandiose plans for Radio Shack. "I remember when Charles told the accounting department to gear up for several hundred new stores a year. They were laughing at him and saying behind his back, 'The man is a maniac.' It really boggled the imagination, because even at that time he was thinking in terms of thousands of stores and people couldn't believe it."

Also getting into the Radio Shack act during this era was Bill Collins, Charles Tandy's boyhood friend.

"When Tandy Leather began to expand nationally, I was interested in putting in paint and wallpaper stores throughout Texas," Collins recounted. "So Charles and I had a lot in common there. We'd have coffee all the time and he'd tell me about his hopes and plans and successes. And sometimes we'd meet for lunch at the Blackstone Hotel."

The two friends would often walk past Leonards Department Store across the street from the Tandy Leather Company, Collins recalled, and Charles would look at it and say, "I'm gonna own that some day."

Tandy also talked a lot in those days about a book called *The Magic of Believing*, Collins said. "He spoke frequently about the theme of the book—that if you believe you can do something and stay with it long enough, you can overcome obstacles and accomplish your goals."

Tandy was totally absorbed in his business, Collins remembered. He never engaged in any sports, never played golf or tennis, didn't fish or hunt. Collins recalled making a small wager with Jim West once that he could get Tandy to play a round of golf. He succeeded in getting Tandy out on the course, but after playing two holes at River Crest Country Club, Tandy found an excuse to call it a day.

"Charles was left-handed, so he had left-handed golf clubs," Collins related. "After I talked him into playing one afternoon, we finished the first two holes. When we got to the third hole, we had a mutual friend, John Roby Penn, who lived right near the golf course, and Charles suggested we park our golf cart and visit Roby for a quick libation. Well, we stayed at Roby's house until about 7 or 8 o'clock that night, and that was the end of the golf game. I don't think Charles ever played golf again. This was 1954, and I think that's the last physical exercise I ever saw Charles take."

In October of 1964, Collins and Tandy were having lunch at the Blackstone Hotel in downtown Fort Worth. Tandy, as usual, was talking of his plans for expanding Radio Shack and the problems he was having finding qualified people to manage the stores he wanted to open.

"Our business was not doing all that well at the time," Collins reported. "I think we had decided to close one or two of them, and I mentioned this to Charles." That was all the opening Tandy needed.

"I've got a great idea, Bill," Tandy said. "You know I'm looking for good people. I'm building a management team that's really gonna take us places. Why don't you join us?"

Collins was receptive. "I had a feeling that there was a lot of future in Tandy Corporation," he said. "We discussed salary and things like that and I told him I would come with him."

Collins joined the Tandy fold on November 1, 1964.

His first day on the job, Tandy informed him: "Bill, you've got to learn the business just like the rest of us."

So Collins started behind the counter as a salesman-trainee in the Radio Shack store in downtown Dallas. "At the time, there were three Radio Shack stores in Dallas, one out in North Dallas, one in South Dallas and one downtown," Collins said. "I worked in the downtown store from November 1 to January 1. Then Charles transferred me to the University Drive store in Fort Worth which did extremely well. It was a large store and had a tremendous business. I worked there two or three months and then Charles told me, 'We're going to open a store in Arlington. Why don't you manage it?'"

Collins opened the store in Arlington, a fast-growing bedroom community located halfway between Fort Worth and Dallas, in April of 1965, the first of many store openings in which he would be involved.

"I not only opened the store, I outfitted it," he disclosed. "At that time, we didn't have total leeway, but as long as the store looked good and you had a good shelving system with your stereos and things of that sort, you were pretty much on your own. The big question was, 'Should the stereos be at the front of the store or the back of the store?' If they were at the back, the traffic would walk by a lot of things that they might buy on the way to the back. All of that was beautifully thought out."

Collins also bought the fixtures himself. "It wasn't like it is today," he said. "They didn't provide the fixtures. I just found some and got approval to buy them. By then, they had ideas about how they liked to display the merchandise. The counter system at that time was what we called an 'against the wall' counter. The door was in front with a plate glass on either side of it. It was a 25-foot front. And as you came in, the counter was to the right or to the left. My parts and pieces was the 27 Series, which was extremely profitable but very labor intensive. We had little cardboard boxes about half the size of a cigar box. You'd just line them up on a table and you'd start with your resistors and transistors and all that, most of which was a mystery to me then."

On June 1, with another couple of month's experience under his belt and the Arlington store beginning to make a little money, Collins received a call from Tandy asking him to come to Fort Worth for a meeting. When he arrived, he found two other store managers, Bill Spears and Ralph Duncan, there.

Collins recalled the meeting. "Charles walked in and told us, 'I want you to go to California.' Well, that was a big move for me because I owned a comfortable home in Fort Worth. Charles told us he wanted each of us to open three stores at sites we selected ourselves, and that we could then choose the best location for ourselves and manage it."

Somewhat reluctantly, Collins agreed to the move, sold his home and headed west.

"We drew for who got first, second, or third choice on where we wanted to locate," Collins recollected. "Ralph Duncan got the first choice. He decided to go to Reseda in the San Fernando Valley, where there was a big, empty W.T. Grant store that he took over. Bill Spears chose Anaheim and I selected West Los Angeles. We were to open our three stores within a period of three months, staff them and then pick the store that we wanted and go from there. We chose the sites and hired the managers with the approval of management in Fort Worth."

Radio Shack already had two very successful stores in California at the time, Collins related, one in Long Beach and one near San Francisco. The San Francisco store was managed by Jon Shirley, who later left the company to become president of Microsoft Corp. Shirley was named district manager when Collins, Spears and Duncan began opening their stores, and the three reported to him.

In choosing a store location, Collins said, "We had to keep in mind that Tandy liked the idea of a high sign on a freeway, a sign that thousands of cars a day would pass. We were able to come up with one of those on the freeway between Anaheim and Los Angeles."

The Los Angeles area, which was in the midst of a growth explosion, was a tough nut to crack, Collins found. "Good locations were very scarce, housing was very scarce. Rent was usually a percentage of sales, and I was going into a new area and had to estimate what the sales might be."

He recalled an occasion when Tandy flew in from Fort Worth and the two of them spent an entire day, from early morning until nearly midnight, driving all over west Los Angeles looking for store locations. The three sites Collins finally selected were on Pico Boulevard near Westchester, in Torrance near the Palos Verdes Estates and in the Ledera Shopping Center near Westchester. He chose the Ledera Shopping Center location for his own store, which proved to be a wise decision. The store had excellent acceptance from the very beginning.

One evening during his first Christmas shopping season in California, Collins was in his store in the Ledera Shopping Center at about 7 o'clock when the phone rang. Tandy was on the line with a question.

"What did you do today?"

Collins, who was "busier than a cat on a hot tin roof," tried to be casual in his reply.

"We did 2," he allowed.

"Goddamn it, 2 what? $2? $200?"

"No, Tandy, we've done $2,000 so far today."

That made Tandy's evening, Collins said. "I'll never forget that."

Another thing Collins hadn't forgotten from that era was the way merchandise was delivered, in sharp contrast to the methods employed later on as operations became more sophisticated.

"They'd send out from Fort Worth all these paper sacks and all they'd have on them was a 27 Series number like 27-104. And gosh durn, we'd receive half a truckload of that stuff, and it took us all day and all night to get the merchandise out of the sacks and put in place. But, as the company grew and they began to do their own packaging, that really cut the labor down. Then we could run stores with two or three people, depending on the size, instead of four or five. I remember having two kids sitting on the floor in the back of the store handling these labor-intensive items. But they were very profitable."

The big ticket items were the stereos, Collins said. "At that time, there were a lot of new speakers coming out and you had to learn the difference between one speaker and the other and the difference among stereos. We had no television."

A memento of Collins' California experience is contained in a recording he made of a talk by Charles Tandy at a store managers' meeting at Green Oaks Inn in Fort Worth in 1971, when Collins was a district sales manager there.

"In 1965, I looked for somebody with stamina to hit these new markets," Tandy told the group. "So I picked three men to go out to California. I worked out a game plan. 'You three guys go out there. I want each of you to open three stores. And of the three stores, you each pick the best one and you run it.' Some of the guys picked the best one and some didn't."

(Laughter.)

"I told them, I'll give you guys an option on 2,000 shares at $32 a share. They couldn't see what they were getting. They couldn't read the crystal ball. These guys were in a position to be regional and district managers on the West Coast. But they didn't say, 'I can get this job done.' I even made a trip out there. I thought they'd got lost. You don't realize what it's like to open a new market. Where you put your first flag down. Anyway, those 2,000 shares would be worth a quarter of a million dollars today."

In later years, Collins remembered the episode philosophically, pointing out that he would have had to go into debt to exercise the option at a time the stock was selling at about half of the option price.

In June, 1965, when Collins went west on his store-opening mission, Tandy stock was selling at around $16, down from a high of 19½ earlier in the year. The price dropped even further as rumors began to abound on Wall Street that Charles Tandy's earnings forecast of $1.50 per share for fiscal 1965 was far too sanguine. This was confirmed when, on August 10, Tandy had the unpleasant experience of issuing a news release dropping his estimate of fiscal 1965 earnings to $1.20 per share. The lower earnings, he said, were the result of expenses incurred by the Radio Shack expansion program.

"The opening and operating expenses related to the rapid enlargement of the Radio Shack store system from 36 units to 57 units were much greater than anticipated, absorbing the earnings recorded by Radio Shack earlier in the year," Tandy declared. "The current expansion program is near completion, however, with the bulk of start-up costs occurring in the year just ended. The objective in fiscal 1966 will be to consolidate the expansion to develop Radio Shack's profitability."

By then, the price of Tandy stock had fallen to 13⅝, down some 30 percent from its 1965 high.

On September 1, earnings of $1.21 per share on sales of $42.8 million, were officially announced. Although below Tandy's original estimate, the earnings still represented a 70 percent increase over the prior year. Sales had recorded a 79 percent increase, boosted by a $15.6 million contribution from the newly-consolidated Radio Shack subsidiary. But all of the earnings had come from the established divisions. The cost of opening 21 new Radio Shack stores, plus adverse year-end accounting adjustments in the operation of the Boston warehouse, had wiped out the operating profit of $560,000 that Radio Shack had racked up during the first half of the fiscal year.

Nevertheless, the modest net profit of $680 that Radio Shack had managed to eke out was a sharp improvement over the net loss of $323,238 it had recorded in 1964 and the whopping $4.2 million it had lost in 1963.

Tandy Leather Company was about to lose its position as the corporate "cash cow" to the upstart from Boston.

Chapter 13

A Champagne Toast at the First of Boston

The trips between Fort Worth and Boston were coming fast and furious. If there had been a frequent flier program in operation in the 1960s, Charles Tandy would have enough bonus points for a first class round trip ticket to Mars.

"Charles was spending ten days in Boston and four days in Fort Worth," Luther Henderson recalled. "By doing this, he had hands-on control of operations of Radio Shack and kept Fort Worth under control, too. None of us on the board ever visualized at that time what size company Radio Shack would ultimately become. But we finally did recognize that it could become, by far, the biggest part of the business.

"If Charles had told us that it was going to be 500 stores one day, we'd have considered that a pretty fair goal for us. Later, when he talked about 1,000 stores, a lot of people thought he was really dreaming." A few of his contemporaries made jokes about what they considered his overly optimistic goals. Henderson described an incident that took place after his purchase of Pier 1 from Tandy.

"We'd gotten in some specimen wooden carvings from the South Pacific. One of them was a life-size figure of a fierce-looking native warrior, probably a Maori, with a very aggressive snarl on his face. We had the idea of giving this to Charles, and we took it up to his office one day while he was gone, and we put a placard on it that read, 'Who says we can't get to $500 million in sales?' Charles just loved it and left it in his office for many months thereafter. It really epitomized his attitude at a time when the company was still at less than $100 million in sales. At that time, $500 million seemed like a very ambitious goal."

Tandy was a very demanding boss, who worked long hours and expected others to do the same, Henderson said. "I never got pushed as hard as most people, maybe because Charles regarded me as a personal friend and as an equal. But he could be brutal to others at times."

"He could be brutal, all right," Bill Michero conceded, "but he tempered his degree of brutality depending upon the individual being brutalized. There are some delicate souls in this world who will wilt at the first harsh word. Then there are others that you need to use a baseball bat to discuss things with. So I'd have to say that Charles had a dial setting for everybody. His technique was to brutalize in public and to pet in private. The point is that he wanted to let you know that you were noticed and loved. What is worse than being ignored?"

Tandy's modus operandi was negative motivation, at which he was a master, Michero said. "So, periodically, he would seek you out and find fault with something you were doing. It didn't matter what. Whatever you did could stand some improvement, and he was the one to provide that improvement, give it that final touch that made it fly. He was the kind of guy who, when he walked into the Louvre in Paris and saw the Mona Lisa for the first time, said, 'There should be a little more orange right through there.'"

Bernie Appel acknowledged that Tandy could be brutal at times, but that underneath his abrasive exterior lay the heart of a pussycat. Appel cited the story of Charlie Levine, a Radio Shack buyer, as an example.

"Charlie Levine was a buyer when I was hired at Radio Shack in 1959. He was a magnificent electronic parts buyer, but he was a very sensitive individual. He had a very sensitive stomach. One day, in a conversation with his wife, she told me that 'Charlie gets very sick whenever Charles Tandy comes to town.' When he knew that Tandy was going to be in Boston on Monday morning, he would get an upset stomach and the dry heaves on Sunday. He couldn't stand the pressure of Charles' way of doing things.

"So one day, I went to Tandy and I said, 'Charles, maybe we ought to fire Charlie Levine.' I said it very facetiously. I really didn't want Charlie Levine fired, of course. 'But,' I told Tandy, 'the problem is he can't stand the way you pick on him. You're killing him. And, yet, he's good. He's gross margin conscious and he's numbers conscious. What can we do about it?'

"Charles looked at me and said, 'I guess I can't pick on Charlie, can I?'

"I said, 'Not in the way you do it.' Remember, this was back in the early '60s, right after he bought us, and he didn't know me from Adam. And he said to me, 'Okay, Bernie, can I pick on you? Do you get sick?'

"I looked him square in the eye and said, 'Charles, you can pick on me all you want, but just keep one thing in the back of your mind. You're gonna get it back from me if I don't agree with you. I'm not gonna sit back and let you yell at me if I disagree with you.'

"He said, 'Okay, we'll see about that.'

"From that day on, in our regular merchandise meetings with all of the buyers sitting there, he never once picked on Charlie Levine again. If Charlie did something wrong, if he packaged two parts in a package when Charles thought it should have been four, if Charlie did anything Charles didn't like, Charles would chew my butt out as if I had done it. Now, Charlie Levine knew he had done it and he knew that he would correct it. But he never got his feelings hurt after that. And this was symbolic of Charles Tandy's management style. As a result of this, Charlie Levine stayed with the company and made major contributions to its growth in electronic parts and accessories. He retired in 1989. But to this day, Charlie Levine has a sensitive stomach."

There was a side to Charles Tandy that few of his associates ever saw, Luther Henderson pointed out.

"He also knew how to stop and relax and enjoy himself for a day or two during periods of greatest adversity. He used to say, 'I can make the greatest playboy in the world for a week at a time, but that's all.' He'd get tired of it. He never took any extended vacations and probably never would if he were still alive today."

Taking a vacation, however, was the farthest thing from Tandy's mind as the calendar year 1965 drew to an end.

The repercussions from his lowered earnings estimate had been felt on Wall Street. Shearson, Hammill, which had been carrying Tandy stock as a "Buy," issued a bulletin on its research wire changing the designation to "Hold," in anticipation of continued "lower-than-expected earnings." Charles' gung-ho Radio Shack store-opening program, which had added 19 stores in July and August alone, was taking its toll on the bottom line. Bowing to pressure from Jim West and other board members, Tandy announced that the "current expansion program would be completed after six more stores were opened by the end of the year."

Radio Shack was now operating stores in 20 states from New England to the Pacific Coast. The state-by-state breakdown was Texas, 16 stores; California, 15; Massachusetts, 13; Connecticut, six; New York, five; Oklahoma, Pennsylvania, Rhode Island and Washington, two each; and Arizona, Colorado, Illinois, Maine, Minnesota, Missouri, New Hampshire, New Mexico, Ohio, Oregon and Virginia, one each.

In addition, the Mail Order Division was serving over 300,000 catalog customers across the country, and the Industrial Division had more than 10,000 industrial and institutional accounts.

A Standard & Poor's report on Radio Shack published on December 22, 1965, noted: "The company engineers, designs and subcontracts the manufacture of its own brand products under the following trade names: Realistic—major components and minor items of audio equipment, including speakers, tuners, amplifiers, receivers, transceivers and tape; Archer—similar products but of a lower price; Micronta—items in photography, optics and test instruments; Radio Shack and Skillman.

"A&A Trading, 50 percent-owned, acts as buying agent for the company in Japan," the report added.

The 50 percent ownership in A&A Trading Corporation had been acquired by Tandy as part of the Radio Shack deal. A&A had been founded on June 6, 1955, by Tadashi (Tad) Yamagata and Milton Deutschmann, each of whom had put up half of the firm's original $20,000 capitalization. Deutschmann had later transferred his 50 percent ownership to Radio Shack.

Yamagata, a native of Honshu, Japan, had come to the United States in 1951 with his American-born wife, Elaine, whose parents were native Japanese. Born in Willow Grove, California, near Sacramento, Elaine was 16 when her father, a physician, decided to return to his homeland in 1938 to practice medicine. When war came with the bombing of Pearl Harbor, Elaine's father was drafted into the Japanese Imperial Navy and was stationed in a naval hospital. Elaine spent the war years in Japan and graduated from Kobe University.

Yamagata, whose father was a Methodist minister, had graduated from Honshu University in the mid-1930s and then had joined the Nissho Company, one of the largest foreign trade companies in Japan. In 1938, he was called to active duty in the Japanese Army and was sent to officer's training school. After receiving his commission a year later, he was assigned to a Transportation Corps regiment then occupying North China and Inner Mongolia. He was discharged from the Army in 1942.

"I was not a professional soldier," he said tersely.

Yamagata then returned to Japan, married Elaine, and headed back to China, where he entered the metal trading business in Beijing. He remained in China until after the end of World War II.

Elaine and Tad had met in Hiroshima before the war. They were introduced by his sister.

"I was quite close to Tad's sister while I lived in Sacramento," Elaine explained. "She was married to the minister of the Methodist Church I attended there, but she returned to Japan after the death of her husband. She was teaching in Hiroshima University and I lived quite close to her. By renewing my friendship with her, I got to know Tad."

After the war, Yamagata became a partner in the Greenfield-Kato Trading Company in Tokyo. Then, in 1951, he moved to New York to represent the firm in the United States. Elaine became active in the business at that juncture because of her fluency in English. The firm initially shipped coal and steel to Japan and imported sundries and binoculars, telescopes and microscopes from Japan. But the Yamagatas found the steel and coal business too unstable, subject to too much fluctuation, and decided to concentrate on general merchandise.

"We started to bring in bicycles from Japan," Elaine recalled, "but the quality was dreadful. We had to repair every one of them. After we sold them, we still had a lot come back. So we filed a claim to Kato-Greenfield in Japan, but they wouldn't honor the claim. So we decided if they wouldn't honor the claim, there was no use continuing the business. So we liquidated it."

One of the Yamagatas' clients, Radio Shack, was importing optical equipment from Japan. Tad and Elaine established a fairly close relationship with Milton Deutschmann, who informed them that he would support them if they went into business for themselves.

"Since they were primarily in the electronics business, they said, 'Why don't you go into the electronics business, too?' Elaine recounted. "So in 1955, we started A&A."

The name had two significances, she explained, "standing simply for America and Asia." But for the Yamagatas, it had a special meaning that only people whose last name begins with a Y can fully appreciate. Elaine explained: "Tad's name starts with a 'Y' and my maiden name was Yamao, so we were always at the end of the line in everything. That's why we chose A&A, so that we could finally be at the very top of the alphabet."

A&A Trading Corporation started out primarily as an import business that dealt mostly in opticals. "We were wholesalers," Mrs. Yamagata said. "We imported the goods at our cost and then sold them to our retail customers. We sold opticals to Radio Shack and to department stores like Macy's and Gimbel's and the May Company."

Their banker at the time was the Bank of Tokyo which had a branch in New York. "The bank was very good to us and helped us finance our imports," Elaine reported. "We continued to import opticals, but we gradually got more and more into electronics. The electronics in the beginning were of very poor quality. We had a lot of problems, but gradually the quality improved."

Tad Yamagata recalled "the unbelievably poor quality" of Japanese products in the 1950s. "It was cheap to buy, but of very bad quality. I had to check all of the merchandise. I even had inspectors in Japan to inspect merchandise before it left Japan. But, at that time, the conditions of transportation were very poor and the merchandise had to go by boat for a very long time through the Panama Canal. We had problems with fungus. I inspected all merchandise when it arrived in New York, so my customers were always satisfied. Radio Shack always wondered why the merchandise I provided was so good, while the merchandise supplied by other importers was so bad. So Radio Shack preferred to do business with me."

One day in 1955, Yamagata received a telephone from Milton Deutschmann's brother, Arnold, who was then a Radio Shack executive. "We're going to Japan," Deutschmann informed him. "We want you go with us."

"And what are you going to do in Japan?"

"We're going to buy electronic goods."

"I'm not qualified to buy electronic goods," Yamagata demurred. "I don't know anything about electronics."

"That's okay," Deutschmann assured him. "We like the way you do business. We can teach you about electronic merchandise."

The conversation resulted in Yamagata's first trip back to his homeland since his arrival in the United States four years before. It was also the first trip to the Orient for Lewis Kornfeld, who accompanied Arnold Deutschmann and Yamagata.

"Lew was a good merchandiser," Yamagata found.

Among the first things the group bought in Japan were speakers and speaker systems that were considerably cheaper than those available in the United States or anywhere else in the world.

"Americans were already importing electronics components from Japan by then," Yamagata observed. "The Deutschmanns knew Japanese components could be used in this country and could be bought at a reasonable price, so they could make a bigger profit on them than handling American-made products. That's how I got into the consumer electronics field. I was very lucky."

When A&A began, it had little business other than Radio Shack, and Yamagata had serious doubts about its viability. "I wasn't sure we could be successful," he admitted. "But Milton Deutschmann promised that Radio Shack would support us." By 1963, A&A's business had grown to a point where Radio Shack was providing only 25 percent of its volume. It was at this point that Charles Tandy entered the picture. Elaine Yamagata recalled her initial meeting with Tandy.

"It was on April 1, 1963, when he suddenly appeared. That was the day when the Radio Shack buyers first met Charles Tandy, and I happened to be in Boston. Our headquarters then were still in New York. My first impression of him was that he was a very dynamic person. Radio Shack had only nine stores and was buying in very small quantities. They weren't too financially stable at that time. Some of the things we had bought and had planned for Radio Shack to buy hadn't been bought. So business was pretty slow.

"And Charles came in. One thing I can remember very well is we had a little walkie-talkie that was selling very well. And he said to get him a quote for 50,000 walkie-talkies. We were really stunned, because 50,000 was not a figure within our common sense at that time. Sure enough, we bought 50,000. We got a reduction in price. A lot of other people were also bringing in walkie-talkies, so it wasn't a hot item by the time our big shipment arrived. But Charles just made the people sell them. That's when the dynamic differences started to happen."

Elaine recalled how she began taking the Eastern Airlines shuttle between New York and Boston more frequently after Tandy's arrival on the scene. "I used to carry a little card that gave the quantities of the merchandise that we were bringing in for Radio Shack, and he would go through the numbers. He would always remember the numbers, and sometimes he would question the buys."

One time, discussing his plans for Radio Shack, Tandy told Elaine he was going to have 400 stores some day.

"I thought to myself," she laughed, 'My goodness, what a Texas brag.'"

Mrs. Yamagata remained grateful to Tandy for staying with A&A

even though the size of the firm was a limiting factor at the outset. But Tandy employed it as the vehicle to achieve one of his major objectives of buying all of his merchandise in Japan.

"He knew that we were small and that there were bigger importing firms in New York," she said. "But he knew he was going to get big, and even though we were still weak, he was going to push A&A and put all of his strength behind us so that we would get stronger, too. We had good contacts in Japan, but when we're buying 500 units and somebody else is buying 10,000, there's a difference. It took a while. For the first year he observed us very closely, really kept tabs on us, and decided to stick with us. After all, he already owned half of us."

Shortly after Tandy's assumption of control over Radio Shack, A&A installed a quality control program under which all Japanese merchandise was inspected before shipment to the States.

"Radio Shack then inspected it when it arrived in the States," Tad Yamagata reported. "If there was anything wrong with it, A&A would repair it on the site so that it wouldn't have to be shipped back to Japan. We couldn't afford the expense of shipping it back, since A&A was so small. So we required any manufacturer who shipped more than $3 million worth of merchandise to stand behind it. If something was wrong, they repaired it. I convinced them it would be smart for them to have their own people on the scene in New York so that they could see for themselves what was wrong. If there was a major problem, they would always have their own people on hand. We agreed to pay for the apartment rental of the Japanese representatives, so they could have a person on the scene. This was a very innovative thing that A&A put in to combat the quality problems."

With the Japanese electronics industry still in its embryonic stage, there were numerous quality problems at the time. Elaine Yamagata recalled an incident when Tandy dropped in unexpectedly at the warehouse in New York and found a large amount of defective merchandise under repair or waiting to be fixed.

"There were lots of CB radios, maybe 100, lined up on the tables and a lot of tape recorders lined up being repaired," she recounted, "and Charles came down to the basement where the work was being done and he said, 'What's going on? Why are these $100 pieces lying on the table?' He was very upset. So the people tried to fix them and get them out as quickly as possible."

Tandy always asked Tad Yamagata to visit the Radio Shack warehouse when he came to Boston. "One day," Yamagata recalled, "he said to me, 'Tad, have you been to the warehouse today?'" Yamagata told him he was planning to do that later.

"No," Tandy said, "I want you to do it now."

"Mr. Tandy, this is not my prime business. My first business is to get the merchandise from offshore," Yamagata replied.

"No," Tandy insisted, "I want you to see the warehouse first."

"But you have a warehouse manager, you have merchandise people. Why don't you ask them?"

"Because I want you to see what's going on."

Now Yamagata understood.

"He wanted me to find out the things that were wrong. I found piles of batteries. Warehouse people always picked the batteries from the top of the pile where they were easier to get to. So all of the old batteries remained at the bottom until their life was gone. I told Charles they had to change the way they picked the batteries or the way of stocking them. We date-coded the batteries, so we could tell when the new ones were being picked for shipment and the old ones were just lying there and going dead."

"Every time Charles went to the warehouse," Elaine said, "he always found something to chew people out about."

He also was a master at putting pressure on the Yamagatas and the Radio Shack buyers to get the lowest possible prices from the manufacturers.

"For example," she related, "Charles got a quotation from a large battery manufacturer in Japan on a quantity of batteries. And he told us, 'You've got to get a better quote than that,' which, fortunately, we were able to do. Radio Shack was not importing batteries at that time, but we did get a very good quote and batteries became and remained a very strong item."

The "battery story" made the rounds at Radio Shack. Bernie Appel remembered the story from the standpoint of the Radio Shack buyers back in Boston.

"In 1965," he recalled, "Charles went over to Japan and met in a hotel room in Tokyo with the president of a company named Novel. They offered him batteries with our name on them, and he made a deal. He got some really high gross margins. When he came back to the United

States, he got all of the buyers together and said to us,'Okay, you guys, I made the first private label deal. You go make the rest of them.' He got the batteries for pennies. It was nickel and dime stuff. But this was his first whack at it. After that, he continually reminded us, 'See how easy it is to buy private label.'"

Mrs. Yamagata's lasting memory of Charles Tandy is of a dynamic man who was also very warm.

"He was very demanding. He was very forceful. He was very inspiring, very smart, very good at figures. He was very nice to us. Sure, he would sometimes tear us apart, but he always put us together and we always left very encouraged. He was a great teacher. He would ask you a question out of the blue, and you wouldn't know the answer. But that's how you learned. He was very good at that. But they were always important questions. He was always pushing and getting others to push us. Even if we were not responsible, he made us feel responsible."

Tad Yamagata added, "He tried to understand the Japanese way of thinking instead of forcing his ideas on people. He listened very well. He understood very well."

In 1968, Tandy Corporation acquired 100 percent ownership of A&A Trading Corporation and the Yamagatas became Tandy employees. Tad held the title of president of A&A Trading Corporation, with Elaine as executive vice president. In 1973, the name of the wholly-owned subsidiary was changed to A&A International. When Tad retired in 1981, Elaine succeeded him. She served as president of A&A International until her retirement in August 1988. The Yamagatas have two sons who work for Tandy Corporation in Fort Worth. Mark Yamagata is a vice president of Tandy Electronics and Harvey Yamagata is director of Tandy Service Plans. Both were born in China while their parents were living there during World War II.

Tad Yamagata retained a fond memory of how Tandy, on occasion, utilized his sense of humor to drive home a point. He gave as an illustration an incident that occurred after Tandy assumed control of Radio Shack.

"Charles acquired Radio Shack in April of 1963, and at the end of the year, in December, I was in Japan. I came back to New York just before Christmas. Mr. and Mrs. Tandy went to Japan for New Year's Eve. He didn't tell me about it in advance, but when he got there he called the

Bank of Tokyo and expected the bank to take him around to see all of the manufacturers who were selling merchandise to Radio Shack. And he expected to visit the A&A office in Tokyo. But most of the companies in Japan close down for the new year between December 28 and January 3, except the banks. They have to collect the money. When Charles came back to the United States, he joked with me.

"He said, 'A&A don't work. The banks in the States are noted for having a lot of holidays. But even the banks were working in Tokyo, but not A&A.'

"He never let us forget that."

The Bank of Tokyo's New York branch figured in a problem that presented itself shortly after Tandy assumed control of Radio Shack. Bill Brown, the Boston banker, relished recalling the incident.

"I got a call from Charles early one morning before I got to the bank," Brown recounted. "When I got in, I was told that Mr. Tandy is eager to talk to you. I called him up."

"Hey, buddy, old partner," Tandy said. "We've got troubles."

Brown said, "You may have troubles, but I don't have any troubles."

"Yes, you do," Tandy persisted, "with the Bank of Tokyo. You didn't renew your letter of credit with Radio Shack and the bank is raising holy hell."

Brown's response was, "I can't help that."

Radio Shack, Brown explained, had been buying merchandise in Japan against letters of credit from the First National Bank of Boston to the Bank of Tokyo. But when Radio Shack had gotten into financial difficulty, the bank had stopped renewing the credit letters. The Japanese suppliers, however, not realizing what had occurred, had continued their merchandise shipments.

"They kept on shipping and shipping and shipping," Brown reported. "So now the Bank of Tokyo had a lot of money tied up in Radio Shack. They had a couple of million in it. I said to Charles, 'We're not bailing them out.'"

Tandy asked Brown if he'd meet him in New York to talk with the Bank of Tokyo representatives, to which Brown agreed. The next day, Tandy and Brown met with the manager of the Bank of Tokyo's New York branch in his office.

"The manager had an interpreter," Brown recalled. "He said he couldn't understand English. Every time I explained to him that we weren't going to issue any letters of credit, that he was unsecured and that he was going to have to fend for himself, he'd tell us through the interpreter that he didn't understand. He kept turning to the interpreter and saying that he didn't understand. Finally, the interpreter told us, 'He isn't going to cooperate. He insists on your letter of credit.'"

At this point, Brown said, "I pulled a Charles Tandy. I stood up and headed for the door. I was halfway out the door when the branch manager grabbed me by each shoulder and pulled me back into his office. 'Where are you going?' he asked. Now he suddenly could speak English.

"I'm going back to Boston," Brown said.

"No, no, no. We will work out something."

Brown modified his position. "The only thing I'll do," he declared, "is I'll permit, if the sales and receipts are adequate over a period of 18 months or so, to pay your backlog, provided you'll continue to ship merchandise to Radio Shack."

The deal Brown made with the Bank of Tokyo was that the bank would receive monthly payments from Radio Shack greater than the cost of the merchandise shipped from Japan.

"Charles said he could live with that," Brown emphasized. "What this meant was that over a period of 12 to 18 months, the backlog would get paid. And since the bank had no other choice, they agreed to it.

"Charles was my kind of guy," Bill Brown remembered fondly. "He'd get right to the point on whatever it was. He didn't beat around the bush. He was bright, he was smart, he knew what was going on, and he knew how to make money. But he could also turn to one of his executives like Charlie Tindall, when Charlie was a senior vice president and chief financial officer, and say, 'Charlie, you dumb shit.' I got used to it after a while, but on the surface it was, 'You dumb this and you dumb that.'"

Brown recalled the time Tandy tried to hire him away from the bank. "He wanted me to come in with him. He offered me all kinds of options to become president of the company. Nobody in the company ever knew this. I said, 'No, but I certainly appreciate your offer.'

"He said, 'Why not?'

"And I said, 'Charlie, this bank has been good to you and you've been good for the bank. You and I enjoy doing business together.'

"And he said, 'That's right.'

"Then I said, 'You know, if I were to work for you, the first time you called me a dumb shit I'd be gone and my options wouldn't be worth anything.'"

Some years later, after the Tandy stock had escalated sharply, had been split and had kept on rising, Charles walked into Brown's office, a big grin on his face.

"Well, you dumb shit," he exclaimed, "if you'd accepted my offer you'd be a damn sight richer than you are today."

"No, Charlie," Brown replied, "I wouldn't still be with you."

Just about noontime on April Fool's Day in 1978, Brown was sitting in his office talking on the phone. He had a luncheon engagement with a bank customer on his schedule and was already running late. Just as he hung up the phone, his secretary walked in and announced that Charles Tandy was in the reception area waiting to see him.

"But I don't have an appointment with him," Brown complained.

"I know that, but he insists on seeing you."

"Fine, send him in."

Tandy strode into Brown's office.

"Do you know what day this is?" he demanded.

"No, should I?"

"It's the anniversary of my buying Radio Shack," Tandy announced.

"Now, Charles reached into his coat pocket and pulled out a bottle of Dom Perignon. Then he reached back into his pocket again and brought out two champagne glasses courtesy of the Ritz-Carlton Hotel. I went to the door of my office and told my secretary to call one of my associates at the bank and tell him to take 'Mr. So-And-So' to lunch, that I was unavoidably detained. By now, Charlie had the bottle opened.

"I said, 'Charlie, I don't drink during the day and I never drink in my office.' And he answered, 'Well, you are today.' So he poured the champagne and the two of us had a drink. Of course, he now offered me a cigar. He used to smoke those cheap cigars. They'd just kill you. And I love to smoke a cigar, but I'd always turn down one of his when he offered me one. I'd say, 'No, thank you, I won't smoke one of those. If you want me to smoke with you, give me a decent cigar.'

"Now Charlie reached into his pocket and he pulled out four or five $2 or $3 cigars and put them on my desk, and he took out one of his darn White Owls, or whatever it was he smoked, and we had a smoke together."

There was a moment's pause and then Brown said, "God, he was fun to do business with."

Chapter 14
"I Wish My Father Was Here Today"

In early February of 1966, Charles Tandy picked up the telephone late one afternoon and dialed the number of his old friend and erstwhile business partner, Phil North. He asked North to join him for a drink at Green Oaks Inn, a splashy new hostelry on Fort Worth's West Side in which North was an investor.

Tandy respected North's business acumen and liked to talk to him about his business. The two met often, usually at Tandy's apartment, where Charles bounced ideas off North. North had built a sizable estate from a series of astute investments after receiving several million dollars from the sale of his stock in Carter Publications, Inc., the owner of the *Fort Worth Star-Telegram*. He had inherited the stock after the death of his father, James M. North, Jr., the newspaper's long-time and highly-respected editor. Although Phil had been groomed to succeed his father as editor of the newspaper, he had left the organization after a falling out with the majority owners and the top management.

Tandy's reason for asking North to meet him at the Green Oaks bar was to offer him a job. "He talked about Radio Shack and told me he really thought he could do something with it," North recalled. "He said that he wanted somebody with him that he could depend on, and that since we'd always worked well together, would I come with him? I told him I wouldn't come with him if he was the last S.O.B. in the world. And Charles said, 'I wouldn't work for you, either. What would you be willing to do?'"

North thought for a moment, then said, "I'll buy Tandy stock and go on your board and work with you in an advisory way provided we agree that neither one of us will sell a share of stock until the price reaches 60 or Tandy Corporation has half a billion dollars in assets or a billion dollars in sales."

Tandy said, "It's a deal."

The two clinked glasses and ordered another round.

At that point, North recalled, Tandy said, "We've got to start paying you something. How am I going to pay you?"

North answered, "At the end of each year, give me an envelope with a check in it."

"But how am I going to know how much the check is for?"

North's answer was, "If it's for the right amount, I'll be back the next day. If it's not, I won't."

Another clinking of upraised glasses solidified the pact, and North joined the Tandy payroll as a consultant "on sort of a daily basis."

North joined the Tandy board on February 19, 1966. Also elected to the board at the same time was Bob Lowdon, the former printing sales-man and Dave Tandy's hunting and fishing companion, who was now president of the Stafford-Lowdon Company.

"The enlargement and diversification of our board steps up the breadth of business experience available to direct the widening activi-ties of the company and we are very pleased to have the leadership of Mr. Lowdon and Mr. North as our company reaches the $50 million mark in annual sales," Tandy said in the news release announcing the new directors.

In the same release, Tandy announced the authorization of 20 new Radio Shack stores and noted that by June 30, 1966, there would be close to 250 Tandy Corporation stores in operation in 125 cities in the United States and Canada, with 150 stores in the Tandy Leather Com-pany craft supply division and 100 stores in the Radio Shack division. "Current projections show that we will have accomplished our objec-tive of increasing both sales and earnings per share over 300 percent in just five years," Tandy added. "This rate of growth continues to be a primary objective of the company."

Shortly after his deal with Tandy had been cemented, North was hav-ing dinner at home when the phone rang. Tandy was on the line.

"I've got a problem," he said.

"What's the problem?"

"The accounting department says that since you come into the office every day, they have to pay Social Security for you. And in order to pay Social Security, they have to deduct it from a salary. So they have to pay you a salary so they can deduct the Social Security."

Tandy paused to let that sink in, then added, "Is it okay if we start you at _____?" He named a figure and hung up. Five minutes later,

North's phone rang again. It was Tandy again. "Is that figure I told you okay?" "I guess so," North responded. North laughed at the recollection. "That was the last time Charles and I ever had a discussion about money."

In North's opinion, one of Tandy's major strengths as a manager was his ability to "play off" people.

"He'd say something outrageous to see if you would react. He wanted you to defend your position or contrary view. He'd play the devil's advocate. He'd think things out loud with you that way, and sometimes he'd reach a consensus that way. He wanted to hear your opinion if you disagreed with him. He enjoyed animated conversation. It might have sounded to others that we were getting ready to have a fist fight, but he wanted people to speak up."

Another of Tandy's strengths was the fact that he knew when to let loose, North said. "He had many people who knew a lot more about their individual jobs than he ever could, and he let them run that part of their job. He didn't try to run everything. He knew that he didn't know everything. Most of all, he knew how to stimulate people to excel, either by persuasion or by kicking them a little bit or praising them, but mostly by just training them. If anybody didn't do their job, he took the blame. He'd say, 'It's my fault for putting that man in the wrong slot or for not training him properly.'"

One of Tandy's favorite expressions during the period he was building Radio Shack was, "If you own all the filling stations, it doesn't matter who owns the refineries," North recalled.

"What he meant by that," North explained, "was that if you own the retail stores, you can buy from the best manufacturers in the world and have your pick of them. And since you have such huge volume, the manufacturers will come to you to show you their best and their newest products. And you'll get them first because you're the biggest. In addition, when you have such big buying power, and it's really a good item, you can tell the manufacturer, 'I'll take six months of your production. You have no credit problem with me, you have no sales expense with me for six whole months. Your line is going to run smooth as silk turning out goods 24 hours a day.' He's going to give you a very low price to get that line going for six months without having to stop it and 're-honk' the mold."

Tandy repeatedly emphasized, North went on, that "When you've got stores everywhere, you can say to people, 'If you buy an item in New York and go to California and it breaks, you can bring it back to any one of our stores and we'll replace it. You don't have to have a sales slip that you always lose just before something breaks or a warranty that always expires the day before it breaks. If it's got Radio Shack on it, we make it good.' You get an awful lot of good will that way."

In the spring of 1966, however, Radio Shack was still a long way from achieving that national presence. There were still a lot of people around the country who had never seen the inside of a Radio Shack store. One of those was John McDaniel, a retired Marine living in Jacksonville, Florida. McDaniel had never even heard of Tandy Corporation or Radio Shack when he talked to a friend in Fort Worth about employment opportunities in the Dallas-Fort Worth area.

"Why don't you talk to the people at Tandy?" the friend suggested.

"I thought he said, 'Candy,'" McDaniel recalled. "I asked him, 'Who's Candy?'"

The friend said, "Not Candy, Tandy."

And McDaniel asked, "Who's Tandy?"

Recalling the incident, McDaniel said, "They didn't have a Radio Shack store where I lived in Florida. But when my friend asked me if I knew of Tandy Leather, I did, because there was a Tandy Leather store there. And he said, 'Well, that's the company I'm talking about. They own Radio Shack, too.'"

McDaniel was looking for a job in the Fort Worth area because his wife's father, who lived there, had suffered a disabling stroke. "We had planned to spend the rest of our days in Jacksonville," McDaniel said, "but Gail's father's stroke dictated we should come to Fort Worth. I interviewed for two jobs when I made the decision to move. One of them was with Collins Radio in Dallas and the other was with Tandy Corporation. I took the Tandy job simply because it was in Fort Worth."

Toward the end of his Marine career, McDaniel had begun studying accounting at night so that, as he put it, "when I did retire, I could do something other than shoot a rifle." He had found employment as an accountant in Jacksonville after returning to civilian life in 1964. But the job for which he interviewed at Tandy was as a check-signer. "A check-signer," McDaniel explained, "is just what the word says. You signed all the checks that went out. Tandy Corporation was smaller then, not very automated, and we signed all the checks manually. Charles liked to have someone that he could depend on to get that final look at the checks before they went out."

McDaniel was interviewed by Charles Tindall, then a vice president and treasurer, who offered McDaniel the job. "We made the deal,"

McDaniel said, "even though Tindall hadn't talked to Charles about it at the time."

The McDaniels arrived in Fort Worth with their wordly possessions on a Saturday in early May. On the following Monday morning, he reported for work. "I worked on Monday and Tuesday," McDaniel related. "This was when the offices were on West 7th Street. Charles had been out of town, and he interviewed me on Wednesday morning after he got back." The interview began at 9 o'clock in the morning in Tandy's office, with Tindall and Jim West also present, and lasted until well into the evening.

Finally, at about 9 o'clock, Tandy turned to Jim West and asked, "Well, what do you think of this guy, Jim?" West said, "I believe I like him."

"I do, too," Tandy said. "Let's hire him."

Tindall, who had been taking all of this in with more than passing interest, now declared with a sigh of relief, "God, I'm glad. He's been working for us for two days."

After working as a check signer for about eight months, McDaniel was moved into the Accounting Department. "We had three accountants at the time in the Radio Shack Division," he recalled. "I was the third. I was an accounting assistant working under the controller. Later on, we split our accounting functions into units and Charles gave me one and he gave someone else one."

McDaniel would go on to become controller of Radio Shack before being named senior vice president and controller of Tandy Corporation, a position he held until his retirement in January of 1989.

Some of McDaniel's early memories of Charles Tandy go back to early 1967 when Radio Shack had about 130 stores on which he was doing the profit and loss statements.

"I found out something about Charles' vision early on," he recounted. "We had started in Boston with just a few stores and we had expanded in Texas and did very well in those stores in Texas and surrounding states. Then we moved on out to the West Coast with stores. When I did those profit and loss statements, I'd add up the profits we'd made in the east and the profits we'd made in Texas and surrounding states. Then I'd get down to the West Coast and lots of those profits evaporated because we had such big losses out there."

McDaniel remembered Charles coming into his office one morning while he was manually doing the P&Ls.

"Well, how are we doing?"

"We were doing all right when I was doing the East Coast and Texas, but now I'm out to Los Angeles and we're losing it all."

Tandy placed a hand on McDaniel's shoulder and said, "You know, I knew we were gonna do that, and we'll keep on doing it for a while. But once we get 50 stores around Los Angeles, then we're gonna start making some profits because we can cover advertising."

McDaniel was frank to admit that from what the profit and loss statements told him, he thought Tandy was out of his mind at the time. "But that was Charles' vision," he said. "He knew where we were going. However, even with his great vision, I don't believe he ever thought he'd wind up with as many stores as he did. But he knew better than most of us how many stores he was going to have. There's no question about that."

McDaniel recalled an incident that occurred a few years later when Radio Shack had about 500 stores and Tandy was pushing Bill Nugent, the senior manager in store operations, to open more and more stores.

"Nugent told him that we had all the stores that we could digest and that the country was saturated."

Tandy looked Nugent in the eye and said, "I've drug you almost to the top of the hill. Can't you take that last step by yourself?"

Another time Tandy told Nugent, after another argument over the store-opening program, "You know, you've fought success so hard, you've almost won."

McDaniel's favorite put down, however, was the needle Tandy inserted into Jim Buxton when Buxton was a regional manager in California. "He had been running very poor sales reports in his region," McDaniel related. "One month his sales were much better and he was bragging to Charles about how well he was doing. Charles was merciless. He said, 'It's hard to fall out of bed when you've been sleeping on the floor.'"

McDaniel's overriding memory of Tandy was that of a man in a hurry. "He was in a hurry to get it done and he understood his priorities."

Shortly after the conversation in which Tandy had assured him they would start making money in Los Angeles after they had 50 stores in the area, Tandy went to Southern California and personally handled the purchase of a small chain of six electronics stores.

"We guys who put the numbers together and handled the assets thought he overpaid for what he got. And he probably knew he overpaid," McDaniel said. "But he was in a hurry. He wasn't buying assets, he was buying location. He didn't quibble much on the purchase. He gave them their price. But what he really wanted was their locations. And, you know, we got rid of their merchandise in a month and put in our merchandise. So we got there a lot quicker his way."

He recalled when a decision was made to go into Memphis, Tennessee, a man named Bennett Hunter was made a district manager and given the chore of opening up the area. "Bennett looked for locations there and kept putting things off and putting things off," McDaniel said. "By most people's measurement, it would not have been inordinately long. But to Charles, he was dragging his feet. So Charles went over to Memphis and in two days came back with five locations. We opened the stores up and that's how we got into Memphis. Charles went there and did it himself."

A new Radio Shack store in that era of the late 1960s opened with $25,000 to $28,000 in inventory, McDaniel reported. The fixed assets ran another $22,000 to $25,000. "But for everything we put into the store in the way of inventory, we had to have backup in the warehouse in about an equal amount. So opening a store in those days cost us about $75,000 to $80,000."

Tandy's policy was to lease real estate rather than buy it. "I don't guess he would ever have bought any real estate if he hadn't been talked into it," McDaniel said. "He felt about buying real estate the way he was about you buying a home. His attitude was, 'Don't buy it, rent it and buy Tandy stock with the money.' He kidded Bill Nugent after Nugent once bought a boat. He used to remind him how much the boat had really cost him in light of the appreciation in Tandy stock. What Charles apparently never understood was that Bill might have enjoyed that boat more than having the stock."

Tandy had a similar attitude about leasing rather than owning warehouses.

"I didn't fault his theory about leasing space," McDaniel said. "But over the long haul, if you have deep pockets, it would be a mistake to go the leasing route. But if you don't have deep pockets, and you want to put your money into opening stores, as was the case with Radio Shack, it was better to lease than to buy real estate. It's true, a person could look back and say, 'Ten years ago we could have bought that for so-and-so.' But we didn't have the money to buy it then. It may have looked like we made some bad calls by not buying that stuff, but the truth is if we'd bought it we couldn't have opened as many stores as we opened. So I think Charles' approach was correct for the time. I think he used his assets wisely."

Charles Tandy's understanding of numbers never ceased to amaze McDaniel. "He understood gross profits and how important they were and how he could increase margins by going private label as opposed to name brand," McDaniel said. "He had great vision in knowing what the cash needs of the company were going to be, and while things might have gotten tight at times, never in all of the times that I was helping with our finances was there a need for us to say to our people paying the bills, 'Hold up these for 48 hours until we get the money.' We never held up any payables or any payrolls one minute, and I think that's one of the reasons we had such good relations with so many vendors. They knew we were good pay. We never put them off. Sure, there were times we had to hustle around to get the money, but Charles saw that as his job and not the accountant's job. And he always had the money there."

McDaniel spoke of companies that made it a practice to pay their vendors and other suppliers as slowly as possible. This was called "riding." Tandy never did that. "As soon as an invoice came in, Charles liked to pay it," he noted. "In the early days, he didn't even want us to hold it until two days before it was due, because he thought we might be one day late if we did that. So we paid them as they came in. Later on, when Charles wasn't watching us that closely, we started riding them as long as we could, but that was just good business. The money was always there."

Tandy wasn't much of a stickler for rules, anyway, McDaniel said. "We operated sans rules most of the time. Charles didn't care about writing memos. He liked to communicate, but he preferred to do it by word of mouth and not by the written message." Tandy would sometimes say to him, "Well, they wouldn't do it this way in the Marine Corps, would they?" And McDaniel would respond, "I'll bet they didn't do it that way in the Navy, either."

McDaniel told of the time Tandy decided he was going to reorganize the company after an analyst had written that the organization chart resembled a bowl of spaghetti.

"In lots of respects, it was like that," McDaniel admitted, "because we didn't even have formal charts of organization. Charles just didn't really believe in that kind of thing. He never got around to it. It just wasn't his management style. He'd much rather just sit there and run the whole company. He didn't like having a big staff and we never had one. Well, this time when he was talking about reorganizing the company, we had five regions covering the United States, and Charles decided he was going to appoint an assistant regional manager for each region who would be responsible, in every way, for half of the stores in that region. But the regional managers were going to be responsible for the advertising and the warehousing."

McDaniel told Tandy, "Charles, that doesn't make a bit of sense. You're giving one guy equal responsibility for half of the stores, but you've got the other guy running the warehousing and the advertising. Don't you think he might be partial to his stores? Especially, when he gets paid on how well his stores do?"

"Well, I think it'll work," Tandy snapped.

"Well, I don't," McDaniel persisted. "If you were in the Navy and you had an aircraft carrier, would you have an admiral for the bow and one for the stern? Which way do you think the ship would go?"

That stopped Tandy for a moment, McDaniel recalled. "But no one ever stopped him for long," he went on. "He informed me in no uncertain terms, 'I don't have an aircraft carrier out there. I've got two PT boats.'"

Tandy had a different management style from anything he ever learned at the Harvard Business School, McDaniel maintained. "He could be rough, but he was also very human. I think the people that he was roughest on were the people in the top end of management, the people who could talk back to him. Charles would come in and get all over me on some subject. But he knew I could fight back on pretty even ground with him and that I had no fear of him. But if he would go out to a warehouse where he'd talk to a guy at a lower economic level, Charles would never put him down, he'd never give him a hard time. He was a heck of a lot nicer to them than he was to a guy like Bernie Appel or John Roach or me. You could always tell by the tone of his voice what type guy he was talking to. I always admired that in him. He never took advantage of anyone who couldn't fight back.

"But even when he roughed you up, after he got through with you, you had the impression that he was trying to teach you, that he was trying to help you, and that he wasn't doing it for any vindictive reason. And he didn't have a long memory of the things that he jumped on you about, and he gave you lots of rope to make your own decisions. I think the public perception of Charles was that he was a great big tough guy. But guys who knew him as I did didn't view him as a great big tough guy at all. I don't know that Charles ever gave me a direct order: 'You've got to do so and so.'"

When he felt Tandy was off base on some directive, McDaniel said he simply ignored it. "I just didn't pay a bit attention to it. He'd give you a lot of rope in that respect and he didn't try to hang you with that rope." He recalled a receivable report he used to make for Tandy. "It was a cumbersome thing to make, its value had since passed and I perceived that we didn't need the report any more. So I asked Charles one day if I could stop making that report. 'Hell, no,' Tandy told me. 'I use that report all the time. I've got to have it.' I knew he didn't use it, so I just quit making it. Over a year later, he asked me for that report one day. He said, 'Where's last month's report?' I answered, 'Charles, I haven't made that report in over a year.' I think he was so embarrassed that he didn't say another word about it."

John Roach also recalled following his own instincts on whether or not to act on the constant stream of ideas, thoughts and suggestions that Tandy threw at his executives. "You knew, and I'm not sure why you knew—I guess your cohorts kept you squared away—that just because Charles suggested that you do something didn't mean a damn thing; and that beyond that, it was up to you to exercise your judgment on whether you ought to do it, knowing that in two or three months, when he thought to ask you about it again, that you would have the wrath of God to pay if you hadn't made the right decision. Even if the right decision was to ignore Charles."

The thing McDaniel remembered most about Charles Tandy, however, was how much he liked to work. "He worked late every night, never going home before 9 o'clock. But he'd come in late, maybe around 11. I was the other way. I went to work early and tried to get home by 6 o'clock. He'd call me the next day and say, 'I tried to get hold of you at 6:30 or 7 o'clock.' I'd say, 'There was no one here, Charles. I'd gone home.' And he'd say, 'Oh, I wasn't worried about you. I knew you'd be back.' He worked seven days a week. Some of the guys who'd accept it, he'd talk to them for an hour on the phone on Sunday. I didn't like to talk business on Sunday, so he quit calling me. I gave him 100 percent during office hours, and I came in on Saturday, as did all the executives. It's easy to understand why we all came in on Saturday. We were a retail company. Stores were open on Saturday. Store managers would call in on Saturday. They'd want somebody to talk to."

* * *

McDaniel's arrival on the scene in 1966 coincided with a high point in Tandy Corporation's financial history, the eclipsing of the $50 million mark in total revenues in the 1966 fiscal year. The principal contributor to the sales gain was Radio Shack, which contributed $20.2 million, an increase of 30 percent over the prior year. Tandy's net earnings and earnings per share were up 51 percent over fiscal 1965.

"The earnings performance," Charles Tandy observed in his letter to shareholders in the 1966 Annual Report, "was in keeping with the growth projections of the company, as a new high of $3,198,154 was recorded. After provisions for Federal Income Taxes of $929,887, net earnings amounted to $2,268,267, or $1.83 per common share on the 1,240,290 shares outstanding at the year end."

Radio Shack, he pointed out, had made its first significant contribution to earnings during fiscal 1966, providing $599,734 of consolidated net income for the year. A pattern had been set. Radio Shack had accounted for 40 percent of the consolidated sales and 26 percent of the consolidated net income of Tandy Corporation. These numbers would continue to grow as Radio Shack would begin to supplant Tandy Leather as the corporate cash cow.

As the fiscal year ended on June 30, 1966, Radio Shack was operating 87 stores in 25 states, an increase of 30 stores from the prior year. The 100-store milestone would be passed in August, and in September ten more stores would be opened in California, Nebraska, Georgia, Missouri, New York, Arkansas and Texas. Also, for the first time, the list of customers receiving Radio Shack catalogs would top the one million mark.

Tandy Corporation now was the recipient of a plug for its stock from an unexpected source, when an advertisement appeared in an astrological publication under a headline that read: "Special Stock of the Month." Tandy stock, the advertisement proclaimed, was coming under a very favorable planetary configuration from Venus, Uranus, and Jupiter. Since Venus was the planet of "artistic and feminine influences"; Uranus, the planet of "electricity, air, and inventiveness, which also rules television and radio"; and Jupiter, the planet of "entertainment and good fortune," this was "a strong combination allied with Tandy Corp.'s activities over the next two years," the advertisement stated. "Increased earnings should reflect in the company's stock, market wise."

Tandy stock, however, failed to react to the plug or reflect its better-than-expected earnings performance. It was trading in the $14 range, or 7.7 times earnings and below its 1965 close of 15¼ in mid-September, when Goodbody & Co. issued a research bulletin calling the stock "reasonably priced and attractive for long-term gains." With the economy slowing down, Goodbody took note of the fact that a good portion of Tandy's sales were to institutions—schools, hospitals, prisons, etc.—which, the report asserted, "had proven to be recession-resistant in the past."

This was the climate that prevailed for a surprising announcement in mid-September that Tandy was entering the nursery business with the acquisition of Wolfe Nursery, Inc., a 40-year-old Stephenville, Texas, firm with annual sales of $1 million. The price was 15,000 shares of Tandy stock, giving the transaction a value of $210,000. Wolfe was the operator of six retail garden centers in Central and West Texas. It specialized in selling hybrid pecan trees grown on a company farm in Stephenville and claimed to be the largest grower of pecan trees in Texas. Wolfe also was a wholesaler of live nursery plants, fruit trees, insecticides, fertilizers, garden equipment, and related items and carried on a wholesale mail-order business.

Why would Tandy buy Wolfe?

The announcement emphasized that the acquisition placed Tandy into "still another major recreational and leisure-time market," and noted that the care and maintenance of garden and household plantings and grounds had become a popular activity for men and women of all ages, particularly in suburban residential areas, as was manifested by the "increasing number of garden clubs, flower shows and neighborhood beautification programs" across the country. Tandy planned an immediate expansion of the Wolfe wholesale and mail order operations and the opening of new retail outlets in the Southwest. Dan Wolfe, son of the firm's founder, would continue to direct operations of the new subsidiary, the announcement said.

The 15,000 shares issued for the Wolfe Nursery acquisition would more than be replenished several months later with the purchase by the company, in the open market, of 39,600 shares of Tandy common stock for its Treasury at an average cost of $14.80 per share. The shares were purchased, Charles Tandy said, "to replace the 15,000 shares issued to acquire Wolfe Nursery and for possible use in future acquisitions." Wolfe Nursery continued as a Tandy subsidiary until February of 1975, when it was sold to Pier 1 Imports for approximately $6.5 million. By then, the Wolfe Nursery operations consisted of 43 retail stores in 12 cities in Texas and Oklahoma.

Wolfe Nursery figured in an amusing incident involving Anne Tandy, the wealthy oil and ranching heiress whom Charles Tandy married after Gwen's death.

"Anne Tandy knew how to hold onto a dime," Eunice West recounted. "She used to buy flowers all the time. Once she bought all these plants at a Wolfe Nursery after Tandy sold it. She was used to getting a 10 percent Tandy discount that was offered to Tandy employees and shareholders at all the Tandy Corporation subsidiaries. Well, on this occasion she had bought over $200 worth of plants. She was paying for them and wanted her 10 percent discount, and they told her, 'No, we're not part of Tandy any more.' So she said, 'In that case, you can take 'em all back,' and she said to her chauffeur, 'C'mon, let's go somewhere else.' The nursery people said, 'Oh, no, come back, come back.' But she left. Later, she told Charles about it, and he really did kid her."

A month after the Wolfe Nursery acquisition, Radio Shack directors approved a rights offering that would raise funds to retire $4.2 million in bank debt and increase working capital. Under the plan, shareholders received rights to purchase three additional shares of Radio Shack common stock for each share held at a price below the current market price of the stock, which was then quoted at $10 bid and $12 asked in the over-the-counter market. At the same time, Tandy Corporation announced it had agreed to exercise its rights to purchase 808,071 new shares of Radio Shack stock, plus all shares not subscribed by other shareholders. The shares were purchased in December at a price of $8 per share, giving the transaction a total value of $6.5 million, the largest single transaction in company history. With the purchase of 133,755 shares to which the rights had not been exercised and another 1,090 shares from a stockholder shortly thereafter, Tandy's ownership interest in Radio Shack stood at 96.2 percent. The remaining 3.8 percent was acquired on May 26, 1967, through the issuance of two shares of Tandy stock for each three shares of Radio Shack stock held by minority shareholders. Radio Shack was then liquidated as a separate corporate entity and, effective June 30, 1967, was merged into Tandy Corporation under a pooling of interests.

* * *

Dave Tandy was in Corpus Christi visiting his daughter, Margueritte Duemke, when the $6.5 million transaction was announced. Dave never forgot the dark days of the Great Depression when he and Norton Hinckley were forced to juggle checks to keep them from bouncing. He was awed by Charles' financial dealings and still agonized over what he feared was his oldest son's propensity for making deals.

Dave was also painfully aware that his time was limited after suffering another in a series of heart attacks. He left the hospital after the latest attack in early December and accepted an invitation from his daughter to spend some time at her home enjoying the balmy Gulf Coast sunshine and seashore. He hoped he might even be able to get in some fishing at his place in Rockport. On December 9, he celebrated his 77th birthday. On Wednesday morning, December 21, 1966, he suffered a fatal heart attack. His body was returned to Fort Worth, where funeral services were held on Friday afternoon, December 23, at the First Presbyterian Church. Burial was in Greenwood Cemetery in Fort Worth. The afternoon of the funeral, offices, plants and stores of Radio Shack, Tandy Leather, American Handicrafts and Merribee Embroidery in Fort Worth closed in his honor to permit employees to attend the services.

An editorial in the *Fort Worth Press* eulogized him:

"The story of Dave Tandy was typical of the American success story, a story built of all the qualities that we hold up to our children as good.

"A Central Texas boy who started from scratch, built small investment into big investment, small business into a major nationwide business, Dave L. Tandy was to become part of the rich tradition which we claim for Fort Worth.

"The name Tandy became synonymous with leather in Texas, then throughout the United States. The story of success was a continuous one, from the Hinckley-Tandy Leather Co., to the Tandy Leather Co., to the Tandy Corp. with several subsidiaries.

"And the distinguished name and tradition is being carried on by an able son, Charles Tandy, who now heads the big business he founded.

"When Dave Tandy died, we lost from the scene in Fort Worth a leader who was prominent among the group of individualists who built Fort Worth and who made it an industrial center to be reckoned with.

"He has earned a prominent niche in our city's history."

Jesse Upchurch recalled that Gwen Tandy and Jim and Eunice West were vacationing in Mexico City when they learned of Dave Tandy's death.

"They were coming to our home for dinner and then we were going to the airport that night to pick up Charles," Upchurch related. "I had lined up a motor coach with a whole Mexican band and all the works to go meet Charles who was flying down from Fort Worth. It was something we did whenever Charles came to visit us. We'd hire a full mariachi band, would have drinks on board a bus we'd rented, make arrangements with customs and immigration so that he walked out of the airport like a prince. We'd have the bus waiting right in the front and the band playing inside the terminal and follow him to the bus. Anyway, I had to go out to do something that night, and when I got back they told me that Charles had called to say his dad had died and everybody had to go to Fort Worth the next day."

The depth of Charles' feelings for his father was demonstrated when he was honored by the TCU Business Alumni Association with its first annual Distinguished Achievement Award at a luncheon at the Fort Worth Club on October 26, 1967, attended by more than 200 of the city's business and civic leaders.

During his remarks, Tandy choked up as he recalled Dave Tandy's influence on his life. Tears filled his eyes as he said, "I wish my father could be here today to see me get this award."

A newspaperman covering the meeting was seated at a table next to one occupied by a group of Tandy Corporation executives. As Tandy cried, the reporter noticed there wasn't a dry eye at the Tandy table. He later mentioned this to W.H. (Pete) Peterson, the dapper executive vice president of the Fort Worth National Bank, of which Tandy was then a director.

"When Charles cries," Peterson quipped, "everybody cries."

Another tragedy would strike a few months later.

Shortly after Dave Tandy's death, Gwen Tandy learned she had lung cancer. She went to Boston General Hospital for treatment and never returned home. She died on April 4, 1967, at the age of 62.

"Gwen Tandy was a very charming person," Eunice West recalled. "She and Charles had a real nice life and they had a fun time together. She was very businesslike, very smart. She liked to talk to men. She liked man talk. She didn't care about getting around a group of women. She was good for Charles."

Gwen Tandy's father-in-law, B.F. Johnston, made his fortune in the Los Mochos Valley of Baja California, Mexico. By 1917, he owned five sugar mills and decided to build one huge complex. So he designed Los Mochos with sugar mills and refineries and built a railroad to serve it. When he died, he left a business empire that included banks, an electric utility company, a telephone company, a railroad, and a hotel.

Upon B.F. Johnston's death, his son, Sherwood, whom Gwen married in 1923 at the age of 18, became the head of the sugar companies and the distilleries. He founded Del Fuerta, the first company in Mexico to make ketchup and tomato sauce, which was responsible for the large tomato and vegetable markets in Los Mochos. The Johnstons lived mostly in Los Mochos, but also had homes in Burlingame, California, an estate in Rye, New York, and smaller places in Mexico City and Cuernavaca. Sherwood Johnston was killed in an airplane accident in 1937.

"B.F. Johnston had connections with banks and was close to the Crocker family in California and had strong connections with Continental Illinois Bank in Chicago and banks in New York and Boston," Jesse Upchurch reported. "As a result, Gwen had solid banking contacts around the country, and this was a good connection for Charles in later years."

Gwen accepted the fact that "Charles lived his business," Upchurch pointed out. "Charles was never looking for some young woman with whom he could raise a family. He knew that would interfere with his business. To him business was his relaxation. It was his life. Gwen accepted that. She might have been inconvenienced at times, but she accepted it."

When Gwen Tandy moved to Fort Worth after the war, "No one knew who she was," her friend, Hazel Vernon, recalled. "And she had to learn to put up with the 14 to 15-hour days that Charles immediately began putting in. And on Sundays, she would go driving with him while he was looking for new store sites. She was a fabulous woman."

Gwen became involved in the performing arts scene in Fort Worth and was a major supporter of the Fort Worth Opera, Fort Worth Symphony, Fort Worth Theatre and the Reeder School of Theatre and Design for children. She organized the Red Balloon Benefit, a fund-raising project for the Scott Theatre, home of the Fort Worth Theatre, and left $250,000 to the Scott Theatre in her will to be utilized as a "panic fund," according to William A. (Bill) Garber, the Fort Worth Theatre's long-time executive director.

Gwen Tandy's estate, at the time of her death, included three million acres of land around Los Mochos, Upchurch revealed. The property she owned in Mexico was sold for $18 million. This did not include all of the land between Los Mochos and Topolobampo that the family donated to the Mexican government.

Charles Tandy took his father's death hard. But Gwen's death totally devastated him.

"He was absolutely distraught," Dave Beckerman said. "He was in tears most of the time. He was just so lost without his wife. He grieved very, very deeply. It was a very sad period in his life."

Beckerman, who was still living in Boston at the time, was given the assignment of making the arrangements for Gwen's funeral in Boston according to instructions left by her before her death.

"She had told Charles she wanted balloons and fireworks, and she also wanted it all recorded on motion picture film so that her grandchildren could look at the film and remember her death, not with sadness, but as a celebration of going forward to a new life," Beckerman said. "She also requested that the music that was to be played was not to be funeral dirges, but, instead, were to be songs that were meaningful to her and Charles. For example, they had met in San Francisco, so she wanted 'I Left My Heart in San Francisco' to be played by the organist."

The funeral was held in a funeral home in Kenmore Square in Boston, which has a park at its center. Beckerman arranged for hundreds of large red helium-filled balloons to be released from the park at the conclusion of the services.

"Then," Beckerman related, "at the last minute, a couple of funny things happened. The morning of the funeral, Charles remembered that Gwen had requested that fireworks be set off. She wanted a Mexican-style funeral with fireworks because she had lived in Mexico a great part of her life." This posed a problem. Where do you get fireworks in Boston, where they are illegal?

"So we came up with the idea that the only people who could tell us where to get fireworks were the police," Beckerman went on. "We had friends in the Brookline Police Department because our Radio Shack store at 730 Commonwealth Avenue was actually in Brookline even though it had a Boston address. Dick O'Brien arranged for a Brookline police cruiser to go into Chinatown in Boston and pick up fireworks from some Chinese merchants. Then the Brookline Police Department arranged with the Boston police, because the funeral was in Boston, that at a given time they would turn their backs to the park."

Beckerman installed men inside the park who were to set off the fireworks and cut loose the balloons at his signal as he exited the funeral home after the services. He also arranged for Jerry Colella, who was then a Radio Shack store manager in Boston and would later become a vice president, to shoot the entire proceedings with a movie camera from the roof of the Somerset Hotel overlooking Kenmore Square. Colella was leaning over the side of the roof with the camera when the fireworks went off.

"He knew nothing about the fireworks, and when I gave the signal and they began exploding, Jerry nearly fell off the roof," Beckerman said.

Beckerman accompanied Tandy when he selected the coffin at the funeral home.

"Gwen was going to be cremated, so that meant the coffin would be, too," Beckerman said. "I saw this terrible funeral home salesman work Charles up from an $800 coffin to a $10,000 coffin that was going to be burned up anyway. After it got to a certain point, I said, 'You know, Charles, I think Gwen would be a lot happier in this very nice $2,000 coffin if she knew the other $8,000 was donated to the Cancer Fund for cancer research.' Charles agreed and that's what was done.

"The fellow from whom we got the balloons found out from the newspapers that this was a wealthy Texan that was being buried. And all of a sudden, the price of the balloons went up from $2 a balloon to $10 a balloon, and there were going to be 300 balloons. And he insisted upon a check. So I made out a check at $10 per balloon and I told him, 'You be at the funeral, and as soon as the balloons go up, I'll hand you the check.'"

Meantime, Beckerman had instructed Carrie Nemser, the Radio Shack controller, to call the bank and stop payment on the check as soon as the balloons were loosed. That afternoon, the balloon supplier called Beckerman.

"What do you mean by stopping payment on the check?" he demanded.

Beckerman then told him, "Our deal was originally $2 a balloon. That means the check should be for $600 instead of $3,000. I'll be very happy to give you a check for $600 or you can take me to court for the $8 a balloon, and I'll be happy to let the people of Boston know what kind of a ghoul you really are."

The man settled for $2 a balloon.

Chapter 15
A Dream Fulfilled

The Forest Park Bowling Lanes on the second floor of the Tandy Mart at 505 South University Drive in Fort Worth were comfortably filled with Friday night patrons on May 26, 1967. Tony Moore, a 17-year-old clerk at the bowling establishment, was sitting at his desk idly paging through a magazine when, at about 10:30 p.m., a small boy rushed up and screamed excitedly, "There's a fire in the restroom."

Seizing a fire extinguisher, Moore ran to the restroom, but was driven back by the flames which were now moving towards the corridor. He raced back to the bowling alley, where about 100 patrons were gathered, and ordered everyone out of the building. He then grabbed the cash box, tore down a flight of stairs and ran outside onto the crowded parking lot.

The first alarm was received at the Fort Worth Fire Department at 10:34 p.m. There would be three additional alarms, and eventually 20 pieces of equipment, including two cherry pickers, and 70 firemen would be on hand battling the blaze. Before it was brought under control shortly before midnight, the fire destroyed the bowling alley and caused severe smoke and water damage to the Tandy Mart. The mart, which opened in April 1962, now housed Tandy Crafts, Tandy Leather and Radio Shack retail outlets, plus an aquarium, coin/stamp center, an import store and a carpet store. Damage to the building, merchandise and equipment was estimated at $500,000.

Shortly after the fire trucks began converging on the conflagration, the telephone rang in Charles Tandy's apartment on Curzon Street interrupting a dinner party in progress.

The caller, a Tandy employee, gasped out the news breathlessly, "There's a fire at the Tandy Mart."

Tandy's dinner guests that evening were Charles Tindall, then vice president and treasurer of Tandy Corporation; Mrs. Tindall, and a young man named John V. Roach whom Tindall was trying to recruit to head Tandy's Data Processing Department. Roach, at the time, was the data processing manager of Texas Consumer Finance Corporation in Fort Worth.

"Tindall had contacted me about coming to work for the company," Roach recalled. "Even though I was from Fort Worth, I didn't know too much about Tandy Corporation, which in 1967 had a good image but not a real high profile. I told Tindall I was thinking about going to work for another company, but that I'd be glad to come out and talk to him. Tindall did a great job of selling me on why I ought to go to work for Tandy Corporation. I told him I was interested, but that I was going to have to make a decision on another job offer soon and that I needed to move forward rather quickly. So, all of a sudden, the phone rings and I'm invited to Charles Tandy's apartment the following Friday night for dinner. When I got to the apartment, the Tindalls were the only other guests. This was not long after the death of Charles' first wife."

The dinner party has remained vivid in Roach's memory.

"I was 28 years old and I'd had only a few job interviews before that, and they all had been career-structured, very professional. But with Charles there was quite a bit of talking, a lot of it not terribly to the point. We started talking about 7 o'clock and we sat down to dinner at 8:30. There was talk about my ambitions, what did I hope to do over the long term, things like that. One of the things I recall I said that night was that I believed that if I made good progress and worked hard and contributed in the way that I felt like I was capable of doing, that by the time I'd been with the company for 10 years I'd be making $30,000 a year."

Over the ensuing years, Roach added with a grin, "Tandy never let me forget that statement."

The interview was still going on over after-dinner drinks when the telephone rang to bring Tandy the news that the Tandy Mart was on fire. Tandy, the Tindalls, and Roach jumped into Tandy's Cadillac and drove down the West Freeway to University Drive.

"The traffic was all stacked up because of the huge fire, so we pulled off, drove through Trinity Park over curbs and through the grass, and

Right, Dave L. Tandy, co-founder with Norton W. Hinckley of the Hinckley-Tandy Leather Company, forerunner of today's Tandy Corporation. The firm opened for business in Fort Worth, Texas, in 1919.

Left, Tandy Leather Company moved to this two-story building at 2nd and Throckmorton Streets in downtown Fort Worth in 1952 after the Hinckley-Tandy split-up.

Right, Charles D. Tandy joined his father, Dave L. Tandy, in the family business upon his return from active duty with the U. S. Navy during World War II. He became the driving force behind the dynamic growth of Tandy Corporation.

Right, gathering of
Hinckley-Tandy Leather
Company employees,
circa 1950. Norton W.
Hinckley is seated front
row, left; Dave L. Tandy,
front row, right; Charles
D. Tandy, second row, left.

Left, home of the Hinckley-Tandy Leather
Company at 15th and Throckmorton Streets
in the lower end of downtown Fort Worth,
circa 1930.

HINCKLEY-TANDY LEATHER CO.

Above, interior view of a Hinckley-Tandy Leather Company
store. The business sold sole leather and other shoe
repair supplies to shoe repair dealers in Texas.

Right, interior of an early Radio Shack store in Boston. Customers were primarily ham radio operators and electronics buffs.

Left, James L. West, left, and Charles D. Tandy study a map showing early growth of Radio Shack outlets across the nation.

Right, former Radio Shack Corporation headquarters in Boston. The near-bankrupt firm, founded in 1921, was acquired by Tandy Corporation in 1963.

Right, 1970s-era Tandy Corporation executives, left to right, James L. West, John A. Wilson, and Charles D. Tandy.

Above, Tandy Corporation headquarters on West 7th Street in Fort Worth prior to opening of the Tandy Center downtown in 1978.

Left, Charles and Anne Tandy break ground for first phase of construction of Tandy Center on July 9, 1975.

Right, Tandy presents bouquet to skating star Peggy Fleming during opening ceremonies at Tandy Center skating rink, 1978.

Left, Tandy shares a laugh at Tandy Center opening with Larry Cole, left, of the Dallas Cowboys and entertainer Lola Falana.

Above, first grade class at Daggett Elementary School in Fort Worth, circa 1924. Charles Tandy is seated first row, second from right.

Above, Charles Tandy, left, and Gwen Tandy, right, with Jessie and Connie Upchurch and the Upchurch children, Kenneth, Jesse, Jr., and Gwendolyn, at the Upchurch's home in Rye, N.Y., Christmas 1959.

Above, Tandy receives honorary Doctor of Laws degree from Dr. James L. Moudy, chancellor of Texas Christian University, at commencement exercises, 1971.

Above, Tandy throws out first ball at opening of Texas Rangers baseball season. Left, Brad Corbett, majority owner of the Rangers.

Left, larger-than-life statue of Charles D. Tandy, unveiled April 15, 1981 near Tarrant County Courthouse in downtown Fort Worth.

CHARLES DAVID TANDY
1918 —— 1978

Left, night view of Tandy Center towers.

Right, John V. Roach, chairman of the board and chief executive officer of Tandy Corporation.

Left, view of Tandy Technology Center, 270,000-square foot research and development facility, opened September, 1991.

we finally got around to the front of the burning building," Roach related.

A newspaper reporter at the scene spotted Tandy and asked him if the mart was insured.

"I hope so," Tandy answered.

"We stood around for an hour or so watching the firemen put out the blaze," Roach recounted, "and then Charles said to Tindall, 'I wonder if we are insured?' And Tindall said, 'I'm sure we are, but I just can't quite remember for sure.'

"So we all piled back into the car and drove down to the company offices on West 7th Street. By now it was nearly midnight. Tindall proceeded to look for the insurance policy, while Charles paced the floor, blowing smoke and encouraging him to hurry and telling him he couldn't believe that he didn't know whether they were insured or not. Periodically, there would be interspersed discussion about my potential job with Tandy. Finally, we got back to Charles' apartment and stood in the yard talking some more. I got home at 2 in the morning."

When he arrived home, Roach was met by his wife, Jean.

"Jean could not understand where I had been," Roach continued. "I had told her I'd be home by 10 o'clock at the latest. It turned out that there were a lot of nights that I wasn't home after that, but at least by then Jean understood the ball game. But now she was pretty curious about what I'd been doing and appeared pretty dubious when I told her about the fire. So to prove that the mart had been on fire, we put our daughter, Amy, who was then 6 months old, in the car and I drove Jean down for a first-hand look."

Roach had found himself thoroughly fascinated by what he called his "seven-hour experience of nonstop Charles Tandy." The following Monday morning, he called Tindall to inform him that he was interested in going to work for Tandy Corporation but that he had another job offer he had to act upon. Roach asked Tindall, "What are you going to do?"

Tindall's reply was, "Charles can never make up his mind on a personnel matter this quickly. I'll do what I can. But I just can't tell you how fast he'll move."

Several days later, Roach was invited to have lunch with Jim West, now the president of Tandy Corporation. "He took me over to the Pig

Stand across the street from the Tandy offices and he talked about the company," Roach recalled. "Of course, I was trying to talk about computers and he was trying to talk about the leather business, so I was never quite sure how well we totally communicated. But before the week was over, in what I later learned was an uncharacteristically short time period, they did offer me a job. I was to come to work at the end of the month.

"Maybe this says something about Charles' management style," Roach added, "but for the entire month I didn't hear from anybody. So on the Friday before I was supposed to go to work, I called Charles Tindall and asked him what time I was supposed to come to work, where my office was going to be, and what I should do when I came in on Monday morning?"

Tindall responded, "Just come in whenever you want to. I'm sure your office will be down where the feller that's been the running the Data Processing Department now is. But Charles hasn't told him yet that you're coming."

Between Friday and Monday, Roach related, "Charles had to face the reality of dealing with the situation and trying as hard as he could to salvage the person I was replacing. But the person decided to leave."

During his first days on the job, Roach found himself nonplussed over the loosely-structured management style that prevailed at the Tandy corporate headquarters.

"It certainly seemed unorthodox to me," he said, "and I think it came as a little bit of a shock. After I'd been on the job for a while, I finally asked who my boss was. And the answer I received was, 'Well, anybody that asks you to do something is your boss.' And, as time went along, I even had to try to figure out who handled my pay situation. That's the person you usually figure is your boss. The bottom line was that I had the same base pay for the next six years, never one cent of increase. And, as time went along, I learned that Charles was the boss and that he made most of the decisions."

John Roach began his career with Tandy Corporation on June 26, 1967, exactly one month after the fire-interrupted interview at Charles Tandy's apartment.

"Charles had asked me what I'd like to become in the company when he interviewed me," Roach recalled. "I said I'd like, after an appropriate period of time, to be something like comptroller of the corporation.

I thought maybe I had that much potential. After Charles' death, it always seemed that I was destined for one of the leadership roles, but I wasn't sure it would be this."

He never dreamed he would one day sit behind the same oversized desk in the same mammoth office overlooking downtown Fort Worth that Charles Tandy once occupied. He was born in Stamford, Texas, and lived there until he was 4 years old when his father, who had operated a meat market in the small west Texas town, moved to Fort Worth and took a job with the U.S. Department of Agriculture as a meat inspector. "This was during World War II, when they put controls on meat, and dad couldn't get enough to support his business in Stamford," Roach explained.

Roach grew up in the Riverside area of northeast Fort Worth and graduated from Carter-Riverside High School. He entered Texas Christian University on a partial academic scholarship and worked at Montgomery Ward unloading boxcars in the summer and ran a freight elevator at night during the school year. One summer he roughnecked in the South Louisiana oil fields. Between his junior and senior year, he worked for Southwestern Bell Telephone Company as an engineer-trainee helping plan where to erect telephone poles.

Roach remembered someone telling him while he was at TCU that one day he could make as much as $12,000 a year as an engineer. "That sounded pretty good," he admitted. "I was convinced I could make that some day."

His first job after graduating in 1961 with a degree in physics and mathematics was as a general engineer at the Pacific Missile Range in California at an annual salary of $6,345. He remained there two years. "It seemed to me that I needed more engineering education or a business education to get into management," he recalled. "Meantime, I had married a Fort Worth girl and both of us were eager to get back home. So I enrolled in the TCU School of Business for an MBA."

Both he and Jean worked while he attended graduate school. During his first year, Roach worked in the TCU computer department, where he received his introduction to computers. The next year, he worked at the General Dynamics plant in Fort Worth.

"I knew that I didn't want any part of the defense industry, so I started looking for another job locally," Roach related. "As a result of having gotten into computers at TCU, I finally landed a job as data

processing manager for Texas Consumer Finance Corporation in 1965."
After two years there, Roach decided to make a change. "Somehow,"
he recalled, "that information mysteriously got to the people at Tandy,
and Charley Tindall called me at home one night and asked if I'd like
to come to Tandy as head of the Data Processing Department."

It would turn out to be a call that changed his life.

*   *   *

Roach couldn't have picked a more eventful time to join Tandy. The
company was moving ahead on so many fronts that it was hard to keep
up with the announcements that seemed to pour out of Fort Worth
headquarters in a steady stream.

Shortly after his arrival on the scene, rumors began circulating
around Fort Worth that a blockbuster acquisition announcement was in
the works that would stun the city. Tandy stock began responding with
sharp price increases. On October 1, 1967, Tandy shot up 4⅛ points
in heavy trading, closing at $39 a share.

At the request of the New York Stock Exchange, Bill Michero, corporate secretary, issued a statement: "Conversations are in progress
with several companies looking toward an acquisition which would expand the national operations of Tandy's Radio Shack Division and add
new operations to the company. We expect to be able to confirm the
success or failure of our current negotiations within about a week."

On Monday, October 16, Tandy stock closed at $42.50 a share, an
all-time high, up $1.75 from its Friday closing price.

The much-awaited announcement leaped off the front page of the
Star-Telegram on October 17, 1967, in bold, black headlines: "Tandy
Buys Leonards."

It was the talk of the town.

For Charles Tandy, who once had worked in the shadow of Leonards
Department Store downtown, it was the ultimate ego trip, the culmina-
tion of a dream he had harbored since childhood.

When Charles was growing up, Leonards had been the place where
everybody shopped for the best bargains in town on everything from
groceries to farm equipment. Leonards was where Charles' mother had
taken him to buy blue jeans for school and dress up clothes for Sunday
School. During his lifetime, Leonards had been the dominant name in
Fort Worth retailing. Its owners, Marvin and Obie Leonard, were prom-

inent members of the powerful Citizens Committee, an elite group of downtown businessmen, bankers and lawyers who epitomized the essence of the Fort Worth Establishment.

It had always galled Charles that Dave Tandy had never been asked to join the Citizens Committee which, for all practical and political purposes, had run Fort Worth from the 1920s to the 1960s until the advent of single member city council districts drained it of its power base. So buying Leonards was another way for Tandy to thumb his nose at the power brokers who had snubbed his father.

The rise of Leonards from a hole-in-the-wall grocery store to a mammoth downtown retail complex was in the best Horatio Alger tradition. Marvin Leonard opened his grocery store on December 14, 1918, in a 25-by-60-foot building he rented for $75 a month at 111 Houston Street across from the Tarrant County Courthouse. His total capital was $835, most of it borrowed. With it he acquired as much merchandise as his limited resources allowed. For counters, he used boards that lay across barrels. His display cases were washtubs. But at the end of his first day in business, he counted up receipts of $195.26, a sum that seemed to him like "all the money in the world." He was on his way.

On November 2, 1919, Obie Leonard, who had been working as a mechanic in a Dallas garage, joined his brother in the store. Soon after that, after considerable agonizing, they decided to expand into a general merchandise business. They began by adding furniture and hardware, then drugs and softwares.

Their slogan was "More merchandise for less money," and they lived up to it. Over the years, their merchandising feats became legends. Once they bought 2,000 dozen pairs of fire-engine red pants from a manufacturer who practically gave them away to get them out of his inventory. Leonards then sold the pants at a giveaway price of $1 a pair.

Recalled Fort Worth attorney Jenkins Garrett, who represented Leonards as general counsel for many years, "For weeks after that, everybody in Fort Worth was walking around wearing bright red pants."

The first Leonards store was outgrown within two years. The Leonards added 15 feet next door, then 25 feet, then a two-story building. In 1930, they moved into their own new building a block away. This building, occupying a full city block, became the hub of their further expansion that included a full-line service station, a complete farm store, a supermarket, an outdoor store, used furniture store, home improvement center, and an auto and boat store. Leonards also offered free parking to its customers on a 14-acre parking lot that was located about one-third of a mile from the main store and from which it operated a free bus service.

During the Great Depression, Leonards stepped into the void caused by the 1933 Bank Holiday. It printed its own scrip, so that cash-strapped wage-earners had a place where they could cash their pay checks and buy groceries and other necessities at the store.

"During the Bank Holiday," said Robert W. Leonard, Obie Leonard's son, "people didn't have a place to cash their pay checks. Leonards printed its own scrip and cashed the checks. Say it was a $25 check, they'd give the guy $5 in cash and the rest in scrip and he could use the scrip to buy anything in the store. Before it was over, I think some of the other merchants began honoring the scrip. They were real innovators," he said of his father and his uncle, Marvin Leonard. "If they'd have had the gall to expand, they'd have been the Sam's of today."

When the Tandy Leather Company moved uptown to 2nd and Throckmorton Streets in 1952, it became a neighbor of Leonards, whose main store occupied the entire block catty-corner across Throckmorton from the Tandy Leather 50-foot storefront. The sprawling Leonards complex loomed larger and larger in Charles' eyes as he passed it every day going to and from work. One day, he promised himself, all that was going to be his.

He made his first attempt in 1959, Bill Michero recalled.

"We were still officing at 2nd and Throckmorton. One afternoon, Charles called to me to come over to his desk. Luther Henderson was already there. He told us he was going over to see Obie Leonard about buying Leonards and he wanted us to go with him. So the three of us walked over to Mr. Obie's office."

After a few minutes of pleasantries, Tandy came straight to the point.

"Mr. Obie," he said, "would you like to sell Leonards?"

Leonard, a man of few words, responded with his usual taciturnity, "Do you have $19 million?"

"No, I don't."

"Well, come back when you do."

"I hope I can."

The entire meeting, Michero recalled, took less than five minutes.

"Then," he said, "we walked back across the street and went back to work."

In early 1963, Leonards made history by opening the world's first electric underground subway system owned by a department store. The $2 million railway system connected the store's 14-acre, 5,000-car parking lot with a huge underground shopping center that was built in the basement of the main Leonards store. Five electric cars, former Washington, D. C. street cars with a capacity of 100 passengers each, operated on two tracks at depths of up to 42 feet beneath the surface of downtown Fort Worth, whisking riders to and from the store at speeds of up to 30 miles. Not only was it an exciting ride. It also was free.

In a skit in the annual Gridiron Show that year produced by the Fort Worth Chapter of the Society of Professional Journalists-Sigma Delta Chi, an actor portraying Marvin Leonard was interviewed by another actor playing the role of a reporter.

"How much do you charge people to ride on your subway?" the reporter asked Leonard.

"There's no charge," Leonard replied. "The Leonards subway is free."

"How can you make any money that way?" the reporter persisted.

"You'd be surprised."

Leonard's answer drew an appreciative guffaw from the audience.

With the opening of the subway and a new three-story building covering an entire city block adjacent to the main store, the Leonards retailing complex had grown to 86 departments occupying more than 500,000 square feet that sprawled over six city blocks on the north end of downtown Fort Worth.

This was the Leonards that Tandy continued to covet.

In the meantime, Charles had become a close friend of the older of Obie Leonard's two sons, Paul. "We used to visit," Paul Leonard recalled. "I used to go over to the Tandy Leather store and visit with Charles and Jim West and Luther Henderson. We were neighbors and friends. That's my earliest recollection of Charles. He was older than I. We went to the same high school, but he graduated in 1936 and I graduated in 1942, so I didn't know him when we were growing up."

In 1964, Marvin and Obie Leonard had severed their longtime partnership to devote themselves to their separate interests. None of Marvin's four daughters was interested in running the department store, while Obie's sons, Paul and Bob, continued to be active in the store's management. In 1965, Marvin Leonard's half ownership in Leonards was acquired by the Obie Leonard family.

On May 28, 1965, Paul Leonard, who now held the title of president of Leonards, was elected a director of Tandy Corporation. Paul Leonard had been aware of Charles' continuing interest in acquiring Leonards when he joined the Tandy board, but the issue lay dormant until the summer of 1967.

"We had decided that we'd like to sell the store," Leonard revealed. "We were in several different businesses by now and our resources were not such that we could grow them all. Financing Leonards tied up a lot of capital because the receivables were between $8 million and $10 million. We were now in the insurance business, the real estate business, the farming business, and the oil and gas business. Really, we were a little conglomerate. And to make the retail business grow demanded all of our assets."

In addition, Leonard went on, "We were late in going suburban with the department store, eight or ten years late. We were not in the forefront of that. We had chosen to stay downtown and we had a very large real estate investment downtown. But the compelling reason we decided to sell Leonards was we didn't have the resources to expand the business in the way we thought it should."

Leonard said he approached Tandy after a board meeting to determine if he was still interested in buying Leonards. "I told Charles that I thought Leonards would be available if he still wanted it, and he said that he was interested. Tandy was the logical choice to buy the store," Leonard continued. "Not only was he in an acquiring mode at the time, he had the creativity and the ingenuity to raise the money to do it."

Negotiations began in earnest. "It became a matter of looking at the numbers," Tandy later recalled.

Since Leonards was a privately-held company, its balance sheet and earnings had never been published. Looking over the P&Ls, Tandy received an insight into the successes and rough spots of the Leonards operation. There were, for example, the large expenditures involved in the construction and operation of the subway, which had cut deeply into earnings.

Initial discussions were built around the idea that Tandy would purchase the Leonards real estate, as well as its name, stock and fixtures, but it soon became apparent that this would involve more money than

Tandy could readily handle or was willing to commit. Another stumbling block was Charles' almost paranoid antipathy to owning real estate. The proposal then narrowed down to the purchase of the business, its stock and fixtures, with the Leonards retaining the land and buildings and leasing them to Tandy.

A snag then developed over the question of receivables. Under the original proposal, the receivables of approximately $10 million were to belong to the Leonards for a number of years, with Tandy taking over the collections. But Charles demurred after a study of the numbers convinced him that such an arrangement was unfeasible. For a while the entire deal was in jeopardy, but Tandy eventually wrung a concession from the Leonards and the receivables became a part of the package.

Clifton O. Overcash, who was a Leonards executive at the time and was later named president of Leonards by Tandy, was convinced that Tandy wanted to own the receivables so that he could convert them into immediate cash to finance the purchase.

"The only way Tandy was able to buy Leonards was to sell the receivables, which he did to Transamerica Credit Corporation, a subsidiary of Transamerica Life of San Francisco," Overcash said. "Charles sold the whole deal to Transamerica and they took over the credit."

When the deal was announced at a press conference at the Worth Hotel in downtown Fort Worth, many people couldn't believe it, Harlan Swain, then the head of the Tandy Leather and American Handicrafts Divisions, recalled.

"The public was absolutely incredulous when the announcement came out that Tandy had bought Leonards," he said. "People thought a mistake had been made, saying: 'The *Star-Telegram* never gets anything right. I'm sure what really happened is that Leonards bought Tandy. Tandy couldn't buy Leonards.'"

At the press conference, Charles Tandy and Paul Leonard announced that Tandy Corporation was purchasing the business and merchandising assets of Leonards Department Store for cash and stock totaling in excess of $8 million, with the actual amount determinable as of the end of October 1967. Tandy would lease the underlying real estate from the Leonards. Also included in the purchase was control of a chain of six Mitchell's junior department stores located in the Fort Worth area.

The price that Tandy wound up paying for Leonards was approximately $8.5 million, of which $7 million was in cash and the remainder in Tandy stock.

"Mr. Obie really didn't want to take any stock," recalled Charles Ringler, who was Leonards public relations manager, "but that was the only way the deal could be made. So he agreed."

One of the first things the Leonards did after the sale was closed was convert their Tandy stock to cash. It turned out to be a costly mistake, in light of the continued rise in the price of the stock and the stock splits that followed.

"The reason we sold the stock was that we thought Tandy was a one-man show," Paul Leonard said. In retrospect, he added, "It was a dumb thing to do. But it's easy to have 20-20 hindsight vision."

Charles Tandy called the Leonards purchase "the largest single acquisition ever undertaken by Tandy Corporation," and noted that it would add over $45 million in annual sales and approximately $1 million in after tax net income to Tandy's consolidated operations. He told the news media that "over 98 years of experience and sales of over $100 million this year are brought together by this transaction," and added that the move "is in keeping with Tandy Corporation's basic objective of a three-fold increase in sales and earnings every five years."

Tandy then added a personal note.

"For 10 years, our store was across the street from Leonards. Sure, we took the location because that was where the traffic was. But Leonards pulled them in and we didn't. Leonards seemed to have some kind of magnet that just pulled in everybody that came near that store."

What he didn't say, one of the reporters would write, "was that even though he eventually moved away from downtown Fort Worth to a new location on West 7th Street, he never forgot that magnet. He never stopped dreaming about it. And, finally, the magnet got him, too."

When asked by a newsman why he had decided to buy Leonards, Tandy replied, "Leonards is actually something over 80 different stores selling under one name. If we find, as we expect to find, that some of the departments that make up the different stores under the same sign have been so operated that they are meeting the needs of the consumer profitably, it may well be that those departments will become the nucleus of new chains."

Tandy welcomed the 1,800 Leonards employees with words about his philosophy of doing business.

"You must have a willingness to share with the people in the company," he said. "The people who work for Tandy are a new breed, filled with the incentive that comes from knowing that the name of the game is to make a buck."

Billy Roland, who was assistant secretary and assistant treasurer of Tandy Corporation at the time of the acquisition, offered his thoughts on Tandy's motivation for buying Leonards.

"What Charles wanted was merchandise that he could put into a nationwide store operation. He knew retailing and he understood buying power concepts of concentration of goods and then dispersing it out through the store system. And he was looking for merchandise that would really sell. That's why he bought Leonards. He saw all those departments in Leonards and he was looking for a way to take any one of those departments or the merchandise out of one of those departments and put it into a chain of stores across the country. Of course, that didn't work out, and Leonards was never profitable after we acquired it. But that was his idea."

Harlan Swain added, "Charles professed to see a great opportunity in Leonards. The way he put it to me was that in a department store you have every line of business there is. So, therefore, ergo, if you have a department store and you are a specialty retailer who knows how to do specialty retailing, you can take this department store and observe each one of its departments and determine which ones you can take and use as a base to establish chains of specialty stores nationwide. This was his theory. He felt like you could take a fabric department of a department store and apply to it the principles of specialty retailing and it can become a chain of fabric stores. And you know, there are chains of fabric stores today. That was his theory, even if it didn't work out."

But, in Swain's opinion, even though the Leonards acquisition never lived up to Tandy's expectations, he did gain one great plus out of the venture.

"What Tandy Corporation really got out of buying Leonards was the publicity. Nobody, even the people in Fort Worth, knew anything about Tandy until after the Leonards acquisition. Tandy was the world's best-kept secret. Suddenly Tandy Corporation was in every newspaper, every TV newscast, was nationally-known, just overnight. It exploded into public consciousness in a way that I don't think you could have done any other way. So I think that's the biggest thing Tandy got out of the Leonards acquisition, because it certainly wasn't profitable on the basis of P&L."

* * *

The fact that Tandy permitted himself to be influenced by something other than Leonards' profit and loss statement was, in John Roach's view, quite extraordinary.

"P&Ls, the profit and loss statements, were the absolute Bible of the company," Roach averred. "Each month, Charles eagerly awaited their coming out of the accounting department. They were widely disseminated, everybody got a copy. He relished getting his a few hours before everyone else, so that he could call you up and ask you a question that you wouldn't be able to answer because you hadn't received your statement yet. This caused all of his people to become focused on the P&Ls. One of the ongoing challenges was did he, in fact, know more than you knew? But that inspired you to just want to try to know something that he didn't know. But you were always amazed at the number of things he knew or that he could deduce. If there was one wrong number in the middle of a report, he'd find it."

About a year-and-a-half after Roach joined Tandy Corporation, the P&Ls figured in an interesting confrontation he had with Charles Tandy. "It showed me a little bit about Charles' very incisive thinking," Roach recalled.

"We had decided that we'd put the P&L statements on the computer because the number of stores was increasing so rapidly. We were probably getting up to close to 300 Radio Shack stores by this time. It was taking more and more time to consolidate all of the P&L statements, and we were getting errors as a result of the growing number of consolidations. The whole procedure was getting to be very difficult. So we did the computer programming and set up the accounting system so that we could run the P&Ls on the computer. And the accountants, all of whom had been exposed to Charles a lot longer than I had, unanimously decided that I was the logical person to tell him about it.

"So, after a meeting one day, I caught Charles and I said, 'I'd like to talk to you about the P&Ls. You know, there are beginning to be problems with the consolidation and getting the P&Ls out on a timely basis is a problem.' I was trying to sell hard because I wasn't real sure that he wouldn't say, 'Let's just keep doing the P&Ls by hand.' He didn't much like computers, anyway. So, in my sales pitch, I finally said, 'You know, Charles, I think we can assure ourselves, as we go down the road, that we'll get the P&Ls out three days sooner if we do them on the computer.'

"He stopped for a minute and he looked over his glasses and blew a puff of smoke from his cigar, and he said, 'We've got a store in Bakersfield, California, that I've known has been losing money for three months. And if you'd gotten the P&Ls out three days sooner, I would have known for three months and three days it was losing money. Hell, Roach, it doesn't make any difference when you get the information out. It's what you do with it after you get it.'"

Chapter 16
A Lingerie Department Loses Its Panties

The same irresistible urge that drove Tandy to *buy* Leonards now manifested itself in his desire to *run* Leonards—his way. Almost before the ink was dry on the purchase contract, he began drawing up plans to go suburban.

"Let's face it," he told a reporter, "the trend is toward branch stores."

He began making changes that altered the complexion of Leonards. This turned out to be a major mistake.

"Leonards was one of a kind, a unique entity, a big tent," Harlan Swain pointed out. "Marvin Leonard had prided himself on the fact that if you couldn't find it at Leonards, you couldn't find it anywhere. Leonards had grown up as a special kind of animal that had everything in stock."

Tandy, on the other hand, with his specialty store orientation, viewed every department as a profit center.

Charles Ringler recalled, "If some things in a department didn't sell fast enough, he got rid of them. You can't do that in a department store."

Ringler cited women's panties as a classic example.

"If panties weren't selling, Charles' approach was to say, 'Let's quit stocking panties.' That's what he'd do with a transistor that wasn't selling in a Radio Shack store. But you can't have a ladies' lingerie department that doesn't carry panties. Charles never quite understood this."

Added Swain, "Leonards had grown and prospered on what to Charles, as a specialty retailer, were ridiculously thin gross margins. And, of course, one of Charles' great obsessions was gross margins, high percentage gross margins. Leonards had been more interested in sales and gross margin dollars than in gross margin percentages, and they are not the same. You can have wonderful gross margin percentages; but if you can't get the sales, it doesn't mean a thing. Charles thought that the same principles of high gross margins and high turn-over rates should be able to be transferred right out of Tandy Leather and Radio Shack into a department store."

It proved to be wishful thinking.

"Charles had done it with Tandy Leather," Swain said in Tandy's defense. "He had discovered that the margins that Hinckley-Tandy lived with in their line of business could be enhanced tremendously. If that were the only company he did it with, it could be suspect to say it could be done elsewhere. But he also had done it at Tex Tan, where they had achieved great margins. And he had done it in Radio Shack. And, certainly, Radio Shack merchandise had been competitive and had been low margin. But he was able to take it and jack those margins up tremendously, not just by upping the price, but through merchandising and selection. So who could blame him for thinking he could do the same thing at Leonards?"

Perhaps, Swain mused, he could have done it by bringing in other people. "Department store people have a mindset to do business in a department store way," Swain observed. "Now, if Charles had replaced everybody in management with specialty retailing people, maybe it would have worked. But he didn't do it that way, and the way he did it didn't work."

Leonards came under Swain's aegis when he was elected a vice president of Tandy Corporation in 1970. He continued in that role until 1974, when Leonards was sold to the Dillards Department Store chain of Little Rock, Arkansas.

One of Tandy's first moves after taking over Leonards was to ask Paul Leonard to stay on as president and chief executive officer. But, by Leonard's own account, Clif Overcash really ran the store from the very outset until 1972 when Overcash resigned.

"I didn't want to have line responsibility for the running of the store," Leonard said. "And Charles' relationship was one of supervising Clif, really. I sat in on quite a few meetings with Clif and Charles out at the apartment. Charles was a figure guy and he wanted increased gross profits right away."

Leonard discovered very quickly that Tandy's management style was a far cry from the paternalistic, benevolent Leonards operation.

"Our philosophy, Uncle Marvin's and my dad's philosophy, was that the department managers were pretty much in business for themselves, and they gave them a lot of autonomy to do the things they thought they needed to do to make money. So there was a loss of that freedom with people. I think it was a shock to the 70 or 80 management people to get into a less people-oriented environment.

"Charles really didn't have the time to be in day-to-day contact with the store employees, as we did. We knew these people, we knew how many children they had, we knew the problems they were having. They were our friends and we loved them like we would members of our family."

Added a long-time Leonards employee, "They didn't pay us anything, but they treated us like family."

Paul Leonard became immediately aware of Tandy's displeasure with Leonards' margins and operating practices.

"Charles, being a figure man, really looked at printouts of inventories and turnover, and he didn't like what he saw," Leonard said. "But one of the things that was a significant drawing card in our store was we worked real hard to have what people wanted when they they came in. So our turnover was not as brisk as it is in a specialty store. For example, a Wal-Mart store turns its inventory 12 to 14 times a year, while we only turned about four times a year. Charles was such a fast-moving, hard-driving guy, he was so successful with Radio Shack, that he thought those same techniques would work everywhere."

Leonard's tenure as store president under Tandy lasted only about seven months. He resigned in May of 1968, but remained as a director of Tandy Corporation for three more years.

"Charles ran a board meeting just like he ran everything else," Leonard said. "He was a take charge sort of guy, who domineered any group that he was in. He was very extroverted. But I've never known anybody that ever worked any harder than he did. I can remember going over to see him at 8 or 9 o'clock at night over at the leathercrafts store. Our store stayed open till 9 o'clock three nights a week, and I was there on a lot of Fridays and Saturdays. He was a seven-days-a-week guy. I never did play with him much, but I understand he played pretty hard, too. He drank a lot of whiskey and smoked a lot of cigars."

Leonard recalled Tandy's barbed-wire side that was so different from the gregarious, charming side that people who knew him socially were accustomed to seeing.

"I saw Charles abuse people badly," Leonard said. "He'd sit there and let them have it without mercy. The way he talked to his executives was just awful. You couldn't imagine the way I saw him abuse Clif Overcash."

Overcash had been running Leonards for three or four years before it was sold to Tandy, he claimed, although he was never given the title of president.

"The Leonards wouldn't let anyone have the title of president except a Leonards family member," he asserted.

Overcash met Charles Tandy in 1959 shortly after joining Leonards, but did not know him very well at the time of the takeover. Overcash had been a vice president and personnel director of Gimbel Brothers in New York City at the age of 28, and then had gone with Litt Brothers Department Store in Philadelphia and Kresge Department Store in Newark, New Jersey, before coming to Leonards.

After the announcement that Leonards had been sold, Overcash recalled, "Tandy called me out to his apartment on Curzon and told me, 'You're my guy. I don't care who has the title.'"

Overcash gained the title of president on May 31, 1968, after Paul Leonard stepped down. He also continued to hold the responsibilities of general merchandise manager.

"We had a lot of meetings," Overcash recalled. "We had a monthly meeting when Paul and I were operating together. The monthly meeting was all buyers and managers. We went over the previous month's figures and what our targets were for the following months. Once in a while Tandy would come in and disrupt the proceedings."

Tandy, Overcash added, was always "real gung-ho," never expressing a negative thought, constantly telling everyone how big Leonards was going to be. Early on, he began searching for vehicles to implement his concept of going national with a chain of stores from one of the Leonards departments.

"We went that way," Overcash related. "We tried it. We opened auto centers. I don't remember how many we had, ten or 12 of them. We had fabric stores. We had ten or 12 of those. The auto centers and the fabric stores were located in Texas primarily, but one auto center was opened in McAlester, Oklahoma."

Neither the auto centers nor the fabric stores developed the way Tandy hoped. As for the effects of Tandy's zealotry to remake Leonards into his image, Overcash said that was an initial sore spot between him and Tandy that eventually led to his leaving the store in frustration. He described what happened:

"Charles and I fought constantly because I wouldn't agree with his trying to make Leonards into a specialty store. I knew it wouldn't work in a department store, especially a department store with the reputation of having this broad stuff. One of the first battles we got into was over flashlight batteries. We had, when we were operating Leonards, probably six, eight, ten or twelve brands of flashlight batteries in stock. Charles said, 'Take all the brands out and put Radio Shack batteries in,' nothing else. That was just typical of him."

Overcash recalled other changes that Tandy instituted.

"In the lingerie department, we used to have four or five different manufacturers of bras and the same in panties and slips. Then Tandy came in and told us to go down to one brand and put our strength in that one. That works all right if you've built your reputation on a specialty store approach. But Leonards had built its reputation and acceptance by having a broad line of merchandise. Leonards wasn't known for being high quality in its merchandise, especially in the soft lines. They were price-oriented. The slogan was 'More merchandise for less money.' So, if you're going to hit the price area, you've got to have something else to go with it, and we had assortments, broad assortments, in the soft lines and the hard lines. We had as good a quality in the hard lines as anybody in the United States—in cookware, sporting goods, hardware, furniture and all that stuff."

When Tandy bought Leonards, Overcash continued, three things happened and all of them were bad.

"One, he sold the credit. That ruptured our business, because Transamerica actually was operating the Leonards credit department and Leonards had had a very easy, soft, 'down South' credit policy before. Now it became a savings and loan or a loan shark credit operation. They ran off millions of dollars worth of business. I never had a more miserable two years in my life on the phone with customers irate over the way they were being treated on their credit.

"The second mistake was trying to operate a department store as a specialty store, which meant curtailing the brands and items you had. Leonards had always had depth and breadth in stock, and Tandy wanted to go into a very narrow merchandising program, the same as a specialty store.

"The third mistake was the blowing explosion of expansion, which was Tandy's absolute dictate. Just for Leonards, for instance, forget auto centers for a minute, forget fabric stores, although we had to blow and go with those and with Mitchell's as well. But we built the Northeast Mall store, we built the Forum 303 store, we built the Irving Shopping Center mall store. That's three major department stores opening in a year-and-a-half to two years' time. Spending a lot of money, a lot of time."

The Northeast Mall store, a 240,000-square foot structure on two levels in Hurst, and a smaller store in the Forum 303 Shopping Mall in the Arlington-Grand Prairie area, were built at a cost of $4.5 million and were financed through a public offering of 300,000 shares of common stock on April 18, 1968. The shares were snapped up at a price of $57.50 per share, prompting some brokers to call the success of the offering "a remarkable display of strength in a stock in which existing equity was being diluted." The Forum 303 store opened on October 31, 1969, and the Northeast Mall store on July 10, 1970.

Overcash insisted he explained to Tandy that the rule of thumb in opening branch stores was that they would lose money the first two years and might break even in the third year of operation. The Leonards suburban expansion program, Overcash summarized, resulted in an increase in total sales from $50 million to $100 million, of which $50 million was unprofitable.

"So," he continued, "we had our credit problem, we had reduced our merchandise and were ruining our image with our customers, and now we were losing tons of money because of an ego expansion program. That's precisely what was happening. And we were also blowing and going with Mitchell's, a junior department store chain that sold ready-to-wear and shoes, no furniture or appliances. We had about six Mitchell's stores when Tandy bought them, and we ended up with about 30. They were located all over Texas and one was in McAlester, Oklahoma. It was forced expansion, that's what it was." Overcash conceded that Tandy had been successfully doing essentially the same thing with Radio Shack. "He thought if he did it with Radio Shack, he could do it with anything. The markup in the department store business was not as great as it was in Radio Shack, and Tandy had gotten additional markup in Radio Shack because he had a bunch of merchandise made in Japan. Also, he didn't have as much competition in the electronics business at that time."

Overcash cited another problem with which Tandy had to learn to contend.

"In a department store," Overcash noted, "if you come down to the bottom line with a three percent net profit, that's outstanding. But Tandy was accustomed to 15 to 20 percent net profit in Radio Shack.

So Leonards really didn't fit his pistol. It was an ego trip for him. He had once sat across the street from Leonards. He looked at Leonards and he dreamed about owning it and its reputation. Everybody in town knew Leonards Department Store. But buying Leonards did put him in the big leagues, volume-wise. It opened up the credit lines for him, it kicked him into more than $100 million in sales immediately."

Overcash's run-ins with Tandy began with flashlight batteries and soon covered the entire gamut of Leonards' operations. There was a plethora of conflicts.

"I believed very strongly in the department store approach if you're gonna run a department store," Overcash related. "You can't run it as a specialty store. And Tandy wanted me to run it as a specialty store. He gave me direct orders six times on those batteries. Finally, Harlan Swain said to me, 'You're gonna get fired if you don't get those batteries out of here.' My secretary said to me, 'You'll get fired, you'll get fired,' because she'd hear us shouting and screaming at each other."

Overcash finally threw in the towel in 1972. He told the newspapers he had resigned because of a difference of opinion over policy. Privately, he said he quit for personal reasons. "It was a matter of honor with me that I'd rather not go into, other than the fact that Charles did not live up to some promises he made to me," he averred.

Overcash reportedly left Leonards a millionaire as a result of investing in Tandy stock with the proceeds of a bank loan that was co-signed by Charles Tandy. He then went on to became a successful investor in nursing homes, apartment houses, office buildings, and shopping centers, and served a term as mayor of Fort Worth.

* * *

In selling the Leonards receivables to Transamerica Credit Corporation a month after buying the store, Tandy received face value for the approximately $10 million on the Leonards books. But more than that, he succeeded in divesting himself of the credit business he detested.

Connie Powell, a merchandiser in the Leonards Home Furnishings Department, recalled Tandy telling him on a number of occasions how much he disliked dealing with accounts receivable.

"Charles' theory was to put the cash in the bank every night," Powell said. "But after the sale of the receivables, the troubles commenced. Transamerica began turning people down for credit, cancelling their credit cards, because they didn't have the right answers on the questionnaires that Transamerica sent out. Transamerica had a checklist that

contained questions about how much a person made and how much
money he owed. Things like that. People became very bitter. And on
top of that, it cost us lots of money in lost sales."

Leonards' customers, Powell said, had a special loyalty to the store
that didn't show up in their credit history. He told the story of going in
to see Marvin Leonard one day for approval of a credit sale for some
furniture.

"What's the problem?" Leonard asked.

"Well, this customer is behind on his payments all over town, to
Monnig's, Stripling's, Penney's, Sears, you name it."

"Is he paying us?"

"Oh, yessir, he's never missed a payment at Leonards."

"Then let him have the furniture."

On big ticket items like furniture, pianos, and appliances, Powell explained, without credit there are no sales. He estimated that Leonards
lost $5 million in sales in the first 18 months after the credit operation
was sold to Transamerica, with most of the losses coming in the downtown store.

Powell recalled Tandy coming into the store after it was sold and visiting with employees, "sometimes chewing us out for not selling more
merchandise. But after he finished chewing you out, he'd smile, pat
you on the shoulder and say, 'When are you gonna come out to see
me?'"

Tandy would call him at the store from time to time, Powell reported,
and tell him to send a TV set out to a rest home or to some needy
shut-in.

"He'd say to have it charged to his personal account. He did that
quite often, with no fanfare. He had a heart as big as a house."

Powell laughed as he described an incident involving Tandy and Phil
North.

"Mr. North was having a cabana built and his swimming pool fixed
up for a big party," Powell related, "but he got mad at the contractor
and threw him off the job before it was finished. We had a Home Improvements Department at the time, and Mr. Tandy called me and told
me to get a crew out to Mr. North's house. He told me, 'Fix it up and
don't worry about the money.' So I sent the crew out and they finished
the job. We sent the bill to Mr. Tandy but he got Mr. North to pay it."

Tandy gave an insight into his disappointment over the way the
Leonards acquisition was turning out at a meeting with a group of store

managers at Green Oaks Inn in Fort Worth in 1971. During the question-and-answer session after he had completed his formal remarks, Tandy was asked by one of the store managers how Leonards was doing. Tandy replied:

"I was trying to create a newer generation of Radio Shacks with a broader merchandise line when I bought Leonards. But it didn't work. Still, Leonards has got $50 million to $55 million worth of volume in it. There's got to be a pony in that pile somewhere. We've got to get some cats who can run that thing right. We're trying to find a route to take to make that thing profitable. That's what we're trying to do."

He never succeeded.

In January 1974, Leonards was sold to Dillard's Department Stores of Little Rock, Arkansas, for 334,445 shares of Dillard's stock worth approximately $4.8 million. Dillard's also paid $300,000 in cash for miscellaneous equipment in the six Leonards stores and two warehouses.

* * *

Despite the initial problems he encountered after the Leonards acquisition, Tandy was not dissuaded from taking a crack at resurrecting another old-line retailing institution in Fort Worth when he learned of its availability in the spring of 1968. The object he now coveted was Meacham's, Inc., a venerable women's specialty department store in downtown Fort Worth. Founded in 1902, Meacham's had once occupied premises at 2nd and Houston Streets, a block south of the Tandy Leather Company site. It had been purchased by Milton and S.J. Amstater in 1937 and had moved into an eight-story building at 5th and Houston Streets in 1954.

Despite its reputation as a top-quality fashion store, Meacham's fell on hard times. Its sales dropped below $2 million. Jack Greenman, a Fort Worth grain dealer and a friend of Milton Amstater's, knew that Amstater was looking for a buyer. Greenman also was aware of Charles Tandy's itch to own everything of consequence in his hometown.

"So I called Charles and told him about Meacham's being for sale," Greenman related.

Tandy's response was, "Meet me for breakfast tomorrow."

Over breakfast at the Fort Worth Club, Greenman told Tandy about the Meacham's situation and caught Tandy's attention with the comment, "The business may not be too good, but it's got a heckuva location." There was no way he could lose, Tandy figured. If Meacham's didn't pan out, its eight-story building in the heart of Fort Worth's central business district would be worth what he planned to offer Amstater for the business.

On June 2, 1968, the announcement of the purchase of Meacham's, Inc., for "near $1 million" was made by Tandy and Milton Amstater. The 65,000 square foot Meacham's Building was included in the deal. At the press conference announcing the purchase, Tandy said, "The downtown area is ready for dynamic development, and the Meacham Building will definitely be a part of that development." Tandy also announced plans for four additional "prestige type" Meacham's suburban stores.

"I think we can support four such stores in the suburbs," he maintained. "Our ladies are well-dressed. I think they will respond enthusiastically to the opportunity of buying merchandise that fits their own personalities from a home-owned company."

This was a not-so-subtle dig at Dallas-based Neiman-Marcus, which had recently opened a specialty store on Fort Worth's far west side.

Matilda Nail Peeler, who was manager of the Galleria Department of the Neiman-Marcus store in Fort Worth before joining Meacham's as head buyer in couture fashions after Tandy bought it, said Tandy's plan for Meacham's was to turn it into another Neiman-Marcus. He convinced Mrs. Peeler to leave Neiman's and help revive Meacham's.

"Meacham's was really run down," Mrs. Peeler recounted. "The merchandise was really off. The fashion world had passed the Amstaters by. On top of that, all downtown stores were hurting. Suburbia was killing downtown."

The news that Mrs. Peeler, an attractive divorcee and former beauty queen (she had been the Maid of Cotton in 1948), was joining Meacham's in a top level job caused many tongues to begin wagging in Fort Worth social circles. She and Charles had been dating regularly after being brought together by Fort Worth socialites Martha and Elton Hyder at a black tie dinner benefitting the Fort Worth Ballet.

Matilda had been divorced from Tully Petty, a Fort Worth advertising man, and Charles was a recent widower who had become Fort Worth's most eligible bachelor. The talk around town was that he had bought Meacham's for her.

Asked about this during an interview, she laughed heartily.

"I know what people were saying at the time, and I wish I could tell you it was true. But the fact is, he was dating Mildred Fender and Brenda Slaughter and a lot of other women at the time. We weren't that serious."

She laughed again.

"Come to think of it, he was dating practically everybody who walked into the store."

She did admit that Tandy had her in mind when he bought Meacham's, but only because he thought she could run it. "As a matter of fact," she added, "when Charles told me he wanted me to run Meacham's, I told him I was afraid I couldn't handle it alone. I asked him to talk to Ann Quinn, who was then the Neiman-Marcus personnel manager, and he did. So Ann came to Meacham's at the same time that I did."

Mrs. Quinn, who would later become a senior vice president of marketing at Team Bank in Fort Worth, joined Meacham's as assistant manager.

"It was a harrowing experience," Mrs. Peeler described her Meacham's tenure. "Charles wanted to compete with Neiman's but he wanted us to run Meacham's the way he ran Radio Shack. He wanted to put furs into Leonards. I told him, 'No woman wants a mink coat with a Leonards label.' But you couldn't tell Charles anything. When I went on a buying trip, he wanted me to buy out New York.

"I said, 'You can't buy high fashion that way.'

"He said, 'We sure can.'"

Mrs. Quinn recalled Tandy asking her before a buying trip, "How much merchandise is Matilda going to buy?"

When she told him, he exploded, "That's not enough to send her to New York for."

"The thing Charles refused to understand," Mrs. Quinn said, "was that you can't buy 300 high couture dresses at a time. But that's the way he was used to buying for Radio Shack."

It was Tandy's Radio Shack orientation, Mrs. Peeler observed, that caused him to open Meacham's suburban stores in the Ridglea and Wedgwood areas of Fort Worth and in the Northeast Mall at Hurst and close the downtown store.

"That was the Radio Shack syndrome," she averred, "have a store on every corner. We really fought going suburban. We had $500 dresses at the Northeast Mall, but the people shopping there were looking for blue jeans, not designer clothes."

The Meacham's acquisition, as was the case with Leonards, never lived up to Tandy's expectations. Its sales remained stagnant and it was never profitable. On June 2, 1972 it was sold to Margo's LaMode, Inc., a Dallas specialty retailer.

Announcing the sale, Dave Beckerman, then a Tandy Corporation vice president with responsibility for Meacham's and Mitchell's, candidly admitted:

"The sale of the Meacham's business, after four years of ownership, is based on our conclusion that the women's fashion business does not lend itself to our areas of expertise."

Beckerman later expounded on the statement.

"The Tandy method of running a business and running stores didn't really apply to Leonards or Meacham's or Mitchell's," he said. "We didn't know how to run a department store, and we still don't. It's not our cup of tea."

Mitchell's operations were discontinued as of December 31, 1973, through the transfer and sale of its inventories to several companies and individuals.

In fiscal 1973, Leonards and Mitchell's had combined sales of $54.8 million, of which Leonards contributed $35.4 million. Their combined losses for the year were approximately $4 million. Their combined losses totaled $11.1 million before they were finally sold, which also marked the discontinuance of the General Retailing Marketing Group.

For Charles Tandy, there would be many additional acquisitions in the offing, new fodder for his insatiable appetite, but there would be no more department stores.

Chapter 17
A Brush With the Grim Reaper

Lost in the outpouring of publicity created by the Leonards acquisition was another development which proved to be of considerably greater significance as far as growth and profitability were concerned. This was the entry of Radio Shack into the dealer store and franchising fields, with the awarding of the initial franchise to Carter L. Wilson of Tyler, Texas, on August 30, 1967.

Jim West explained the rationale behind the move in a newspaper interview.

"Radio Shack has grown from nine stores to 160 stores in the past four years," West said. "In looking for just the right kind of people to operate our stores, we find there are many who would like to come with us, but as owners rather than as employees. This is the reason for the initiation of the franchise plan."

According to Lew Kornfeld, who was then Radio Shack's vice president for merchandising and advertising in Boston, Charles Tandy had been considering going into franchising for some time.

"He had the idea quite early on that we could expand more rapidly and more cheaply if we went into franchising; that we could, in effect, open new stores at half the cost of opening company-owned stores."

By early October of 1967, the first three of a projected 300 franchise stores were operating under the new program. They were located, in addition to Tyler, Texas, in Watertown, Maine and Trenton, New Jersey.

Bruce Russell, who had been named director of franchise operations in Boston, was quoted in *Audio Times*, a trade publication based in New York, as stating that responses had been received from prospective franchisees in 44 states and six foreign countries to a Radio Shack flyer outlining the franchising plan.

Under the program, Radio Shack provided the franchise stores with inventory that was shipped within seven days after the signing of the franchise agreement. Franchise stores agreed to stock about 2,000 items with a total retail value ranging from $20,000 to $30,000, with Radio Shack "marketing engineers" assisting the franchisee in selecting the inventory. The program also included an arrangement whereby, if the store became "unbalanced" on some items, it could return "overstocks" in exchange for items needed. Included in the franchise package was assistance from Radio Shack in store layouts, fixturing, advertising and promotion, and store operation. Franchise stores also received "full representation" in Radio Shack advertising, including being listed along with company-owned stores in the ads. Radio Shack also mailed its flyers to franchise store customers "on a regular basis" from Fort Worth.

"We feel we have a real winner in this program," Russell told *Audio Times* in an article that appeared on October 15, 1967. "The profit potential for the man who has one of our franchises is darned good. People who go along with us will make out well. We're very serious about this effort." He also disclosed that Radio Shack, under "very special circumstances, would offer some financial assistance to those wanting a franchise."

Franchises initially were put into larger cities where company-owned stores were not being opened. However, with the inauguration of the dealer store program in 1972, the solicitation of new franchisees was halted.

Dealing with experienced, successful retailers in the dealer store program posed fewer problems than coping with franchisees, most of whom had no prior retailing experience.

Anthony A. Bernabei, a Princeton graduate who had grown up in New Jersey and had joined Radio Shack in 1969 after working in pre-Castro Cuba and on Wall Street, had been named head of the Franchise Division in 1970. Bernabei claimed credit for selling Charles Tandy on the dealer store program. He said the idea initially came up during a conversation with Bob Lynch, his assistant in the Franchise Division.

"We were talking about doing a dealer program and I said, 'I don't think we're ready for that yet.' But later we went to see Charles and I wrote a one-page memorandum saying, 'Charles, I think we're mature enough to start a dealer program in cities of less than 20,000 population where the nearest Radio Shack store would be so far away that it wouldn't impinge on the marketplace.' I said I thought we could have

2,000 of these stores across the country. We showed the memorandum to Charles on a Wednesday, and on Thursday or Friday we went to Granbury and signed the first deal. The guy we signed up sold refrigerators and ranges and what-not. I don't remember the exact details, but he had to pay, like $500, and then he put out his Radio Shack dealer sign."

Granbury is a small town about 30 miles southwest of Fort Worth, and was "way out of any geographical or demographical competition with Fort Worth," Bernabei noted. Nevertheless, concern was immediately expressed by the district and regional managers in Fort Worth over what they perceived as an invasion of their territorial rights. As the program developed nationally, Bernabei added, "every other regional manager saw it as a threat."

Lew Kornfeld also claimed credit for the origination of the dealer store program. "It was my idea," he maintained. "There may be others who claim it, but I know I had the idea (I don't know if I had it alone) because I had always tried what I called 'wholesaling' my unique imports from the Orient in order to get the volume up to where the price would be lower. I even had people like Allied Radio as customers. So I'd had some experience selling product to others. To me, it was obvious that we could do [the dealer store program] without making anybody angry, especially since we sought dealers in towns where there wasn't enough population for us to open a Radio Shack store."

The object of the program, Kornfeld said, was to have the dealers add the Radio Shack line to the lines they were already selling. "These people were already established in business," he pointed out. "They were credit-worthy. All they had to be was convinced this was a good thing for them, and it was. So we switched from franchising over to dealer operations." The dealer stores, operated by independent radio, television, and appliance retailers, offered a new, untapped market for Radio Shack merchandise. And since they did not pose the problems confronted in the franchise operations, they thrived. They were added at an average of 175 per year and by 1982 there were 2,000 of them selling Radio Shack merchandise in the hinterlands. Their sales were helped by Radio Shack's national television advertising.

"Our TV ads increased our awareness," Kornfeld noted. "We were more credible when we knocked on a prospect's door. Our signed-up dealers reported seeing our TV commercials and doing more business, and our network TV's reach was so total there was no part of the country our advertising didn't penetrate."

* * *

Meantime, back in Fort Worth, Charles Tandy was in the process of negotiating another deal.

"If you drink a lot of milk," he once told an associate, "you oughta buy a cow."

The sentiment entered into his decision to buy the Stafford-Lowdon Company of Fort Worth in January, 1968: "If you're doing a lot of printing, you oughta buy a printing business."

Bob Lowdon, who had been a favorite fishing and hunting companion of Dave Tandy's, had become the president of Stafford-Lowdon, the firm that had been doing printing for Tandy Corporation since the Hinckley-Tandy Leather Company days. Lowdon was also a Tandy shareholder, having bought stock at Dave Tandy's invitation during the American Hide & Leather era. He had joined the Tandy board in 1966 at Charles' invitation.

In late 1967, Tandy approached Lowdon about buying his company.

"We were doing a lot of printing for Tandy and they were spending a lot of money with us," Lowdon recalled. "We had the equipment for the bigger jobs that they needed, and Charles figured he'd make a profit two ways by buying us—the profit we were making on the printing we did for Tandy and the profit we were making from our other business. I remember he used the term, 'double dip.' He was going to get a double dip by buying us."

Stafford-Lowdon's volume was about $7 million and its pre-tax earnings were approximately $600,000. "We were profitable," Lowdon said, "but not nearly as much as we became later on after Tandy bought us. He wanted to expand everything that was profitable. He was smart as a whip and he really knew how to make money."

Stafford-Lowdon was purchased for approximately 100,000 shares of Tandy stock worth about $5.6 million and Lowdon became one of Tandy Corporation's largest individual shareholders. He used his influence to convince most of the other Stafford-Lowdon owners to retain the Tandy stock they received in the transaction.

"I was convinced Tandy was going to make more money all the time," Lowdon said. "Over the years, the people who didn't hang on to their stock were sorry. Some people could hardly wait to sell their stock, and I'm sure they wake up screaming at night. Horace Porter sold his stock right away after he sold Royal Tile to Tandy. The Leonards sold their stock right away, and Hugh Wolfe could hardly wait to get his hands on that stock so he could sell it after he sold Wolfe

Nurseries to Tandy. Charles tried to talk them out of it. He told them they were making a bad mistake, but they wouldn't believe him. It cost them all a great deal of money."

Tandy later would grouse to some of his confidants, as Tandy stock continued to hit new highs, that he'd paid too much money for Stafford-Lowdon because he had bought it for stock instead of cash.

Lowdon, who retired from the Tandy board in 1990, recalled how frustrated Tandy became when one of his own executives failed to follow his dictates about buying stock in the company. One of the culprits who incurred Tandy's ire was his longtime friend, Bill Collins.

"When I first went out to California after joining the company," Collins recounted, "Charles said to me, 'Be sure and buy some stock.' But after selling my house in Fort Worth and moving my family out to a more expensive place to live, I needed to get the most out of every dollar I could. So, two years later, I still hadn't bought any stock. When Tandy found out about it, he called me up and said, 'Now, damn it, get on the ball and buy some stock.' I said, 'All right, but things are mighty tight. I can't afford it.' His answer was, 'Goddamn it, do it.' So I did it. Later, of course, I was very glad I had."

Dave Beckerman recalled one of the first meetings held for Radio Shack store managers after Tandy assumed control. "He told the group that he liked his people to be invested in the company," Beckerman related. "Then he held up a sheaf of Tandy stock certificates and said, 'I've got this stock here and I can arrange for loans for all of you to buy some.' Tandy's initial deal," Beckerman continued, "was that we could buy Tandy stock, which was then selling for around $6 a share. If, at the end of a year, if we were dissatisfied, he would buy it back from us at the price we had paid for it, plus our brokerage fees. I didn't have much money then," Beckerman continued. "My old Radio Shack stock had gone down the drain. But I went out and bought 500 shares of Tandy, which was a lot of money for me. I had a negative net worth then, so it wasn't easy for me to raise the money to buy the 500 shares. But I did buy it. Today that $3,000 investment would be worth over $2 million."

Beckerman recalled an incident that took place after his Tandy stock had made him a millionaire on paper in the early 1970s.

"I went to a liquor store, bought a bottle of Dom Perignon, had it chilled, and at 5:30 that afternoon drove out to Tandy's apartment on Curzon Street. I put the bottle on the table and opened it and I poured us both a glass. Then I raised my glass in a toast and I said, 'Charles, I brought this bottle along because I want you to know that today I counted up my net worth and it's in excess of a million dollars. You know, Charles, I think that for as long as I've worked for you, I've wanted to have enough money to be able to tell you to your face to go fuck yourself. But now that I have enough money, I've somehow lost the desire."

Tandy almost fell off his chair laughing.

Dave Christopher, who joined Radio Shack as a part-time employee during the 1966 Christmas season and would go on to become president of A&A Trading Corporation and a senior vice president of Tandy Corporation, remembered his initial exposure to Tandy's passion for getting his employees to buy stock.

"It was at my first store managers' bonus meeting," he recalled. "There was no question what Mr. Tandy wanted us to do—buy stock in the company. He had lots of support from the audience. Typically at those meetings there were a number of old Tandy hands, old Tandy Leather employees, who had seen this pressure and were well-versed in it. They would get up and give testimony as to how great the program was and how everyone really needed to participate. They were the first ones to raise their hands and say they wanted to buy more stock. It made newcomers like me figure, 'Gee whiz, these guys know a lot more about it than I do. They must be smart. And I just heard Charles Tandy tell us how great it's gonna be, so I'd better buy some stock.'

"The program he outlined was essentially that we could buy stock by putting down 25 percent of the total purchase price and that the Fort Worth National bank would carry the balance on a personal note at the prevailing interest rate until the next year's bonus time rolled around. That got to be kind of a vicious cycle, because you'd end up each year owing 75 percent of what you'd committed to in the prior year, and you'd keep on doing it year after year. So you always owed 75 percent of what you'd bought.

"Since the stock was going up, everybody could calculate pretty easily that they were coming out ahead on this routine of buying more stock on credit each year. Everything looked great for a long time. There was a lot of growth in the company, a lot of expansion, a lot of opportunities. A lot of guys got promoted to bigger jobs, bigger paychecks, bigger bonuses, and the tendency was to buy more shares as you made more money. A lot of people even bought additional stock by borrowing money from their local bank using the stock they already owned as collateral. All this was looking real good until 1970 when things started to hit the skids. The price of the stock began falling and people started getting calls from their banker for more collateral because the value of the stock wasn't high enough any more to cover their loans.

"In my particular case, I had a banker who called me a number of times for more collateral. The first time he called, I brought him the title to my wife's automobile. Before things were over, I had another call and had to go down and sign a chattel mortgage for my furniture. Things really got a little scary." Fate finally smiled on Christopher in 1974. He was transferred from Kansas City, where he had been a district manager since 1970, to a similar position in New York City.

"I was able to sell my house in Kansas City very easily, and when I got the equity out of it, I was able to pay off my banker," Christopher said. "This got me out of hock to him and put me in a nice position compared to a lot of my peers who had no more collateral to put up and had no option but to sell their stock. It was not the best of times for a lot of people. Those who were able to survive look back and laugh now. But you have two camps. There were those who did have to liquidate and had to sell all their stock just to come out of it.

One of those who had to sell most of his stock to stay solvent as the price plunged to $9 a share was John Roach.

"Charles was very aware of what was happening," Christopher said. "There were a number of people who defaulted on loans. They just walked away from them, and Charles had no choice but to make the loans good. I assume he picked up whatever stock there was for himself. About that time, when things hit the bottom, we were starting to get a little heat from the Securities and Exchange Commission. Even in the case of the Tandy Investment Plan, for some people the value of the plan was less than they had put in even after the company's matching contribution. The company finally offered to let anybody out of the plan and to regain all of their investment, plus six percent interest. I don't think too many people took advantage of that. I think there were only a few people who had less value in the plan than what they'd put into it."

* * *

Tandy shares had closed at an all-time high of 55 as 1967 drew to a close. It was one of the biggest winners on the Big Board, having risen

270 percent from its 1966 year-end closing price of 14⅞. Of all the 1,400 issues listed on the New York Stock Exchange, Tandy ranked 17th in largest percentage gain in the price of its stock.

Newsweek business columnist Clem Morgello observed, "Tandy Corp. is not a turnaround situation itself. But it specializes in finding and buying ailing companies in the retail field (example: Radio Shack) and putting them into the black—and it enjoys the extra advantage of lower taxes because of the tax-loss benefits it picks up at the same time."

In January, 1968, an ebullient Charles Tandy established a new Radio Shack beachhead in the heart of Manhattan with all of the swagger of Douglas MacArthur wading ashore on his return to Manila.

Full-page advertisements in *The New York Times* and other Big Apple dailies heralded the grand opening of the Radio Shack store at 348 Fifth Avenue on January 31, 1968. New York's First Lady, Mary Lindsay, wife of Mayor John Lindsay, assisted by a beaming Charles Tandy, cut a strip of magnetic recording tape, in lieu of a ribbon, formally opening the newest Radio Shack outlet. The site, on the west side of Fifth Avenue between 34th and 35th Streets in the shadow of the Empire State Building, had been the home of a Tandy Leather Company store. The leather goods operation was moved to another floor in the same building.

As the customers entered the new store they passed displays of lower-end merchandise, such as transistors, then filtered through several parts gondolas, and eventually came out into an alcove featuring hi-fi equipment. There they found a surprising array of name brand products rather than the usual house brands found at other Radio Shack outlets. Charles Tandy told media representatives that the move was an effort to gauge the profitability of name brand merchandise. On hand for the opening were a number of leaders of the high fidelity industry including Avery Fisher, president of Fisher Radio Corporation and Harold Schulman of United Audio, who helped demonstrate their equipment to the hundreds of New Yorkers who thronged the store. Representing Radio Shack were Lew Kornfeld, Dave Beckerman and Sol Baxt, head of lease operations in the Macy's stores.

The Radio Shack expansion program in the Big Apple received another boost on February 6, 1968, with the signing of an agreement with Friendly Frost, Inc., of Westbury, New York, to establish Radio Shack consumer electronics departments in 26 Friendly Frost major appliance stores in the metropolitan New York City area. The move was expected to add approximately $5 million in annual sales to Radio Shack.

The Friendly Frost deal followed on the heels of Radio Shack's acquisition of the retail division of Terminal-Hudson Electronics, Inc., of New York City. The division consisted of 14 leased departments selling consumer electronics equipment in major East Coast department stores including Macy's in New York, Bamberger's in Newark and John Wanamaker's in Philadelphia.

On February 15, 1968, a headline declaring, "Tandy Aim: 1,000 Outlets in 5 Years," appeared over an article in *Audio Times*, a New York-based industry publication. The article advised that Charles Tandy's timetable for opening his 1,000th Radio Shack store was February 1, 1973. Tandy was quoted as stating, "I'm 49 years old. I want to wrap this up. We're going to have 1,000 Radio Shack stores, leased departments or franchised stores by the end of five years."

The article also quoted Tandy: "We are very profit-oriented. Show me any other major audio retailing outfit making 10 percent. We plan to get into some phase of manufacturing, but the fact that we don't have a factory doesn't mean a thing. We have the same characteristics as a manufacturer in that we design and engineer many of our own electronic products and have them made for us. Right now our fall merchandise is all committed for manufacture in Japan. We work one or two years ahead."

Radio Shack, Tandy added, enjoyed its "unique" status as a producer and merchandiser. "We can talk to manufacturers on an equal basis in regard to advertising," he said, "because Radio Shack, in effect, advertises its own products, just like any big-name producer. And when it comes to advertising the products of other manufacturers that we carry in our stores, we can give a manufacturer a program that most outfits can't."

Publication of the 1,000-store forecast was followed by a special Tandy Corporation shareholders meeting in Fort Worth on February 18, 1968, at which stockholders approved a management request for an increase in the number of authorized shares of common stock from 2,000,000 to 5,000,000, and the authorization of 1,000,000 shares of new preferred stock. The increased shares, the company said, would be available for future acquisitions.

On June 24, 1968, *Barron's*, a leading financial publication, featured

Tandy in an article titled, "New Breed of Merchant Prince," which began: "You don't have to be a giant conglomerate (or one which covets
the role) to come up with an expected merger or two these days. Take
the case of Tandy Corp., an erstwhile Fort Worth specialist in leather
goods now transformed into a sprawling retail chain."

The article noted that Tandy's "bootstrap" operation had grown to en-
compass a chain of amateur-electronic hobby shops, another of junior
department stores, and Leonards, "the Fort Worth equivalent of Macy's." It added that the Meacham's acquisition earlier that month had
caused "eyebrows to be raised" in some quarters.

"If nothing else," the writer, Joan Greene, asserted, "The move rein-
forces the old shoemaker's proud claim to being the No. 1 merchant in
its hometown." Referring to Tandy's "unique" corporate philosophy,
Ms. Greene wrote, "Since its first big move into leathercrafting, the
firm never has lacked for imagination, enterprise and a talent for doing
the unexpected. Postwar development of its chain of small hobby
shops, with mail order units, led in turn to its initial important acquisition, Radio Shack, which, incidentally, also provided a $4 million tax
loss. With sales rising from $20 million to over $100 million and pre-
tax income from $1 million to a projected $8 million in just the past
five years, Tandy must be doing something right."

The *Barron's* earnings forecast for fiscal 1968 proved to be right on
the money.

For the year ended June 30, 1968, Tandy reported income before federal income taxes and extraordinary credit of $8.1 million or $3.99 per
share, compared to $3.5 million or $2.06 per share for the prior year.
Net sales totaled $111.9 million, up 84 percent over the previous year's
record high of $60.7 million. Net income was enhanced by the utiliza-
tion of $4.2 million of tax loss carry-over during fiscal 1968. Had this
not been applied, net income per share would have been $2.74.

The question posed to Tandy with increasing frequency was, "What
are you going to buy next?"

Bill Aguren, business columnist of the *Fort Worth Press*, thought he
knew the answer. On July 19, he published a rumor that Tandy's next
takeover candidate was none other than Montgomery Ward.

"The rumor, coming on the heels of Tandy's acquisition of Leonards
and Meacham's here, has brought chuckles in Fort Worth business circles for several weeks," Aguren wrote. "However, the new *Texas Business & Industry* publication, in its July issue, reports there is talk,
which Tandy does not deny, that he has his eye on 'one of the nation's

biggest and oldest mail-order-retail corporations—one with $1.3 billion in assets last Feb. 1.'"

The magazine did not name Montgomery Ward, Aguren noted, but stated that the company in question had a Fort Worth installation almost directly across the street from the Tandy Corporation headquarters. Everyone in Fort Worth, of course, knew that Montgomery Ward had a major retail and mail order complex on West 7th Street.

Although he never really considered buying Montgomery Ward, which even for him would have been quite a mouthful, Tandy got a kick out of the rumors that added to his celebrity status as a wheeler-dealer.

On Tuesday, August 6, the *Wall Street Journal* reported that Tandy had been talking with Rexall Drug and Chemical Co. about a merger and quoted Bill Michero as stating, "There have been no meaningful conversations and nothing is imminent."

The *Journal* article then added, "Told of Mr. Michero's remarks, a Rexall spokesman said no talks about a possible merger had taken place with Tandy, but that Tandy had approached Rexall expressing an interest in acquiring Rexall's drug division. Rumors about a possible merger of Tandy and Rexall circulated after Tandy shares reached a 1968 high $80.625 on the New York Stock Exchange last Thursday. The issue traded as low as $45 earlier this year. Yesterday, it closed at $79, up $1 from Friday's close."

Meanwhile, the pace of the acquisition program continued unabated, with four firms joining the Tandy fold. They were:

Bona Allen, Inc., of Buford, Georgia, a saddlery manufacturer and producer of finished leather products for general and industrial use, in June for $4 million in cash and notes. Bona Allen was a longtime supplier of leathers to Tandy Leather Company and Tex Tan.

The Magee Company, Inc., of Pocahantas, Arkansas, a manufacturer and wholesaler of picture frames, for cash totaling approximately $1.5 million, in July.

Royal Tile Manufacturing Company of Fort Worth, manufacturer and marketer of ceramic tile, for approximately 9,000 shares of Tandy Corporation common stock, in September.

Color Tile of Denver, Colorado, the largest importer of ceramic and mosaic tile in the nation and operator of 14 stores in the West and Midwest retailing home improvement and beautification materials with sales of $6 million, for Tandy stock valued in excess of $3 million, in November.

Also, in July, 1968, Radio Shack opened a large regional warehouse in the Los Angeles suburb of Garden Grove, California, a further indication of the growing emphasis on developing sales on the West Coast. The new facility was Radio Shack's third regional warehouse, supplementing the existing ones in Boston and Fort Worth. Its opening followed by several months the creation of a new Radio Shack Western Region headed by Jim Buxton, the former supervisor of the San Antonio Division.

Buxton was hardly thrilled over being transferred from Texas to California. He was looking forward to a banner year in San Antonio in 1968 because the city was celebrating its 250th birthday with Hemis-Fair '68, the first world's fair ever held in the Southwestern United States.

The Radio Shack store in the Tandy Wonderland Mart that Buxton opened in 1963 was one of the top volume leaders in the country and had been the first outlet in the chain outside of Boston to hit $1 million in annual sales.

"I was doing great," Buxton emphasized, "making decent money, and I liked San Antonio. I was content to stay right there." Best of all, Buxton added, Tandy left him alone. And that was the way he liked it.

"When I first came to work," he explained, "Charles promised me, 'Buxton, you make me money and I'll leave you alone.'"

Tandy lived up to his word until January of 1968, when Buxton received a telephone call from him telling him his presence was urgently needed in Fort Worth.

"When Charles called me and told me to come up to Fort Worth, I was concerned," Buxton recalled. "When he took me to dinner, I was worried. He'd always take you out to dinner to tell you about a new job he had in mind for you."

The new job Tandy had in mind for Buxton was resuscitating California, where Radio Shack was losing money hand over fist. Buxton told Tandy to find himself another candidate, that he was happy in San Antonio and wanted to stay there. Surprisingly, Tandy didn't press the issue. That should have given him a forewarning on what was to come.

The next morning, Buxton got up, packed his suitcase and took a cab to the Tandy headquarters.

"I walked into Charles' office and I asked him, 'Have you decided who you're going to get to do the job?'"

Tandy looked up from the P&L statements he was perusing and peered at Buxton over his spectacles.

"I'm sending you," he said firmly. "But this time, by God, I'm not asking you, I'm ordering you to do it."

It was take-it-or-leave-it time and Buxton took it.

"So I went to California," he said. "I took over the new Western Region, one-third of the United States. I didn't want to do it, but Tandy made me do it, and it turned out to be the best thing that ever happened to me."

The Western Region had no way to go but up; it had already hit bottom. When Buxton arrived, there were 33 stores in operation, none of which had ever made a penny's worth of profit. The region was awash in red ink. Buxton established the regional headquarters in March of 1968 in a new warehouse that was under construction in Garden Grove. The 72,000 square foot facility also housed the executive, supervisory, and advertising offices, quality control laboratories, and a 6,000-square-foot model store where new merchandise, fixtures and promotional techniques could be tested.

"We outgrew the warehouse almost immediately," Buxton recalled. "We really went ahead fast. We opened the warehouse in July of 1968, and it was obsolete within a year." During that period, more than 50 new stores were opened on the West Coast and district offices were established in Los Angeles, San Francisco, and Seattle. In choosing new store locations, Buxton said, "We looked for concentrations of people and income."

In the booming Pacific Coast economy, these were not difficult criteria to meet.

* * *

Back home in Fort Worth, Charles Tandy now was enjoying the acceptance and respect that had eluded him for so long. Suddenly he was in demand as a speaker before business and civic groups and as a guest in the best homes in the city. His new status was manifested by his being asked by Walter R. Humphrey, editor of the *Fort Worth Press*, to author a guest editorial that appeared on the afternoon of August 5, 1968.

"One of the most pungent and profound statements ever made about our American society was contained in the title of a song written by Roger Miller a couple of years ago: 'Squares Make the World go 'Round,'" Tandy editorialized.

"These six words clearly state a simple fact of life. This fundamental fact has been almost shouted down and forgotten in recent years while the news media have been filled with the noisy efforts of nations, groups and individuals trying to achieve goals by almost any means short of working properly for them. I believe it's time to reappraise the role of the 'Squares' of the world.

"A generation ago a man was complimented to be considered 'square.' He was proud to make a 'square deal,' 'shoot square,' and be 'square with the world.' Somehow, though, the word was gradually twisted in everyday usage until it became an adjective of contempt. It became 'square' (or not 'in') to aspire to manly responsibilities, to rise to the aid of a fellow human being, to practice simple honesty, to be a builder of something.

"The 'Squares,' nevertheless, have continued to be dependable, rather than dependent. They have continued to act, rather than to react. They have continued to perform with pride, rather than to avoid. They have continued to stand out as individuals, rather than to submerge in the crowd. In other words, there have always been men of dignity and maturity who have seen to it that the needed and progressive work of the world was accomplished.

"The man who is 'Square,' as always, is the guiding strength of his family, his community and his nation. He also brings this strength to his work or profession. He is the builder, and he is the one who earns any lasting progress that is made. I have had the experience of working with thousands of men during my lifetime, and I agree with Roger Miller that 'Squares' do make the world go 'round."

Aligning himself with the "Squares" did nothing to diminish Tandy's standing in the archly-conservative Fort Worth business community. Buttressing the free enterprise system against the inroads of creeping socialism was a favorite Tandy topic in his platform appearances, and he now demonstrated his support in a more tangible way.

Since the death of Dave Tandy in 1966, Charles had been seeking a suitable vehicle to honor his father's memory. He found it in the endowment of the David L. Tandy Professorship of American Enterprise Management in the M. J. Neeley School of Business at Texas Christian University. Announcement of the establishment of the professorship was made on September 18, 1968, by Charles Tandy and Dr. James M.

Moudy, TCU chancellor, following a meeting of the Tandy Corporation Board of Directors in Fort Worth.

During a brief ceremony at the board meeting, Dr. Moudy commented, "We who knew Dave Tandy well appreciate this living memorial to a man whose business judgment provided the base from which Tandy Corporation has grown and prospered."

Dr. Ike Harrison, dean of the business school, said the professorship would enable the school to recruit another outstanding professor of management. One of the activities of the new professor would be the encouragement of young men and women to aspire to positions of business leadership, and he also outlined a plan under which promising candidates for master's degrees would serve as interns with top business executives of regional firms, under the supervision of the new Tandy professor.

Charles Tandy was on his way to gaining the same kind of status in his hometown accorded other legendary figures like Amon Carter Sr., Sid W. Richardson, and John B. Connally. One reason was the performance of the stock that bore his name on the New York Stock Exchange, where Tandy was finally getting the recognition its bullish board chairman thought it was due.

During the summer and early fall of 1968, the stock had enjoyed its own private bull market. In September, it reached an all-time high of 80⅝, which provided an auspicious backdrop for an appearance by Charles before the New York Society of Security Analysts on September 13. Tandy was in especially fine fettle as he addressed the prestigious body in a private dining room overlooking Lower Manhattan.

Calling fiscal 1968 "the most profitable and productive year in the history of Tandy Corporation," Tandy informed the analysts that the company's net worth had more than tripled during the year, from $11.9 million to $43.4 million, as a result of the retention of earnings of $6.1 million, the sale of 300,000 shares of stock with proceeds of $16.5 million, the issuance of common stock in connection with acquisitions valued at $6.5 million, and the issuance of 189,145 shares of common stock due to the exercise of warrants totaling $1.2 million. This reduced to 30,532 the number of common shares subject to the exercise of warrants at a price of $9 per share, with the remaining warrants due to expire on December 31, 1969.

Tandy also waxed bullish on the company's growth, noting that the number of retail outlets had reached 465 as of June 30, 1968, compared with 327 on the same date the year before, with the largest increases coming in the Radio Shack Division.

"Radio Shack now operates 260 retail outlets in 44 states, an increase of 104 over the previous year, and is participating in a vigorously growing segment of our economy, in which per capita sales are rising and will continue to increase," Tandy said. "The division's sales have grown from $12 million to $40 million in the past four years." Most of the merchandise sold by Radio Shack, he pointed out, was being marketed under private brands and manufactured to company specifications in the United States and Japan.

"Our company entered fiscal 1969 with a much broadened base of merchandising capability and opportunity, an adequate and strengthened financial condition and structure, and a seasoned operating organization," he declared. "These are our key assets. The policies and objectives which had produced a successful record of growth since 1960, when the present management assumed operating control, should become increasingly effective when applied to the greater size and scope of the company's total marketing effort.

"Our policy of retaining earnings for reinvestment to support continued expansion of operations will continue. Programs to improve sales and profitability will continue to be pursued. Acquisitions suited to enhance existing operations, or to develop new marketing dimensions, will continue to be sought out. The coming fiscal year offers opportunity to add substantially to the company's continuing record of growth and performance, and management looks forward enthusiastically to the challenge."

*   *   *

Little more than a month later, Tandy Corporation would face the prospect of losing its leader.

Charles celebrated his 50th birthday on May 15, 1968, with the help of his brother, Bill. The competitive fires that once had flared between the brothers had died down. Bill had joined the Tandy board in 1965 and had become one of Charles' valued confidants. He was considered an asset on the board by the other directors because of his lack of reticence in speaking up when he disagreed with the always opinionated chairman. Charles, in turn, had proved helpful, through his many contacts, in steering business to Bill's construction firm in Tulsa.

On the morning after Charles' birthday, the two brothers, each holding a big cigar and smiling broadly, were pictured in the *Star-Telegram* standing in front of a billboard that proclaimed in large type: "Charles is 50!"

The caption underneath the photograph said that Bill Tandy had denied all knowledge of the billboard that had appeared in front of Tandy headquarters on West 7th Street or of a number of 2-inch ads that had been scattered through that morning's *Star-Telegram* carrying the same "Charles is 50" message enclosed within a heavy black border.

One thing was readily apparent to anyone looking at the picture. Both brothers had eaten too much birthday cake. Charles, especially, looked like he had put on a lot of weight. In fact, just like the Tandy stock, Charles was hitting new highs daily on his bathroom scales. It was hardly a new problem. All of his adult life, Tandy had been fighting a personal "Battle of the Bulge" with his waistline, and his eating and drinking habits made weight control all the more difficult. From time to time, he embarked on reducing regimens, which included betting Bill Tandy on who could lose the most weight within a certain time period. Occasionally, Charles also put in a stint at a "fat farm" in California.

The health spa Charles frequented in California was not cheap, Billy Roland reported. "It cost him about $1,000 a pound," said Roland who wrote all of Tandy's personal checks.

With his weight having ballooned to 235 pounds, Tandy spoke frequently about his need to undergo another session at the health spa, but he was always too busy to do anything about it. It would take a heart attack in Boston on October 8, 1968, to slow him down.

Dave Beckerman recalled the event that traumatized the company.

"Charles was in Boston on one of his regular visits when he had the heart attack. Then, while he was in the hospital, he had a second heart attack. I'd gone to the hospital to visit him. I'd visit him or somebody would visit him every day to get marching orders for the day."

Beckerman arrived at the hospital about 7:30 or 8 o'clock in the morning. He found Tandy's room unoccupied and the bed made. A nurse's aide was in the room and Beckerman asked her, "Where's Mr. Tandy?" Charles had had another heart attack that had almost proved fatal.

"They really thought they'd lost him," Beckerman said. "It took about six or seven minutes before they were able to resuscitate him."

The news of Tandy's heart attack caused a near panic in the corporate headquarters in Fort Worth. The first concern, of course, was for Charles' well being, but running a close second was the fear of what the impact would be on the price of the stock. The decision then was made to sit on the news pending any further developments.

But there was one problem. Tandy was scheduled to be the featured speaker at a black tie dinner at the Fort Worth Club on October 29, when Tandy Corporation was to be honored by the Newcomen Society in North America, an organization devoted to business history. Tandy's absence would have to be explained and someone else would have to deliver the Newcomen Address, a history of the company. The decision was made for Jim West to read the speech, which was "ghostwritten" by Bill Michero.

That night, as the 300 guests entered the ballroom of the Fort Worth Club, they were handed a brief statement informing them that Charles Tandy would not be able to be present that evening, as scheduled, and that his place on the program would be taken by Jim West.

"While in Boston on a business trip," the statement declared, "Mr. Tandy went to a clinic for a regular checkup. His doctors expressed concern at his overweight condition and insisted that he stay at the clinic for several days until he reduces his weight to 195 pounds. He is now at 210 pounds."

Reporting on the memo the next morning, the *Star-Telegram* stated that it had learned, "This means that in a matter of three weeks, Tandy has 'peeled off' some 25 pounds."

Tandy was quoted in the story as having told friends in Fort Worth, "These doctors are pretty tough. But I've decided to go along with them. Already I feel a great deal better, and I'll be back there pitching as soon as they release me."

At the dinner, a message from Tandy was read by Sam B. Cantey III, the secretary of the Fort Worth Chapter of the Newcomen Society.

"I firmly believe that to make money for a company and its stockholders, a man must first make money for himself," the message read. "All of our key management men from division heads to store managers are on a salary plus bonus incentive, with bonuses tied directly to profits. This past June, the company paid out more than $2 million in year-end bonuses to more than 500 men and women in the organization. That's one out of every ten employees.

"When we look at potential acquisitions, we also look for the fresh talent in those organizations. We intend to realize a high percent return on investment for each acquisition and know full well that motivating the people is as important as analyzing the balance sheet."

Tandy then added:

"I believe we have laid the foundation for a $1 billion organization. At our present rate of growth, we can hope to achieve that goal. We have the dream, the organization and the resources to accept the challenge. The opportunities are everywhere. We believe we're only beginning."

Jim West, after tracing the corporate history from the Hinckley-Tandy days, noted that Tandy Corporation's growth had been maintained at about a 25 percent compound rate in sales and earnings for the past seven years. He then delineated the company's fundamental policies:

"Financial policy? Instead of dividends, we believe our shareholders would prefer to see plow-back of earnings leading to capital gains.

"Bank borrowing? We borrow as much as we need to finance seasonal requirements.

"Acquisition policy? We consider no acquisition unless we can see the possibility of at least 25 percent profit on assets before tax.

"Inventory policy? We stock only those items that prove to have fast profit-making ability.

"Compensation policy? We pay our managers generously. None have an employment contract, but all are motivated by a profit-oriented bonus formula."

Naturally, there was talk around town in the aftermath of the meeting that Tandy was in the hospital for more than a weight-reduction program. There were rumors that he had suffered a heart attack, but all were promptly denied. The local newspapers made no effort to delve into the matter further in spite of the fact that two months would elapse before Tandy would return from Boston. And there was no apparent concern on Wall Street, where the stock continued to make new highs, closing at $93 a share on the day of the Newcomen dinner.

On November 20, Harold Monroe wrote in his daily financial column in the *Star-Telegram*, "Tandy Corp. reached an all-time high of 96 and closed there for a rise of 3 points on the day. An associate of Charles Tandy, board chairman, was in touch with him Tuesday at the home of his brother, A.R. (Bill) Tandy in Tulsa, where he was reported in good health and 'rarin' to go.' He has cut his weight by 36 pounds to 199 pounds since he went to a Boston hospital last month for a checkup and was told by his doctors he'd have to 'peel off a lot.'"

After leaving the hospital in mid-November, Tandy spent a week recuperating in the Florida sunshine. Dave Beckerman flew to Miami with him and then drove him to Key Largo, where Tandy checked into a resort hotel.

"A funny thing happened that first night in Key Largo," Beckerman recalled. "I wanted to go to bed, but Charles said, 'No, let's have a drink first.' So we went to the bar. "It was a horseshoe-shaped bar, with the bartender in the middle. So we're sitting at the bar and there was a feller on the other side of the horseshoe hiccupping like crazy.

"Charles says to the guy, across the horseshoe, 'I can get rid of those hiccups for you for 20 bucks.'

"The guy says, 'I bet you can't.'

"Charles laid a $20 bill down on the bar and the guy with the hiccups laid $20 down on the bar.

"Charles said to the bartender, 'Give him a tall glass of water.'

"Now Charles walked behind the guy and told him, 'I'm going to press your ears; and while I press, you drink the water.'

"The fellow drank the glass of water and found the hiccups gone. What Charles did was close off the eustachian tubes, I guess, by putting enough pressure on them.

"Anyway, Charles then picked up the two $20 bills and gave them to the bartender.

"That was Charles just out of the hospital."

Tandy returned home to Fort Worth on Saturday, December 7, after an absence of two months. That night he was the guest of honor at a dinner party at the Fort Worth Club given by Continental National Bank Board Chairman Robert P. Dupree, a close friend. Dupree had invited some 25 couples to the dinner, telling them only that he was going to have a "mystery guest."

In an account of the dinner party, Harold Monroe wrote, "Dupree was hoping that Tandy had changed so much that nobody would recognize him. But it didn't work out that way. Charles Tandy at 194 pounds is still Charles Tandy—trimmer and sleeker, but still the same exuberant personality who has continued to amaze the financial world with the increases in the sales of his business (and the price of Tandy stock) every year.

"Even when he was in that Boston hospital, he couldn't quite keep his mind off business," Monroe reported. "There was a day when top executives of a major Boston retail concern were sitting around his bed, complete with their accountants and reams of paper and charts and tabulations. 'I almost made a deal,' Tandy said, 'but another company that was able to use its own office and its full staff of accountants sort of sneaked in ahead of me. I still think my offer was better than theirs, but I'm not worried. There are still a lot of fine companies all over the United States that would make very good Tandy divisions, and there's still time to bring them into the fold.'"

Tandy told Monroe he was "rarin' to go," but that his doctors had insisted he limit himself to "a couple of hours a day at the office" until around the middle of January.

"That's not for me," he growled. "When I do go back to work, I'm going to work full time."

But although he was not quite cleared to go back to the old grind full time, he was keeping in touch with things, Tandy insisted. He spoke about a shopping center being planned on the western outskirts of Fort Worth.

"We're thinking in terms of making it a complete shopping center, like the original Tandy Mart, but consisting solely of Tandy-owned enterprises. It will sell everything from trees and shrubs to sophisticated electronic equipment. We haven't put the numbers together yet, but we know where we're going."

The complex, which would be named Tandy Town, would soon become a reality on U. S. Highway 80 West, featuring a Radio Shack and a Wolfe Nursery among other corporate entities.

Tandy also had a word of warning for the employees of the far-flung Tandy divisions.

"I've been telling them that while I was away, they took 41 pounds of my sweetness away. And so they might find that all that's left is meanness."

Monroe wasn't buying any of that.

"None of the Tandy employees believe him," he wrote. "They think he had a lot more than 41 pounds of sweetness in him."

The fact is, Tandy would come back from his brush with the grim reaper more propulsive then ever.

Mary Frank recalled, "After his heart attack, I think that's when he really began to hurry up and finish up, to pull things together. He was afraid time was going to run out on him. That's when he appeared driven, rushing between Fort Worth and Boston all the time."

Bill Michero saw to it that Tandy was greeted with all of the ceremony due the commander-in-chief upon his return to active duty. "In the early years of the company," Michero explained, "Charles was able to get away with running things with a military style of leadership: 'I've got three gold braids on my shoulder and you've just got one on your sleeve.'" So, in honor of Charles' return, Michero designed a flag with a Tandy logo.

"This was a holdover from our Navy time when you ran up the flag to designate that the senior officer was present," Michero added. "When he was gone, you hauled the flag down. Well, we hung up the flag outside of Charles' office on the day he came back to work."

A short while later, Tandy appeared in Michero's office with the flag under his arm.

"Michero," he snapped, "I don't want anybody to know where I am, and you know that. And you can take this flag and stuff it."

Then he grinned.

Chapter 18
"What Are You Gonna Buy Next, General Motors?"

A leaner, meaner Tandy came back to work full time shortly after the arrival of the new year. He swaggered into the office sporting a tan and a new dark grey suit.

"This is the only suit I have that fits me right," he said proudly, as he showed off his new svelte figure.

He was welcomed back with the news that his hometown was honoring him with two awards—Top Male Newsmaker of the Year by the Press Club of Fort Worth and Outstanding Salesman of the Year by the Sales and Marketing Executives of Fort Worth.

Tandy received the Press Club award in absentia at the annual Newsmakers Ball at Ridglea Country Club on February 8, 1969. He was on hand, beaming broadly, however, on February 11 when he accepted the Salesman of the Year Award in the Crystal Ballroom atop the venerable Hotel Texas in downtown Fort Worth.

In making the presentation, Lewis H. Bond, then the president of the Fort Worth National Bank and the previous year's recipient of the award, called Tandy a man "cut from the great American dream." He described Tandy as "a man who sells merchandise that won't come back to customers that will."

Walter R. Humphrey, editor of the *Fort Worth Press*, devoted his front page column, The Home Towner, to a paean to Tandy. He wrote:

"Charles Tandy has been both a buyer and a seller these past couple of years. The companies he has bought have helped make Tandy Corp. one of the giants in the commercial field. And when you hear that Tandy Corp. will have around $180 million in sales this year, you can't have a lingering doubt about this super-salesman.

"Charles Tandy has sold Fort Worth in a big way while he has been expanding this unusual empire of his. He has made Fort Worth the headquarters of his far-flung operations and the Tandy Corporation name on the Big Board in Wall Street has no other reference point but Fort Worth. He and his associates have put this city on the map in a new way, with the acquisition of Leonards, Meacham's, Stafford-Lowdon and other enterprises here at home bolstering their nationwide operations. It is difficult to see how anyone else could have been selected as Fort Worth's top salesman for last year."

Noting that Tandy had been honored by the Sales and Marketing Executives, an organization his father had helped found, Humphrey added, "This surely must have been a compliment above so many others he has received in his rise to fame. He has built quite an empire on the firm foundation laid by Dave Tandy in the leather business. With imagination, vision and daring, he has spread out from this good base into many new fields, selling thousands of products."

The column concluded, "He moves ahead with purpose, but keeps the common touch, the down to earth qualities which make him popular, not resented, exciting in what he's doing but neither arrogant nor vain about it. Yes, the Salesman of the Year is quite a guy, easy to know and impossible to dislike."

Things had never looked so good. Sales and earnings were booming and Tandy stock was running rampant.

Propelled by the announcement of 79 percent increases in sales and earnings for the first six months of the 1969 fiscal year and amid rumors of an impending stock split, the stock hit a new all-time high of $103.25 per share in mid-February.

The two-for-one split, the first in the company's history, was approved by the board at its regular meeting on February 20. At the same time, holders of the remaining warrants due to expire on December 31, 1969, were advised that, as a result of the split, the purchase price of the stock issuable upon exercise of the warrants would be $4.50 per share rather than $9.00 per share.

On April 8, the effective date of the split, Tandy stock closed at an all-time high of 110½.

Tandy now was having the time of his life going around town saying, "I told you so," to people who had failed to follow his advice to buy Tandy stock.

His former partner in the ladies' belt business, John Justin, recalled ruefully that, despite Charles' urgings, he'd never bought any Tandy stock.

"I guess I never really believed what he was telling me," Justin said. "I could have made a lot of money if I'd listened to him."

The late William M. Fuller, a prominent Fort Worth oilman, recalled eating lunch with Tandy at the Fort Worth Club. After lunch, Tandy invited him to his office.

"I want to show you something," he told Fuller.

At the office, Tandy pulled a sheaf of papers out of his desk. They contained sales and earnings projections for Tandy Corporation.

"All of the lines headed straight up," Fuller said, laughing as he recalled the scene. "I couldn't believe what I was seeing. I thought to myself, 'These can't be right. Nothing goes straight up like that, except a rocket ship.'"

Fuller eventually became a Tandy shareholder and shared in subsequent stock splits, but he acknowledged he missed the boat by not clambering aboard earlier.

Elton Hyder recounted with a chuckle, "Charles loved to call me when the stock was going up and brag about how many millionaires he'd made that day. But when the stock would go down, I'd call him and ask him, 'Charles, how many millionaires have you unmade today?' He'd get madder'n hell."

James S. Garvey, Fort Worth grain operator and rancher, carried a vivid recollection of Tandy holding court in front of the Fort Worth Club on a wintry afternoon before a group of shivering business and professional men.

"Charles was saying, 'I told you guys to buy my stock, but you wouldn't believe me.'" Garvey said.

Bernie Appel recalled how Tandy enjoyed needling employees who had ever exhibited a lack of faith in his vision. During the period when Radio Shack was still losing money, Appel had confronted Tandy with his concerns over the company's lack of profitability.

"I went into his office," Appel recalled, "and I said, 'Charles, this is crazy. How are you ever going to pay us the bonuses you're promising us when we're never going to make a profit? We can't make a profit because you're opening all these stores all over the country. That's what's draining the profits. How are you gonna do it?'"

It was about 9:30 in the morning when Appel entered Tandy's office.

"He was drinking black coffee, as he always did," Appel remembered. "He kept me in that office all day long. He didn't let me go to lunch. He had me going absolutely crazy. I sat there listening in on telephone calls from the bank, everything that was going on. Whoever came into his office, I sat there and listened to the conversation."

At about 7:30 that night, one of the Radio Shack executives stuck his head into the room and saw that Appel still sitting there.

"Bernie," he asked, "what are you doing here? You were here when I came in this morning."

Appel answered, "I'm still trying to get an answer out of Mr. Tandy on how I'm ever going to make any more money at the rate we're going."

"Has he let you have dinner?"

"What dinner? I haven't had lunch yet."

Tandy looked up from some papers he'd been perusing.

"Okay," he said to Appel, "let's go have dinner."

After dinner, while Tandy savored a brandy and a cigar, Appel made one final try.

"Charles," he said, "you haven't answered the question I asked you this morning. How am I ever going to make more money?"

Tandy puffed on his stogie, exhaled a cloud of pungent smoke, and said, "Don't worry about it. Stick with me and I'll make you rich."

"That was Charles Tandy," Appel added. "You couldn't argue with him. A year later we got our bonuses. He gave us our bonuses and took them back and put them into Tandy stock. He believed heart and soul in the company and he got us to invest in it."

Tandy enjoyed his role as Fort Worth's most eligible bachelor.

"After Gwen's death, every single woman in town tried to date him, and some were more vigorous in their pursuits than others," Phil North reported. "But he was very adroit in dodging them. He went with a number of real attractive ladies and he had several dates with Arlene Dahl. I remember one time we were in New York and Arlene was supposed to meet us someplace and she didn't show up. Charles just got furious about it, although I'm not really sure he knew who she was."

The movie actress figured in another Tandy story told by Elton Hyder.

"We had gotten Charles a date with Arlene Dahl to go to a party at George Ann Carter's (Mrs. Amon G. Carter, Jr.) house. About 75 to 100 people were there. A very pretty party, small tables. Charlie fell sound asleep at the table. Arlene was about the maddest red-headed woman I ever saw."

Eunice West recalled being concerned over the intensity with which Tandy was playing the dating game.

"All the young girls in town were chasing Charles, and he was living quite a life for a man who had just had a bad heart attack. I told him, 'Charles, you've got to calm down, you're just going too fast. You have to stop all this running around. Make up your mind and marry one of them.'"

Tandy answered, "Don't worry about me, Eunice. If I ever marry again, I'll marry an older woman."

He may already have made up his mind.

On June 12, 1969, he married Anne Burnett Windfohr, the owner of a vast oil and ranching empire in northwest Texas and the doyenne of Fort Worth society. Tandy had just turned 51 and Mrs. Windfohr, the widow of Fort Worth independent oil operator Robert F. Windfohr, was 63 when they were joined in matrimony by the Rev. Louis F. Martin at St. Andrews Episcopal Church in Fort Worth.

The granddaughter of legendary cattleman Samuel Burk Burnett, Anne virtually grew up in the saddle. She was as much at home on the range as in the drawing room of her palatial home.

As a youth, Burk Burnett rode the fabled Chisholm Trail through Fort Worth, driving herds of Longhorns north to the Kansas railheads. The family holdings his granddaughter inherited included the vast 6666 Ranch in King County, Texas, and the two Triangle Ranches in Wichita County and Panhandle, Texas. Burk Burnett won the 6666 Ranch in a high-stakes poker game and named it after his winning hand.

The wedding of Anne Burnett Windfohr and Charles Tandy was big news in Fort Worth, not only because of the prominence of the principals and the disparity in their ages, but because of the fact that it came as such a surprise. No one knew they had even been dating.

"They were very, very quiet about it," Phil North said. "In fact, they never had a date in Fort Worth."

North was sworn to secrecy by Tandy when he informed him about the impending nuptials. North's wife, Janice, didn't learn about it until several weeks later.

"It's time we told Janice," Tandy said to North. "Why don't you tell her that Anne wants her to come over for a drink this afternoon."

"So we went over to Anne's old house, the new one wasn't finished yet," North said. "We walked in and there was Anne wearing the new diamond ring that Charles had gotten at Harry Winston. Then we went over and looked at the new house."

Eunice West received the news of the impending nuptials in a telephone call from Charles on a Saturday evening.

"I want to tell you something," he said. "I'm over at Anne's and we're going to get married. She wants to talk to you."

Anne came on the phone, Mrs. West recalled.

"She told me that they were going to marry, and then she said, 'It will more than likely be a convenience marriage because there is a lot of difference in our ages. But we can travel and go places together.'"

Elton Hyder recalled he was in Tandy's apartment on Curzon when he learned the news.

"Charles said, 'I've got something to tell you,'" Hyder recounted. "I looked over in the corner at Anne and I said, 'You're gonna get married.' And she said, 'that's right.'"

The wedding preparations were carried out under security precautions almost as tight as the D-day invasion of Normandy.

"They didn't want any news to leak out in advance," Phil North disclosed, "so we had somebody from the county clerk's office come to my living room the night before the wedding and they sent the marriage license out to my house."

The ceremony was held in a small side chapel at the church. Bill Tandy was the best man. Eunice and Jim West, Connie and Jesse Upchurch, Janice and Phil North, and Mary Louise Tandy, Bill's wife, attended. Also present were some of the cowboys from Anne Burnett's ranch. The group, including the bride and groom, went to Ridglea Country Club for dinner.

When the news of the nuptials broke, it became the number one topic of conversation in Fort Worth. One of the better lines that made the rounds was that it was the first marriage that ever had to be approved by the Securities and Exchange Commission.

Lewis Bond, Tandy's banker, told an associate that he had seen the Windfohr-Tandy pre-marital agreement and that it contained more pages than the prospectus the bank had filed with federal agencies prior to its conversion into a holding company.

Other friends like wealthy oilman W.A. (Tex) Moncrief, Jr., had a lot of fun needling Tandy about his marital obligations, particularly in light of his heart condition.

"I was with Charles at Anne's house right before the wedding," Moncrief recalled with a laugh, "and I told him to be sure and take his doctor along with him on the honeymoon."

The newlyweds spent their honeymoon at Dave Tandy's old house in Rockport. The site was definitely not the Pierre in New York, the Crillon in Paris, or the Hassler in Rome, which were more to Anne's style, but Charles was quite vehement that a lengthy absence from the office at that time was simply out of the question.

Phil North, who owned a vacation home in Rockport not far from the Dave Tandy place, was at home in Fort Worth when he received a phone call from Tandy on the third day after the wedding.

"Will you come down here and talk business to me?" Tandy pleaded.

North said he replied, "Charles, you're on your honeymoon. I'm not gonna do it."

But Tandy was not about to be put off.

"So the next day I went down to Rockport and spent part of their honeymoon with them," North said.

Elton Hyder reminisced about accompanying Anne and Charles to Rockport on one occasion and watching her do her morning calisthenics.

"She was a good-looking woman who worked hard at keeping in shape. She had a great figure," Hyder said. "She also had a lot of style. I can remember her driving around town in a Duesenberg and a Rolls-Royce. And the I.M. Pei-designed house she had built was really spectacular."

The "mansion," as the house was known around Tandy corporate headquarters to differentiate it from the "apartment" on Curzon, featured a magnificent salon with ceiling that soared to a height of 150 feet. "There was a tremendous tree growing in the room that was about 60 feet tall," Hyder said.

"The house was really spectacular," he continued. "I have the dining room chairs that Anne did the crocheting for. She did beautiful crocheting. There are 24 chairs and they are beautiful. I bought them at Sotheby's when her estate put them on sale. She had a little pool of water in the house that you couldn't see, and some people walked into it. And she had these gorgeous paintings. Anne had beautiful taste, truly beautiful taste. A lot of the paintings were Picassos and a lot were Impressionists and there were some Georgia O'Keeffes. And they bought a big Buddha when they went to Japan, a magnificent thing. It was a very spectacular house. In some ways it looked more like a museum than a home. There was a lot of marble and a beautiful driveway. Pei was very proud of it."

Ed Bass, one of the four billionaire Bass brothers in Fort Worth, recalled visiting the house with his parents, Nancy Lee and Perry Bass, while it was still under construction.

"Anne was showing us around," Bass said with a grin, "and when we came to one of the bedrooms, she said, 'And this is baby's room.' I thought she was talking about Little Anne, her daughter. Later I discovered that she was talking about Charles. She called him 'Baby.'"

Eunice West recalled that for years after the wedding there was talk in Fort Worth that Charles had, for a second time, married an older woman for her money.

"I know that people said that," Mrs. West said, "but Anne did not help Charles. I know for sure she didn't. Charles had enough money of his own when he married Anne. They didn't need each other's money. It was that sort of a marriage. She didn't need Charles and he didn't need her. So it worked out nicely that way. Gwen, of course, had helped Charles by putting up her money when he was fighting for the company, but their marriage was entirely different.

"Anne would entertain for Charles at the big house. She told me once while I was visiting there one evening, 'This is my house. Charles doesn't own any part of the house. All he does is pay for the food when I entertain for him.'

"But they had a good marriage. Charles was busy and he didn't have a lot of time to go to places with Anne that she wanted him to go. She had a lot to take off of him and he had a lot to put up with, too. It wasn't all roses, but it was a nice marriage.

"And she was a lot of fun. I always enjoyed her so much, because not having grown up in Fort Worth, there were a lot of people I didn't know. I'd get with her and she'd tell funny things that happened to people and about the old families here."

As for Charles' preference for older women, at least as marriage partners, Mrs. West thought it might have had something to do with the fact that his mother was such a dominant factor in his life while he was growing up. Perhaps, he was seeking a surrogate mother to fill the void left by the death of Carmen McClain Tandy?

Phil North, however, believed that Charles' choice in spouses was dictated by the fact that he was really married to his business.

"I think he felt that if he married someone his own age, she would demand more of his attention, have him rushing around to parties and things that would distract him from business. I really think that he didn't want to spend as much time on things that newlyweds do. It just didn't appeal to him."

Anne Burnett Tandy was an outspoken, salty-tongued, strong-willed woman who was as accustomed to dominating the scene as was her charismatic husband. She was so accustomed to occupying the spotlight that she was not above upstaging her husband at social functions.

When the two were jointly honored with the prestigious Golden Deeds Award of the Exchange Club of Fort Worth in 1974, the master of ceremonies, Bayard H. Friedman, board chairman of the Fort Worth National Bank and a former mayor of Fort Worth, brought down the house that filled the ballroom at the Fort Worth Club with a line from Confucius:

"Sad is the hen house when the hen crows louder than the rooster."

No one, however, laughed more heartily than the two honorees.

It was a volatile marriage, as one might have expected when two people accustomed to speaking their minds and possessing massive egos got together. Sometimes their arguments reached Olympic proportions. One night, after a particularly heated encounter earlier in the day, Tandy suffered a major indignity, being locked out of the house. Compounding the affront was that the fact that Bob Hope was an amused observer.

Hope was a frequent visitor in Fort Worth during the '70s as a result of his investing in oil deals with independent oil operators like W.A. (Monty) Moncrief, Sr. and J. Lloyd Patton. On one occasion, when Hope was in town to see Patton about a wildcat he was preparing to drill, the two repaired to the Fort Worth Petroleum Club, where they were joined by Elton Hyder, Jr. and Tandy. It was a pleasant evening, with each of the men around the table in the club's comfortable bar trying to outdo Hope in telling jokes. Finally, around midnight, Hope said he was ready to call it a night.

"Where are you staying?" Tandy asked him.

"The Fort Worth Club," Hope responded.

"The hell you are," Tandy declared. "You're going home with me."

After demurring initially, Hope finally acquiesced to the insistent Tandy. They got into Tandy's Lincoln Continental and drove out to the mansion. Hope whistled in appreciation when he saw the edifice.

Tandy parked the car in the driveway and strode to the front door. He inserted the key into the lock. Nothing happened. He kept on trying, but the lock wouldn't budge. Now he tried the door bell. It rang loudly. But again nothing happened. No one answered the ring. Now a red-faced and frustrated Tandy began pounding on the door and calling out for someone to open it. There was no response.

Watching what was transpiring, Hope couldn't resist inserting the needle. Leaning his head out of the car, he said to Tandy, "Sure, you live here..."

What had happened was that Anne had ordered the locks changed on all the doors of the mansion after her embroglio with Charles that morning. Both he and Hope wound up spending the night at the Fort Worth Club.

One of the first things people noticed about Charles after the wedding was a change for the better in his tailoring.

"Anne was always after him about his rumpled appearance," Phil North recalled, "and she finally had a commercial pressing machine installed in the house."

She also began a campaign to upgrade his wardrobe by buying suits for him.

Bill Roland, who wore the same size suit as Charles, a 48 long, related an incident when Anne had bought Charles four suits at Brooks Brothers in New York. The suits were in the back seat of Tandy's Lincoln Continental when he parked next to Roland's car on the Tandy parking lot on West 7th Street. Tandy walked into the office where he encountered Roland.

"Do you want some suits?" he asked. "Anne bought me four suits in New York and I don't like any of them. You can have them all."

Roland wasted no time in taking Tandy up on the offer.

"The second Mrs. Tandy desired her husband to look more like a millionaire industrialist and less like a millionaire Texan, starting with his shoes," Lew Kornfeld wrote in his book, *To Catch a Mouse*.

"You know these damned Gucci loafers aren't built for a man of weight," Kornfeld quoted Tandy as complaining. "Yesterday Anne made me buy six pairs...and whoee-ee, do you know the price tag?"

But Mary Frank remembered a company Christmas party of that era when Charles showed off his new footwear.

"We were dancing and he stopped on the dance floor and he said, 'How do you like my new shoes?' You know, like a kid. And I said, 'They're really good looking, Charles.'

"'They're Guccis,' he said, and he started dancing."

Tandy's personality changed along with his wardrobe after his second marriage, Miss Frank opined.

"I think Anne Tandy changed him," she said. "I think he got tougher after he married her. You know she could be as tough as one of her cowhands, and that's not a reflection against her. She could be the epitome of grace and charm; but when she had to, she could fight it out with her meanest cowhands. She worked a lot on the dress angle for Charles. He began dressing better and looking less rumpled."

* * *

On April 9, 1969, Tandy Corporation filed a registration statement with the Securities and Exchange Commission for a proposed public offering of $40 million of 5 percent convertible subordinated debentures. The proceeds, the statement said, would be used to open 410 new Radio Shack stores and 50 franchised Radio Shack dealer outlets during the 1970 and 1971 fiscal years and finance the construction of two new Leonards suburban department stores. The debentures, due in 1989, were convertible into common stock at a price of $64.50 per share. They were sold on May 20, 1969 through an underwriting managed jointly by Eastman-Dillon Securities Company, E.F. Hutton & Co., Inc. and Rauscher Pierce & Co., Inc.

An industry publication that interviewed Lew Kornfeld and Dave Beckerman at the time of the public offering, commented: "Radio Shack is opening stores so fast that the number has to be counted on a daily basis."

Beckerman noted that prior to Tandy's acquisition of Radio Shack, mail order comprised 60 percent of Radio Shack's sales volume.

"Currently," he pointed out, "since we have put stores out where the customers are, mail order is 10 percent of our volume. This is a decentralized operation and every store handles its own mail order business."

"We don't refuse mail orders in any store of the Tandy divisions," Kornfeld interjected. "We write copy directly at getting mail orders, but we don't make a fetish out of the mail order business. We don't say we won't return to a centralization of mail order, but we are a specialty store operation and the large mail order houses are department stores. Mail order requires an apparatus—people to open letters, answer them, handle returns. We had this, but we purposely dismantled it and distributed it over our stores so that it would not be a significant overhead factor for any of them."

Kornfeld divulged that one of Radio Shack's most popular items, its Science Fair electronic kits, was being manufactured in Fort Worth and that the company was taking a "hard look" at acquiring other manufacturing facilities in the United States. "There is no limit for manufacturing in the United States and abroad," he went on. "Tomorrow is beginning. Manufacturing might lead to wholesaling to broaden our distribution. There could be an effort as well on imports. We are now in all components except TV and consoles and it is fair to surmise that we will go into these in some manner in the next year or so...imported and made to our specifications.

"Our philosophy has been," Kornfeld continued, "that we don't look on imports as having a connotation of cheap merchandise. We do not aspire to carry discount house, low-priced merchandise. We could not have nationalized our Realistic brand if we had put price ahead of quality and style."

He cited two examples.

"Look at our new Push 'N Play radio. This is a take-off on a European model, but it's made to our specification. It has FM and AM, AC and battery. It has three pre-selection tuning controls and pushbuttons, one for AM, two for FM. It's priced at $49.95. Then there's our omnidirection high fidelity loudspeaker which we manufacture in Tokyo. It will sell for $19.95. Most loudspeakers, to do some good, have to be placed against a wall, but this one can be placed on a desk or hung on a wall or from the ceiling."

Summing up, Kornfeld declared, "These things make it easy for us to open new stores and not be looked on by the local gentry as 'Who dat?' The cognoscenti of electronics know that we've been around and they know what track we're on."

By the close of the 1969 fiscal year on June 30, Radio Shack was operating 454 retail units in 46 states, including 39 leased departments, an increase of 194 retail outlets over the number in operation a year earlier. In addition, there were 31 independent dealer stores associated with Radio Shack under franchise agreements. Total sales of the Radio Shack Division had increased 67 percent to $67 million. It was now apparent that Radio Shack was becoming the driving force behind Tandy Corporation.

Tandy's net sales also showed a healthy 53 percent increase to $180 million during the year, while net income rose 23 percent to $7.8 million. Earnings per share registered a 40 percent increase to $1.97, excluding the 1968 extraordinary tax credit of $1.9 million or 61 cents per share.

"The operating results of the past year are very satisfactory and demonstrate that vigorous expansion and earnings progress have continued to be maintained in good balance," Charles Tandy informed the shareholders. "Significant investments also were made to enlarge the production and sales capacity of several of the marketing divisions. These enlargement programs are designed to enhance future earnings, and a portion of that enhancement should begin to be realized during the coming fiscal year. We are pleased with the prospect of establishing new records in fiscal 1970."

The "enlargement programs" to which Tandy was referring were the Color Tile and Royal Tile acquisitions and two smaller deals that added Creative Decorative Company, Inc., of Glendora, California, and Johnal's, Inc., of Miami, Florida, to the fold. Creative Decorative, acquired for $450,000 in cash and notes, manufactured household decorative items and distributed them through home furnishings dealers. Johnal's, which was bought for $30,000, manufactured household decorative merchandise which was to be marketed by the Magee Company's sales organization.

Additional acquisitions were in the offing.

In September, two R.E. Cox & Co. department stores in Texas, one in Stephenville and one in Marlin, were acquired at a cost of approximately $200,000 in cash and were added to the Mitchell's Junior Department Store Group.

In October, J.M. Bucheimer Co. of Frederick, Maryland, an 85-year-old firm nationally known as a manufacturer of specialty leather goods, primarily for sportsmen and for law enforcement uses, was acquired in exchange for 12,904 shares of Tandy common stock. Bucheimer, which had 1969 revenues of $4.3 million, maintained manufacturing facilities in Frederick, Maryland; Cameron, West Virginia; Valencia, California; and St. Catherines, Ontario, Canada.

Also in October, the Woodie Taylor Company of Fort Worth, operator of food, candy, soft drink, cigarette and other coin vending machine services in the Fort Worth area, including retail, warehouse, plant and office spaces occupied by Tandy Corporation, was acquired in exchange for 8,333 shares of common stock.

Lunching at the Fort Worth Club or at social functions, Tandy would glow as people came up to him to ask, "What are you gonna buy next, Charles, General Motors?" In truth, Tandy was finding the acquisition game a lot more fun than Monopoly. All you needed was lots of stock with which to play. With five million shares authorized and 3,981,945 shares outstanding, Tandy decided he needed a bigger cushion.

Shareholders learned of his plans to increase the number of authorized shares from five million to ten million when they received their proxy materials for the annual meeting to held at the Sheraton Hotel in Fort Worth on November 13, 1969. The additional stock was needed, management said, so that it would be available for issuance "in connection with future financing, investment opportunities, acquisitions of other companies, and stock dividends or distributions."

The stock market interpreted the news bullishly when it was made public on October 14. Tandy stock was heavily traded and reached a new post-split high of $63 per share, a gain of $2.25 on the day.

The increase in the number of authorized shares was overwhelmingly approved by the shareholders at the annual meeting, which was marked by the absence of the chairman of the board. Jim West presided in Tandy's stead. A brief news item had appeared in the *Star-Telegram* on Friday, October 31, reporting that the newspaper had learned Charles Tandy had been hospitalized several days earlier "because his doctors insisted he should rest."

In fact, Tandy had been admitted to All Saints Episcopal Hospital on the morning of October 26 after suffering a severe heart attack. The heart attack was complicated by an acute gall bladder attack that took place in the hospital a week later.

"It was a pretty touchy medical problem because gall bladder surgery would have been very difficult and very dangerous," Dr. Robert W. (Bobby) Brown, the former New York Yankees third baseman and Tandy's cardiologist at the time, recalled. Fortunately, Tandy responded to treatment by Dr. Robb Rutledge and the surgery was averted.

The diseased gall bladder was later removed by Dr. Rutledge on October 12, 1972.

Bobby Brown, who became the president of the American Baseball League after he retired from his medical practice in Fort Worth, remembered the irrepressible Tandy conducting business from his hospital bed after his 1969 heart attack.

Brown said of his former cardiac patient, "He would be very cooperative as long as he could have a phone and as long as his lieutenants or his business associates could come in and see him once a day, where he could really keep track of his company and keep running it. In essence, he would have a board meeting in his room in the coronary care unit every morning. The nurses would sit there transfixed just looking at the monitors and looking at him in there talking to his people. It was just a very unusual circumstance, but that was the only way he'd stay in. And as long as he could do that, he was very content."

Tandy was "totally immersed in his business," Brown continued. "He had very few interests otherwise. He didn't like sports particularly and he hated exercise. He was basically a sedentary person that loved figures and loved reading his *Wall Street Journal* and looking at his company reports and issuing orders for his company. It was all-consuming in as far as the business was concerned. His idea of a vacation was just to do more business. He was not one to want to go to Aspen or Vail or to the Caribbean. He would do it to be with people or if he was under duress, but it was only for him to transfer his office to that place and continue on with his business. He wasn't interested in the beach or the snow or things like that."

Asked if he had tried to get Tandy to cut down on smoking and drinking, Brown replied: "Here again, what you tried to do was have him practice moderation, because if you made things too tough for him or you made things too difficult for him to adhere to, he just would throw over the traces and go his own way. As long as you had reasonable limits on him, he would cooperate fully."

However, in a report he wrote after Tandy was admitted to All Saints Hospital on July 21, 1976 with a recurring cardiac rhythm problem, Brown noted: "He has not taken care of himself. He has put on some 23 pounds of weight since his infarction in 1969. He has been ingesting too much food, too much alcohol. He smokes 15-20 cigars a day and drinks perhaps 15 cups of coffee per day."

Tandy, Brown said, was a probable candidate for by-pass surgery, but refused to have any coronary angiography.

"He didn't want to know how bad or how good his coronary arteries were," Brown revealed. "He told me right off the bat that he didn't want any diagnostic tests where they put dye in your coronary arteries, because he wasn't interested in any kind of surgery."

The coronary infarction and gall bladder attack in 1969 had kept Tandy hospitalized for nearly a month until November 21, but as he began feeling stronger and was moved from the coronary care unit into a two-room hospital suite, he immediately converted his new surroundings into an auxiliary office.

Rachel Barber recalled being summoned to the suite to report on how she was progressing on an assignment for Meacham's that Tandy had given her.

"He had a monitor on his heart, but he was keeping up with everybody," she said, "always asking questions, 'How is this going, how is that going?'"

Bill Roland walked into the suite one afternoon to find Tandy, hooked to a monitoring device, sitting on his hospital bed and chatting animatedly with Jim West, Bill Michero and Douglas Manning, a Tandy vice president.

"I'd seen Brad Corbett coming down the hall with a young woman dressed in a sort of a tow sack," Roland said. "Then Brad paused at the door and brought the girl in."

Brad Corbett was then the chairman of the board of Robintech, Inc., and later would become the majority owner of the Texas Rangers American League baseball team. He and Tandy had become close friends.

"Brad was carrying a bottle of champagne and he brought the girl into the suite," Roland related. "Before we knew what was happening, the girl took off her dress. She had a bikini on underneath. Then she sat down on Charles' lap and put her arms around him."

Janet Lesok, then a newly-hired 21-year-old secretarial employee who later became Tandy's personal secretary, recalled her introduction to her future boss.

"I was a 21-year-old messenger-type girl, taking his mail and the P&Ls to him in his suite at All Saints. The first time I saw him, Mrs. Tandy was there, and he was talking on the telephone and you could hear him all the way down the hall."

Each time she arrived at the suite, her arms full of papers, Janet had to talk her way past Anne Tandy.

"Mrs. Tandy didn't want people bothering Charles with company business, but there was no way she could stop it," Mrs. Lesok said.

When Tandy left the hospital, he was ordered by Dr. Brown to remain away from the office for several weeks. After soaking up some Arizona sunshine, Charles returned to Fort Worth and began working out of his apartment on Curzon, which he had retained as a retreat after his marriage.

"He used the apartment as an office and he immediately began wheeling and dealing," Janet Lesok recalled. "We worked off a little orange card table in the den. His maids, Annie B. and Laura, who had been with him for years, ran the apartment and prepared his lunch. I ran between West 7th Street and Curzon four or five times a day. Charles was crazy about the maids and always took real good care of them. He put them in the employee savings plan and they had company cars. I remember the time Annie B. got into financial problems and got out of the employee savings plan, cashed it in. He hit the proverbial ceiling when he heard about it. 'This is not set up to be borrowing from, like a bank,' he told her. He went on and on. He saw to it that she eventually got back into the plan."

The maids loved to watch soap operas on television, which reminded Janet of an incident she said typified Tandy's lack of pretentiousness.

"One day when Charles had a high-powered meeting going on at the apartment, I walked into the kitchen at lunch time. The maids had the TV going, so I joined them. There we were, all three of us, watching the soap opera with our elbows on the table and our bottoms sticking out behind us.

"Charles walked into the kitchen and said, 'If I'm not disturbing you ladies from all this important business...'

"And with that, he dropped his pants and stood there in his drawers.

"'I've ripped my pants,' he said, 'and I wonder if one of you ladies is not too busy to sew them up so I can get back to my goddamned meeting...'

"I was in shock. Those two ladies never even blinked. They just took the pants. I never took my eyes off the television set. And after they repaired the pants, he just put them on and went back to his meeting. He didn't miss a beat, never took the cigar out of his mouth."

Chapter 19
"Bernie, I'll Build You Your Own Synagogue"

Tandy's brush with the Grim Reaper had at least one salutary consequence. It convinced him that he could no longer put off moving the Radio Shack headquarters from Boston to Fort Worth.

On numerous occasions over the years, Tandy had broached the subject to Lew Kornfeld, whose response was predictably negative. The fact that Tandy had not pushed the issue was a strong indication that he did not consider the move important enough to risk losing Kornfeld and other key members of the Radio Shack team. So he had continued the wearing regime of dividing his time between Beantown and Cowtown. But in the aftermath of his latest heart attack, he decided the time had come to put his foot down.

"He'd been talking to me about moving to Fort Worth since 1963," Kornfeld remembered. "But I loved where I was living in Belmont, a Boston suburb, and so did my family. No one else among our key people in Boston wanted to move to Fort Worth and I told that to Charles each time he brought up the subject."

By the fall of 1969, however, the growth of Radio Shack put a strain on its cramped facilities in Boston. Kornfeld found himself facing the prospect of having to rent additional office space for his buyers and for the rapidly-expanding advertising department. For the first time, he found himself actually considering that it might make sense to consolidate all of the Radio Shack operations in Fort Worth rather than expand into new office space in Boston. But he still wasn't convinced when Tandy again brought up the subject after his heart attack.

"I was visiting him in the hospital," Kornfeld recalled, "and he said to me, 'I wish you'd move here.' And I answered, 'Oh, Charles, we've been over this before.'"

To which Tandy replied, "I guess you can't make people do what they don't want to do."

As Tandy spoke those words, Kornfeld related, "I saw an awful blip appear on the monitoring machine to which he was hooked up. That's when I knew I was going to move. I don't want to overdramatize what happened. Keep in mind that I already was facing the spectre of having to move the Boston offices, and the fact was that things were being run more and more from Fort Worth. But I couldn't help being frightened by what I saw on the machine. I asked Charles to excuse me for a minute and I walked to a nearby public telephone and called my wife.

"'Ethel,' I told her, 'Charles wants me to move to Fort Worth and I owe it to him to do it.'"

Mrs. Kornfeld, however, extracted a promise from her husband that he would insist that the move not take place until the following June, when their son was due to graduate from high school.

"At that point," Kornfeld said, "it occurred to me that this was a propitious time to hit Charles with another matter. So I went back to his hospital suite and told him I would move to Fort Worth after my son's graduation in June 1970. Then I said there was something else I wanted to talk to him about."

"What's that?"

"I think you should make me president of Radio Shack."

There was a brief pause as Tandy mulled it over. Then he said, "Okay."

The prospect of eventually having to relocate to Texas had been hanging over the Radio Shack offices like the sword of Damocles ever since 1963. When the sword finally fell on the 20 families who were asked to make the move, their reaction was less than euphoric. To them, Fort Worth still seemed like a frontier outpost and Texas presented a totally alien culture.

"We had to do a selling job," Kornfeld said, "and it wasn't easy."

Kornfeld and Bernie Appel and their wives were invited to stop over in Fort Worth while en route to Acapulco on a brief vacation in December, 1969.

"We couldn't have chosen a worse time," Kornfeld said. "We'd been telling our wives about the great climate in Fort Worth. But, as luck would have it, we arrived in a blizzard. The weather in Fort Worth was even worse than what we'd left behind in Boston."

"It was the week before Christmas, and Charles had us over to the big house for a big dinner," Bernie Appel said. "After dinner, I got locked in a room with Phil North and James West and they beat the hell out of me. They really worked on me to convince me to move to Fort Worth. I told them some of the things that were worrying me about the move, and that's where a funny incident happened between me and Charles Tandy.

"The morning after the big dinner," Appel related, "Charles called me at Green Oaks Inn. I remember it was a very cold, very windy morning. He got me on the phone and he said, 'Bernie, what's this bullshit I hear that you don't want to come to Fort Worth?'

"My answer was, 'Charles, I didn't say I didn't want to come to Fort Worth. What I said is that I want to meet with the rabbis and the head of the community center and find out if I can make some sort of a Jewish life here for my children.'

"That's when he said to me, 'Bernie, if you don't like the synagogue we've got here, I'll build you your own.'"

That rejoinder, in Appel's opinion, typified Charles Tandy.

"He was a man who didn't have a biased bone in his body, a lovely human being who really cared about people, no matter how rough he could be on you."

"He was very proud of us," Appel continued. "After we arrived in Fort Worth, he introduced us to people in the community. He said he wanted us involved in the community. He felt that it was important that his people should be involved in community activities, in their churches, the Arts Council. At a party he gave to introduce us to Jewish community leaders, he told Arthur Ginsburg, a prominent Fort Worth businessman, 'I'm gonna make these people wealthy, so you take good care of them.'" When Appel wanted to join a country club, Tandy was his mentor and his reference. "He called the manager of the club," Appel said, "and told him, 'Never mind about any kind of a waiting list. You take good care of my executives.' He went to bat for us every single time. Then he'd come in and beat the hell out of you. But that was the way he taught you."

Before the decision to move the Radio Shack headquarters to Fort Worth was finalized in late 1969, Tandy was engaged in another acquisition project, this one involving Allied Radio Corporation of Chicago, then the nation's number one distributor of electronics products, with sales of approximately $90 million.

Tandy had made a pass at Allied Radio back in the early '60s prior to his takeover of Radio Shack and had been curtly rebuffed. Allied subsequently had been taken over by James J. Ling, the swashbuckling corporate raider from Dallas, whose highly-leveraged empire was now hemorrhaging red ink. Faced with having to sell off some of his subsidiaries to satisfy his creditors, Ling approached Tandy about taking Allied Radio off his hands.

"The problems of the Ling organization were getting more and more publicity," Bill Michero recalled, "and it was apparent that he had to get rid of some of his assets. We were so busy with our own business that we wouldn't have pursued the Allied thing if Ling hadn't gotten into so much financial trouble."

It was easy to understand Charles' interest in adding Allied Radio to the Tandy fold.

As Lew Kornfeld explained, "He adored the idea of buying out this prestigious company that was bigger than we were and was also our largest direct competitor."

Tandy also saw in Allied an immediate entry into the Chicago area that Radio Shack had not yet penetrated in a major way. Allied, at the time, had 41 company-owned retail stores located primarily in the Upper Midwest, plus a national mail order business.

"Charles thought it was a natural way for us to occupy a whole new country," Kornfeld pointed out. "We were expanding rapidly by opening new stores on our own, but an even quicker way to expand was to buy already existing stores."

Kornfeld was in Tokyo on a buying trip in early April of 1970 when he was awakened from a sound sleep by the ringing of the telephone in his hotel room.

"It was 3 o'clock in the morning, a terrible time for me in Tokyo, but a convenient time for Charles in Fort Worth," Kornfeld noted.

"Guess what I just did?" Tandy asked.

"You've bought Allied."

"Yep."

The telephone call provided Kornfeld with what he termed "a final glimmer of opportunity" to head off the scheduled Radio Shack move to Fort Worth.

"Charles," he said, "as long as you now have Allied and they already have their headquarters established, why don't we move Radio Shack to Chicago instead of Texas?"

There was silence on the other end of the line. Then Tandy said, "No, you're still coming to Fort Worth."

The announcement that Tandy Corporation had purchased the business of Allied Radio from LTV Ling Altec, a subsidiary of Ling-

Temco-Vought, Inc., of Dallas, hit the financial press with a surprising impact on April 14, 1970.

The size of the transaction—approximately $25 million, of which $11 million was in cash and the remainder in the assumption of Allied Radio liabilities—was the largest in Tandy history.

"We had to sell some stock the following year to pay off the obligation," Bill Michero noted.

Commenting on why he had bought Allied Radio, Tandy told a reporter from *Investor's Reader*, "We have done an entirely different acquisition job than Litton or LTV or Boise. We have sought things that were similar or of a compatible nature. The profit goes up faster and you take less risk when you put things together right. Right now, the energies and efforts of our company are centered on electronics. Allied fits so perfectly with Radio Shack that when you put them together you have got a good match."

The article quoted Tandy as stating he had decided to eliminate cameras from the Allied stores in line with his firm belief in specialty merchandising.

"You wouldn't go to Wolfe's Nursery to buy ladies underwear," he said.

Looking back on the Allied Radio acquisition, Lew Kornfeld said he was unalterably opposed to the deal and that he tried, in vain, to talk Tandy out of making it. Kornfeld compared Allied Radio to the Maginot Line in France in World War II.

"They were entrenched in an obsolete retailing technique, still sticking mostly to mail order. I thought we could move around them easily."

A decision now had to be made about what to do with the Allied Radio name.

"Whatever we do," Tandy had told a reporter, "we will certainly continue the Allied name. We will maintain the name with our own identification or we will combine it either with the corporate Tandy name or Radio Shack. The name has too much going for it to scrap."

The announcement that the name of the Radio Shack Division of Tandy Corporation had been changed to Allied Radio Shack was made on May 5, 1970.

One of the first things Kornfeld did after moving to Fort Worth and assuming the presidency of Allied Radio Shack was to buy vanity license plates for his car. They read, "ARS-1."

Shortly after that, Tandy walked into Kornfeld's office.

"I just saw your car out front," he said.

"Oh, yeah, my ARS-1."

"Kornfeld," Tandy said, "you don't even know how to spell ass."

Kornfeld took over his new job with a sense of deja vu.

"Ironically," he said, "I now had back all of the problems of the 1958 to 1963 period. I had all of the name brands back. I had all the repair problems Radio Shack used to have. I had all of the old mail order problems. I had all of Allied's private label stuff. And I had an industrial division to contend with again after we had finally gotten rid of Radio Shack's. I had everything back.

"But we all finally agreed after some experimentation that we would change Allied to all private label merchandise, to 2,400 stockkeeping units, and that the Allied stores would operate the way Radio Shack operated. So the net result of the acquisition would be that we would wind up with 41 new Radio Shack stores in Illinois and wherever the Allied stores were located."

Allied's substantial mail order operations were quickly dismantled for the same reason that Tandy had taken Radio Shack out of the mail order business. So much of the electronics equipment being shipped at the time was extremely fragile and highly susceptible to breakage. In addition, Allied's industrial division was moved to Fort Worth as a new Tandy division, with George Steeves, a Radio Shack employee for 21 years, being named president of the new Allied Electronics Industries Division. The division later was sold.

One of those intimately involved in the tedious process of meshing Allied with Radio Shack was John Roach, who was then manager of the corporate computer center. To him fell the responsibility of integrating the Allied operations into the Tandy computer systems. Thus, he found himself flying between Fort Worth and Chicago on a regular basis for several months.

Stamped indelibly in Roach's memory is what transpired during his first visit to the Allied offices in the company of Charles Tandy.

"When we arrived at the Allied headquarters, we were told we had to put on identification badges," Roach remembered. "The guard at the front desk handed Charles a badge. He didn't like it, but he put it on. Then we proceeded to the president's office."

Roach grinned at the recollection of what happened when Tandy stormed into the office of Allied president Shelby Young and saw that the 35-year-old executive wasn't wearing an ID badge.

"Charles' first words were, 'Where's your goddamn badge?'"

"This was to a guy who's been working for him now for only several hours and has never met him before," Roach said.

After the initial flurry of activity subsided, Roach had a respite of several months until a major accounts receivable problem cropped up in Allied's industrial division.

"It became my problem as far as Charles was concerned," Roach reported, "because accounts receivable are run off on the computer. The fact that Allied had sold things to people that they shouldn't have and didn't collect from them the way they should have were all secondary to Charles. So, he tried to make me feel that it was my problem. My sense is that he didn't have anybody else to place the blame on."

For the next six months Roach flew to Chicago every other week, working with the Allied accounts receivable people to get the accounts in reasonable shape, "the best that I really felt I could," he added.

But during that six-month period, the fiscal year-end bonus time arrived.

"For some reason," Roach related, "Charles and I had a lot of trouble about bonuses, particularly in the early years. His feeling was that computer people were just staff, that they were not contributing to making sales, and that they should be paid like staff people. Yet, he did everything he could to keep you from being a staff person by forcing you into operations."

For the first few years of his employment, Roach permitted Charley Tindall and Billy Roland to submit his bonus request to Tandy for his approval. But, he added, as time went on, he decided that he would be better off bargaining for himself.

"They weren't doing all that great for me," he noted.

"So I'd go up to see Charles and I'd give him a bonus schedule for everyone in the computer center," Roach continued. "Typically, it would take four to six hours talking about what we ought to be doing as a company, then go back to talking about the bonus schedule a little bit and discussing how the bonus tied into the big plan. Finally, arduously, I'd get the schedule approved, with a lot of help from Lew Kornfeld and Bill Nugent and Carroll Ray and others. They'd keep telling Charles he ought to pay us what I was asking and Charles would keep trying to hold the bonus down.

"One morning during the Allied thing," Roach went on, "I went to see Charles with my bonus schedule. I was due in his office at 8:30. I got there at 8:30 sharp. He arrived about 1 p.m. That was typical and didn't come as any great surprise to me at all. So there we were, just the two of us, all that day, just arguing back and forth on every subject known to man, occasionally having a fairly heated discussion. Finally, at about 7 o'clock, he says, 'Okay, dammit, just write down whatever number it is that you want.' So I wrote down a number and he said, 'Great, now get back to work.'"

This was around August 15, Roach recollected. Several days later, as the people in the corporate office began receiving their bonus checks, Roach became concerned when his check failed to arrive. He began making inquiries, and finally asked Janet Lesok, Tandy's secretary, if she knew what had happened to his check.

"He's got it," she informed Roach. "He asked me for it."

"Now," Roach revealed, "you didn't necessarily see Charles every day. Particularly, when he was staying out at the apartment, you might not see him for a week or two. Several weeks went by and the check didn't show up. More time passed and the check still didn't show up. Finally, I managed to get in to see him and asked him about the check, and he told me, 'Well, you're not through with last year's work yet. The accounts receivable isn't finished.'"

Roach now had reason to be concerned.

"We were all indebted for stock at the bank," he recalled, "and I couldn't pay off my note that was due. Time went along. One day I went to Janet and I said, 'Why don't you tell Charles to call the bank. They're getting tired of my excuses and I don't think they believe me anymore.' I was saying that because I wanted to get that bonus check loose. I wasn't having as much trouble with the bank as I was having trying to get the check loose. Meanwhile, while Charles was holding court with various people in his office every day, he'd pull my damn check out of his pocket and wave it around at everybody and say, 'Now, if you were tough, if you were a real boss, if you had guts, you could handle your people like I do. I get my work done.' Then he'd put my check back in his pocket."

Roach continued, "September went by. No check. Keep in mind that I was getting more than half of my pay for the whole year in the bonus, because I never got any base pay increases. Now, it was months past the end of the fiscal year and still no bonus. Finally, one day, when Charles and Bill Nugent were flying up to Chicago on the company plane, I hitched a ride and went along. They attended to their business and I went to Allied and worked there all day and then met them back at the plane that night.

"After one or two bourbons, Charles finally pulled the damn check out of his pocket. It was dog-eared, wrinkled, kind of curled up. He slammed the check down on the little table of the airplane and said, 'Here, take the damn thing. You haven't earned it, but I don't want to hear any more about it.'"

* * *

The Allied Radio acquisition by Tandy Corporation created a firestorm of media speculation about the implications of the merger for the consumer electronics industry.

Audio Times, a major industry publication, said the purchase had caused "shock waves from Fort Worth to Chicago, with reverberations from coast to coast." *Audio Times* added, "At one time, Allied Radio, with its huge catalog operation, was the leading retailer of high fidelity components. Today, with 41 retail stores and a major catalog operation, it is still one of the biggest retail audio operations in the nation. Some observers believe the combined Radio Shack-Allied operations might account for as much as 10 percent of retail high fidelity component sales.

"Allied Radio and Radio Shack were rivals for many years, principally in mail order. Each restricted its retail operations to a limited geographical area. After Charles Tandy bought Radio Shack, he expanded the small chain into the largest chain of retail electronic stores in the world. Radio Shack operates 660 company-owned stores and has 80 franchised affiliates. Allied began a rapid expansion of its company-owned stores in the last two years and has plans to continue opening many new units."

Merchandising Week, a Chicago-based publication, trumpeted, "With its purchase of Allied Radio last week, Tandy Corp. of Texas has emerged as the powerhouse in the retail audio field, and the move dramatizes some significant changes taking place in that area. Tandy already owns Radio Shack, a division with 660 wholly-owned retail stores and some 80 franchise outlets and leased departments. Allied now has 41 retail stores mainly located in the Midwest. The only remaining competition in the field of any size is Lafayette Radio, which now has 34 stores along the Mid-Atlantic region of the country."

Home Furnishings Daily warned: "Tandy Corp.'s purchase of Allied Radio Corp., Chicago, could create a private label giant and result in the loss of millions of dollars of business for United States brand name stereo manufacturers. This was the fear of manufacturer-suppliers of the Allied chain during the Consumer Electronics Show in Chicago.

Most of the suppliers felt it is a 'foregone conclusion' that Allied will eliminate U.S. brand components and compacts from its national consumer catalogs by 1971."

The newspaper quoted a manufacturer, "What could really be scary is that combined buying clout. Whew! They'll be able to command even more respect from Japanese manufacturers."

Lew Kornfeld said he brought up the possibility of anti-trust problems arising from the Allied acqustion during his middle-of-the-night telephone conversation with Tandy from his Tokyo hotel room.

"Anti-trust is liable to come after you," he said he told Tandy.

Tandy's confident reply was, "You know how we're going to handle that? We're going to put these two companies together in such a way that the government won't know where to start looking."

As it turned out, Tandy's confidence in his ability to thwart the anti-trust forces was somewhat overblown.

For one thing, Herschel C. Winn, who was the first in-house attorney hired by Tandy Corporation in 1968 and later became a senior vice president and general counsel, pointed out that the Allied acquisition was made during a period when the federal government was "very active" in anti-trust cases.

John Roach noted that the three dominant consumer electronics companies at the time were Allied Radio, Lafayette Electronics, and Radio Shack, so that it was not particularly surprising that a merger between two of the top three firms caused the watchdogs in Washington to begin licking their chops.

Whatever the case, the Department of Justice lost no time in zeroing in on the deal, requesting its Anti-Trust Division office in Chicago to look into the potential restraint-of-trade ramifications of the acquisition.

On May 25, 1970, only a month after the announcement of the merger, *Electronics News*, an industry publication, reported that a letter had gone out over the signature of Richard W. McLaren, an assistant United States attorney general, to some 25 companies requesting "facts and figures on the consumer electronics specialty market and soliciting reasons why the merger would lessen competition or tend to create a monopoly."

Among the companies contacted were Lafayette Radio Electronics, Harvey Group, Harrison Radio, Arrow Electronics, Gem Electronics, and Burstein-Applebee, the publication said.

"Spokesmen at the firms declined to reveal their position regarding the Justice Department's request," the story added. "It was apparent, however, from several firms that the Tandy deal engendered some apprehension."

The article quoted one company spokesman as saying, "It will certainly give Tandy more leverage in dealing with suppliers. The company is now much bigger than many of the companies whose products it is carrying. You can figure out the implications yourself."

In an anti-trust matter, Winn pointed out, "You have to have a market. So the Justice Department conceived the idea of a consumer electronics specialty store market that applied to Tandy."

On May 16, 1971, the U.S. Department of Justice filed a civil anti-trust suit against Tandy Corporation in federal district court in Chicago, charging that the Allied Radio acquisition violated the anti-merger section of the Clayton Anti-Trust Act. The suit further charged that Tandy's acquisition of Allied's electronic products business illegally eliminated competition between the two companies; that it might make it more difficult for new competitors to enter the business, and that it might encourage similar mergers. The government asked that Tandy be ordered to divest itself of the assets it had acquired from Allied and that it be enjoined for five years from acquiring any other electronics products retailer without prior approval of the Justice Department or the Court.

"At the same time," Lew Kornfeld reported, "we began emptying the Allied stores of their merchandise and opened Radio Shack stores nearby."

Herschel Winn added, "We were opening new stores at a rapid rate and it was economically better for us to agree to a settlement. Why spend a lot of money fighting the case, when you could open up that many more Radio Shack stores very quickly?"

On December 28, 1971, Tandy Corporation announced it agreed to the entry of a consent decree filed with the United States District Court, Northern District of Illinois, not to contest the complaint filed against it by the Justice Department. The decree, which was entered on January 28, 1972, called for the divestiture within two years of the 36 remaining retail stores acquired as part of the Allied purchase.

Under the terms of a plan approved by the Justice Department, 27 of the stores were sold to Schaak Electronics of Minneapolis between January 14, 1974 and June 4, 1974.

"The sale was structured so that Schaak Electronics could buy the stores in steps," Winn recalled. "They were supposed to buy them in two steps, but they couldn't manage the last bunch of nine stores. So we went back in and had the decree amended. We just ran out the store leases and didn't reopen in those nine locations. That's the way it was ultimately resolved."

The divestiture was no great blow, Winn pointed out. During fiscal 1973, the 36 Allied Radio stores had aggregate sales of $9.8 million and income before taxes, interest and administrative expenses of only $257,180.

Charles Tandy took note of the Allied Radio problem at a store managers' meeting in Fort Worth in 1971.

"I'm waiting for the federal government to tell us what they want us to do," he told the gathering at Green Oaks Inn. "You never make any money fighting fights. We won't fight unless they want us to give away 300 stores. Then I'll get into a scrap. But if they ask us to divest ourselves of 38, 39 stores, we've already done the job. We've got the market. We've done what we wanted to do."

In a talk at Brigham Young University in March, 1973, Tandy touched on the anti-trust proceedings.

"We bought Allied Radio Corporation in 1970," he declared, "but the government has asked us to divest ourselves of it. Allied has 37 stores against our 2,000, so it is a rather unfair charge to say we are restraining trade. I mean, 37 stores just can't do that much business against 2,000! But I'm not going to fight the government. I'll go right along with the federal decision like a lamb."

Meanwhile, Tandy's nonelectronics acquisition efforts also continued, with the purchase on April 30, 1970, of Collins of Texas, Inc., a manufacturer and marketer of quality ladies' handbags and related accessories of leather, fabric and wool, with annual sales of $2.3 million. The purchase price was 45,815 shares of Tandy stock valued at $1.5 million.

Later in the year, when it became apparent that more management depth was needed at the corporate level, five new Tandy group vice presidents were named in September, 1970. They were David Beckerman, Douglas Manning, Lewis Shows, Harlan Swain, and John Wilson.

Prior to his promotion, Beckerman had been vice president of Radio Shack's Eastern Region; Manning, vice president and general sales manager of Tex Tan Western Leather Company; Shows, president of the Tex Tan Welhausen Division; Swain, president of Tandy Leather Company and American Handicrafts Company; and Wilson, vice president of Tandy Leather Company and American Handicrafts Company.

The promotions were primarily the result of concern over Tandy's health, but they also served to mollify some hurt feelings over Lew Kornfeld's ascendancy to the top Radio Shack job.

In an interview published about a month after the promotions were announced, Tandy said the new group vice presidents had been elected as part of a reorganization designed "to bring sales up to $600 to $700 million. We have taken the best men from our operating divisions. They are all in the late 40s or early 50s."

A proud and seemingly fit Charles Tandy presided at the annual meeting in Fort Worth on November 12, 1970. Tandy elaborated on the record highs of $253.3 million in net sales and $9.1 million in net income that had been previously announced and lauded "another outstanding performance" by the Allied Radio Shack Division, whose sales had accounted for approximately 40 percent of the company's total sales volume and had contributed approximately 54 percent of the sales increase.

"Counting the Allied Radio contribution," he added, "the Allied Radio Shack Division's sales rose 55 percent to $101 million during fiscal 1970."

At the fiscal year-end on June 30, 1970, the number of retail outlets of all Tandy divisions had reached a total of 991, up from 710 a year earlier. Most of the gain came from the Allied Radio Shack Division which closed the year with 674 retail units, up from 454 the year before. This included Radio Shack's entry into the Canadian market with the opening of three stores in Toronto in June, plus 99 associate (franchise) stores.

"Strong emphasis will continue to be placed on consumer electronics in fiscal 1971," Tandy told the shareholders, "with current plans calling for the opening of 300 additional company-owned and associate Allied Radio Shack outlets during the year."

Tandy's once "impossible dream" of 1,000 stores was about to become a reality.

Chapter 20
Zsa Zsa Misses a Ribbon-Cutting

Jim Buxton's relationship with Charles Tandy dated back to 1955 when he clerked in the Tandy Leather Company's store in Amarillo. It had been less than amicable at its best and stormy at its worst. There was a two-year period during the early 1960s when the two didn't speak.

"This was while I was managing the Tandy Mart in San Antonio," Buxton explained. "Charles had written my bonus plan out on a slip of paper at the start of the year. If he'd have let the darn thing alone, I'd have been paid more than he was that year. Of course, he couldn't tolerate that. So he tore it up. He'd never changed anybody else's bonus before, but he changed mine. We got a little crosswise over that. We didn't speak for about two years. I recall going up to Fort Worth for his father's funeral, and I never even went by the office. Dave Tandy and I had had a real rapport, and Charles didn't especially like that, either," Buxton asserted. "When I'd have an appointment to see Charles in Fort Worth, Dave would spot me and call me into his office and we'd chew the fat for a couple of hours. Charles would get real mad over that."

"Mad" was the operative word in Buxton's relationship with Tandy.

"He motivated me by getting me mad," Buxton said. "I'd get mad and I'd get just like a bulldog. But he knew I liked to make money, so he gave me a rabbit to chase and he knew I'd chase it. In all the years, he never set foot in one of my stores except once when he was in San Antonio working on buying Tex Tan. He'd rented a car and he came into my Tandy Leather store and said, 'Take me to the airport.'"

So it came as a total shock to Buxton when Tandy handed him the plum of opening the milestone 1,000th Radio Shack store in the spring of 1971.

Buxton was dispatched to California in March 1968 to try to breathe life into the ailing Western Region. Under his direction as regional manager, the number of Radio Shack stores in the region had increased nearly five-fold from 33 stores to 150 stores by November 1970.

Whether the distinction of opening the 1,000th Radio Shack was given to him in recognition of the job he had done on the West Coast or was merely simple chance, Buxton never discovered. It was typical of Tandy, he figured, to hand him the coveted assignment without telling him why. But when he spoke about the store that opened in Garden Grove in May 1971, it was with untypical warmth.

"It was a gorgeous store, the prettiest store the company had up to that time," he said. "Charles was really excited about the opening. He was planning to attend the opening ceremonies and bring a bunch of people with him on the company jet. But something went wrong with the plane and he didn't make it. Maybe it's just as well. It could have been a real fiasco. We had lined up Zsa Zsa Gabor to cut the ribbon and we had advertised it extensively. So there were thousands of people at the ribbon-cutting. But no Zsa Zsa. We were going out of our minds about what to do. Fortunately, I had a real bright advertising man by the name of Bernie Elfman whom I'd hired and brought out to the West Coast from New York. He was one of the best in the business."

Elfman now rode to the rescue.

"We had a real cute receptionist in the office, a redhead, cute but dumb," Buxton continued, "and when we finally gave up on Zsa Zsa getting there, Bernie went over to the redhead and told her, 'Stand up on that desk.' So she stood up on the table. She was wearing a long skirt, and Bernie took a pair of scissors and made a mini-skirt out of it, or, to be more accurate, a mini-mini skirt, by whacking the bottom of the skirt off. Then he took her outside to cut the ribbon and we didn't have a single complaint. Zsa Zsa called 30 minutes later and said, 'I've hurt my back, I can't make it.' I informed her the show had gone on without her."

*   *   *

With the Radio Shack store opening program rolling along in high gear, an intriguing question began to assert itself. How many Radio Shacks was enough? How many stores could be profitably digested? Bill Michero, who had been promoted to vice president and corporate secretary, addressed the question in a talk to the St. Louis Society of Financial Analysts on April 1, 1971.

"Our projections are for expansion of the Consumer Electronics Division to 1,000 retail units by June and to a total of 1,500 units within three years," Michero told the group. Then he added, "Our research indicates that this country can hold 1,500 of our prototype stores."

Of the 300 new stores scheduled for opening during the 1971 fiscal year, 200 would be company-owned, with the remainder associate stores, and one-half to two-thirds of the new outlets would be located in shopping centers, Michero said. "We prefer strip front centers," he disclosed. "We like identification, and the merchants like us because we are not a parasite. We do not rely on walk-by traffic. Each one of our customers comes specifically to our store. In addition, shopping center sites are much more easily and quickly opened than lone-standing sites."

All of the new stores, Michero emphasized, would be of the typical 2,500-square foot Radio Shack variety, rather than the 10,000-square foot stores favored by Allied Radio. "We thought that we might do a few 'bull' stores in accordance with the Allied Radio prototype operation," Michero said, "but as we measured more accurately the return of these stores we have not pursued them. Most of the former Allied stores are on short-term leases and they will not be reproduced."

Of the Allied stores that Tandy acquired, Michero added, "The ideal arrangement for us would have been to purchase the stores without their inventory. The Allied concept was a supermarket that required a lot of footage and a lot of stock. The Radio Shack store requires less capital, is more efficient, easier to supervise and more profitable. We can build three Radio Shacks for one Allied."

Looking back upon Michero's prediction that 1,500 stores was the maximum number of Radio Shacks the country could absorb, Herschel Winn noted that this was a pretty bold forecast at the time. "But as we kept on growing, we kept on changing the numbers," he disclosed. "Each time someone set a number as to the optimum number of Radio Shack stores we could have, that number would be met and a new optimum number would then be handed down."

* * *

In the spring of 1971, Tandy stock was a hot item on the Big Board. Charles Tandy's personal holdings of some 240,000 shares had increased in value to some $12 million. Investors snapped up a public offering of 800,000 shares of Tandy stock at the 1970 year-end at $49.75 per share. The company utilized the $37.9 million proceeds of the offering to pay off short-term bank loans that had funded the year's store expansion program.

The January, 1971 issue of *Fortune* magazine named Tandy Corporation the nation's No. 1 retail merchandiser and one of the 40 top corporations in the country.

Forbes magazine ranked Tandy fourth among the outstanding performers on the New York Exchange as a result of the whopping 555.7 percent increase in the price of its stock over the 5-year period between 1966 and 1970. *Forbes* also ranked Tandy first in 5-year sales growth and in 5-year earnings per share growth among the nation's top retailers.

An article about Charles Tandy in *Investor's Reader*, published by Merrill Lynch, Pierce, Fenner & Smith, noted that "Texas millionaires traditionally think big, but big can be relative. Charles David Tandy, the 52-year-old chairman of Fort Worth-based Tandy Corp., says when he came to his father's wholesale leather business in 1947 after Texas Christian University, Harvard Business School and the U.S. Navy, his aim was 'to build a big company with sales of $1 million.' When he achieved that, he figured, 'If I could earn $1 million before taxes, I'd be doing good. My next goal was $100 million volume. Now it's a billion. I have learned to move the figures far enough away.'"

Tandy Corporation was featured in a column in *Barron's* by Alan Abelson, who recalled an earlier *Barron's* story that described Tandy as a specialty retailer of leather handicraft and hobby items.

"Well," Abelson now wrote, "Tandy has spread its wings and grown mightily since then. The company is now heavily in consumer electronics. Its progress has enjoyed considerable investment recognition. The stock, which could be had for 8 in 1967, has sold as high as 66½. Last week, it traded around 48. At this level, it commanded a not inconsiderable PE (price earnings ratio) of 21. Bulls on Tandy look for another solid earnings gain in the current (1971) fiscal year."

In an appearance before the Dallas Association of Investment Analysts on January 20, 1971, Tandy noted that Tandy Corporation sales soared 60 percent over the past six-month period in the face of a general falling off of retail sales nationally. "We don't expect a 60 percent gain in profitability, because of (the cost of our) new store openings," he told the group. "But from what I've seen of our earnings, I'm tickled to death." He then asked, "Why are we able to do better than retailing in general? The answer is that we are staying with smaller ticket items.

For example, the average ticket item at Allied Radio Shack brings in $5.80."

He also gave credit to the company's stepped-up advertising programs.

"I wasn't impressed by our sales figures for the six days following Thanksgiving 1970," he informed the analysts. "So I released $750,000 for the advertising budget and that brought sales up to expectations. At Tandy, we reserve a certain percentage of our sales which goes into advertising. It is one of our musts, one of our biggest items and we believe in it. We know if we don't do the advertising, we won't have our sales. We have learned without question that if you are going to maintain your gains and if you are going to maintain the improvement in your sales, you've got to advertise. Just because you have sales running well, that is not the time to slow down."

When he took over Radio Shack, Tandy told the analysts, "They thought a four or five percent advertising budget was a good one. Right now we are running close to a nine percent advertising budget as a percent of sales."

In January, 1971, Tandy stock got another boost when the prestigious Putnam Vista Fund of Boston added it to its list of ten largest investments. Tandy joined such select company as Xerox, IBM, Western Union, Philip Morris, and Burroughs in the Putnam Vista portfolio.

One note of sadness, however, interrupted the flow of happy tidings. This was the untimely death of Bill Tandy at the age of 49 on February 15, 1971, after a heart attack. Bill had become a successful businessman in Tulsa, and at the time of his death was president of the Southern Mill & Manufacturing Company there. He was survived by his wife, Mary Louise; a daughter, Carol, and a son, Alfred R. Tandy, Jr. Over the next few years, Charles Tandy devoted himself to keeping Bill's business moving for the benefit of his brother's wife and children.

* * *

In the spring of 1971, Tandy stock, along with the market in general, was benefitting from a pump-priming program that President Richard M. Nixon initiated in anticipation of the 1972 presidential election.

This moved Humphrey B. Neill, publisher of a Washington newsletter, to pontificate: "So why shouldn't the stock market stampede when it becomes evident that a conservative Republican president is ready and willing to spend the country into prosperity? Alexander Hamilton did it, too. The contrary idea that Mr. Nixon would go to any lengths to prevent a depression is a notion hard to accept, but I believe it now is evident. A depression on top of a hated war could tear this nation to pieces."

The "stampeding" stock market, to which Neill referred, helped propel Tandy stock to a new high of 74 by late April. So when the Tandy Corporation board convened on April 29 for its regular quarterly meeting in Fort Worth, one of the items on the agenda was a proposal from management for a two-for-one stock split. The split, subject to shareholder approval of an increase in the number of authorized shares of common stock from 10 million to 20 million, was okayed by the board. A special meeting of shareholders was called for June 18, 1971, to consider the increase in the number of shares.

The board also approved a call for redemption of the entire $40 million issue of five percent subordinated debentures due in 1989. Debenture holders were given the choice of redeeming the debentures for cash at 104.75 percent of their face value or of converting them into Tandy common stock at a price of $62 per share.

On June 18, shareholders overwhelmingly approved the increase in the number of authorized shares, paving the way for the two-for-one stock split which became effective on July 28, 1971.

The call for redemption of the debentures resulted in the conversion of $39,890,000 of the $40 million face amount into 642,728 shares of Tandy common stock, with only $110,000 in debentures being redeemed for cash on June 15, 1971.

As far as Tandy investors were concerned, it was obvious that as long as the stock continued its bullish course, redemption could wait.

As for Charles Tandy, it was like getting a second dessert. He was getting his cake and eating it, too.

He also was reveling in his new status as an honorary Doctor of Laws bestowed upon him by his alma mater, TCU, in the spring of 1971. "Not bad for a guy who once flunked out of Rice," he chortled after the ceremony at the commencement exercises.

At a gathering of students in the M. J. Neeley School of Business at TCU, Tandy gave the group a sampling of his business philosophy.

"The customer is our boss," he declared. "He is trying to tell us something, so we can't argue. We want to know exactly what will make him happy, and we ask him just that. Usually, when a man complains to the president of a company, something definitely is wrong somewhere. But this type of complainant usually becomes our best customer and biggest booster."

Then he added, "At Tandy, we welcome young people with all their ideas, because a company that will not accept change will not succeed."

*   *   *

One thing that was not about to change, however, was Tandy's appetite for acquisitions. It manifested itself once again on July 1, 1971, with the purchase for $3.7 million in cash and stock of P.J. Parker, Inc., of Rochester, New York, whose principal asset was Hickok Manufacturing Company, producer and marketer of a nationally-known brand of belts, billfolds, men's jewelry and other accessories. Hickok had reported a net loss of $500,000 on sales of $18 million for the year ended December 31, 1970, but Lewis D. Shows, the Tandy Corporation vice president who represented the company in the negotiations, was confident he could turn the operation around with an infusion of cash and marketing savvy.

"The acquisition will provide Hickok with the capital requirements to support expanded merchandising programs required in the rapidly-growing men's fashion market," Shows said in a press release announcing the purchase.

Shows also announced that the Hickok offices and its key executives, including its president, William Wright, would move to Arlington, Texas, between Fort Worth and Dallas, before the end of the year and that the Hickok leather goods operations would relocate from Rochester to Arlington by July 1972.

One of the things that Tandy inherited in the Hickok acquisition was the Hickok Belt Award for the outstanding professional athlete of the year. The annual award, a $30,000 diamond-studded belt, was started in 1950 by Raymond T. Hickok to honor the year's outstanding professional boxer. Hickok, an avid boxing fan, reportedly began the award named in honor of his father, S. Rae Hickok, as a means of meeting his ring idols in the flesh. But over the years, the scope of the award enlarged to include all professional sports.

Despite the fact that Charles Tandy was totally disinterested in sports, professional or otherwise, he permitted himself to be talked into presenting the Hickok Award to golfer Lee Trevino at a dinner at the Holiday Inn Downtown in Rochester on January 31, 1972. Trevino, who had won the United States, British, and Canadian Opens in 1971, was the first professional golfer to receive the award, winning out over a field that included basketball player Kareem Abdul-Jabbar, heavyweight boxing champion Joe Frazier, and baseball Hall of Famer Roberto Clemente.

Despite the auspicious start, the Hickok Award failed to survive the change in ownership. The members of the Rochester Press and Radio Club, under whose aegis the Hickok Belt had been presented over the years, voted to drop their backing of the event after the Trevino presentation. "After that," said Phil North, who had accompanied Tandy to Rochester for the award presentation, "we let the thing die a natural death."

There was another unforeseen fallout from the Hickok acquisition. Unbeknownst to Tandy management, the Hickok retirement benefits, including group insurance programs for retirees, were insufficiently funded. When this fact was discovered shortly after the takeover, Tandy cancelled the programs. But the funds that were already in the pension fund were not affected. Herschel Winn described what happened.

"We didn't think we should have to pay out of our pockets what Hickok had promised to pay its retired employees. But Hickok had not funded the promises. So we terminated the plan. This meant that if I was getting a pension of $100 a month, I now would get $88 a month. So they sued us for the unfunded portion of the plan."

By an unfortunate coincidence, from Tandy's standpoint at least, Senator Jacob K. Javitz of New York was leading an effort to impose federal vesting and funding requirements on new and existing pension and profit-sharing plans. In a speech on the Senate floor that got widespread media coverage, Javitz used the discontinuance of the Hickok pension plan as an example of the abuses he wanted to correct. The action by Tandy, Javitz maintained, meant that 350 retired Hickok workers would take a 12 percent cut in their pensions and 400 Hickok employees with rights to Hickok pensions would receive nothing at all. Javitz noted that Tandy was doing better financially in the current year than it had done the year before, so that its decision to phase out the Hickok pensions was not based on any lack of earnings.

An editorial in the *Rochester Democrat and Chronicle* declared, "Because of tottering or bankrupt pension plans, 36 million workers out of 40 million promised pensions are doomed to little or nothing according to some estimates. It isn't necessary to look any further than Rochester to find an example. When the parent Tandy Corp. of Fort Worth took over the Hickok operation here, it assumed its liabilities and obligations. One of those obligations was to continue to fund the pension plan. The employees have been badly let down."

Tandy's position was that the contract did not require such an obligation.

The suit was eventually settled after Hickok was spun off and became a part of Tandy Brands in 1975.

Although Charles Tandy was not directly involved in the Hickok matter, his lack of enthusiasm for employee benefit plans other than stock-buying programs was well known within the company.

"He was never a big believer in those sort of things," recalled John McDaniel, who helped institute Radio Shack's first comprehensive group health insurance program in 1967. McDaniel, who later became a Tandy Corporation senior vice president and controller, added:

"Charles believed in the company stock and he wanted everybody to buy it. He wanted everybody to be in the savings plan and later the stock purchase plan. But other benefits, such as hospitalization insurance, he didn't really believe in. We'd tell him we had to have hospitalization in order to attract good employees, but Charles insisted it wasn't necessary in Radio Shack."

McDaniel said that he and Bill Nugent, who was then a Radio Shack division manager, finally took matters in their own hands and signed a group health insurance contract with Aetna.

"We didn't have Charles' approval to do that and we knew that he would find out about it," McDaniel said. "But he never said a word to us after he found out."

Later, however, Tandy went to great lengths to needle McDaniel and Nugent about the plan's provisions, especially the $100 deductible. "A hundred bucks is reasonable for lower paid employees," he told them, "but executive types like you should have $1,000 deductibles."

Bill Brooks, who was the Aetna division manager in Fort Worth at the time the contract was signed, recalled that Tandy Corporation had an "employee pay all" group health insurance plan with Prudential in the early 1960s, but that it was limited to top executives.

"Several years later," he said, "Billy Roland extended the plan somewhat, with Aetna as the carrier." Brooks told of the trepidation he experienced when McDaniel and Nugent installed the comprehensive group insurance plan in 1967. "I was afraid I'd lose all of my Tandy business when Charles found out about it. But he never said a word to me."

Jim Buxton had a more painful memory of the lack of an employee group insurance program in the early 1960s.

"I had attempted without success to interest the company in putting in a group insurance plan," he recalled. "Then, I guess, it was around Easter of 1961, when I was a Tandy Leather district manager and managing a Tandy Leather and American Handicrafts store in San Antonio, one of my sons had an accident while mowing a neighbor's lawn. The mower mowed some of his toes off and he was in the hospital for three months. I went broke over that, not having any insurance, but I raised so much heck that they finally put in an insurance program a few years later. Luther Henderson brought the policy to me and threw it down on my desk." This was the "employee pay all" group insurance plan with Prudential that was limited to top executives.

Buxton's two sons, Tom and Dick, who began their careers sweeping out their father's leather store in San Antonio, followed in his footsteps as Radio Shack employees, Tom as a vice president in real estate and store planning and Dick as a group manager in international franchising.

* * *

Fiscal 1971 proved to be another year of growth for Tandy. Each of its four major marketing groups registered significant increases in sales over the prior year.

Consumer Electronics led the way with a 56 percent increase, followed by Hobby and Handicrafts, up 36 percent; Manufacturing and Distribution, up 35 percent; and General Retailing, up 20 percent. Combined sales rose 41 percent to $356.9 million, while net income increased 24 percent to $11.3 million, or $1.25 per share.

The Consumer Electronics Group, with sales of $161.6 million and earnings of $15.7 million before taxes, extraordinary items, interest charges and administrative expenses, provided 45 percent of Tandy's total sales and 60 percent of its earnings.

In announcing the fiscal 1971 results, Charles Tandy took special note of the "strong performance" of the Allied Radio Shack Division, calling its contributions to earnings "particularly gratifying in the light of the vigorous expansion program which continued throughout the year."

The Allied Radio Shack expansion program added 219 company-owned retail outlets and 81 associate stores during the year, bringing the number of company-owned stores to 893 in 48 states and Canada, and the associate store total to 180. The grand total, as of June 30, 1971, now stood at 1,073.

Overall, Tandy Corporation ended fiscal 1971 with 1,451 company-owned and associate stores.

The Hobby and Handicrafts Marketing Group, which included Tandy Leather, American Handicrafts, Wolfe Nurseries, Merribee and Color Tile, grew from 282 units to 400 during the year.

The General Retailing Group, which included Leonards, Meacham's and Mitchell's, opened 23 new outlets, including two full-line Leonards suburban department stores and 15 Mitchell's junior department stores, bringing the number of outlets in the group to 58. But the General Retailing Group continued to remain unprofitable, posting a loss of $2.3 million.

Tandy took note of the loss in the 1971 Annual Report.

"The General Retailing earnings performance reflects the burden of the very vigorous suburban store expansion program pursued during the past two years," he commented. "The Company generated greatly increased overheads in connection with these moves into new trade areas, and sales levels were not yet developed commensurate with the increased expenses. The suburban expansion program was undertaken in the knowledge that it would have a negative effect on earnings until sales of the new retail outlets reach the projected levels."

Tandy was a bit more bullish about the outlook for the Consumer Electronics Group.

"The past three decades have witnessed an unprecedented growth in the use and popularity of consumer electronic products," he noted. "The development of efficient sound recording and reproduction systems, household electronic devices and the profusion of parts and equipment to service and improve their performance has created an industry and a burgeoning market which barely existed thirty years ago. Our Consumer Electronics marketing group serves this growing segment of the economy through our Allied Radio Shack Division. Our program involves designing and selecting products which bring the latest technological advances and the greatest possible value to our customers. By continuing to utilize marketing techniques which offer the utmost in service and individual attention to each customer, we are confident we will continue the pattern of impressive gains shown by our Consumer Electronics Group during 1971."

As 1971 drew to a close, there remained one event that would provide the icing on the cake to what had been an especially rewarding year for Charles Tandy. Perry R. Bass, the patriarch of the billionaire Bass family of Fort Worth, was elected to the Tandy Corporation board. Bass, the nephew of the legendary Fort Worth wildcatter, Sid W. Richardson, was a leading independent oil operator and successful investor in his own right, a renowned yachtsman who served as Ted Turner's navigator in international yachting competition, and a philanthropist noted for his support of education and the arts.

Bass was not only one of the nation's wealthiest men, but he and his wife, Nancy Lee, sat at the apogee of Fort Worth society. Two of their four sons, Sid R. Bass and Robert M. Bass, were already beginning to carve out identities of their own as savvy investors, whose individual fortunes would one day exceed $1 billion. The Bass' two younger sons, Lee and Ed, though lesser known outside of Fort Worth, would become involved in a variety of business undertakings and Ed Bass would gain widespread recognition as a result of his sponsorship and funding of a biosphere project in Arizona in 1991.

When Charles Tandy approached him about joining the Tandy Corporation board, Perry Bass at first demurred. "I told him that I was in the process of getting off boards rather then joining them," Bass recalled. "But then Anne called me and said she wanted me on the board so that she would have someone on the inside that she could turn to in the event that something happened to Charles."

Having Perry Bass accept the invitation to join his board provided Charles Tandy with the ultimate gratification of his ego. It gave him a special status in his home town that had somehow eluded him. The ambitious young man who once had vowed that one day he would turn his father's leather business into something really big had finally arrived.

He had come a long way from 15th and Throckmorton.

Chapter 21
Disaster in a Rice Field

It was chilly outside, with the wind whistling in from the north, but inside the Tandy hangar at Meacham Field in Fort Worth on Monday morning, January 18, 1972, things were warm and cozy and the coffee in the percolator was piping hot. The seven passengers who would be flying to Victoria, Texas, that morning aboard a Gates Learjet owned and operated by Tandy Corporation were enjoying a final cup before boarding the aircraft in anticipation of the scheduled 7 a.m. departure. They began gathering shortly after 6:30 a.m., but the crew arrived well before 6 o'clock to conduct their pre-flight checks and file their flight plan.

At 6:04 a.m., Glenn Alvin Clifton, chief pilot of Tandy Corporation, received a weather briefing from the Fort Worth Flight Service Station that indicated considerable cloudiness along the route to Victoria. The report gave the prevailing visibility there as five miles, and forecast it would decrease to no less than three miles. This was well above the minimum requirements of a 400-foot ceiling and one-mile visibility for an authorized landing of a Learjet at the Victoria airport.

Clifton filed an Instrument Flight Rules (IFR) flight plan to the Victoria County-Foster Airport, estimating a flight time of 45 minutes and specifying three hours of fuel on board the aircraft. The designated alternate airport was Austin, Texas.

At 6:45 a.m., the seven passengers began boarding the Learjet and buckled themselves in. Promptly at 7 a.m. Clifton taxied out of the hangar. At 7:04 a.m., the plane was airborne.

Clifton, 52, a World War II Army Air Corps pilot, had been a pilot for Tandy Industries, a company owned by Bill Tandy in Tulsa, for nine years before becoming chief pilot of Tandy Corporation in April of 1971. He qualified on Learjets while in the employ of Tandy Industries. He had a total of more than 15,500 hours of pilot flying time to his credit.

Clifton's co-pilot was Cecil Swanner Gibson, 29, who also had flown for Tandy Industries in Tulsa before joining Tandy Corporation in November 1971. Gibson had more than 2,100 hours of flight time in his pilot's log.

The seven passengers aboard the $1.5 million jet, a 1970 Model 25, that brisk January morning were Lewis D. Shows, a Tandy Corporation vice president, and his wife, Jane; William H. Wright, president of Hickok Manufacturing, Inc., and his wife, Barbara Jane; and three other Hickok executives, Harry McLean, merchandise manager; Richard J. Braun, production manager; and James W. Toombs, purchasing manager.

Shows and the four Hickok representatives were scheduled to attend a meeting with Tex Tan Welhausen executives in Yoakum, Texas, at 10 o'clock that morning. They were to be met at the Victoria County-Foster Airport in Victoria and driven the 40 miles north to Yoakum, where the Tex Tan Welhausen headquarters were located. Clifton had decided not to land at the Yoakum airport because its runway was not long enough to accommodate a jet. Victoria, on the other hand, had an 11,000-foot runway.

Mrs. Shows was making the flight because she was planning to visit her husband's ill mother at her home in Beeville, 35 miles southeast of Victoria. Mrs. Wright was planning to visit friends in Yoakum, where she and her husband had lived briefly while he was a Tex Tan Welhausen vice president.

Shows, 52, was a rising star in the Tandy corporate hierarchy. He had joined Tex Tan Welhausen in Yoakum in 1946 after service as a captain in the Army Air Corps during World War II, had become a sales manager in 1959 and been promoted to president in 1961. He moved from Yoakum to Fort Worth in July 1970 after being named a vice president of Tandy Corporation. His responsibilities at the corporate level included overseeing the Manufacturing and Distribution Group that included Tex Tan Welhausen, Tex Tan Western Leather Company and Hickok. Shows had played a major role in the negotiations for the Hickok acquisition in July 1971.

Wright, 55, moved to Rochester from Yoakum after taking over the Hickok presidency in September 1971, but his stay in upstate New York was short-lived. He returned to Texas in December 1971, when the Hickok executive offices were transferred to Arlington. Wright joined Tex Tan Welhausen in 1959 as a sales representative in San Francisco and was promoted to Western regional manager in 1966. He was vice president of sales and merchandising of Tex Tan Welhausen in Yoakum when he was tapped by Shows to become president of Hickok.

McLean, Braun, and Toombs were among the 30 Hickok executives who made the move from Rochester to Arlington after Hickok's sale to Tandy Corporation.

After takeoff, Clifton turned the plane's nose in a southeasterly heading and began his ascent to the 29,000-foot altitude for which he had been cleared by the Fort Worth Air Route Traffic Control Center. The next 28 minutes were uneventful as the graceful jet homed in on its destination.

At 7:32 a.m., Clifton contacted the Houston Air Route Traffic Control Center to receive clearance to begin his descent into Victoria. He was cleared to 24,000 feet. Three minutes later, he was cleared to 10,000 feet and was given the current Victoria altimeter setting of 30.03 inches of mercury. Houston provided the Victoria altimeter setting because the Victoria control tower had been closed due to a lack of traffic. At 7:39 a. m., Clifton reported he had just passed through 15,500 feet and was granted clearance to descend to 5,000 feet.

At 7:40, Houston Traffic Control transmitted a special weather observation for the Victoria airport: "Sky partially obscured, 2,000 scattered, estimated 8,000 broken, one-quarter of a mile visibility with fog, wind calm."

Clifton responded to the message that visibility at Victoria had dropped below the one-mile minimum level: "Tango Charlie, Roger, we'll go take a look at it...stay with you...."

At 7:41:10, Clifton reported he was at 9,000 feet and descending. At 7:41:40, he reported he had just passed through 8,000 feet. He was then cleared by Houston Control for the approach to the Victoria airport.

At 7:44, Houston Traffic Control queried Clifton about the weather conditions he was encountering.

He answered, "Tango Charlie, we can't tell. We're still at 3,000 feet."

Houston radioed, "Radar contact is lost five miles northwest of Victoria. What is your present altitude?"

Clifton replied, "Three thousand, Tango Charlie."

That was the final radio transmission.

Raymond Krawietz, owner of a farm northeast of the Victoria airport and close to the airport's approach-zone area, was in the kitchen with his wife when he heard the sound of an airplane overhead.

"It was coming in real low and it sounded like it was going to take the roof off the house," Krawietz later reported. A few seconds later, he heard a loud noise that shook the farmhouse "like there had been an earthquake." An electric clock in the kitchen stopped at 7:45 a.m. as the house began to shake.

Krawietz's wife said, "That plane just crashed."

Krawietz went outside but couldn't see anything because of the dense fog that enveloped the area. He told a National Transportation Safety Board investigator that the fog was so thick he could barely see 100 feet in front of him. But that did not deter him from climbing into his pick-up truck and driving to the fence line on his property. He could see parts of the wreckage of an airplane and "little fires burning about every 30 feet or so." He also saw an electric utility pole that had been knocked down.

"I came right back and called the Department of Public Safety, then went back and followed the crash path," Krawietz later related to *Star-Telegram* reporter Jim Marrs. "It looked like the plane hit the ground first and came back up. The left wing hit the power pole and it went right on through my fence and ended up in this other rice field. I followed the crash path and found the bodies. It looked like there were nine."

The twin-engined jet first struck the ground about 10 yards inside of Krawietz's property line, leaving a hole about two-feet deep. It then smashed through a fence, sheared off a power line pole and disintegrated as it plunged through a plowed rice field belonging to a farmer named Roy Scherer. The two largest remaining parts of the plane, which caromed more than 400 yards through the rice field, were an eight-foot section of the cockpit and a slightly smaller piece of the tail structure.

The site of the crash was exactly 1.7 nautical miles short of the airport runway, the National Transportation Safety Board stated in its official report on the accident.

There were no survivors.

The Shows left three children, two married daughters and a son. The Wrights were the parents of twin sons. McLean, 40, was survived by a wife and four children, ages 4 to 11; Toombs, 52, by a wife and a daughter; and Braun, 34, by his wife and three small children. Clifton was survived by his wife, a son and a daughter. Gibson was unmarried.

The news of the crash stunned everyone in Tandy headquarters in Fort Worth. Bettye Elliston, who was then Jim West's secretary, recalled how the switchboard lit up with calls after the first reports were aired that a plane carrying a group of Tandy executives had gone down. Ms. Elliston, who joined Tandy in 1968 and become Bernie Appel's secretary after Jim West's retirement, said that many callers were concerned stockholders seeking details of the accident. Other callers were newspapers, radio and television stations and news services from across the country seeking further information and the names of the victims.

"Janet Lesok, Charles Tandy's secretary, and I were sitting together when the phones started ringing off the walls," Ms. Elliston said. "All of the officers up on the second floor came out of their offices and stood behind us offering their moral support, as we tried to answer all of the calls."

Tandy, who usually arrived late in the morning, had not yet arrived. When notified, he took the news so hard that his cardiologist, Dr. Bobby Brown, was called and looked in on him later that morning at Tandy's apartment on Curzon.

When the news of the crash hit Wall Street, Tandy stock sold off sharply on rumors that Charles Tandy had been killed. The stock dropped 2½ points, from 41½ to 39, in a matter of minutes, but recovered somewhat after the announcement was made that Tandy had not been aboard the aircraft. The stock closed at $40, down $1.50 on the day.

By 10 a.m., Bill Michero was aboard a jet belonging to Anne Tandy's Four Sixes Ranch bound for Victoria to handle arrangements for the shipment of the bodies to funeral homes in the cities where the funeral services were to be held and to take charge of personal effects found in the wreckage. The men were quickly identified by wallets and other documents found on the bodies. Mrs. Shows' body was identified through a 2½ carat diamond ring found on her finger. The identification was made by a Victoria physician, Dr. Charles Borchers, the son-in-law of Carl C. Welhausen of Yoakum, a Tandy Corporation vice president and director and a former president of Tex Tan Welhausen.

A bizarre sidelight to the disaster was later recalled by John Roach, who had invited a group of friends to his home the night before the crash to attend a birthday dinner party for his wife, Jean.

"Everyone at the party knew that I was supposed to leave on a trip the next morning," Roach related. "When the news broke that a Tandy plane had crashed, they all assumed I was aboard."

Roach did fly to Baltimore on the morning of January 18 on a commercial airline flight. Upon his arrival at the airport, he rented a car.

"I found out about the crash when I turned on the car radio," he said.

On August 9, 1972, the National Transportation Safety Board issued a report attributing the "probable cause" of the accident to the "lack of altitude awareness on the part of the flight crew while descending into known weather conditions which were conducive to a rapid deterioration in forward visibility. The action of the crew," the report continued, "might have been influenced by a visual, illusory effect produced by a shallow layer of dense fog, combined with the relative position of the sun."

The Safety Board recommended that the Federal Aviation Administration ensure the widespread dissemination of Advisory Circulars and Air Carrier Operations Bulletins which emphasized the hazards associated with weather conditions characterized by a "partial obscuration caused by shallow dense fog."

The report noted, "If the preflight forecast had indicated that the visibility at Victoria was expected to drop to between one-quarter and one-eighth mile in fog by arrival time, it is conceivable that the pilot might not have initiated the flight, or might have planned his flight to the alternate destination. Regardless of the forecast, however, the pilot was informed that the visibility had dropped to one-quarter mile in fog prior to initiation of the approach. The Board believes that the pilot used poor judgment in attempting the approach under the weather conditions which prevailed."

On January 27, 1972, Charles Tandy announced the election of John Cosby as a vice president of Tandy Corporation and president of Hickok Manufacturing Company. Cosby had succeeded Lewis Shows as president of Tex Tan Welhausen in 1970 when Shows moved to Fort Worth to become a Tandy Corporation vice president. Cosby began his career with Tex Tan in 1948 as a sales representative in the Pacific Northwest after serving four years in the U.S. Army during World War II.

At the same time, Arthur A. Tolbert, a longtime employee who had joined the company as a factory worker in 1933, was elected president of Tex Tan Welhausen Company, succeeding Cosby.

The vacancies caused by the plane crash in Victoria were filled from within. But for top management, it was a sobering reminder of the importance of maintaining a strong cadre of support strength on the corporate ladder.

*　*　*

Out in the field, however, it was business as usual. And in the executive suite in Fort Worth, Tandy was still wheeling and dealing.

On February 5, 1972, he announced the acquisition of Vit-A-Way Corporation, a 30-year-old Fort Worth manufacturer and distributor of mineral and vitamin feed supplements for the livestock industry, with plants in Denison, Texas, and Albuquerque, New Mexico.

Tandy called the $750,000 cash acquisition "another expansion of our agribusiness," which now included Tex Tan Western Leather Company, Bona Allen, Inc., and the J.M. Bucheimer Company.

Leo Potishman, a former grain dealer who had founded Vit-A-Way in 1942, said he had had prior offers to sell the company but had waited until an organization came along that had the resources to expand the manufacturing and marketing of the products.

"Money doesn't mean as much to me as will the satisfaction of watching something I founded and built continue to grow," Potishman told James E. Vance, a *Star-Telegram* agricultural writer.

Vit-A-Way, however, did not fit into the Tandy picture as Charles had hoped. Its sales never exceeded $3 million, and it was sold to the SuCrest Corporation on February 26, 1975.

On May 4, 1972, Tandy announced another deal that appeared to some observers to make even less sense than the Vit-A-Way acquisition. This was the purchase of 14.26 percent of the outstanding stock of Kimbell, Inc., a Fort Worth-based holding company, for $8.5 million in cash and notes. Kimbell owned and operated a chain of Buddie's Supermarkets, and a number of Thrifty Drug Stores and Jetton's Cafeterias in the Fort Worth area. The stock was purchased from J.C. Pace, Jr., who was then the president of Buddie's Supermarkets and a Kimbell director.

Tandy called the purchase of the Kimbell stock an investment in its growing merchandising operations, an optimism which some members of the financial community and at least one of his directors failed to share. Phil North said he tried to discourage Tandy from making the deal, basing his argument on the fact that the gross margins of grocery chains were very low in comparison to the numbers to which Tandy was accustomed.

"We'd have been better off buying our own stock," North said, "but Charles was hot to do this, and the board went along with him. This was typical of the board's reaction to everything he presented. For the most part, the attitude was that Charles knew what was best for the company, and most of the time he did. Sure, he'd made an occasional mistake, but when you were doing as many things as he was, there had to be an occasional loser."

Bill Michero was having a hamburger with a New York securities analyst, Robert J. Schweich of Wertheim & Co., when the news of the purchase of the Kimbell stock broke.

"The guy just went berserk," Michero said with a chuckle. "He just went ape. He'd been touting Tandy stock. Now he could hardly wait to get to a telephone to tell his office to dump the stock."

Why did Tandy buy the Kimbell stock, which it sold back to Kimbell, Inc., in December 1977 for $8.5 million in cash, the same price it paid for the stock five-and-a-half years earlier?

It was reported that he had entertained the possibility of putting Radio Shack departments into the Buddie's supermarkets, but it was an idea that never came to fruition.

Bill Michero contended that the purchase was "more of a social decision than a business decision."

Some of Fort Worth's wealthiest families were represented on the board of the Kimbell Art Foundation, the beneficial owner of the majority of the Kimbell stock. The foundation built the world-renowned Kimbell Art Museum in Fort Worth. The museum was named for Kay Kimbell, the founder of Kimbell, Inc., who left his entire estate and extensive art collection to the foundation upon his death in 1964 and directed the foundation trustees to build a museum of the "highest quality" for the benefit of the people of Fort Worth. The trustees selected Louis Kahn, the noted Philadelphia architect, to design the internationally-acclaimed museum building.

Charles and Anne Tandy were among the guests from the cream of Fort Worth society and art patrons and critics from across the nation and abroad at the black tie gala that highlighted the festivities surrounding the opening of the Kimbell Art Museum on October 4, 1972. One of the local guests remembered chatting with Hilton Kramer, then the art editor of the *New York Times*, at the opening night party.

"Kramer just couldn't get over the fact that this jewel of a museum could be built in Fort Worth, Texas," the Fort Worth resident recalled. "He was awed by the collection of art that had already been assembled and by the money that was available to add additional works from around the world."

* * *

Charles Tandy for vice president?

Someone had to be joking. But there it was, an article in the *Audio Times*, that speculated on that possibility. The fact that the date the article appeared was April 1, 1972, was considered by some to be highly appropriate. The headline over the story declared: "Industry Figures Enter Politics." Under a Washington, D.C. dateline, the article began:

"President Richard Nixon is known to be contemplating Charles Tandy as his running mate in the next presidential election to replace Spiro Agnew.

"'It makes sense,' said a presidential spokesman. 'Tandy has 1,500 Radio Shack stores alone—and lord knows how many Tandy Craft Centers. Just the exposure in their windows alone would be enough to cinch the election.'

"Meanwhile, informed Democratic sources say IHF prexy Walter Goodman is considering entering the next primary in a bid for the U.S. presidency.

"'It's probably an easier job than running the Institute of High Fidelity,' Goodman told *Audio Times*. The IHF president said he was certain he could do a better job than the present administration. 'Of course, I'd hate running against Charles Tandy. He's my friend.'"

Charles Tandy never expressed a great interest in partisan politics, although he was a conservative on fiscal issues and on government interference with the free enterprise system. He never minced any words when expressing his opinion about politicians. His favorite target was Congress.

"Congress is not responding to what we, as the core of the American people, want," he told an interviewer, Tina Flori, who was writing an article about him for the TCU student magazine. "Congress does it all in the guise of 'That's what the people want.' But the people don't know the price they're going to pay for it. The public isn't informed, they're lied to. Government officials say they're not going to tax the people, they're going to tax business. Well, the only thing business can do is put it back in the price of the product. Hell, there ain't no such thing as a free ride.

"They've lied like hell about Social Security. That thing is bankrupt. If that was me handling the Social Security program, I'd be in jail. It'd make Billie Sol Estes look like Jesus Christ. I've had a Social Security card since June 2, 1937, and they've spent all the money I've sent them. They don't understand sound fiscal policy. Give me twice as many salesmen and we'll make this government economy spin like you've never seen it spin.

"But politicans think, 'No, don't excite the public. We might not get elected next year.' Hell, you can't get elected unless you lie to everybody. The best thing that John Connally ever said was to limit the terms of Congressmen and the President. Get them out of there and make them live with the laws they've passed."

Nevertheless, when it served his purposes, Tandy was not averse to seeking the aid of his Congressman. Former Speaker of the House Jim Wright of Fort Worth recalled an incident that took place back in the 1950s shortly after he had been elected to his first term in the House.

"Charles was incensed over a surtax that had been imposed on certain types of leather goods," Wright recounted. "He called me about setting up a meeting with the appropriate bureaucrat in Washington so that he could present his side of the issue. I made the arrangements. I'll never forget the day of the meeting. Charles barged into the bureaucrats' office carrying a hundred-pound hide on his shoulder and threw it down on his desk. Now that he had gotten the guy's attention, he proceeded to tell him what he thought about the surtax. Obviously, he knew how to add weight to his argument."

* * *

Tandy Corporation closed out the 1972 fiscal year on June 30 with net earnings of $1.41 per share on sales of $423.2 million. While net earnings had risen 39 percent, net income per share had grown only 13 percent. The per-share earnings had been dampened by a 23 percent increase in shares outstanding as a result of the acquisitions.

Nevertheless, Charles Tandy, commenting on the year in his letter to shareholders in the Annual Report, called it "the most productive" in the company's history and the tenth consecutive year of "unbroken advances." The company, he said, had successfully dealt with problems posed by the temporary closing of domestic ports, the revaluation of foreign currencies and the wage-price freeze that had been imposed during the year. "The orderly marketing processes of several divisions were strained at various times," Tandy wrote, "but the impact of the new economic conditions had been largely assimilated as the year drew to a close."

As of June 30, 1972, Tandy reported, the company was operating 1,943 retail stores, a net increase of 592 units over the past 12 months. He called the opening of "almost two stores for each business day of the year, a record for the company, and possibly a record for any merchandising organization."

Of the 592 new retail outlets opened, 435 were in the Consumer Electronics Group, which again led all other groups in sales and profitability, accounting for 43 percent of sales and 64 percent of earnings. The new units brought the number of company-owned stores in the Radio Shack Division to 1,328 in the 48 continental states, the District of Columbia and Canada. Not included in the total were 215 associate stores and the 37 Allied Radio stores destined for divestiture.

Phil North, however, had another memory of 1972, one not nearly as sanguine as Tandy's.

During the summer of 1972," he recalled, "we were opening two Radio Shack stores a day and were ordering merchandise to stock the stores. Suddenly, we found we were literally out of money. The loan limits of the Fort Worth banks were not anywhere close to what we needed. We called the Republic National Bank of Dallas and they told us they'd loan us $10 million if we'd put two of their people on our board and promise not to open any more stores. Charles told them that was not an acceptable solution to the problem.

"So he and I went to Chicago to talk to the banks up there. When we called Continental Illinois, they told us not to even bother coming to see them. They weren't interested in lending us any money. The First of Chicago invited us to come over, but they spent the entire time talking about how much bad paper they had from other companies and why they weren't making corporate loans.

"Charles and I went outside. We had our coats slung over our shoulders and we looked up at the temperature on the Prudential Building, I guess it was, and it said 104 degrees. It felt like it was hotter than that. The next bank we called was the Harris Trust Company and they said, 'Come on over and we'll take you to lunch.' They not only took us to lunch, but they loaned us their limit. As I recall, it was $6.5 million, which tided us over this very difficult period."

Tandy was sobered by the experience. "He vowed never to let the company get into that kind of shape again," North said. Shortly thereafter, a five-year agreement was negotiated with a group of banks for a $50 million revolving line of credit that provided the capital to fund further expansion.

On August 14, Tandy stock was the recipient of a major boost in Dan Dorfman's "Heard on the Street" column in the *Wall Street Journal*.

"The phrase 'specialty retailer' turns a lot of investors on, and for good reason," Dorfman wrote. "Big money has been made in the stocks of a variety of such merchants—from discount druggists to catalog merchandisers. Now A.G. Becker has come up with what it believes will be another investment winner in the field, namely consumer electronics, or, more specifically, the home audio equipment market. And in this vein, the brokerage concern is voicing enthusiasm for Tandy...a nationwide specialty retailer of such equipment."

The Becker plug for Tandy, written by Christopher C. Stavrou, stressed Radio Shack's ability "to increase sales, maintain gross margins and consistently increase its market penetration at the expense of other retailers." It noted that Radio Shack was "aggressively opening new units," and predicted the company would continue "its excellent growth record." Stavrou strongly recommended the purchase of Tandy stock and forecast the price would move to the mid-50s six to nine months down the road.

Stavrou was equally bullish about the consumer electronics industry as a whole.

"The generation that began as the postwar baby boom and was brought up on stereo and hi-fi sound in the 1960s now is entering an age bracket with increasing purchasing power," he opined. "This customer will continue to respond favorably to the advances in audio equipment technology, notably improvements in sound fidelity and increasing miniaturization and reliability of components and parts. Over the past ten years, sales of home audio equipment grew 171 percent, from $726 million in 1961 to about $2 billion in 1971. In terms of consumption per U.S. household, the advance was 126 percent to $30.18 from $13.33 in the same period. Over the past five years, according to the Electronic Industries Association, dollar sales of radios, phonographs, tape equipment and other products, such as transceivers and hi-fi components, grew 51 percent."

At Tandy headquarters in Fort Worth, the column evoked an appreciative response. Finally, it seemed, somebody on Wall Street was articulating what Charles Tandy had been preaching since 1963.

Chapter 22
Radio Shack Goes International

The seven men seated in the living room of the spacious apartment on Curzon Avenue knew that something was up. They had heard the rumors about an overseas venture. Still, the tension in the room was strong enough to feel as Charles Tandy rose to his feet. He stood in a corner of the room, his cigar clutched in his left hand, his glasses perched on his forehead. Sir John Gielgud never occupied a center stage with more aplomb.

"We're going international," Tandy emoted. "We're going to open Radio Shacks all over Europe, and you guys are going over there to do the job."

One of the men in the room would later recall that he couldn't help thinking, as Tandy made his pronouncement, of a newsreel he had seen in the early days of World War II of Adolf Hitler standing in front of a map that covered the wall behind him and proclaiming: "Today Germany, tomorrow the world!"

But this time there were no "Sieg Heils" reverberating through the room, only the bemused looks on the countenances of the seven men making up Charles Tandy's audience on that chilly January morning in 1973. They had received telephone calls several days earlier summoning them to a meeting in the apartment on Curzon. They had no inkling of why they were wanted in Fort Worth.

Some guessed about what was to transpire. Now they had it straight from Tandy's own lips. They were going to blaze a new trail for Radio Shack into the Old World.

The men who were present in the room that blustery January morning had been recruited from the top echelon of the Radio Shack marketing ranks. Three of them, Jim Buxton, Ken Gregson, and Dean Lawrence, dated from the Tandy Leather Company days. Buxton was now a Radio

Shack regional vice president in Southern California; Gregson, a regional vice president in Columbus, Ohio; and Lawrence, a former assistant regional manager in Chicago, was now the general manager of the Allied Radio Division.

The others in the room were Bruce E. Russell, Richard J. O'Brien, Jon A. Shirley and Tony Bernabei. Russell joined Radio Shack in 1966 as director of franchise operations and was now a regional vice president in Boston. O'Brien joined Radio Shack in Boston in 1956 as manager of the mail order department and was now a regional vice president in Philadelphia. Shirley began his career in 1958 as a department manager of a Radio Shack store in Boston and was now merchandise manager of the Radio Shack Division in Fort Worth. Bernabei, who had been with Radio Shack since 1969 and served in mergers and acquisitions and as head of the franchise department, was a regional vice president in Fort Worth.

Tandy laid out the program for the group.

"Those marketplaces overseas are primed and ready for us. It's a huge market and it's high time we tapped into it. We've been wanting to expand our horizons. Now is the time to do it."

It was Tandy at his upbeat best.

"What we've done here we can do there. What has worked for us in the States will work over there. We know how to sell. We know how to make money. That's what counts. Sure, there are those who are opposed to our going overseas, who feel we're doing fine on our own turf. So why take on the headaches and the risks of expanding overseas?"

His answer: "The time to do it is when you're riding high, when you can afford it. If we wait until later, it may be too late." Tandy reminded the men in the room that they were part of a management team he had personally hand-picked and developed over the years.

"When you've brought people to a certain level, you've got to have things for them to do," he asserted. "You've got to have places to move them, offer them new challenges and new rewards. If you don't use them, you'll either lose them or they'll dry up and stagnate. You people are supposed to have some moxie. Now's your chance to show it."

The fact was that Tandy had been unable to find places for most of the seven in his planned centralization of Radio Shack operations.

Tandy told the group that a new International Division was being formed and that it would be headed by Russell, who would carry the title of division president. Russell would be moving from Boston to Fort

Worth, from where he would oversee the overseas operations. Bernabei, Buxton, Gregson, Lawrence, O'Brien, and Shirley would become
vice presidents of the International Division and would be heading
overseas with their families.

There were still a lot of questions, including the key one of where the
European invasion would commence.

Jim Buxton's recollection was that Tandy "left it pretty much open
where we should go," and Ken Gregson claimed the credit for suggesting that the operation should begin in Belgium or Holland.

"I'd already decided in my own mind before I got to the meeting that
Charles was going to tell us he wanted to open in Europe," Gregson recalled, "and I'd already picked out where I wanted to go. I wanted to
go to Antwerp or Brussels, and the reason was that Holland and Belgium were the two smallest countries in Free Europe, they were the
easiest to move money into and out of, and they each had a major port,
Rotterdam and Antwerp. Because they were small countries, their governments and agencies would be easier to deal with, and their laws
were such that we could do more there than we could do in the larger
European countries."

After long consideration of the pros and cons of both countries, Gregson said he finally gave the nod to Belgium. "I just decided we should
go to Brussels," he recounted, "and that's what I finally told Tandy at
the meeting."

When Tandy asked what had led him to his conclusion, Gregson answered, "A number of things. First of all, Belgium is the smallest country in Europe. We won't be dealing with state governments, as we do in
the States. We'll be dealing with federal governments. And since Belgium is the smallest country, it'll be the easiest to deal with."

Then he threw in the clincher.

"NATO is in Brussels," he declared. "There must be a reason for that.
SHAEF is in Belgium, at Mons. There must be a reason. Belgium has
been overrun by so many people over the years, that a Belgian just kind
of shrugs his shoulders and says, 'Ach, so take it or leave it.' So, in essence," Gregson concluded, "Belgium would be the easiest country to
set up in. By far, easier than Germany. By far, easier than the other
countries."

When someone asked why not start out in the United Kingdom,
Gregson replied that his research indicated it would be more difficult to
set up an operation and do business there.

"You've done some homework," Tandy acknowledged.

"I had been around Charles for so long," Gregson recounted, "that I could see the handwriting on the wall. I knew he had a vision of building a worldwide company. He wanted worldwide recognition, and to gain that he had to go international. We were already doing the job in the States. We were already in Canada. What else was there for us to do when we were enlarging our scope but go international? I came to Fort Worth thinking that's exactly what we were going to do."

Before leaving for the meeting he convened a family council attended by his wife, Faye, and his children, Kenneth, 15, and Lisha, 13.

"I told them I believed that Charles was going to want me to go overseas and help put together an international division for Radio Shack," Gregson said. "This was a big step for us as a family. It meant going to a foreign country to live, and I wanted to know how they felt about it before I committed myself."

Kenneth asked his father how long he thought the assignment would last. Gregson figured about two years, and Kenneth said, "This is an opportunity to live overseas that I'll probably never have again." Lisha got up and put her arms around her father. "Dad," she told him, "you haven't made any mistakes yet that I know of, why should I worry about it now." Faye Gregson threw her hands up and said resignedly, "Whither thou goest, I goest." She had followed her husband on a succession of assignments in the 20 years he had worked for the Tandys, first for Bill and then for Charles. She didn't relish pulling up stakes and moving to a foreign country, but this wasn't the time to put her foot down.

Gregson's homework, which had impressed Tandy, was not wasted on his colleagues. Although a long discussion ensued, in which everyone spoke his piece, it was finally decided that Belgium would be the country in which the European operation would be launched.

"We agreed we were all going to Brussels," Gregson said.

But it turned out, Tandy had other plans for one member of the group, Dean Lawrence. Tandy informed Lawrence he had another destination in mind for him. When the significance of what Tandy was preparing to tell him hit Lawrence, he said, "Charles, you wouldn't."

"Why wouldn't I?"

"Charles, you couldn't."

"Why couldn't I?"

"You don't really want me to go to Japan?"

"Why not? We gotta do business there, too."

Tandy's choice of Lawrence for the Tokyo assignment was based primarily on the fact that he had been stationed there during World War II. Lawrence was not particularly happy about going back, but finally agreed. His stay in Tokyo would be of short duration, however. Soon after his arrival he informed Tandy there was no way he was going to be able to open any stores in Japan and make any money under the government restrictions on foreign operators. It was a story other American businesses encountered before and since. It was all right to buy in Japan, but virtually impossible to sell anything there.

Tandy took the news calmly.

"No problem," he told Lawrence, "ships sail in more than one direction." So Lawrence and his wife, Sara Mae, and their four children waved goodbye to Tokyo and headed south to Sydney, Australia, where their welcome was considerably warmer.

With the decision made that the overseas venture would commence in Brussels and Tokyo, planning for the operation got under way and continued in Fort Worth for the next week.

"We really got down to brass tacks," Gregson said. "All of us remained in town, holding meetings every day. We also were checking with people about how to do business in Belgium, what we were going to need when we got over there. We checked with the banks about currency regulations. Dick O'Brien and I went to New York to look into the types of transportation we'd be utilizing—barge traffic, truck traffic, ocean traffic. There were a million things we found that we had to brush up on, things we were going to have to do."

In late January, 1973, Bernabei, Buxton, Gregson, O'Brien, and Shirley took their wives on a two-week visit to Brussels.

"We wanted to show them the lay of the land," Gregson said. "Our wives, of course, were concerned about schooling, about housing. They needed to find out about these things and help make the decisions about them, because once we got over there and started putting the operation together, we weren't going to be able to take the time to do that. They were going to have to do their thing while we were doing our thing. So it was important that everything was jelling right.

"When we got there, we checked with people at J.C. Penney and Sears, who were operating over there. We met with the banks, with lawyers, with other people who could help us. We had to select a law firm and selected Coudert Brothers. It was a business fact-finding trip for the guys and a living fact-finding trip for the gals. We had to find out what the price of housing was, about the kinds of leases they had over there. We found out that you took pictures of the house you leased before you moved in and took pictures when you moved out. It was another world over there and we were going over stark cold blind."

Jim Buxton, his wife, Jody, and their two sons, Dick and Tom, were the first of the Tandy group to settle in Brussels. The Buxtons rented an apartment. Tony Bernabei and his wife, Olivia, and Jon Shirley, his wife, Mary Lee, and their three children followed in late February. They set up housekeeping in rented houses.

The Gregsons returned to Columbus after the Brussels junket and put their home up for sale and made arrangements to take their children out of school. While in Brussels, they rented a house and enrolled the children in St. John's, a small private school in Waterloo that was affiliated with St. John's University in Washington, D.C., and was, therefore, accredited in the States.

"It took about 30 days for the house in Columbus to sell," Gregson said, "so it was March when we finally moved to Brussels. It was a total change for us, a total change in lifestyle, food, in everything."

From the outset, it was supposed to be a team effort, Gregson recounted, with each member of the group having a special area of interest: Bernabei in opening stores, Shirley in merchandising, O'Brien in advertising, Gregson in store locations and Buxton in distribution and warehousing. That was the game plan.

"We had a lot of people pulling at us," Gregson said. "The Yamagatas (of A&A Trading Corporation) wanted us to go the United Kingdom because they said we couldn't get licenses to import goods into Belgium. I told them, 'No, the reason you want us to go to England is that you think it's easier from your standpoint. I've been assured we can get licenses in Belgium.'"

Then Buxton decided he wanted to go to England, Gregson reported, "because he found out they spoke English there." Buxton had a problem, Gregson said. "He wasn't going to deal with people in another language."

Buxton agreed that he began pushing for England after he began encountering unforeseen difficulties operating in Belgium.

"The first thing we ran into that Charles never realized," Buxton said, "is that you can't take your money over there. You can borrow all right, but at 21 percent. We couldn't stand that. Also, I was trying to get merchandise into Belgium, and they had more damn restrictions than you could shake a stick at. I had a beautiful location picked out for a warehouse in Antwerp and I had plans drawn for it. But we kept having problems and more problems.

"So I went to England, where you could speak the language and everything was great. The only restriction we had over there was in pocket calculators. I called Charles and told him, 'We're all pulling in opposite directions. No one is seeing eye-to-eye on anything. The smartest thing in the world for us to do is go to England, get used to this foreign country where all of us can speak the language, and we can make this thing profitable in a year. Then we can take on another country.'"

Of the group that Tandy sent to Europe only Bernabei could speak any language other than English. With a degree in modern languages and literature from Princeton, Bernabei was fluent in seven languages. He had lived in nine countries and served in Army Intelligence during World War II, interrogating German and Italian prisoners.

Buxton recalled asking Tandy why he selected Bernabei, a relative newcomer to the company, to be part of the initial overseas contingent, and Tandy replied, "Because he's the only guy we've got who can speak the language." Then, Tandy added, "None of you guys knows which wines to order with the food over there. Bernabei is the only guy we've got who can do that."

Bernabei was never quite accepted into the Tandy hierarchy, perhaps because of his Ivy League background and the fact that he was an outsider whose corporate roots were neither in the Tandy Leather Company nor Radio Shack. He was recruited by Bill Tandy and joined the organization after Charles' heart attack in October, 1968.

Bernabei was then with C.I.T. Educational Buildings, Inc., a subsidiary of C.I.T. Finance, in New York. He and Bill Tandy had worked together on a dormitory building program for small colleges, with C.I.T. providing the financing and Bill's company, Southern Mill and Manufacturing of Tulsa, doing the construction.

"One day I was in Bill's office in Tulsa," Bernabei related, "and I told him that I wasn't really happy with my situation at C.I.T. And he said, 'If that's the case, you ought to talk to Charles Tandy.' Bill had been expressing concern to some of his fellow directors about what he deemed to be a lack of management depth in the company. He had really been shaken by his brother's heart attack."

Bernabei's initial meeting with Tandy took place in Tandy's hospital room in Boston.

"My first impression of Charles Tandy was of him sitting in his pajamas on the edge of the bed with a yo-yo that he played up and down, thinking of it as a product that you possibly could sell batteries for because it had a light in it. He was always intrigued by that sort of thing. And I thought, 'Dear me, what am I getting into? Here's a guy playing with a yo-yo who's just had a heart attack!' Well, we talked and talked. And he said, 'If everything goes well, I'll give you some stock.' He didn't mean he'd give it to me. I'd have to pay for the stock ultimately."

The announcement that Bernabei joined Radio Shack in a new staff position as executive vice president was made in a news release on March 23, 1969.

The word around Tandy headquarters in Fort Worth was that Bill Tandy had sold his brother on bringing Bernabei into the organization. Jim Buxton offered this scenario:

"Bernabei was really hired by Bill Tandy who sent him to Fort Worth to be executive vice president of Tandy Corporation, but when he got there Jim West wouldn't let him have the job. So they made him executive vice president of Radio Shack with no duties."

Bernabei said that after he accepted Charles Tandy's offer to join the company, he spent "some time with him trying to find some sort of slot in corporate headquarters. When he named me executive vice president of Radio Shack, I really didn't understand the implications of what executive vice president meant. Years later I realized that the message in the corporate world is that the executive vice president is going to be the president of the company. But that never occurred to me. I just plowed ahead doing the things that needed to be done. Because the organization was in place, my first job was in mergers and acquisitions."

His major acquisition was of Antennacraft Company, Inc., of Burlington, Iowa, a manufacturer of television antennas, for $1.2 million in cash and notes in May 1970. He was named a regional vice president of the Central Region in 1972. He recalled bragging to Tandy after his first year on the job that his was the best region in the country, with $35 million in sales and $3.5 million in pre-tax profits.

Chomping on his cigar, Tandy retorted, "Bernabei, have I done anything to keep you from doing $70 million?"

Bernabei reported that before going overseas, each member of the task force signed a contract stipulating he would serve abroad two years at the same salary he was receiving in the job he was relinquishing.

"Charles' attitude was that we could move into any country and do exactly the same things that we did in the United States," Bernabei opined. "But it just wasn't to be. Some specific instances are that in the United States we did the five-cell flashlight battery promotion and one year gave away two million flashlights. The gimmick was that we gave away five-cell flashlights that cost us only 90 cents and the profit on the five batteries we sold to go with the flashlight was a lot more than the cost of the flashlight. That was a marvelous promotion like the battery card, where you came in once a month and got a free battery. But once we got you in the store, you usually bought something."

The problem was that promotions like these were illegal in Germany, Bernabei found after setting up operations in that country.

"In Germany," he said, "you couldn't use the battery card. You couldn't use the flashlight promotion because the very strong lobby of the small store owners had established a law that you can't give away samples. Charles couldn't understand that.

"'What do you mean you can't use the battery card? Why can't you give away flashlights?'"

Another successful stateside Radio Shack promotion, giving lifetime guarantees on hi-fi speakers, also couldn't be employed in Germany, Bernabei recalled, because of another law that banned guarantees. Bernabei described the case that precipitated the enactment of the legal barrier.

"There was a guy who rebuilt chimneys, and what he would do is rebuild a chimney and give a 20-year guarantee. And the German lawyer asked him, 'How long have you been in business?' And he said, 'Ten years.' And the lawyer said, 'How can you give a 20-year guarantee if you've only been in business 10 years?' And that's how the law got on the books."

There were other problems, too.

In Germany, the Tandy group encountered a strong "nationalistic attitude," Bernabei said, "where consumers just wouldn't buy a product that wasn't German-made. It had to be Blaupunkt or another German manufacturer."

In Belgium, he pointed out, there were French-speaking areas and areas where Walloon was the prevailing tongue. Sending a catalog printed in French to a Walloon-speaking individual meant he not only would not buy your product but would probably bad mouth you, to boot.

"We all lived in Brussels. We had a central warehouse at Naninne, just outside of Brussels, that supplied all of Europe. We opened stores in Holland, Belgium, Luxembourg, Germany, and, eventually, France. We couldn't go into Italy because the law wouldn't permit it. And we were also in England. We had our own warehouse in Birmingham that supplied all of England. We called our stores, Tandy, because, in Germany, especially, Radio Shack would not come out so good."

Gregson spoke of the feelings of optimism that pervaded the group before it began encountering the realities of operating on foreign soil.

"We knew there was going to be a lot of competition over there. There was Blaupunkt, ITT, Siemens, Philips, and others. But they weren't merchandising the way we were. They didn't do business the way we did. We saw a huge marketplace in Free Europe, a common market they were trying to put together, of 290 million people. We knew there were national border problems to overcome that we didn't have in the States. We didn't know what the difficulties were going to be. We'd just have to go over there and find out."

They quickly found out that space was at a premium in Europe.

"We were used to running 2,500-square foot Radio Shack stores in the U.S. In Europe we were going to have to do with 1,000 square feet," Gregson reported. "We had lots of shopping centers and malls here. They didn't have them in Europe. So it was really a totally different kind of operation."

In addition, Gregson said, Tandy didn't earmark any funds or give them a budget with which to work. He remembered an occasion during the second year of the European operation when Tandy complained to him, "Gregson, I knew this was going to cost us money, but did it have to cost this much?"

As he began looking at potential warehouse sites in Europe, Gregson couldn't help being influenced by the successful Radio Shack practice of operating central warehouses from which it shipped merchandise to stores across the United States.

"We had found it was cheaper and more efficient to do it that way," he said. "When we got to Europe, we decided to set up a central warehouse in Belgium from where we should ship into all of the other countries. People didn't understand. They would ask, 'Why would you take it from Germany, buy it in Germany, take it to Belgium and ship it back into Germany?' Our answer was, 'That's the way we do it.' We could actually show them how we saved money by doing it. We could control the inventory better and we could get better use out of our money."

The site that was selected was in Naninne, 42 miles south of Brussels.

"It's right on the north, south, east and west highways and it's right on the River Meuse," Gregson said. "It was ideally located. We could get to France from there, to Holland and to Germany and to Luxembourg. We'd use the port of Brussels."

There was another plus to the choice of Naninne as the site for the warehouse and the headquarters for the operation, according to Gregson. Naninne was French-speaking, but the first store to be opened in Belgium was to be located near Antwerp in a Flemish area.

"So we could say to everyone we weren't playing favorites," Gregson said. "We were supplying jobs in both the French and the Flemish parts of the country. This would keep us from getting involved in this French versus Flemish business."

The first hurdle that had to be overcome was getting permission to locate the operation in Naninne and secure the necessary import permits.

"It helped that our lawyers, Coudert Brothers, had an office in Brussels and had connections with Rene Close, the governor of the Province," Gregson disclosed. "We convinced the authorities and the governor that we were the kind of people they wanted. We were a clean industry, nonpolluting. We weren't into heavy manufacturing. We didn't generate noise. Most of all, we were going to supply jobs, which was what the country desperately needed."

The operation began in a rented, 30,000-square-foot building while the new warehouse was being built. Gregson now encountered some problems with the contractor about the type of structure he wanted.

"I didn't want a warehouse that was going to last 300 years, which was the way they built things there," he explained. "I wanted something which was utilitarian. I found out there was a strand steel type erection, with the skin and the insulation available from Luxembourg, and I convinced the contractor to check with them. We wanted a cement slab poured and then the steel skin put up. The contractor's response was, 'But the building won't last.'"

Gregson finally convinced the contractor that the building would probably not be used for longer than 20 years and that by then something entirely different would probably be needed.

The first store opened in August of 1973 in Aartselaar, near Antwerp on the main highway to Brussels. It bore the name, Tandy International Electronics.

"Charles wanted Tandy in the name," Gregson said. "He wanted to establish a name, so that later it might be possible to utilize it with other things like Tandy Leather."

The first store was twice as large as the average 1,000-square-foot outlet that was opened in Europe because of the fact that Gregson was able to make a deal with a former Tandy subsidiary, Pier 1 Imports.

"Pier 1 had a store in Aartselaar in a building that was too large for them," Gregson reported. "So we made a deal to take 2,000 square feet of their space, and we put in a wall to separate the two operations."

Gregson remembered another problem that arose from the fact that everyone was on vacation while he was trying to get the store ready for the August opening.

"In July everybody goes on vacation, and I had to literally build the store from scratch with the help of three young Flemish men that I got hold of because all of the building trades and everybody else were on vacation and I couldn't find a carpenter anywhere."

So Gregson and his helpers put in the partitions, the vinyl asbestos tile flooring, the showcases and the shelving by themselves. They even had to find the aluminum extrusions to put in the glass showcase tops.

"We worked around the clock to get the store ready," Gregson recollected.

To expedite the delivery of the first shipment of merchandise from Houston, Dick O'Brien sat on the dock in Brussels to make certain the two containers cleared customs and were trucked to the store in Aartselaar.

"Now," said Gregson, "comes the funny part. We got two containers of U.S. merchandise that ran on 110 volts and 60 cycles, and we were in Europe where everything was 220 volts and 50 cycles. This was really hilarious. Our merchandisers were real geniuses. European television sets are totally different from what we have in the States, but they sent all of the television supplies, connectors and everything else for U.S. television. Every turntable they shipped turned at 60 cycles, not the 50 we needed. That was easy to correct. We could get adapters to adapt them down to 50. Okay? But what do you do with a clock? We could buy transformers and take 220 down to 110 and operate the clocks. So we bought transformers and we put adaptors on the turntables."

Gregson vividly remembered trying to explain to a customer that there would be no problem with a clock-radio because it was 110 instead of 220.

"I told him I would give him this transformer to go with it, so it would operate," Gregson related. "And he told me in his broken English that things ran on 50 cycles in Belgium and that this was a 60-cycle clock."

Gregson said that he laughingly told the customer, "Don't worry, I'm not going to charge you for the clock, and, besides, it will tell the correct time every six hours."

The customer laughed and bought the clock-radio.

The first advertising they did used the word "Sale" which turned out to be illegal and caused them to be hauled into court.

"It seems," Gregson explained, "that there are certain 'Sold' periods in Europe, in January and July, when you are permitted to slash prices and say, 'Sale.' But after you do that, the merchandise that was 'on sale' has to be taken to the storeroom and not be shown again until you have another 'Sold' period. This prevents you from raising the price of the marked-down merchandise."

They also gave away free flashlights at the opening, which was unheard of in Europe, and incited Belgian flashlight manufacturers to haul them into court on the grounds the Americans were taking away their livelihood.

"In France," Gregson recounted, "we couldn't say things in a certain way because they've got people who look after the French language and if you say the wrong thing, you're in court."

They had less of a problem in Belgium, where the officials they dealt with seemed to appreciate the fact they were trying to learn the rules and abide by them. Their attitude was, "We know that you're trying. And as long as you're trying, we won't have a problem."

The opposite was true in Germany. There, Gregson said, "if you broke the rules, you broke the rules. The theory was, you should know the rules. If you didn't, that was too bad."

In Holland, most of the difficulties they encountered stemmed from the fact they were competing on the home turf of Philips, the mammoth consumer electronics company.

"Every time we got ready to open a store in Holland," Gregson revealed, "Philips would have the local magistrate or other authority come down and slap us with a rule they said we had broken, like we didn't have the right kind of a back door. So we couldn't open the store. They were doing their damnedest to keep us from operating. So I got mad, and in one day we opened three stores in Eindhoven, which is their headquarters. We had the mayor's nephew install the back doors, so they wouldn't find anything wrong with them. So, of course, they found something wrong with the stairways to the basement and some other stuff."

Gregson sighed as he recounted the incident.

"Those were the kinds of problems we were facing every day," he said, "and nobody in the States could understand this. The people in Fort Worth were constantly on our backs asking, 'Why can't you do this? Why can't you do that?'"

* * *

By 1974, the group that had left Fort Worth a year earlier with such high hopes and unanimity of purpose was no longer a unit. It had been dissolved, with different people setting up shop in different countries.

Tandy chastised them, "You went over as a team but you can't function as a team because everybody feels they have to be territorial."

"We broke up the group because there seemed to be a few problems we couldn't solve," was Gregson's appraisal of what happened.

"Dick O'Brien was gonna worry about England. We'd sent him to England because we'd decided we couldn't ship across the Channel with all the problems that entailed. I'd gone over to England with Dick and we'd put in a warehouse in Birmingham and started opening stores. Dick was running that operation, but was still living in Brussels.

"Tony Bernabei was sent to Germany, but also continued to live in Brussels. We tried to get him to go to Frankfurt because that was where the American community was. But Tony made a tour and decided that he was going to put in an office in Duesseldorf. So he put in the office there and started opening stores in Germany. The merchandise was shipped out of the warehouse in Belgium. And I'm running Holland, Belgium and France from Belgium and Jon Shirley is in Belgium with me as merchandiser and advertiser."

Jim Buxton returned to the States in the latter part of 1973 to become involved with another project, Giant Store Corporation of Boston, and Tony Bernabei returned home in 1975. In 1976, Bruce Russell was relieved of his duties as president of the International Division and Dick O'Brien was supplanted by Carroll Ray and Bob Bourland in England.

Meanwhile, Gregson developed diabetes.

"The change of lifestyle and all the rest had worked havoc with me," Gregson said. "At one point, I dropped down to 138 pounds. Everybody kept telling me I was crazy, that I shouldn't stay over there, but my attitude was that I had gone over to do a job and I wasn't coming back until the job was done. Charles was worried about my health and tried to get me to come home. He insisted I come back every six months for a visit. One time Faye and I were visiting with him in his office and he said to me, 'When are you gonna come home?' And before I could answer, he looked at Faye and said, 'He's a hard-headed sonuvabitch, isn't he?' And she said, 'It's your fault. You raised him.'"

Gregson told about a conversation with Tandy on one of his trips home when they began reminiscing about the old Tandy Leather days. Gregson recalled how he had to carry bulky 100-pound rolls of cowhide up and down a narrow flight of stairs in the store he managed in St. Louis during the 1950s and '60s.

"Charles knew what I was talking about," Gregson said, "because he'd seen me do it, wearing a brace on my leg. And he asked me if I remembered how many steps there were on that staircase going down to the basement. I told him, 'I sure do. Do you?' And he said, 'There were 16 steps.' And he was right. There were 16. And I said to him, 'I'm sure glad you remember.'

"And Charles said, 'I watched you carry a lot of leather up and down those steps.' And I said, 'Yes, by God, and never once did you put out your hand to help me.' And Charles looked me in the eye and said, 'Gregson, I wasn't about to put out my hand to help you because I didn't want you getting lazy.' And then he added, 'But you don't know how happy I am that you don't have to go down steps like that anymore.'"

Gregson remained in Europe until May of 1979. The European operation finally showed an overall profit during his last year there.

"It took us five years to get profitable," he recalled. "Germany was not profitable when I left. France and Belgium were profitable. Holland still had some problems. The bulk of the profitability was in Belgium."

In Australia, where Dean Lawrence set up shop in Sydney in 1973, progress had been steady, if not spectacular. By the time Dave Christopher supplanted Lawrence in January of 1977, there were about 100 Tandy Electronics stores in operation, all on the eastern coast, in Sydney, Melbourne, Adelaide, and Brisbane, where most of the population was concentrated. There were no stores on the west coast, where Perth was the only market.

Christopher, who had been a Radio Shack district manager in Kansas City and a regional manager in New York, had just been transferred to Fort Worth as a divisional manager, when he volunteered to go overseas.

"Along with the promotion to divisional manager," Christopher explained, "came an oath that if we accepted the job, we also accepted the fact that at some point in our divisional manager career we would be assigned overseas. I was very antsy about the overseas assignment. So I decided the best thing to do was tell Bill Nugent, then the executive vice president of Radio Shack, that I wanted the first overseas assignment that opened up. I didn't care where it was, I just wanted to go. At that time, Ken Gregson was in Belgium and I understood that his health wasn't real good. So I thought there was a very good possibility I would go to Belgium. I even encouraged my wife to take French lessons."

Mrs. Christopher had just signed up for the course when Nugent broke the news to Christopher that he was in line for the next overseas assignment which was going to be in Australia. This was in early October of 1976, and Christopher was told he would be leaving for Australia in January.

Tandy's response, when he learned from Nugent that he had selected Christopher for the Australian assignment, was to exclaim: "I know you haven't taught him anything, so you'd better send him to me on Saturdays so I can teach him what's really going on."

So Christopher began going to Tandy's office for Saturday classes. It turned out to be an interesting, if somewhat unusual, experience.

"I was unsure what the format was going to be," he recalled. "Was I going to be taught as if I was in school? Or was I going to be asked a lot of questions? As it turned out, the Saturday sessions entailed just sitting in one of the chairs in front of Tandy's desk. He had a constant parade of people coming through his office. It might be John Wilson wanting to talk about Color Tile. It was just one person after another who would kind of line up outside his door. Charles would listen to their problems and I'd just sit there listening to one subject after another.

"They'd talk about Color Tile, Tandy Leather, Merribee, and just change from person to person, and I was just listening. I wasn't expecting that. But what Charles was doing was giving me a chance to see first-hand how a chief executive dealt with problems. I was amazed at his ability to change subjects, from what was going on in this company to what was going on in that company, to handle this kind of problem to that kind of problem. He was absolutely on top of everything. When somebody called him on the phone, Charles would put him on the speaker. Of course, they had no idea who was listening in on the conversation. Charles didn't seem to care."

For three months, Christopher spent his Saturdays with Tandy.

"I'd usually get there at 8:30 or 9 o'clock," he recounted. "Charles was never there. He would come in about 10 o'clock and go practically all day. People would quit coming into his office around 5:30 or 6, and then Charles would sit around and shoot the breeze about what was going on. His wife would usually starting calling around 6 or 7 and ask him when he was coming home. He'd say, 'In a few minutes,' or 'we're about to wind up,' and he'd carry on for another hour or two. Sometimes it would take two or three more phone calls, 'Are you through yet?' 'How much longer?' 'We're supposed to be at so-and-so's right now.'

"Those Saturday sessions would end somewhere between 6 and 10 o'clock at night. We'd go to the Fort Worth Club for lunch, have a sandwich or a hamburger. On a few occasions, he wanted to go and visit stores late on Saturday afternoon. We'd get in his car and I'd drive. We'd drive around and he'd pick a store and we'd stop and he'd go in and start asking the store manager, if he wasn't busy with a customer, how he was doing. He'd ask him questions about his P&L. It was absolutely an experience to see the man operate."

Tandy never did talk to Christopher about Australia. But, in retrospect, Christopher conceded, he learned a great deal about running a business. "I got the sense," he added, "that Tandy was trying to teach me lessons. He was taking me into his confidence on things that were going on. When someone left his office, he'd often continue talking about the problem they'd been discussing."

Australia, when Christopher arrived there in early 1977, was still unprofitable. Business was "pretty good," Christopher found. Australia had always enjoyed better sales than most of its European counterparts, better by comparison when translated into U.S. dollars. It was losing money mostly because of low gross margins.

"The stores and the product line were essentially the same as in the States," Christopher found. "Dean had done a good job establishing the stores and establishing procedures. We rented space for the stores which were a little smaller than those in the States. The business hours were very odd. There was no shopping in the evening. By law, the stores could be open only one night a week and that was on Thursdays. The rest of the days they had to close at 5:30. On Saturdays, they had to close at noon. Sunday shopping absolutely was not allowed. It was very different from the U.S. at that time, where shopping hours were expanding like crazy and it was becoming very common to be open every night of the week. And in some places, where the laws permitted it, we were opening on Sunday."

In Christopher's first year at the helm, Australia turned a profit, and he recalled a meeting in Fort Worth with Tandy and Nugent upon the conclusion of that first profitable year.

"Nugent was very pleased, of course, that Australia had gotten profitable," Christopher related. "One of the reasons it had gotten profitable was that I immediately went in and propped up gross margins on merchandise. We'd wound up raising prices like crazy and, furthermore, we'd gone through a devaluation of the currency that had further driven up prices. As a result we were just barely making last year's sales.

"I can recall Nugent being so proud and telling Charles how smart he had been in picking me to go to Australia, because I'd had this big turnaround and gotten the thing profitable," Christopher continued. "And Charles just looked at him and said, 'Yeah, but the son of a bitch has got a sales loss.'"

Christopher returned to Fort Worth in July, 1980 and was placed in charge of all international relations, including corporate responsibility over A&A Trading Corporation. He was named president of A&A Trading in 1989 and in 1992 was promoted to executive vice president of Radio Shack with responsibility for merchandising and advertising, while retaining his position as president of A&A Trading.

In 1986, Tandy Corporation spun off its retail operations in Australia, Canada, the United Kingdom and Europe as a new publicly traded company named InterTAN. Each Tandy shareholder received one share of InterTAN stock for each 10 shares of Tandy Corporation stock held as a tax-free dividend.

Management's rationale for the move was that it would permit Tandy to concentrate on maximizing the opportunities afforded by its domestic operations and give InterTAN the flexibility of aggressively adopting solutions to its specific problems.

A total of 2,119 company-owned and dealer/franchise retail outlets was spun off to InterTAN, including 888 in Canada, 826 in Europe and 336 in Australia, plus 69 export dealers.

The profitable Canadian operation had not been a part of the International Division until the spin-off. It was included in the package in order to make it more attractive to investors.

Dave Christopher added his perspective on the venture that had begun so auspiciously in Charles Tandy's apartment on that chilly January morning in 1973:

"Charles had the vision that these guys to whom he'd assigned responsibility had enough experience to be able to do the job and that it should be virtually no problem. His attitude was, 'If we can do it here, why can't we do the same thing over there?' But he found out it was a huge problem. It cost us a lot of money and we learned a lot of lessons about doing business in those countries."

In a *Fortune* magazine article published in December, 1976, Irwin Ross wrote:

"Tandy Corp.'s foreign operation, begun in 1973, is another potential source of profit, if and when it gets turned around. With 353 stores in Australia and Europe, it has yet to make money and last year racked up an operating loss of $8.5 million. Once again, Tandy blames the people he sent over to run the stores. 'I feel the European market is as big as the U.S.,' he says, 'but being successful there is another chapter we haven't written.'"

Unfortunately, the chapter would not be written during his lifetime.

Chapter 23
A 'Giant' Deal Falls on Its Face

It was deja vu at the First National Bank of Boston. The bank was in big trouble with a loan, and once again it had turned to Tandy to bail it out.

The ailing company was Giant Stores Corporation, a 40-store discount department store chain in New England that also operated 14 Summit catalog showrooms in New Jersey, 43 Dairy Mart convenience-food stores, a health and beauty aids wholesale operation, and two import companies. At the time the First National Bank brought Tandy into the Giant Stores picture, it and two other lenders, the State Street Bank of Boston and the Prudential Insurance Company, stood to lose $31.5 million in loans they had made to the discount retailer over the previous three years.

Giant had already approached a number of other mass merchandisers to feel out merger possibilities, among them Zayre, King's Caldor, J.M. Fields, and K-Mart. All had backed off after scrutinizing the numbers. "A look at the books was all we needed to make up our minds," one major discounter was quoted in *Home Furnishings Daily*.

In March of 1973, Giant management forecast "substantial losses" estimated at about $4 million for the 1972 calendar year. Following this announcement, Giant board chairman Theodor Kaufman and vice chairman Alfred Bloom resigned their positions, and Jack H. Shapiro took over as president and CEO.

When the First National Bank offered Charles Tandy the opportunity of acquiring Giant Stores in the spring of 1973, his first thought was to utilize Bill Tandy's old company, Tandy Industries, Inc., of Tulsa. Charles had assumed the title of board chairman of Tandy Industries after Bill's death.

"It was sort of like letting the scrubs play the first quarter of the football game," Phil North explained. "If the project fell on its face, Tandy Corporation would be protected. If it turned out to be a winner, Tandy Corporation had the capital to move it along."

In early April of 1973, rumors began circulating that Tandy Corporation was looking into acquiring Giant Stores. On April 6, Jim West issued a statement, "There's been some talk and we may be talking about some sort of plan, but that's no indication that we are necessarily going to buy."

When the rumors began hitting where it hurt the most, in the price of Tandy stock, Bill Michero was forced to make a more definitive statement. On April 10, after Tandy tumbled three points, Michero attributed the sell-off to the "confusion" between Tandy Industries and Tandy Corporation.

"I want to make it clear that we are not crawling into bed in any respect with Giant Stores Corp.," Michero declared. "We were evaluating the possibility of sub-leasing some of the Giant premises for whatever of our operations we thought might do an effective job there."

Michero emphasized that Tandy Industries was not a part of Tandy Corporation, but was primarily involved in pre-fab housing and building college dormitories and hospital facilities.

The deal that was worked out called for Tandy Industries, the First National Bank, State Street Bank, and Prudential to provide a three-year revolving line of credit of up to $8 million, or $2 million each, to Giant Stores, secured by substantially all Giant assets, including inventory.

Tandy Industries would provide management consulting to Giant and, in turn, would receive warrants to purchase a majority of outstanding Giant stock at $3 per share or book value as of June 30, 1973, whichever was lower. In addition, Tandy Industries was to receive a call at the same price per share on shares of the company held by its former management and certain stockholders. Exercise of the warrants would give Tandy Industries control of Giant Stores and its $50 million in sales. The word among the wise was that with Tandy Corporation's financial clout and management behind it, Giant could turn into another steal.

The majority of the outstanding Giant loans of $31.5 million were extended 10 years to June 30, 1983, with no amortization during the first three years.

By an interesting coincidence, the date of the agreement, April 1, 1973, was the 10th anniversary of Tandy's acquisition of Radio Shack.

"Charles had been up in Boston piddling with the Giant thing for about 30 days," Jim Buxton, who later became involved in the project, reported. "The First National Bank of Boston had asked Charles to come in and take a management deal, and he did it with Tandy Industries. Giant was a $50 million company," Buxton added. "They had stores like a small K-Mart, about 40,000 to 60,000 square feet. They sold everything. Beautiful. They caught Charles' eye. They were operating from New Jersey to Maine, all over New England. They had Giant stores, galleries, tobacco stores, dairies."

Buxton had been in Europe when the Giant deal was made. Later that year he was talking to Tandy via transatlantic cable. It was a Tuesday, he recalled, and they were going over what was happening in Europe, when he said to Tandy:

"I understand you've tied into another monster back there in Boston."

Tandy's response was, "Yeah, get yourself on an airplane and be here Friday."

What Buxton found when he arrived was a company with a serious cash flow problem and liabilities that outweighed assets by about two-to-one.

"We tried real hard to make it work," Buxton said. "It was a chain that we could have done a world with. We worked on it, worked on it, trying to spin things out of it, but it just wouldn't fly. There was no way to make it go. We worked real hard to get our money out of it and then exercised our option to get out of the management contract and shut it down."

Mary Frank, who also was involved in the Giant project, recalled that "it was the same kind of business like Edison's, and it was going broke." But Tandy, she added, "saw in it the possibility of another Radio Shack."

Tandy then put together a strike force made up mostly of accountants, and sent Miss Frank with them to the Giant headquarters in Chelmsford, Massachusetts.

"My assignment was to put out a catalog," she said. "This outfit had not made a catalog and I hadn't done one for 10 years. I thought Charles was out of his mind. But he said, 'Your job is to put a catalog together.' And we did. It was ready to go to press. It was at the printer's, one of the best jobs I ever did, when they said, 'Stop.' Charles decided there was some monkey business going on in the company and he pulled out. Then everybody came home and that was the end of that."

The Giant Stores venture came to an end with the resignation of Tandy Industries from its management agreement on October 25, 1973. Giant Stores eventually filed for protection under Chapter 11 of the Federal Bankruptcy Act, listing $50.5 million in debts. Creditors were told they could expect between 8 and 10 cents for each dollar owed from the sale of assets. The sole survivors of the company were five Summit catalog showrooms in New Jersey.

The October, 1973 issue of *Boston* magazine, in a lengthy article by Gerry Nadel, recounted the Giant story. This is how Nadel described Charles Tandy to his readers:

"That's Tandy of Texas, boy. Tandycrafts Tandy. Radio Shack Tandy. Giant Stores Tandy. The guy holding together the whole ball of wax. And you'd better get the message. He's the same Charles Tandy who bailed the First National out of that Radio Shack mess ten years ago. In fact, that's how he got into this...invalid is too mild a word. Sinking ship, maybe. A sinking ship with gunpowder in the hold and a fire on deck. And they called in Tandy...A very memorable man, $500 million a year memorable, and now when the Boston bankers found themselves in $50.5 million worth of Giant trouble, they remembered the man who'd bailed them out ten years before. Tandy's little stint of Samaritanism ten years ago got him Radio Shack—a thousand stores today. This time the betting was that Tandy might walk away with all that would be left worthwhile of Giant."

Unfortunately, this time there was nothing worthwhile remaining.

* * *

Meanwhile, Tandy Corporation continued to rack up double-digit gains in sales and earnings, reporting a sales increase of 22 percent and a 24-percent rise in net income for the quarter ended March 31, 1973. The gains were not reflected in the price of Tandy stock, unfortunately. Much of the merchandise that Tandy purchased came from overseas, so the value of the dollar impacted the cost of goods. A devaluation of the dollar in mid-February of 1973 caused a one-day drop of 3⅝ in the price of the stock to a new low of 34. Only a month earlier, the stock had stood at 42⅝.

In the face of the reaction on Wall Street to the devaluation, Charles Tandy issued a statement, "We don't believe this devaluation is going to have a hard impact on us. We bought merchandise in anticipation and in sufficient quantity to see us through a turnaround."

He added that the ability of the consumer electronics industry to offer goods at a wide range of prices would help meet price increase pressures and possible consumer reaction.

In late February, Tandy had sat down with a writer from the *National Tattler* for a wide-ranging interview. Admitting that he once had planned to retire when he reached the age of 40, he added, "But I found out that I was just learning what I was supposed to do. My early plans were to work like hell, make some money, and retire and enjoy it. But I found the enjoyment I got from money was not based on having it or spending it, but on working with it and making it do things and grow—making people perform and grow. I've had much, much more enjoyment after age 40."

Tandy said there were two secrets to his success.

"First, there is the knowledge that there is the opportunity to succeed," he observed. "Second, there is something that has not been properly emphasized—selling."

To make his point, he asked: "What is a politician, a banker, a lawyer? He's a salesman first. A banker has got to sell his services. You can be the best lawyer in the world, but you aren't going to be very successful with no clients. Billy Graham is the perfect example of a salesman. He's selling his product with all kinds of belief and determination."

Selling, Tandy contended, should be one of the first moves for a person starting out in life.

"When you sell something, you then appreciate what it costs and what efforts are needed. Being a salesman, you can excel in many lines of business. Young people should look at selling as an opportunity for training, because they are going to be salespeople, one way or another, for the rest of their lives."

In addition to selling the virtues of salesmanship, Tandy was also on a Radio Shack store-opening tear.

In April of 1973, 27 stores were opened. In May, 40 more stores were added, bringing the total close to 2,000. Once again the question arose: How many Radio Shacks could the country accommodate?

Charlie Tindall, who once had talked of a maximum of 1,500 stores, was now expanding his horizons. In an interview with *Chain Store Age,* he said he believed there was "room enough for more than 3,000," adding that Tandy was planning to open Radio Shacks at a rate of 500 to 550 units each year "from now on."

Asked what would happen when the saturation point was reached, Tindall emphasized that the company was already engaged in exploring new worlds to conquer overseas.

But despite the new store openings and strong sales and earnings, Tandy stock continued its downward slide. On August 21, 1973, it closed at a new low of 18½ on heavy volume, propelled by what Bill Michero called the "snake-in-the-grass" syndrome. He had coined the expression in an interview with Reuters News Service.

"The snake," he explained, "is the fact that Tandy belongs to a group of companies called specialty retailers—a group once loved and presently being shunned by some investors and analysts." What had happened, Michero groused, was that one specialty retailer had been experiencing problems, and now all members of the group were suffering from the fallout.

"It's the way the market is," Michero philosophized. "Our stock held up for a long time, but then we really got shot."

The principal bugaboo being attached to Tandy stock was that its earnings, which had been growing at more than 20 percent annually, would come under pressure when the economy started to slow and consumers stopped having as much discretionary income to spend on Radio Shack staples such as stereos and tape recorders. Another problem was the fact that Tandy was a major importer of products from Japan and thus would be hurt by the recent revaluations of the yen.

Two Dallas analysts, Lynn McCormick of Eppler, Guerin & Turner, Inc., and John McStay of Underwood, Neuhaus & Co., disagreed with this scenario.

"Just look at Tandy's earnings progression during the last economic slowdown," McCormick said, "and I really think that any fears about its performance in the near future, if indeed there is a slowdown, have been greatly overdone. So, too, have any questions about its dependence on Japanese products been greatly overdone. Tandy stock is underpriced and I'm recommending it."

Dismissing the concern over discretionary income, McCormick pointed out that the average purchase at a Radio Shack store was between $10 and $15.

"Such a purchase is not like the choice of buying a car or a boat in a recession," he added.

McStay opined, "Tandy is not alone in selling Japanese-made products. So if it has to raise its prices, so does everyone else, which is pretty much what happened in the last yen revaluation."

Both analysts noted that Tandy had been decreasing its dependency on Japan as its major supplier by diversifying its manufacturing operations into South Korea, Canada and the United States. Radio Shack was now importing only 50 percent of its product mix, while an increasing number of items were being produced in company-owned facilities in the United States. Radio Shack was now operating plants in Texas, Illinois, Iowa, and New Jersey, including new audio tape, wire and cable manufacturing facilities and an antenna plant in Fort Worth.

Manufacturing plants included Tandy Instruments, Tandy Electronics, Tandy Audio, Tandy Wire & Cable, Tandy Antenna, Tandy Magnetics, Tandy Crystal, Plastellite and Community Sign, all in Fort Worth; Gavin Electronics in New Jersey; Antennacraft in Burlington, Iowa; TCE-Japan in Tokyo; TCE-Korea in Masan, South Korea; and ARC in Kagoshima, Japan and Masan, South Korea.

Discussing the growth of the manufacturing capability, Lew Kornfeld commented, "We are simply applying the Tandy method of vertical integration to our business—making what we sell and aiming at 100 percent somewhere up the line. Aside from profits, the motives are simple: (1) to gain the skills in design and technology required to keep us in a position of leadership; (2) to achieve product exclusivity, and (3) to reduce dependency on the ability of external suppliers to keep pace with our needs. The archaic notion that retailers can't be producers has been dispelled by our accomplishments to date."

Charles Tandy told an interviewer from *Audio Hi-Fi* that he insisted the company determine from retail experience if a product was a "fad or permanent" before tooling up to make it. Then, he said, "cost-win"—the start-up expense versus total dollar volume and profit of the product—was tallied.

In-house manufacturing, Tandy said, afforded greater flexibility in designing product lines and improved communication between the retailer and the supplier. But the most important advantage was the cost reduction obtained by "eliminating the markup for the middleman."

Tandy pointed out that most of the hi-fi receivers sold by Radio Shack had been made for some time by Tandy plants in Japan and Korea; that antennas for radio, TV, and CB were being made in the United States, and that wire, cable, and replacement crystals also were made by Tandy and sold by Radio Shack.

"If you sell enough hamburgers," he quipped, "eventually you would do well to enter ranching."

In late September of 1973, *Financial World* noted the beating Tandy was taking on Wall Street in spite of its impressive growth and earnings performance.

"If one had to choose from among a multitude of factors that have been responsible for shareholder frustration this year, prime among the list would have to be the way stocks have skidded even though company earnings have soared. And Tandy Corporation's stock simply has to be considered one of the best examples of this malaise. Not only have Tandy's sales and earnings grown steadily year after year for the last decade, but the outlook is for more of the same in spite of tough competition."

The article described how Tandy's book value per share had jumped 1,400 to 1,500 percent in the last decade. Yet, between 1972 and 1973, its stock had slumped by 65 percent and its price/earnings multiple had plunged from 35 to 10.

An investor buying Tandy would be getting a "volatile security that fairly crackles with static," the article concluded. "It is no sleeper. If the company's future is as good as its past, and that, of course, will have to be proved, the depressed Tandy common stock could well sound a better tune for its shareholders in an improved stock market environment."

* * *

Despite the down market as the year drew to a close, Charles Tandy was as upbeat as ever as he raised a glass of Dom Perignon to toast the advent of 1974 at a New Year's Eve gathering with a group of close friends.

For Tandy personally, 1973 had been a rewarding year. There had been some ego-satisfying recognition, including a flattering invitation from David Rockefeller to join the prestigious Advisory Board of Rockefeller University, a research institute that had been founded by John D. Rockefeller, Sr.

During the year, Tandy had added another leading Fort Worth businessman to his board, William C. Conner, chairman of the board of Alcon Laboratories, Inc. Alcon, a pharmaceutical firm specializing in ophthalmic products, was started by Conner and Robert D. Alexander shortly after World War II in the back room of their ethical pharmacy. The company was sold to Nestle, Inc., in 1978 for more than $400 million. Conner remained a Tandy director until his death in January, 1992.

Tandy also had been elected president of the Fort Worth Exchange Club, the most select organization of business and professional men in town. And he had been tapped for the presidency of the Fort Worth Art Museum, an indication that some of Anne Tandy's interests were beginning to rub off on him. Tandy, in fact, was particularly proud of his wife's art collection which graced the walls of the mansion they shared. This, however, led Tandy into artistic circles he had not previously frequented. And one night, it led him into a classic bit of one-upmanship at the expense of a pompous art collector.

The man, who had already antagonized everyone in the room with his continual references to his art collection, turned condescendingly to Tandy and asked him whether he collected art.

"In a small way," Tandy responded. He then whipped a couple of sheets of paper out of his coat pocket and began to read off a list of names of artists whose works decorated the walls of his home in Fort Worth. The names included Braque, Chagall, Gauguin, Picasso, Leger, Miro, and Toulouse-Lautrec, among others.

The man who had asked the question slunk away, having finally met his match.

Shortly after the start of the new year, Tandy finally made a personnel move he had been putting off for some time out of deference for his feelings for Jim West. On February 28, 1974, he announced that West had been named to the newly-created position of vice chairman of the board of Tandy Corporation and that John A. Wilson had replaced him as president and chief operating officer. Wilson, who had been with the company since 1951, was the corporate vice president in charge of the Color Tile, Wolfe Nurseries, and Royal Tile operations.

West, whose seniority dated back to 1930, had become a legendary figure at corporate headquarters where tales of his frugality abounded.

He once kept Charles Tandy and a group of company executives waiting and shivering outside a restaurant in Chicago one wintry evening while he went over the check item by item, causing Tandy to note drily:

"We may all get pneumonia out here but Jim's gonna make sure we weren't overcharged."

As a store manager, West was taught to hold down expenses. He automatically turned out the lights when he left a room, even the bathroom. Sometimes this meant that someone still in the bathroom would be left in the dark. This could prove to be embarrassing at times. C.O.

Buckalew, who for many years ran the computer center operation, told Herschel Winn of an occasion when he had been left in the bathroom with the lights out when Charles Tandy walked into the room.

"Hey, Buck," Tandy asked him, "what are you doing here in the dark?"

West was approaching his 71st birthday when he relinquished the corporate presidency to assume the more or less honorary role of vice chairman. Eunice West had been urging her husband to retire, and now he finally acquiesced.

"I had him write out a retirement letter and give it to Charles," she recounted. "That same day, Charles came to the house and sat down in the den. He took the letter out of his pocket and tore it up. And he said to me, 'I know who was behind this letter. Don't you ever do that again. Jim West will be with me as long as he can walk to that office.' Oh, Charles was so angry with me."

West retired in 1981 at the age of 78 upon the completion of his 51st year with the company. He died on November 11, 1983, at the age of 80.

"He put everything he made back into the company," Mrs. West recalled. "All of his net worth was in Tandy stock."

In March of 1981, West gave away $15 million in Tandy stock to 11 Fort Worth institutions. The major bequest of $12 million went to Texas Wesleyan University to build the Eunice and James West Library. Other recipients were Texas Christian University and the University of Texas at Arlington, which established chairs in their business schools, and W.I. Cook Children's Hospital, Junior Achievement, Boy Scouts, Girl Scouts, YMCA, Happy Hill Children's Camp, the Fort Worth Boys Club, and Fort Worth Girls Club.

West downplayed the importance of the gifts.

"We have no children," he said in a newspaper interview, "and we both feel that wealth must be used properly. You know, these days the effort to protect your wealth becomes harder and harder and more trouble than the money is worth. So why put yourself to all that trouble when you can use your money to bring happiness to many people?"

Then he added, "Oh, they won't remember me too long even if my name is on the library. You just want to leave the world a little better off than when you arrived."

Although the Wests lived in a comfortable home in a fashionable area of Fort Worth, their neighbors were surprised at their affluence when the bequests were publicized.

"My friends said to me, 'You could have been riding around in a Rolls Royce,'" Eunice West remembered. "Well, the material things didn't mean a thing to us. We were blessed with our health and you can't buy that."

In the early part of 1992, as the result of a gift of $9.3 million from Eunice West, ground was broken for the James L. West Presbyterian Special Care Center in Fort Worth. The facility will be devoted to caring for persons with Alzheimer's disease and other dementia, and assisting their families.

* * *

In early 1974, at the urging of Charles Tandy, the Tandy Corporation board of directors belatedly addressed the problem of the continuing disappointing performance of the company's stock. At a board meeting on April 4, 1974, the directors approved a program to reduce the number of shares outstanding by up to two-million shares through an exchange offer for a new issue of subordinated debentures.

The offer permitted shareholders to turn in all or part of their holdings of common stock to the company and receive 20-year subordinated debentures, callable after two years at 105, and bearing an interest rate of 8½ percent. The face amount of the debentures was to be 22 percent above the market price of the common stock on the effective date of the exchange offer, but not to exceed $35.

On April 18, the exchange offer was amended to fix the face amount of the debentures at $29 per share and increase the interest rate from 8½ percent to 10 percent. Despite the higher interest rate and an extension of the deadline from June 30 to August 9, the exchange offer fell short of the 2-million share goal. A total of 1,218,772 shares of common stock was tendered in exchange for $35.3 million of the newly-authorized 10 percent subordinated debentures. The shares acquired in the exchange were subsequently retired.

In a talk to New York securities analysts, Charles Tandy explained the rationale behind the exchange offer.

"One of the functions of the offer was to recognize and respond to the growing importance of current yield within the investment community and among individual investors," he declared. "The flight of investment monies from equities to high-yielding short-term debt vehicles needs no repeating here, but our management was keenly aware that many of our long-standing shareholders were being trampled in the stampede.

"The exchange offer gave our shareholders the opportunity to change vehicles, and those who did are still ahead of the game at this time. It was interesting that almost no institutional shareholders participated in the exchange and that only 1,218,000 shares came in while the offer was prepared to accept 2 million shares."

During 1974, Tandy Corporation also had acquired 579,300 shares of its common stock in the open market at a cost of $12 million, or an average price of $20.76 per share. The highest and lowest prices paid were $30.75 and $17.50 per share. These shares also were retired.

Tandy's purchase of its own stock was noted in a *Wall Street Journal* article on June 20, 1974 that declared:

"The hundreds of companies that began buying back some of their own stock on the open market generally cite similar reasons: With stock prices so low, buybacks were an economical way to obtain shares for making acquisitions and fulfilling employee stock-option plans. Usually left unsaid was that buybacks can boost the price of the stocks, or at least keep them from falling as much as they otherwise might."

But as the 1974 fiscal year came to a close, Tandy stock was still trading in the $24 to $25 range.

The company's 1974 performance was impacted by the loss of $7.1 million, or 67 cents per share, from the sale of Leonards and the discontinuance of the General Retailing Marketing Group. But net sales from continuing operations rose 27 percent to $579.1 million and net income from continuing operations increased 29 percent to $27.5 million, or $2.59 per share.

Radio Shack again was the star performer, recording a 34 percent gain in sales and a 50 percent jump in earnings. The Radio Shack Division now was producing 62 percent of Tandy Corporation's total sales and 78 percent of its total divisional income.

No wonder the Annual Report declared, "As Radio Shack grows, so grows Tandy Corporation."

Chapter 24
A Triple Play for Tandy

Who would have believed that in the recession year of 1975 a rather innocuous item called a citizens band radio that had been around for more than a decade would suddenly bolt out of nowhere to become the newest national fad since the hula hoop?

"It's unreal what's happening," said Robert Katz, a Radio Shack buyer, about the CB radio phenomenon. "It's our fastest-growing item."

He wasn't talking about a hula hoop-priced product, either. Buyers of CB radio equipment were spending anywhere from $60 for a 3-channel set to $350 for a 23-channel unit with sidebands. But, in spite of the faltering economy, CBs were selling like hot cakes.

Propelled by the CB boom, Radio Shack sales were on an upward track, in sharp contrast to the generally drab retailing picture nationwide. While other retailers were singing the blues and pulling in their horns, Radio Shack was opening new stores and giving face-lifts to its old ones.

"I don't think this country's in as bad a shape as our commentators would have us believe," an ebullient Charles Tandy told the members of the Downtown Fort Worth Rotary Club. "Our business has been good," he added, "and that's nationwide."

For the first nine months of the 1975 fiscal year, Tandy Corporation reported a 33 percent increase in sales and a 50 percent increase in earnings.

"We have been told that our Radio Shack sales record this past year has been remarkable," Charles Tandy declared in a talk to a group of Los Angeles bankers and financiers. "We have been told that our results have been impossible in view of what has been happening to the grand old names of retailing. Current economy efforts by consumers, and the cost savings attached to do-it-yourself products, have produced these results. Citizens band has reached boom proportions and now represents 13 percent of Radio Shack sales, while areas of high unemployment, such as Detroit, have shown higher sales gains than other areas."

Radio Shack opened five new stores in the Detroit area in February 1975, in the face of what the *Detroit News* called "the economic woes" being experienced there. The new outlets brought to 33 the total number of Radio Shack stores in the Detroit area, with seven additional stores scheduled to open by the beginning of June.

Sales in the Detroit area were running up to 40 percent ahead of the prior year, Mark L. Seaman, the Radio Shack district manager there, reported.

Where hand-held calculators had once been the hottest-selling consumer electronics products, CBs were bigger. *Forbes* magazine noted citizen band radio sales had exploded to the forefront, growing by better than 30 percent a year compared to 13 percent for calculators.

"A CB radio is nothing more than a simpler, cheaper version of a police or commercial two-way radio," *Forbes* reported. "Retail sales of CB radios were no more than $140 million in 1973. In 1975, they'll reach $350 million; next year $500 million. By 1980, enthusiastic CB makers are talking about sales of $1 billion."

What was behind the sudden upsurge? CB radios, after all, had been around since 1959, when Radio Shack's first Realistic CB transceivers hit the market. Industry sources attributed the interest to the OPEC oil embargo of 1973 that spawned long lines at the fuel pumps and the 55 mph speed limit. Truckers began using CB radios to find out where they could get gasoline and where police radar traps were located. This received a great deal of publicity and got the public interested. The Federal Communications Commission helped by cutting the price of a five-year CB radio license from $20 to $4. Between 1972 and 1975, license applications zoomed from less than 15,000 per month to more than 200,000.

The CB radio boom even spawned a new language.

"Breaker, breaker, c'mon. This is Pig Pen. There's a Smokey Bear at pogo stick 227. You smooth talkers show your double nickels now or pay the big dime at the northbound bubblegum machine. C'mon you 18-wheelers. 10-4."

"Gotcha, Three Little Pigs. This is Big Bad Wolf huffin' at your back door. Slow twin buffaloes it is. Your rockin' chair buddy appreciates that. 10-4."

Translated, one trucker was warning another that he had spotted a highway patrol car near mile-marker 227 and suggested he slow down to 55 mph (two buffalo nickels).

"It's not very often you get a hula hoop in this business," Bill Nugent told *Denver Post* writer Bill Strabala. "We're able to sell everything we can get. But it has grown to more than just a thing to warn you where Smokey is. Americans like to jabber. And it helps pass the time on the road. But there's a safety factor, too, if you've got a flat or other trouble. CBers are nice people. They like to help. And you can also learn what's ahead in heavy traffic."

Strabala wrote, "While the truckers and an increasing number of 'four-wheelers' (passenger cars) are tuned in to their CBs, companies like Tandy Corporation, parent company of Radio Shack, are tuned to their cash registers. Radio Shack, probably No. 1 in the CB and electronic gadgetry markets, has increased its sales threefold in the past year within the CB market alone and expects to double its present volume during 1976. And that's a 'big 10-4,' or OK, as country singer Dave Dudley says in one of his truck-driving songs."

Even Charles Tandy had gotten into the act. His "handle" on the CB radio in his car was "Mr. Lucky."

"Mr. Lucky" was at his swaggering best as he delivered his "What Recession?" pitch to a gathering of the New York Society of Securities Analysts in February, 1975. Announcing plans to open 30 to 40 new Radio Shack stores in the New York metropolitan area in 1975 and 1976, Tandy informed the group:

"After years of unprofitable operations, this district finally turned a profit last year—about 1.5 percent on sales. But to take our message to the public in New York's expensive advertising media, we need more stores. The planned additions will increase the number of Radio Shack outlets in the New York area to more than 130. Then we will be able to buy more television and radio time and more newspaper inserts because the saturation of the market with our stores will justify the expenditures."

Tandy told the analysts that Radio Shack planned to open 400 stores nationwide in fiscal 1975, but that the expansion was flexible in light of the current state of the economy.

"In some areas we may not open as many units as planned," he said. "I don't care if the regional manager only gives me 10 stores where he was supposed to open 25 stores, so long as he gives me 10 winners. I don't want 25 if 10 are going to be losers."

Tandy conceded that Radio Shack had not yet learned how "recession-proof" its business was. But, he added, "We do know that in times of economic anxiety, and even in bad weather, people tend to spend more time at home. And that is where our 'do-it-yourself' customer lives."

He gave the analysts the following profile of a typical Radio Shack customer: A male, with a median age of 30, a high school education, household income of $10,000 and over, whose average purchase was $10.25, and who liked to do his own maintenance, repair, and improvement on electronic devices and communications equipment. He liked to save money and "downtime" by avoiding service calls and repair bills.

"We are not looking for the guy who wants to spend his entire paycheck on a sound system," Tandy reported. "The kind of customer who walks through our door is one who wants the maximum amount of listening pleasure without it costing him an arm and a leg. Most importantly, his repeat purchase pattern is high, a 60 percent repeat purchase factor every six months. One reason for this is that many of the Radio Shack products are of a consumable nature, such as blank recording tapes, vacuum tubes, batteries and outdoor antennas."

There were currently nine-million copies of the latest Radio Shack catalog in customers' hands, Tandy informed the analysts.

"If you will analyze the catalog in detail, and, by the way, we do just that to develop it, you will find that the merchandise selections and pricing points are slanted very strongly towards the needs of the 'do-it-yourself' customer. We are in the 'do-it-yourself' business. The line is limited to about 2,400 items and their unit retail price breaks down this way: 72 percent of the items retail from $0-$5; 16 percent from $5-$20; 6 percent from $20-$50; 3 percent from $50-$100; and 3 percent from $100 and up.

"This explains the viability of our typical store size which has a 25-foot front. It explains how we are bringing into a neighborhood trade area a selection of wanted products which are not readily available elsewhere. It explains how our sales personnel can become effectively knowledgeable of this limited number of items in a reasonable period of time. It also explains why some people are puzzled on their first visit to a Radio Shack store because they presume it to be a traditional audio shop. The product mix tells you that Radio Shack is much more than that.

"When we try to measure Radio Shack's markets, we are talking about a product line and marketplace which barely existed 30 years ago, products and supplies which were rarely available to the public 20 years ago, and a field of merchandising which began to take on the appearance of an industry a little over 10 years ago. Today, the United States consumer electronics market is growing at an annual rate of 10 to 15 percent after eliminating price inflation, and will top the $6 billion mark in sales in 1975."

A fundamental factor in the company's growth was its compensation policy, Tandy asserted.

"It is the reason we have attracted, held, and advanced so much dedicated talent over the years. Starting from the simple premise that for an employee to earn anything for the company, he must first earn something for himself, we long ago established a program of profit-sharing formulas as far down into the organization as possible. This calls for profit-center measurement throughout the company at every store, factory, warehouse and staff position. This is one reason we produce over 5,000 profit and loss statements within the company each month.

"The compensation program provides a nominal base salary, plus an earnings formula designed to deliver substantial additional income in relation to profits produced by each profit center. Admittedly, this approach to compensation does not appeal to everyone. But for that individual who prefers to be compensated for his ability, it works very well. That is the type of person our system has always attracted."

But finding qualified managers for the new stores was becoming a "tough nut to crack," Tandy conceded. The company took on 160 college graduates in the 1974 fiscal year and hoped to double that number in the current year, Tandy noted.

But, he revealed, "because expansion has been so rapid, training for the new managers is being held to a minimum. So the store manager has to be self-driven. If he runs too many price-cutting or giveaway promotions on his own, store profits and his income will suffer. If this begins to cut too deeply, then the district manager and the store manager get together to work out the problem. Other profit-shrinking problems such as theft by employees or customers are dealt with in a similar fashion. The inexperienced manager is not simply left to sink or swim."

During a question and answer session, Tandy was asked how many Radio Shack stores the U.S. could support. He responded, "Five years ago, some of my people thought 1,500 was the outside number. Now they're talking about 6,000."

Whether it was Tandy's oratory or merely the fact that the stock market was chalking up solid advances, Tandy stock rebounded sharply during February, 1975. The stock was trading in the $16 range when Tandy made his appearance before the New York securities analysts, after trading as low as 11⅝ earlier in the year. But by the end of February, it was up to $28 a share, making it the 15th largest gainer among all stocks on the Big Board for the first two months of 1975.

Harry Laubscher of Blyth Eastman Dillon & Co. was especially keen on Tandy, calling its shares undervalued and "especially attractive for potential capital appreciation" because of its rapid expansion. He forecast fiscal 1975 earnings of $3.75 per share and fiscal 1976 earnings of $4.40 per share.

Laubscher was impressed with Tandy's track record over the past 10 years, during which it had racked up annual growth rates of 35 percent in revenues, 41 percent in net income and 29 percent in earnings per share. He predicted new sales and earnings records in the current year and said the company was capable of 15 percent annual growth in per-share earnings over the next five years.

"Another positive factor," Laubscher added, "is the fact that Tandy has been eliminating some of its general merchandising operations which have been a drain on profits and management time."

The jettisoning of the marginal operations had begun on February 26, 1975, when Tandy announced an agreement in principle to sell its Wolfe Nursery Division to Pier 1 Imports for $6.5 million in cash. Wolfe Nurseries, which had been acquired in 1966 for 15,000 shares of Tandy stock valued at $210,000, now operated 45 retail stores in 12 major cities in Texas and Oklahoma.

The day after the Wolfe Nursery sale was made public, Tandy announced the sale of Vit-A-Way, Inc., to SuCrest Corporation. Vit-A-Way, which had fiscal 1974 sales of $3 million, had been acquired in February, 1972 for $750,000 in cash.

Then, on April 23, came the announcement that an agreement had been reached under which Tandy would sell the assets of Corral Sportswear Company and its two divisions, Western Leather Company and Buckboard Company, to El Dorado International, Inc., of Minneapolis.

Corral Sportswear, a manufacturer of casual leather coats and jackets and leather accessories for men and women based in Ardmore, Oklahoma, had been a part of the Tandy stable of companies since 1961.

John Wilson said that the sale was made "so that the capital assets of the company could be applied toward the larger and more rapidly-expanding operations of Tandy Corporation."

As a result of the 1975 divestitures, plus the sale or discontinuance of Leonards, Mitchell's, and Meacham's over the prior two years, the non-electronics operations of Tandy Corporation were drastically reduced. Meanwhile, Radio Shack was expanding faster than ever.

What was going on? Was Tandy Corporation shedding its traditional stripes? Bill Michero offered an insight.

"In the bundle of companies we had left, there were still about 15 that were viable business enterprises and difficult to evaluate in terms of a sale. So the thought of a spin-off developed, and we worked on it for about a year-and-a-half. Then the decision was made to create the Radio Shack operation as a clean play, without all of this other clutter around it. So we moved everything out that was not electronics."

John Wilson recalled the genesis of the spin-off plan.

"We first started talking about it one evening in Charles' office. He said to me, 'What the hell's wrong? Why aren't we being recognized?' He was talking about Wall Street. We both agreed that the reason we didn't have the kind of recognition we wanted was that we were a conglomerate and conglomerates had lost favor. We talked about it a number of times after that, and we both agreed that the spin-offs were something that we ought to do. So Charles took it to the board and the board said, 'Okay, let's go.'"

The impactful announcement that would signal a turning point in the history of Tandy Corporation was made on the afternoon of May 27, 1975, in a press release that declared:

"The Board of Directors of Tandy Corporation, following a meeting in Fort Worth, today announced tentative approval of a plan which would separate the business of the corporation into three distinct publicly-held companies. The plan calls for the issuance to shareholders, in the form of a tax-free dividend, of the common stock of two new companies to be drawn from the handicrafts and from the leather products operations of Tandy Corporation.

"The resulting two new companies will be named Tandycrafts, Inc., and Tex Tan-Hickok, Inc. Tandycrafts' primary operations will consist of the Tandy Leather, Color Tile, American Handicrafts and Stafford-Lowdon Divisions. Tex Tan-Hickok's primary operations will consist of the Tex Tan and Hickok Divisions. Tandy Corporation, under the plan, would carry on the consumer electronics (Radio Shack) operations as its sole business.

"The purpose of the plan is to provide more intensive and distinct management leadership of the three basic and diverse businesses of the company, each of which has reached substantial size in recent years. It will set out clearly the operating and financial progress of the three businesses, each with a distinctive growth pattern. It will provide shareholders with three clearly-defined investment vehicles, each with a simplified corporate structure and business direction. The plan also underscores management emphasis in developing the principal businesses of the company.

"Before the plan can be formally adopted, various regulatory and statutory matters must be determined. Assuming such matters are determined favorably, the plan is scheduled to be adopted and implemented within the next few months."

The more limiting Tex Tan-Hickok name was changed several weeks later to Tandy Brands, Inc.

An announcement on August 12 spelled out the details of how the new shares in Tandycrafts and Tandy Brands would be spun off. Each Tandy shareholder would receive one share of Tandycrafts stock for each two shares of Tandy stock held, and one share of Tandy Brands stock for each 10 shares of Tandy stock held.

Initially, Wall Street wasn't sure what to make of the announcement.

On May 28, the day after the spin-off announcement, Tandy stock sank 2⅝ to 35⅞ in active trading. But by late October, the stock had surged to 48.

John Wilson recalled that he bought some Tandy stock in 1974 at $27 and watched it plummet to $9 a share by the end of the year.

"Charles couldn't believe what was happening," he remembered. "Our sales and earnings were going through the roof and our stock kept on going down. But after the spin-offs, it started going up and it kept on going."

In a letter to shareholders, Charles Tandy reported on the rationale behind the spin-offs:

"In the years between 1960 and 1972, the company made many additions to its merchandising operations. With the passage of time, and with the regular evaluation of all operations within the company, those operations likely to make a material future contribution to the company were generally identified by 1973. Tests of return on capital and potential market position were among the criteria used in determining the most productive marketing directions available to the company.

"In 1973, your management commenced a program of reducing the variety of merchandising activities in which the company was engaged, so that the company's financial resources and executive experience could be channelled toward greater effectiveness. Since that time, the program has seen removal of the General Retailing Group and its associated projects, and the sale or liquidation of a number of other operations, including six during the past year. These actions have moved the company into a new alignment which recognizes its three primary marketing strengths: consumer electronics, 'do-it-yourself' merchandising, and leather products marketing."

A further insight was contained in the Prospectus Summary filed with the Securities and Exchange Commission:

"It is believed by Tandy's management that the separation and spin-off will provide a more intensive management leadership of the three basic and distinct businesses now operated by Tandy, and will provide a better framework for management decisions concerning the employment of capital and the operations of the separate businesses. It is also believed that the operational and financial progress of the three businesses, each with a distinctive business direction, will be more visible to stockholders, and therefore a stimulus to the executives to show growth and improvement. In addition, the separation will permit a clearer basis for evaluation of the businesses of the three corporations by employees, the public and the investment community, which Tandy expects will be of particular advantage at such time as additional capital may be required."

Bill Michero put it in simpler terms, "Because we were made up of so many kinds of businesses, it was an awkward company to measure and evaluate."

Michero spoke knowledgeably about another compelling factor behind the spin-off—the decline of handicrafts from the major position it occupied in the marketplace when the Tandy Leather Company was enjoying its spectacular growth in the 1950s and '60s.

"A lot of things impacted it," he said. "We now have a generation of television watchers who have no interest in or time to do handicraft things. We've also had a demographic phenomenon of a lower birth rate where youth groups, such as Scouting, began a major decline in enrollments. School budgets over the last 15 years have been leaning away from the old handicrafts things that were taught in the industrial arts and art sections from elementary school on up. There's a long list of reasons why handicrafts no longer are an expanding universe."

Stanley Lanzet, an analyst with Kidder, Peabody, a Wall Street brokerage firm, offered an additional insight: "Investors have tended to view Tandy as a company with one major attraction (Radio Shack), plus a number of small, mostly unknown parts that detract from the overall valuation placed on earnings."

His opinion was echoed by Robert J. Schweich of Wertheim & Co.: "If Tandy Corp. can stand as a pure operating company, the Street will take more of a liking to it. In addition, there's a lot more potential in the stock when evaluated on the basis of Radio Shack's performance. It is capable of achieving at least 25 percent earnings growth in fiscal '76 and '77, and over the next two years has the potential of doubling its current multiple."

On October 1, 1975, the Internal Revenue Service ruled that the shares of Tandycrafts and Tandy Brands stock to be issued to Tandy Corporation shareholders would not constitute taxable income, paving the way for the spin-off to become effective on October 31, 1975.

As a result of the unbundling, 11 former operating entities of Tandy Corporation were transferred to Tandycrafts, Inc. They were Tandy Leather, American Handicrafts, Color Tile, Royal Tile, Stafford-Lowdon, Bona Allen, Magee, Merribee, Woodie Taylor Vending, Automated and Custom Food Services, and *Decorating and Crafts* magazine.

Tandy Brands began operations with six former Tandy Corporation entities—Tex Tan Western, Tex Tan Welhausen, Hickok Manufacturing Company, J.M. Bucheimer, Collins of Texas, and Western Sales.

The spin-offs involved people as well as operating entities.

John Wilson, who had been elevated to the presidency of Tandy Corporation only a year-and-a-half earlier, was among the executives spun off. Wilson resigned as president and chief executive officer of Tandy to become president, chief executive officer, and a director of

Tandycrafts. The position he vacated was not filled until 1978, when Charles Tandy assumed the title of president in addition to that of chairman of the board and chief executive officer.

"Wilson's background was in the crafts business, in Tandy Leather Company, and he had been very important in the development of the Color Tile programs. So he was made a part of the crafts bundle," recalled Bill Michero.

Michero and Billy Roland were spun off to Tandycrafts, Michero as vice president, secretary and treasurer, and Roland as assistant secretary and assistant treasurer. They had held the same titles at Tandy Corporation. Roland would later return to Tandy Corporation. He retired as a vice president in 1985 after 31 years' service.

Herschel Winn, who had been assistant secretary and corporate counsel, succeeded Michero as vice president and corporate secretary.

Douglas H. Manning and John Cosby resigned as Tandy Corporation vice presidents to assume new executive positions with Tandy Brands, Manning as president and chief executive officer and Cosby as vice president, secretary and treasurer. Joining them on the Tandy Brands management team were William M. Manning, president of Tex Tan Western; Carson R. Thompson, president of Tex Tan Welhausen; Adolph D. Weiss, executive vice president of Hickok; Richard S. Bowlus, president of J.M. Bucheimer; and Frank A. Dromgoole, president of Western Sales.

Charles Tandy, who wound up with four percent of the outstanding stock of Tandycrafts and Tandy Brands by virtue of his ownership of Tandy Corporation shares, assumed the title of board chairman of both companies. He received approximately 185,000 shares of Tandycrafts stock and 37,000 shares of Tandy Brands, with an initial market value of approximately $2.7 million, as a result of the spin-offs.

Tandycrafts' stock began trading on the New York Stock Exchange on a "when issued" basis on October 17 at a price of $13 per share and Tandy Brands began trading over-the-counter at $7 per share. When Tandy Brands was listed on the American Stock Exchange in 1976, Charles Tandy became the only individual ever to have his family name listed twice, once on the New York Stock Exchange and once on the Amex.

As a result of the spin-offs, Tandy Corporation surrendered approximately 27 percent of its net sales, 24 percent of its total assets and 24 percent of its earnings. This reduced its fiscal 1975 net sales from $724 million to $528 million; its total assets from $414 million to $319 million, and its net income from $3.81 per share to $2.88 per share. Tandy also spun out the 851 company-owned hobby and handicrafts retail outlets it was operating in the United States and Canada.

As part of the agreement, Tandy Corporation advanced $6 million to Tandycrafts and $1.25 million to Tandy Brands for operating purposes. In return, Tandycrafts assumed $15 million of Tandy Corporation debt and Tandy Brands assumed a $3 million note payable to Tandy.

Tandy Corporation was now totally in the consumer electronics business, with Radio Shack as its dominant entity. Radio Shack emerged from the spin-offs with 3,865 retail outlets, including 2,651 company-owned stores, 1,036 dealer stores and 178 franchise stores in the United States, Canada, and abroad.

Also left in the Tandy corporate fold were A&A International, Allied Electronics, Antennacraft, Community Signs, Gavin Electronics, Plastellite Company, Tandy Cable, Tandy Communications Antennas, Tandy Crystal Center, Tandy Electronics, Tandy Fabrications, Tandy Instruments, Tandy Magnetics, Tandy Speakers, Tandy Wire, and TC Electronics.

Commenting on the spin-offs, *Forbes* magazine noted, "The plot is simple: to let Radio Shack stand alone—and proud. What's the redeployment deal worth to shareholders? Charles Tandy's eyes light up behind his half-glasses when he recalls how generously the market values other specialty retailers. Look, he says, at fashion retailer Petrie Stores, with a price/earnings ratio of 20, or Longs Drug Stores, at 27. Surely, the new Tandy Corp. built on Radio Shack should sell at a P/E of 18 to 20 rather than its current 11. If that happened, an investor would in effect be getting Tandycrafts and Tandy Brands free."

As it turned out, that was exactly what happened.

*   *   *

While Charles Tandy was making national news with the splitting of Tandy Corporation into three separate corporate enterprises, he was also making local headlines with the announcement that the long-anticipated Tandy Center Project in downtown Fort Worth was finally going to leave the drawing board and become a reality. A beaming Tandy made the announcement in May, 1975 at the Golden Deeds Awards

Banquet of the Exchange Club of Fort Worth, at which he and Anne Tandy were jointly honored as the city's outstanding citizens.

"This is one of the big days of my life," Tandy told a packed ballroom at the Fort Worth Club. "I met with my board of directors this morning, and they agreed with everything I wanted. They have agreed to let us go ahead and build a new headquarters for Tandy Corporation in downtown Fort Worth."

The project actually dated back to 1973, when Tandy Corporation purchased an eight-block site in downtown Fort Worth for $11 million in cash and notes and announced a $100 million joint venture with Ogden Development Corporation of Los Angeles. The initial phase of the joint venture, the announcement said, would include a 35-story office tower, a 700-room luxury hotel and an enclosed shopping mall. Charles Luckman Associates, internationally-known planning and architectural firm, would create the master plan. Tandy Corporation said it would occupy 100,000 square feet in the office building.

The announcement stressed that the commencement of construction of the project would depend upon the availability of financing on suitable terms and the completion of other arrangements with developers, architects, builders, lenders and investors. The project, however, quickly ran into several snags.

In March, 1974, after a splitting of interests between Ogden Development and Charles Luckman, Charles Tandy reported he was "now talking with other groups about the project." Bill Michero's recollection was that after the Tandy group spent six months working with Ogden's property development division, "Ogden decided to abandon the program."

In the May, 1975 announcement, Charles Tandy reported that Tandy Corporation would go it alone in building the Tandy Center. He said the initial plans for the building had been scaled down somewhat from the original plan, but would still constitute a major addition to the city's skyline.

"I'm a little embarrassed it's not what it started out to be, but it's going to be a start," he added.

Ground was broken for One Tandy Center, a 320,000-square-foot, 19-story office tower, on July 9, 1975. Construction began simultaneously on an adjoining three-level shopping mall with 135,000 square feet of retail space, an ice skating rink on the street level, a two-level parking garage to accommodate 300 automobiles, and banking facilities.

Wearing a white suit and with a white hard hat sitting jauntily atop his head, Tandy sounded a nostalgic note to the several hundred business and civic leaders and city and county officials attending the groundbreaking ceremonies, reminding them that the site of his new corporate headquarters was only a block away from the two-story building at 2nd and Throckmorton Streets that had once served as the home of Tandy Leather Company.

"When the plans for this development first evolved about three years ago," Tandy told the gathering, "the idea was to develop an eight-block area all at once. But after going outside the area and getting another firm to come into the venture, difficulties arose, and the original plan became unfeasible."

Now, with Tandy Corporation projecting $700 million in sales and $40 million in profits after taxes for the current fiscal year, he said, he had been able to persuade his directors to move ahead with the development project in two phases, the second of which would include a 20-story office building and the first new department store to be built in downtown Fort Worth in more than 40 years. The 120,000 square foot department store was to be located in the three-level shopping mall and occupied by Dillard's.

Ground was broken for Two Tandy Center on October 14, 1976, with Charles Tandy, Jim West and Carrie Nemser, a Radio Shack vice president and 22-year employee, wielding the spades.

Janice Williams, a *Star-Telegram* business writer, recalled the events leading to the construction of the Tandy Center in a story published in November of 1978.

"They laughed privately or jeered openly, and even the most dedicated city boosters quivered for fear the dream would fall apart, when Charles Tandy announced his intention to reshape the city's downtown skyline. But then the dreamers watched it happen, bit by bit; the scoffers did a turnabout and Tandy himself lived long enough to realize his fondest ambition.

"What he did—with the same driving force that reshaped a tiny family-held corporation into a billion dollar international empire—was turn an aging, decrepit part of the city into a glittering array of new construction that embraces two high-rises, downtown's first new department store in nearly half a century, and a galleria of shops and stores topped by a reflective dome.

"All of this came about swiftly, in terms of construction time, once Tandy got the wheels in motion and began work on the eight blocks adjoining the Courthouse square on the south. After his initial announcement with Ogden Corp. of Los Angeles as a joint-venture partner, there was a long hiatus in which nothing occurred.

"Then, as Tandy candidly reported, 'difficulties arose,' and the agreement was off. At that point, he decided to undertake the entire redevelopment alone on a 'pay-as-you-go' basis—and was proud of the fact that Tandy Corp. needed no mortgages, no insurance companies, no outside financing for the project."

The summer of 1975 was a rewarding time for Tandy Corporation stockholders. On July 30, the *United States Investor*, published in Boston, carried the following bullish item:

"One of the Big Board's biggest winners of 1975 is Tandy Corp. Its shares have more than quadrupled in price this year on strong earnings and word that Tandy plans to split the company into three parts....With its outstanding record, Radio Shack alone is expected to command a higher multiple than its current P/E."

Over the next few months, Tandy continued to receive upbeat appraisals and "buy" recommendations from brokerage houses and financial analysts such as Dean Witter & Co., Kidder, Peabody and Co., Blyth Eastman Dillon & Co., the Securities and Commodities Corporation of Northport, N. Y., Desmond J. Heathwood, Jerome H. Buff, and Merrill Analysis, Inc. Investors apparently were paying attention.

On October 3, the Associated Press reported that Tandy climbed 2¼ to 40¾ on news that the Internal Revenue Service decided its planned spin-offs of two of its operations would not be treated as taxable income for shareholders.

In mid-October, Radio Shack announced it was discontinuing its quadraphonic line to place more emphasis on high-end stereo components.

"We'll sell anything people want," Charles Tandy was quoted in *Home Furnishings Daily*. "If they change their minds, we'll be the first to admit we've made a mistake about 4-channel systems and go back into it with our tail between our legs."

Radio Shack reported a 29 percent increase in sales of hi-fi receivers in September over the same month in 1974 and a 28 percent increase in speaker sales. But those gains paled in comparison to the 124 percent increase racked up by CB radios.

"We more than doubled CB sales last year and we're going to try and double them again in the coming year," Charles Tandy told *Home Furnishings Daily*, adding that he was anticipating CB sales of $114 million for the first eight months of the current fiscal year.

Another bullish scenario appeared in column by a Wall Street money manager in *Financial World* in November:

"Speaking of specialty retailers, a lot of smart guys are looking at the Tandy situation. The company has recently spun off two of its operating divisions to shareholders, leaving it essentially with its Radio Shack consumer electronics retail division. Oppenheimer is impressed with the core business and is adding the company to its recommended list. Earnings growth at Tandy appears to be quite viable because over 75 percent of Radio Shack stores are less than five years old, and they should grow very rapidly as they mature. This is a higher ratio of young to mature stores than that of any other large retailer we know.

"Tandy's record in recent years has demonstrated its ability to generate consistent earnings growth, particularly in the recession year of fiscal 1975, when both comparable store sales and earnings showed good increases. In the field of consumer electronics, the company is the dominant factor by a wide margin, which gives it greater flexibility and opportunities regarding manufacturing and marketing than its competitors."

The writer's optimistic forecast proved to have a spark of prescience when Tandy reported December sales in excess of $113 million, a record for any single month in the history of the company and a 50 percent gain over December 1954 sales of $75.5 million, restated to give effect to the Tandycrafts and Tandy Brands spin-offs. Sales of CB equipment were strong during the month, but sales of merchandise other than citizens band increased 39 percent over the prior year.

Tandy stock also received a boost from the announcement of another two-for-one stock split in the form of a 100 percent stock dividend which was to be effective January 9, 1976, to stockholders of record on December 12, 1975.

A further sign that Tandy was moving into the investment limelight was the announcement that options on its common stock would begin trading on the American Stock Exchange on January 19, 1976.

At the annual meeting on November 24, an openly jubilant group of shareholders greeted Charles Tandy with an enthusiastic round of applause as he stood at the microphone and called the year "another one of record advance of Tandy Corporation."

The shareholders had good reason to feel benign.

Tandy stock was one of the big gainers on the New York Stock Exchange during 1975, posting a spectacular increase of 352 percent from a low of 11½ to a year-end closing high of 52. Of the 2,137 issues traded on the Big Board, only one posted a greater percentage gain than Tandy. That was Best Products, a catalog and showroom retailer, whose stock rose 523.8 percent from 2⅝ to 16⅜.

In addition, Tandycrafts closed out the year at 13½ and Tandy Brands at 8. This meant that a person buying 100 shares of Tandy stock at 11½ wound up the year with stock in the three corporations worth $5,955, a net gain of $3,205 or 365.6 percent, over the initial investment of $1,150.

Participating in the gains were more than 7,000 Tandy employees who had signed up for the Tandy Corporation Stock Purchase Program that was instituted in May of 1975. The contributory program, including employer contributions related to length of service, provided for regular purchase by employees of the company's stock at the monthly average price.

Chapter 25
The CB Radio Bubble Bursts

Radio Shack was now the name of the game. The only game.

Of course, Tandy would continue to keep an eye on what was going on at Tandycrafts and Tandy Brands and the corporate offices of the new offshoots would remain in the buff-colored brick and glass building on West 7th Street that housed the headquarters of Tandy Corporation. But the old feeling that everyone was playing for the same team was gone. For some of the old-timers like Bill Michero and John Wilson, it wasn't an easy adjustment.

Perhaps it was no coincidence that Charles Tandy ensconced himself in a new bailiwick downtown, a ground-floor suite in the Fort Worth Club Building formerly occupied by a Christian Science reading room. There, he claimed, he could concentrate on running Radio Shack without being subjected to the distractions and interruptions that plagued him at corporate headquarters. Now he could pore over his profit-and-loss statements, conduct meetings, rail at his executives in person and over the telephone, and play the genial host to the people he wanted to see. He claimed he loved his new-found freedom so much that he even refused to have his secretary, Janet Lesok, on the new premises.

"One woman in my life bossing me around is enough," he said grinning broadly, in recognition of Anne Tandy's penchant for running everything she touched with the iron hand of a boss wrangler on one of her ranches.

When he moved into his new office, Tandy assigned John Ellis, a longtime employee, to screen his telephone calls and visitors. But, as it turned out, Ellis was often away on other assignments, leaving Tandy to answer the phone himself. A visitor walking into his office unannounced one day found him talking on the telephone.

"No, madam," Charles was saying, "Tandy Corporation does not sell bird cages."

On another occasion, Tandy found himself trying to cope with three telephone calls, two on hold and one on the line. Then, with a laugh he turned to a visitor and remarked, "This is a multi-million dollar company. As you can see, I'm perfectly organized."

"He never kept to a schedule," Janet Lesok recalled. "The people who were scheduled to meet him for a 9 o'clock meeting would see him sometimes just before lunch. They'd sit there, afraid to move. We all had to wait our turn. I would need signatures. Sometimes I sat through entire meetings just to catch him to sign a piece of paper or a check so that I could go down and cash a check for him.

"When I first started working for him, when I'd ask him in whose office he was going to be, he'd test me by saying, 'Bob Lynch,' knowing full well he wasn't going to Bob Lynch's office. He wanted to see if I could find him. He also did that with hotels. 'I'll be staying at the Plaza,' he'd say when I knew he was going to be at the Regency in New York. When I'd reach him there, he'd say, 'Goddammit, Janet, how did you find me?' Finally, after about two years, he gave up trying to fool me. But it always annoyed him that I was able to keep up with him."

Mrs. Lesok discovered early on that Tandy was not the kind of boss who buzzes his secretary over the intercom and says, "Miss Smith, would you please come in and bring your notebook." She learned very quickly that he was not going to give her dictation or talk into a recording machine.

"What you had to do," she said, "was listen to him talk enough, know he would talk to someone in one voice and to someone else in another voice, and be able to compose letters in the proper voice for each person. Now, if they were long, business-type letters, they were written by other people in the company for his signature. But any of his personal notes, just memo-type things, I would write."

She also was in charge of sending gifts to friends of Tandy's around the country like restaurateurs Bob and Pete Kriendler, the owners of the '21 Club' in New York.

"The Kriendlers just absolutely adored him," Mrs. Lesok related. "If his plane landed at LaGuardia at midnight, he would call. If the restaurant was closed, they'd open it up for him. They loved western wear, the vests, the hats, and the boots, and we were forever shipping western goods from Tex Tan and the other western wear companies up to the Kriendlers."

Another good friend who called Tandy frequently was automobile magnate Henry Ford II.

"Mr. Ford always made his own calls, never placed them through a secretary," Mrs. Lesok reported. "We also sent him lots of western stuff. That's what I was there for. To remember to do these little nice things, because Charles didn't have time to think about them."

Jesse Upchurch recalled that Henry Ford telephoned Tandy quite often to congratulate him on the company's performance. He remembered one year when Tandy Corporation had racked up profits of $50 million to $60 million and the Ford Motor Company's electronics division had lost about $50 million to $60 million. Tandy called Ford and asked him if he would sell the Ford electronics division to him. "Maybe I can turn things around," Upchurch said he told Ford.

"I think Ford believed him," Upchurch said. "As a matter of fact, I think they came very close to making a deal. And Charles could have financed it, because he had a lot of people who believed in him who would have financed any venture he wanted to go into."

The people who believed in Tandy had ample reason for their trust.

Radio Shack sales were booming in the aftermath of the spin-offs, sparked by the CB radio boom. The month-by-month increases over the prior year were hard to believe—57 percent in January 1976, 60 percent in February, 58 percent in March, 42 percent in April, 40 percent in May, 41 percent in June. Fiscal 1976 sales were on the way to exceeding $740 million, more than the 1975 sales of $724.5 million that had included the Tandycrafts' and Tandy Brands' contributions.

The store-opening program was proceeding at a dizzy pace that would find Radio Shack opening nearly 1,200 company-owned and dealer outlets in the U. S. and Canada during the year ended June 30, 1976, bringing the number of retail outlets in North America to 4,599 and the number worldwide to 5,154. Especially significant was the fact that the expansion program was now being financed entirely out of the cash flow generated by the existing stores.

Asked by an interviewer how many stores he was shooting for, Tandy replied, "I feel that we can have 2,000 more."

Profits were continuing to soar, heading towards a record $3.55 per share from continuing operations in fiscal 1976, an increase of 126 percent over the prior year.

* * *

More recognition came Tandy's way.

In January, 1976, he became the first recipient of the Spirit of Enterprise Award of the Fort Worth Chamber of Commerce. In March, he received the Dateline Award of the Advertising Club of Fort Worth for focusing national attention on the city. Later that month, he was named outstanding chief executive officer of the year in the merchandising and services category by *Financial World*. The selection was made by a panel of judges composed of 48 securities analysts. Other CEOs honored included John Swearingen of Standard Oil (Indiana), Donald T. Regan of Merrill Lynch, Walter A. Haas, Jr., of Levi Strauss, and Joseph F. Cullman 3rd of Philip Morris. In October, he received the 1976 Business Executive of the Year Award and entered the Business Executives Hall of Fame at Texas Wesleyan University in Fort Worth.

He continued to broaden the membership of his board of directors in an attempt to quiet the concerns in some Wall Street circles that the board was loaded too heavily with inside directors. In May, Donald L. Bryant of New York City, executive vice president and special assistant to the chief executive officer of the Equitable Life Assurance Society, was elected a director.

Tandy was discovered by the business and financial press, and suddenly the flamboyant, cigar-smoking Texan was the focus of newspaper features and magazine articles about his climb from rags-to-riches. Writers were popping into Fort Worth in a steady stream, looking for an unexplored angle or a previously unpublished recipe for his success.

Visiting journalists found him in his downtown hideaway in the Fort Worth Club Building, seated behind a large walnut desk, a big smile on his face, exuding charm, ebullience, and the aroma of 20-cent cigar smoke. On a coffee table nearby was a witch's head, dubbed "Miss Radio Shack," with a "Pull Me" tag dangling from her mouth. One pull and the visitor was sprayed by a stream of water spouting from the gap-toothed orifice.

"It's only water," Tandy would howl, his booming laugh nearly drowning out the cackle that emanated from the witch's mouth.

Decorating his desk was a plastic female breast, a gift from Anne Tandy. When Tandy pressed the nipple, a gong would sound signalling that it was coffee time. Another knickknack on his desk was a small peanut-filled burlap bag bearing the legend, "Nutz 2 U."

"Tandy seems incapable of giving anyone a frosty welcome," Irwin Ross wrote in the December 1976 issue of *Fortune*. "He has about him the warmth and exuberance often associated with Texans, but speaks with barely a trace of a regional accent. Talk is both vocation and avocation with him. Ask him a question about his business and he is delighted to respond for half an hour, not without eloquence and in sentences that march in disciplined order. When new visitors arrive, he often waves them to seats to listen to his dialogue with prior arrivals. He also has the greatest difficulty ending a conversation. The result is that he is late to most appointments, often by as much as an hour."

John Merwin, writing in *D* magazine published in Dallas, informed his readers in a June, 1976 article, "Had you bought one share of Charles Tandy's stock in 1975, at its low of 11⅝, a year later that stock would be worth approximately $88. Lots of Tandy employees, little old widows and various other investors are happy about that. Look at Tandy's own numbers. The value of his personal shares leaped in a year from a mere $4.3 million to $32 million."

"I was a poor boy. I'm rich now," Tandy admitted. "I've been rewarded for what I do, but the opportunity is there for all. I have said many times that I can't make enough money to satisfy myself by working only 40 hours a week, and I'm interested in other people who want more money and are willing to work for it."

Although his salary was still only $75,000 a year, Tandy's total compensation in fiscal 1976 amounted to $614,700 as a result of bonuses. The board raised his salary to $250,000 in fiscal 1977, and his total compensation amounted to $688,000.

To an interviewer from *Time*, Tandy pointed out that a major reason for Tandy Corporation's success was the fact that everybody was attached to a profit and loss statement.

"The majority of a man's income comes from bonuses—that's after performance, not before," he stressed. "I want people who live for and will die for this work. If they don't want to do that, let them work for Sears."

Chain Store Age said about Tandy, "He couldn't care less if his managers had three heads. He only looks at their numbers." And looking at Radio Shack's numbers, the publication added, "It's tough to imagine a more successful specialty store chain. For instance: Radio Shack has been popping out new stores at the rate of three-a-day (average size

2,200 square feet), generating 30 percent or better yearly sales gains while compounding earnings nearly 50 percent a year since 1970. A typical new Radio Shack store in its first year of operation produces $300,000 in total sales and $60,000 in operating profits on an initial merchandise investment of $150,000, for a gross margin of 52 percent and a 32 percent return on investment."

But it was Ross' article in *Fortune* that painted the most complete portrait.

"To the people who work for him," Ross wrote, "Tandy is an unrelenting taskmaster, the kind of boss who will call up a district manager to explain a drop in sales and who insists that people work long hours, including weekends, if that's what it takes to get their job done. Because he likes to work on Saturday morning, he expects his executives to show up, too. On his orders, corporate headquarters remain open on Saturdays from 9 to 1."

"Very seldom does he give a compliment," Ross quoted Bill Nugent. "He always has something to criticize. One month this year, we ran a 60 percent sales increase over the year before. Tandy's response was, 'Why didn't we sell more merchandise?' He was only half-kidding."

Ross cited examples of what he called Tandy's "insensitivity to other people's feelings," such as dressing down an underling in the presence of a third party, and making "jocularly disparaging remarks about associates, again in their presence." He described an incident at a social gathering, where Tandy called his top financial adviser, Charles Tindall, "a dumb bookkeeper," in a voice heard around the room.

But the other side of the coin, the article continued, was that Tandy was the guiding force behind "a giant machine for the creation of millionaires, a project close to Charles Tandy's heart." Ross told of instances where Charles dug into his own pocket to help associates enlarge their estates, citing as an example his loaning $50,000 to a newly-hired executive to buy Tandy stock. After three stock splits, the shares were now worth more than $1 million. In 1971, Ross added, Tandy made similar loans totaling $1,760,000 to five newly created vice presidents.

"Charles Tandy has far outdistanced the field," Ross wrote, "and he has done it with a chain of small stores that are rather unimpressive in appearance and often staffed by inexperienced sales people. His secret lies not in a lot of inventive new techniques, but in the speed, boldness, and scale of his operation. Tandy has expanded faster, advertised more, and enforced more strenuous controls than any of the competition. Even when the Radio Shack stores were losing money a dozen years ago, he was putting in new outlets. By fiscal 1969, when the chain was grossing only $65 million, he amazed the industry by opening nearly 200 new company-owned stores. He has continued opening new company stores in the U.S. and Canada at an astounding rate of better than two each working day. No retail corporation, food chains aside, has spawned company-owned stores at such a clip."

* * *

Just before the publication of the *Fortune* article, however, Tandy would face the unpleasant task of publicly acknowledging that a three-month internal investigation by the company had uncovered several isolated instances of "improper or questionable" transactions by company employees in the United States and abroad over the preceding five-year period.

The disclosure was made in a news release on November, 10, 1976, that stated, "While no pattern of illegal or improper conduct has been found, nominal gifts, merchandise discounts and cash payments were made in foreign countries where such practices are customary to expedite normal business operations, and gifts of merchandise were given to postal employees in a foreign country to facilitate the mailing of advertising at reduced rates."

In addition, the news release declared, "Merchandise gifts were given to personnel in the tax assessor's office in Orange County, California, in connection with a claim for tax exemption, and political contributions were made to one of those persons in his subsequent campaigns for election to the U.S. House of Representatives. The total value of the gifts, discounts, and payments amounted to $23,500 and the contributions totaled less than $7,200."

The news release added, "Tandy Corporation has terminated the making of such political gifts and contributions, and management has recommended to the board of directors that it reiterate corporate policy in a formal resolution and written directive to all company employees, stating that all personnel are expected to comply with the law and to adhere to high ethical standards in Tandy's business operations and transactions."

Subsequently, U.S. Rep. Andrew J. Hinshaw, Republican of California, was convicted of accepting merchandise from a Tandy Corporation employee while serving as tax assessor of Orange County in 1972. Hinshaw, who was elected to Congress in 1976, received a sentence of one to 14 years.

On November 16, 1976, an editorial in the *Fort Worth Star-Telegram* discussed the disclosures and commended Tandy Corporation for its handling of the matter.

"In this age when many big businesses are viewed with suspicion, it is refreshing that Tandy Corp. initiated an extensive internal investigation of its own international activities," the editorial said. "It is commendable that Tandy took action to find and correct questionable practices—to reveal rather than conceal. That kind of open, truthful approach is fitting for a firm headquartered in Fort Worth, Texas."

* * *

But by now, Tandy had something else to worry about—a widespread fear that the CB radio boom might be coming to an end. His concerns had been mounting since the spring of 1976, when Tandy stock began plummeting upon publication of the company's nine-month figures that revealed a 180 percent increase in sales of citizens band radios. By late May, the stock had fallen some 20 percent from its high of 47 earlier in the year.

On June 1, Tandy stock dropped 1⅝ to 35, and on June 5 it was off 3 more points and was the most active issue on the Big Board, which caused Clayton Reed, a financial columnist, to speculate in print, "You're wondering about CB manufacturers as a stock buy? You may be too late. True, sales and profits of companies like Hy-Gain Electronics, Tandy Corp. (Radio Shack), Pathcom Inc., Regency Electronics, Gladding Corp., E.F. Johnson Co. and Dynascan Corp. have doubled, even quadrupled recently, and could do so again. Wall Street, nonetheless, remains skeptical. Price-earnings ratios generally are low. There are reasons beyond the 'fad' fears. General Electric and RCA, which abandoned the market years ago as unpromising, are jumping back in. And integrated circuitry is on the way—remember pocket calculators? All this will chop prices and could make the CB market die of its own weight."

But it was a ruling by the Federal Communication Commission (FCC) on July 27, 1976, that caused the real panic in the CB marketplace. The FCC ruling authorized an increase in Citizen's Band radio channels from 23 to 40, effective January 1, 1977. That precipitated a flood of dumping of 23-channel radio sets. In Lew Kornfeld's view, "This put a screeching halt to the two-year seller's market in CB radios."

In his book, *To Catch a Mouse*, Kornfeld elaborated. "Pre-boom, CB had ambled along at 4-6 percent of Radio Shack's growing business. From 1972-1976, this 4 percent sleepyhead matured to a vast and treacherous monster. During several quarters of fiscal 1976 and 1977, it soared to over 20 percent of our sales and twice to as high as 28 percent. Then the public's passion for mobile chit-chat cooled at a pace and in a manner as predictable as what usually happens when torrid affairs with gadgets go sour."

The day after the FCC announcement, Tandy stock was the second most-actively traded issue on the New York Stock Exchange, falling 2¼ to close at 32⅛.

The following afternoon, Charles W. Tindall, Tandy's chief financial officer, told the Dow-Jones News Service that he knew of no reason for the stock's weakness and that he saw nothing but good news in the FCC's ruling permitting more CB radio channels. "It creates a whole new category of merchandise for us to market," Tindall contended. "Once the 40-channel unit is being marketed," he added, "the 23-channel models will still be the most popular CB models, primarily because of the price difference which could amount to $30 to $40 a set."

Wall Street took the statement with a grain of salt.

As Tindall's remarks went across the Dow-Jones wire, Tandy stock was trading at 30⅛, off 1¼, after hitting a low of 29⅜ earlier in the day.

CB manufacturers, Tandy included, began a frenzied rush to get their new 40-channel radios ready for FCC approval prior to January 1. Radio Shack was first in line at the FCC on September 10, 1976, when the agency began receiving 40-channel models for certification. The first five radios delivered to the FCC's laboratory for testing were from Radio Shack.

In the meantime, prices on the existing 23-channel radios were beginning to slide. A Radio Shack advertisement in the *New York Daily News* in September announced a "price slash" from $109 to $99.

Describing the situation to a group of securities analysts, Lew Kornfeld predicted there would be more price erosion. "But," he contended, "we are better able to advertise and are in a better position to sell than our competition, meaning we can meet erosion vigorously and with great effect."

There was no stemming the slide in the price of Tandy stock, however.

On Wednesday, October 6, 1976, Tandy directors received notification of a special board meeting to be held on the following Wednesday morning, October 13, in Fort Worth. On Friday, October 8, there was unusually heavy trading in Tandy Corporation $35 October options on the American Stock Exchange. The heavy trading in Tandy options continued on Monday and Tuesday, October 11 and 12, and trading in Tandy common stock also was unusually heavy on the New York Stock Exchange on both days. Concerned over the abnormally high volumes, the governors of the American and New York Stock Exchanges halted trading in Tandy options and Tandy stock on Tuesday afternoon, October 12, pending an announcement by the company. At the halt, Tandy stock was trading at 32⅝ on the NYSE, up ¼, amid rumors that the stock was being quoted off the floor at 36 to 39.

Shortly before noon on October 13, the financial wires began circulating an announcement from Fort Worth that the Tandy board had approved a plan granting stockholders the right to exchange their Tandy shares for a new issue of $40 subordinated debentures paying 10 percent annual interest. The offer was subject to a minimum of 500,000 shares being tendered by the offering's expiration date of December 17, 1976. If more than 1.5 million shares were offered for exchange, the company reserved the right to accept some or all of the excess shares or reduce the subscriptions on a pro rata basis.

Tandy stock opened for trading on the New York Stock Exchange on Thursday morning, October 14, on a block of 150,400 shares at 34⅞, up 2¼ from the last sale on Tuesday afternoon, as investors jumped eagerly on the opportunity to acquire stock at a price in the mid-30s that could be exchanged for debentures worth $40 and that also paid 10 percent annual interest. Then, just before the close of trading on Thursday, October 14, the Securities and Exchange Commission announced that it had ordered an investigation of possible insider trading and/or manipulation in Tandy stock and Tandy options.

Responding to the SEC announcement, Charles Tindall issued a statement that the company knew of no insider trading in its stock or options, but was investigating the possibility of an information leak.

"We have no indication of insider trading by any directors or officers of the company," Tindall declared. "We polled employees at our Fort Worth headquarters and found none of us in Fort Worth bought any stock or options in October." He added that the company was polling its directors about their recent stock purchasing activity.

"It looks like there could have possibly been a leak about the pending exchange offer in view of the heavy volume in Tandy October options. It does look suspect," Tindall conceded. He indicated a leak could have occurred during the preparation and printing of materials related to the exchange offer, pointing out that the materials had been delivered to the printer over the weekend.

In an interview with *Dallas Times Herald* business writer Richard Bonner on October 15, Herschel Winn, vice president and corporate secretary, said the company polled 14 of its 15 directors and found that none of them had bought Tandy October options. The remaining director was on a hunting trip and could not be reached. Winn emphasized that the term "insider trading" did not necessarily mean trading done by a company insider or on information given by a company insider.

"It includes trading by anyone who gets inside information with or without the consent of the company or company employee," he said.

Winn declined to speculate on a rumor that a relative of a Tandy executive might have committed the leak by disclosing to social contacts that "good" news was imminent from the company.

At the annual meeting in Fort Worth on November 12, Winn informed the shareholders that to his knowledge no Tandy officer or anyone in a management position had been involved in insider trading.

Winn did report, however, that one Tandy employee and four former Tandy employees had given depositions to the SEC regarding option trades they had made just prior to the public announcement of the exchange offer on October 13.

The SEC subsequently filed complaints against six individuals for using "non-public" information to benefit themselves in buying Tandy options. The profits they accrued, according to the SEC, ranged from $14 to $1,844. A federal court order later required five of the six to divest themselves of the profits generated by their trades and to pay nominal fines.

On November 22, 1976, the SEC gave its approval to the debenture exchange offer, opening the gates to an ocean of shares that began flooding in for exchange. By the December 17 deadline, a total of

5,386,125 shares, or about 30 percent of the 17.9 million Tandy shares outstanding, had been tendered. The company agreed to accept 2,450,975 shares for exchange, including all tenders of 50 shares or less. Tenders of more than 50 shares were accepted on a pro rata basis. The 2,450,975 shares were exchanged for $90,039,000 in debentures and were retired.

The offer achieved two of the company's long-range goals—to reduce the number of odd-lot holdings, thereby trimming the expense of furnishing annual reports and proxy statements to holders of less than 50 shares, and to boost per share earnings by shrinking the amount of common stock outstanding. Charles Tandy called the reduction in the number of shares a plus for the company and for its stockholders.

"At prices prevailing in recent years, which have been quite modest multiples of current earnings relative to historical norms," he told shareholders, "the purchase of shares with borrowed funds will enhance the future return on equity and earnings per share growth because the profit margins of the Company are in excess of the interest costs of the funds borrowed."

Robert Metz, a *New York Times* financial writer, observed that the exchange offer showed that Tandy management was so sure that its shares were undervalued that it was willing to go into debt to buy them up. "This is the second time in just over two years that Tandy has moved to reduce its equity," Metz noted. "Mr. Tandy's frustration is perhaps understandable in terms of the past. As recently as 1972, Tandy shares traded at a price-earnings ratio of 35. At recent prices, the stock was trading at nine times the most-recently reported 12-month earnings."

"The public was the real winner," Charles Tandy said of the exchange offer. "They came in like a flock of geese. It was very attractive to the little guy. When interest rates declined, investors scrambled to pick up the 10 percent paper."

Tandy stock also was a winner.

On December 20, it was the most active issue on the Big Board, gaining ⅞ to 38¾ after the company announced the tendering of the 5,386,125 shares. By late January of 1977, the stock climbed back to the mid-40 range amid good reviews from the investment community. Oppenheimer & Co., Inc., for example, announced it had increased its fiscal 1977 earnings per share estimate for Tandy Corporation to the $4.90 to $5.15 level because of the decrease in the number of shares outstanding and improvement in the company's long-term outlook.

"Since Tandy's exchange offer expired December 17, 1976, the stock has outperformed the market," Oppenheimer said. "Our December 2, 1976, Tandy report was much too cautious in its opinion that the stock was fairly priced near term because: (a) the stock had run up after the announcement of the exchange offer and (b) we thought investors might negatively interpret indications that total demand for CB had peaked, unrelated to the 40-channel introduction. In retrospect, we should have stressed that the favorable longer term fundamentals outweighed the near term uncertainties, which investors now seem to be recognizing."

*　*　*

On January 1, 1977, when the first 40-channel CB radios hit the marketplace, Radio Shack sold the first set.

The coup was pulled off by Chick L. Whitfield, the owner of a Radio Shack dealership in Tamuning, Guam, who made a special trip to Japan during December and picked up a supply of 40-channel radios. Whitfield then placed them on sale in his store at 12:01 a.m., January 1, Guam time, which was 13 hours ahead of the arrival of the new year on the mainland.

On January 10, *Time* magazine carried a story with a photograph of a beaming Charles Tandy holding a 40-channel CB set in his hands.

"The ubiquitous (more than 5,000 U.S. and Canadian outlets) Radio Shack claims 15 percent of the market in Citizens Band radio equipment," *Time* reported. "CB enthusiasts accounted for almost 25 percent of the chain's $742 million in revenues last year. Experts forecast sales this year of at least 10 million of the new CB models, and Radio Shack is set to take home to its parent, Tandy Corp. of Fort Worth, an increasing share of the industry's profits."

The sales bonanza never materialized, however.

Bernie Appel, who was then Radio Shack's vice president of merchandising, attested to this in a newspaper interview in which he admitted, "The 40-channel demand has not been as significant as anticipated." Appel then added, "The current stock of 23-channel sets is being sold at extraordinary values."

He wasn't exaggerating. Discounting on 23-channel sets soon began running rampant. Tandy saw a silver lining among the clouds, however.

"Because we were selling to the ultimate consumer as well as to our dealers," he would later recall, "we were able to spot at an early date the growing glut of 23-channel equipment in the marketplace before many of the independent CB manufacturers, and act accordingly. By moving aggressively with early price promotions, we were able not only to dispose of our remaining 23-channel units relatively quickly at acceptable gross margins, but were also in a position to purchase and sell substantial quantities of distress close-out units of branded manufacturers at very attractive prices and profit margins. In the process, we significantly increased our market visibility and store traffic which had a spill-over effect on the sales of other product lines."

Tandy confided to John Roach, "I'd much rather buy the distressed merchandise and sell it myself than have my competitors selling against me at cut-rate prices."

Lew Kornfeld estimated that Radio Shack bought upwards of a million close-outs and resold them profitably at discounts of up to 50 percent during fiscal 1977.

Robert E. Keto, a longtime Radio Shack employee who became president and chief executive officer of InterTAN Inc., recalled accompanying Tandy to a speaking engagement before a group of analysts in Atlanta during this period.

"Charles told the analysts that he was going to sell 1.6 million CBs," Keto said, "and one of the people in the room asked him how he knew he could sell that many."

Tandy's rejoinder was, "Listen, wiseass, I've got them and I'll get rid of them. I just haven't decided the price yet."

But the heavy markdowns on the 23-channel sets were taking their toll on the price of Tandy stock. On April 20, 1977, after the announcement of flat third quarter earnings despite a 27 percent increase in sales, Tandy stock dropped 1½ to 32¼. The same day, a Japanese CB radio manufacturer announced it was cutting its production by one-third because of "demand uncertainty" in its major market, the United States. L.F. Rothschild & Co., a New York brokerage house, issued a report that spoke of "investor concern about CB radio price competition and its possible impact on Tandy's earnings growth."

In mid-May, with the price of the stock still falling, Charles Tandy ordered full page ads taken out in key newspapers across the country that proclaimed in bold type:

"On May 2, 1977, the Standard & Poor's Outlook published a list of New York Stock Exchange companies with 10 years of unbroken earnings growth. Of more than 1,500 common stocks, only 90 survived the S&P computer screening. The 90 stocks were then ranked according to 5-year growth rates. Guess which company was No. 1."

Heading the list of 90 companies was Tandy Corporation with a five-year growth rate of 48 percent.

Investors apparently weren't impressed.

On June 7, Tandy dropped 4½ points to 23⅝ on the report that sales at Radio Shack stores in existence more than a year dropped 5 percent during the month of May. Overall, Radio Shack sales rose only 10 percent during the month. The news shocked Wall Street which had come to expect monthly sales increases from Radio Shack of 25 to 30 percent.

Garland Asher, who was then Tandy Corporation's director of financial planning, said there was a simple explanation for the failure of May sales to show a larger gain. "We're in a transition period involving CB sets—a transition period expected to continue another two months. Sales are slow because so many 23-channel sets are on the market at low prices. We think sales of the new 40-channel sets will climb after the transition period."

On June 8, Tandy retreated another 1½ points to 22⅛, bringing its two-session plunge to 6. During the day, the stock traded at a new low of 21 for year, down more than 50 percent from its 1977 high of 42⅞.

On June 20, Charles Tandy moved to stem the tide with a tender offer to buy 3.5 million shares of Tandy stock at $29 per share. In announcing the offer, Garland Asher stated, "We're not a CB house. We're just a peddler...an electronics retailer. But the stock market has branded us a CB company. And because so many of the CB manufacturers are in trouble, they've brought our stock price down, too."

Tandy stock jumped 3⅛ to 27½ on news of the tender offer. A total of 5,426,000 shares was tendered by the July 12 expiration date, of which 3.5 million shares were accepted and retired. This reduced the number of shares outstanding to approximately 12 million.

Charles Tandy rationalized the move in an interview in *Forbes* on July 15. "We're predicting earnings of $4.10 to $4.40 for our fiscal year that ended June 30," he said. "To finance the $29 offer price, we're paying prime rate for the money, or 6.5 percent. On $29, that interest cost is about $2 pretax, or $1 a share after taxes. So, for $1 in interest cost we're buying shares that earn better than $4 and are spreading the gain over the other shares."

Tandy Corporation's fiscal 1977 earnings totaled $4.17 per share on sales of $949.3 million. The figures showed, beyond a shadow of a doubt, that Radio Shack was a whole lot more than a CB radio purveyor. But Wall Street wasn't listening.

In Fort Worth, where there was an old saying, "When Tandy stock sneezes, Fort Worth catches cold," there was a lot of sadness among the tapewatchers in the brokerage house boardrooms.

But among veteran stockbrokers like Franklin Halsell of Merrill Lynch's Fort Worth office, it was a case of history repeating itself one more time. Halsell had been watching the Tandy roller-coaster ride for too many years to throw in the towel now. One of his favorite expressions was, "Nobody ever got rich betting against Tandy." The time to buy, he told his customers, was now when the stock was a bargain.

The investors who followed his advice wouldn't be sorry.

Chapter 26
The Birth of the TRS-80

At 5 o'clock in the afternoon of a sunshiny day in June, 1975, John Roach pulled his car into a parking slot in front of the modest Tandy corporate headquarters on West 7th Street and made his way to his small office on the second floor of the two-story structure.

Roach had served two years as vice president of distribution for Radio Shack. He had just returned from an extended out-of-town trip and dropped by his office to check his mail before going home. He arrived to find the gossip mill working overtime with the news that Radio Shack's vice president of manufacturing had just quit his job. Roach was not particularly surprised.

"The guy had been hired for the job from the outside and had never really fit in," Roach would later recall.

Now Lewis Kornfeld poked his head into Roach's office. "I'm glad I caught you," Kornfeld said. "Charles wants to see you first thing in the morning."

Roach arrived at Tandy's office at 9 o'clock the following morning. He was still waiting when Tandy finally strolled in at a little after 10. He came right to the point.

"I've got a new assignment for you," he told Roach. "I'm putting you in charge of manufacturing."

Shaking his head incredulously as he recalled the incident, Roach said, "What you've got to realize is that I had never been in a manufacturing facility in my life, especially not a Tandy facility, and I didn't know anything about cost accounting."

At that time, Radio Shack owned and operated 17 factories in the United States, Canada, Japan, and South Korea which produced more than $80 million worth of consumer electronics products annually and employed nearly 3,000 people. The plants turned out about 20 to 25 percent of the products sold in the more than 2,500 Radio Shack retail outlets in the U.S. and Canada and the approximately 350 Tandy International Electronics stores in England, Belgium, Holland, Germany, and Australia.

"But Charles had told me I was now in charge of manufacturing," Roach said, "so I got busy trying to do that."

One of the things Roach concluded right off the bat was that the Radio Shack manufacturing operations lacked an in-house engineering capability.

"There were a few engineers around in a couple of our plants," Roach said, "but we really didn't have much of an engineering group for an operation our size. The first thing I did was try to put them together in a sort of central group to handle the development of new products." One of the group's initial efforts was to develop a new line of calculators. "The calculator was kind of the latest thing then," Roach pointed out, "so we were trying to build calculators, among other things."

At that time, there was no such thing as a cheap computer. The least expensive models cost $50,000 to $100,000. There were some mini-computers in the marketplace, but their cost was prohibitive, running into the hundreds of thousands of dollars.

"Computers were then considered a rare species of creation, requiring an extremely cool and clean environment, special handlers, and large capitalization," Lew Kornfeld said. "The cost of making, selling and maintaining them was believed irreversibly high, and there was no large existing library of software. But two critical computer components, the cathode ray tube for displaying and the keyboard for manipulating data were already in 1975 at surprisingly affordable prices."

Radio Shack already had employees on its payroll who enjoyed putting "computer parts jigsaw puzzles" together, Kornfeld continued, including some who "prowled the industry for things to add to Radio Shack's unique 'Parts Place' category of components."

One of the most avid of these computer hobbyists was Donald H. French, who worked as a buyer for Bernie Appel in the Radio Shack merchandising department. French had become totally immersed in the fascinating new world of do-it-yourself computer-building, subscribing to all of the magazines devoted to the subject. He assembled working computer models from electronic kits already on the market. Soon he was engaged in a one-man crusade to convince the decision-makers in the company that Radio Shack should get into the computer kit business. His pitch now caught John Roach's attention.

"He was getting all of these magazines talking about kitted computer parts," John Roach remembered. "I mean, it was a real hobbyist thing. French would talk to members of our engineering group about what he was reading in the magazines and what he was hearing from people on the grapevine. Pretty soon all of us were kind of talking about it, and we decided, well, maybe, we ought to build our own computer kit."

The project made little progress until the spring of 1976, when Roach and several of his engineers took a trip to the Silicon Valley of northern California to visit some semiconductor manufacturers. "We were really looking primarily for parts out of which we could make CB equipment and telephones," Roach said, "because we wanted to start manufacturing telephones and CB was still going strong. But we did, of course, still have a continuing interest in computer kits."

One of the companies Roach and his engineers visited was National Semiconductor. There they were told that the person in charge of computer parts was not available, but that they could talk with one of his electronics engineers.

"The guy they brought out to see us was really excited about computers," Roach said. "One of the things he told us was that there was a computer store just down the street that we should be sure to visit. So, after we finished our business at National Semiconductor, we walked down the street to the computer store. This was one of the first computer stores in the country. Of course, it didn't have anything in it that looked like a computer. It just had some printed circuit boards, some bins with parts in them, and things like that. But, lo and behold, who did we find when we got there but the guy from National Semiconductor who had been talking to us earlier. I kind of got the feeling that he was interested in going to work for us, so I suggested to the head of the Radio Shack engineering group that he get in touch with the guy."

A month later, Roach asked the engineering group head, "Have you had that guy in for an interview yet?" The answer was negative. "My sense was that he really didn't want to have the guy in," Roach recalled. "So I told him, 'I want that guy in my office Saturday morning.' Saturday morning, the guy shows up, and he comes to work for us."

The 24-year-old engineer was Steve Leininger. He would become, in John Roach's words, "a one-man band" in the development of the TRS-80 personal computer.

The push to come up with a marketable, low-cost, small computer kit began in earnest. Roach assigned a design and engineering team that included Steve Leininger and Don French. Because of lack of space, the unit was initially housed in a former automobile salesroom.

The task force began its labors amid mounting pressures for the development of a new product that would hopefully supplant the CB radio. In addition, Radio Shack badly needed a product that would showcase its technological capabilities as part of its ongoing effort to upgrade its image.

"People still thought of us as 'Nagasaki Hardware,'" Lew Kornfeld explained.

Then there was the pressure being applied by Charles Tandy, whose constant refrain to Kornfeld and Roach was, "Let's get off our asses and come up with some new products."

The quest for the new computer kit continued into 1977.

"The task force was trying to develop the mechanical designs, the cases, what we were going to do for a monitor, because monitors just weren't around as they are today," Roach recalled. "We seemed to be going back and forth, in a sort of hit-or-miss process, trying to come up with something that we thought we could sell, that might be an offering."

Meanwhile, Bernie Appel suggested the idea of developing a fully-assembled small computer rather than a kit.

"The problem was," Roach declared, "that there wasn't anybody else out there that was reputable at all that wanted anything to do with making a simple computer. In fact, the people who were really in the computer business thought it was a totally worthless idea, because you couldn't have all of the sophistication in a simple computer that they thought you had to have to sell anything."

According to Roach, the critical decision to build a wired, complete system rather than a computer kit was made by Kornfeld and Bernie Appel. "It was an especially gutsy step," Roach said, "because the market was entirely kit up to that time."

Recalling the decision, Bernie Appel said, "The TRS-80 was not a long range plan, a 'let's go after a market' type thing. It was an idea that a couple of our people thought about. It was talked about in the industry. It was brought to me by one of my buyers. I looked at it and I said, 'If you're gonna make a $500 to $600 item, don't sell it as a kit. Make it a wired unit that works.' Lew Kornfeld concurred."

With their hopes finally realized, Leininger and French and the other members of the development team went back to work with renewed enthusiasm. Periodically, Leininger and French would come over to Roach's office to show him the latest fruits of their labors.

"They'd say, 'Well, here's what we can do,'" Roach recounted. "But I was mostly worried about price. Radio Shack had never sold anything costing over $500 in its life. I was scared to death that the public wouldn't buy the product, no matter how great it was, if it was priced over $500. So I would send them back and say, 'This is too expensive.' 'We can't get there with this.' 'Yeah, we can accept this idea and that idea.' 'That makes a lot of sense, but...'"

Slowly the negatives were whittled away, costs reduced, designs scrapped, and new ones drafted. Selection of a microprocessor, the heart of the microcomputer, was a key decision. Imbedded on a tiny silicon chip, the microprocessor contains the elements that enable the computer to handle data, make calculations, carry out stored instructions and perform the other functions it is designed to do. After a lengthy search, a Z-80 microprocessor manufactured by Zilog, a semiconductor company in the Silicon Valley, was chosen.

Another cost-saving move was a decision to go into the marketplace for a monitor rather than tool up and produce one internally.

"A number of manufacturers of video monitors were offered orders in lots of 1,000," Lew Kornfeld reported, "but only RCA showed any interest. RCA not only agreed to supply us with the monitors, 12-inch black and white TV receivers without tuner, speaker and certain other circuitry, but the silver gray case that was included served us as a style and color guide for the rest of the system. The computer itself, consisting of the Zilog Z-80 and support parts, was located in a separate keyboard cabinet."

The TRS-80 was developed for less than $150,000, including tooling costs," John Roach revealed. "That was a small investment for the significant role that computer had in spawning a new industry. But the low-cost development was necessary for such a high risk product in what was then an uncertain market. For example, the black and white monitor sourced from RCA was a discontinued television cabinet available in 'Mercedes Gray' or 'Woodgrain.' We took what was available to save costs. This explains our often-cussed gray color in later years."

About the silver gray color, Lew Kornfeld added, "I strongly approved its selection on the principle that we didn't want something as serious as a computer to go to work in racing stripes. I felt it had to look sober, dignified, and impressive."

The handmade model of what was to become the TRS-80 was finally assembled in January of 1977. "It had a case and a keyboard and had some reasonable resemblance to what we initially came out with," Roach recalled. "On the breadboard, meaning a hand-wired thing, underneath the table and under a black cloth, we had the guts of the computer. We set it up in what was the only conference room in the company at the time, on the second floor of the building on West 7th Street. Lew Kornfeld looked at it. He was excited about it."

Recalling the development of the handmade model, Kornfeld noted, "Whenever I'd see the breadboard, I'd say, 'We'll order it the day it can play chess with me and nobody from engineering has to hold the wires together or tell me, 'honest, boss, it was working just a minute ago, but...' Then came the day it would play chess, and, finally, the day our little group said there would be a working TRS-80 prototype ready to be approved for production early that afternoon."

It was now time to secure the boss's blessings on the project. Kornfeld recalled the historic day in the spring of 1977 that Charles Tandy was first shown the prototype of the machine that would blaze the way for the mass-marketing of personal computers.

"As I crossed over the windowed landing separating my grungy office from our grungy, windowless conference room," Kornfeld recounted, "I looked out and saw Tandy getting into his black Continental."

Kornfeld charged down the flight of stairs to the street level and bolted out the front door in time to intercept Tandy as he was backing his Lincoln out of his parking slot.

"Charles," Kornfeld panted, "I need you to come upstairs to bless a new project. It might be a real, exclusive winner."

"What is it?"

"A computer, a little desktop computer."

"A computer!" Tandy blared. "Who needs a computer?"

Kornfeld admitted that no one really knew if a market existed for a small computer.

"I told him that there were no known customers asking for one; that it was virtually impossible to identify buyers; that we had no opening or quantity set beyond what would be needed to buy parts economically, but that we were considering at least 1,000; that all we had was a very rough idea of parts and labor costs, so a selling price had yet to be firmed up. But I guaranteed not to give away gross margin to prove any points."

As he and Tandy walked up the stairs to the conference room, Kornfeld offered one final admission.

"Charles," he said, "this is the first product I've ever been involved with that has so many fundamental unknowns. But there is also one known. If the project does succeed, it would be like inheriting a Boeing 747 and, having decided to keep it, you're going to need spare parts, aviators, ground crew, hangars, extra long landing strips, and God knows what else, including lots of money."

When Tandy and Kornfeld entered the conference room, they found an assemblage on hand that included John Roach and Bernie Appel. Tandy seated himself at the head of the large oblong table that dominated the room.

The presentation began.

"First there was a kind of sales pitch by the technical people and the merchandising people," Roach recalled. "Through it all, Charles was puffing on his cigar and just kind of shaking his head. Typically, he didn't get involved in merchandise. He was not technical at all."

When the demonstration ended, there was a moment of silence. All eyes were riveted on Tandy. The tension in the air was excruciating. Then Tandy blew a cloud of smoke at the ceiling.

"It's interesting," he said. "It's different." He looked around the room. "How many of these do you think we should buy?"

Numbers were thrown out and Lew Kornfeld reiterated the 1,000-unit minimum he had mentioned earlier.

"Okay," Tandy said, "let's go with 1,000 machines. If we can't sell them, we can always use them in the stores for inventory."

As Tandy left the room, there was much handshaking and backslapping. "Everybody was happy," Roach said, "because now the development team knew it was going to get to build a computer."

A few days later, Roach walked into Kornfeld's office and told him, "Lew, we can't build 1,000 machines. In order to really meet our cost targets and get tooling and everything that we need to do, we're going to have to build 3,000 machines."

"That's fine," Kornfeld responded. "Let's build 3,000."

In his book, *To Catch A Mouse*, Kornfeld later wrote: "Radio Shack certainly hadn't determined the size of a possible microcomputer market when it put the TRS-80 into production in Fort Worth. The first production plan was for only 1,000 computers. The second production plan was for 3,000 computers. Neither the fiscal 1977 ad budget nor the fiscal year budget for the year beginning July 1, 1977 included funds dedicated to promoting the PC.

"But by September 1, 1977, when we saw everything was coming up roses, we hired new hands, rented new spaces, changed the rules for permissible dollar inventory levels in the stores, reserved a large ad a month for the TRS-80 in the monthly flyer, and included it in newspaper ads and inserts."

It was Kornfeld who named the product the TRS-80—"T" for Tandy and "RS" for Radio Shack. The "80" came from the Z-80 Zilog microprocessor.

"I decided to use Radio Shack instead of Micronta, our usual brand for serious technical items," Kornfeld said, "because here was a unique chance to make Radio Shack a manufacturing name in addition to its fame as a retailer."

Now began a race against time to bring the TRS-80 to market.

"The pressure of the upcoming electronics shows and the awareness that Commodore International and Apple were also about to bring out microcomputers, and the difficulty of keeping important secrets secret, convinced us we needed a firm kickoff date," Kornfeld disclosed.

The Warwick Hotel in New York was chosen as the site and August 3, 1977 as the date of the unveiling. But by early June, the TRS-80 production line was still dormant. Kornfeld, who had been promised he would have 50 units in hand by the beginning of June, was beginning to feel like a general anxiously awaiting the arrival of his missing army as D-Day approached.

Meantime, a decision was made to market the TRS-80 at a price of $599.95. Kornfeld described the reasoning behind the $599.95 price tag.

"Discovering that our price margin would not be torpedoed at $599.95 and on being assured by our factory that cost reduction would result from mass production and after tool cost write-off, I froze the price at $599.95 against all temptation, even after a savvy computer parts retailer reckoned that $1,000 to $1,200 was not only attainable but reasonable in view of the scarcity of competition. But on or near the market in modest quantity were the Commodore 'PET'; Apple II, which had color but lacked a video display and was more money; the Compucolor 8001 at $2,750, 'America's lowest-priced personal computer system with color vector graphics'; Processor Technology's Sol 20, advertised as 'The Small Computer' for $995 kit and $1,495 fully wired (less monitor); and a few others. Now did not seem to be the time to play 'Bet the Bank!' The one hundred dollars or more per system we might make if the business was out there might just be enough to kill the product. Why risk killing a product with so much going for it in technology, prestige and price?

"Note: Our median sales ticket at the time was a skimpy $29.95.

"In addition, whenever anyone produced a rabbit out of his hat in consumer electronics, 10 other companies would display their version of the bunny at the next industry show, and two would claim to have fathered it. Hence the rest of my rationale for $599.95. Hopefully, our modest price would help discourage the loft operator and low-ball importer from taking a ride on the high tech bandwagon for a few years."

Roach revealed an interesting sidelight to the TRS-80 story involving William H. Gates, who co-founded Microsoft Corporation in 1975 at the age of 19 and went on to become a multi-billionaire after Microsoft became the number one developer of computer software.

"Our original BASIC interpreter was written in-house, as there was not much else available," Roach reminisced on the 10th anniversary of the introduction of the TRS-80. "The debugging of that first BASIC almost led to a delay in the introduction, but at 3 o'clock one morning—just in time—that last 'bug' was found.

"As interest and momentum in the fledgling microcomputer industry began to increase, we invited Bill Gates to offer his Microsoft BASIC as Level II BASIC for the TRS-80. Microsoft was just a handful of people in those days led by Gates' dreams. The boyish Gates made an urgent trip to Fort Worth during the week of a family member's wedding to negotiate and 'sell' his BASIC. His BASIC was great, as was his grasp of software; but his negotiating was a little less than confident. With his one-and-a-half page agreement and a little negotiating, we agreed on a one-time charge. Later, when we introduced the Model III, Gates suggested that, perhaps, Microsoft should also receive a royalty or some additional compensation. It did. Bill and Microsoft have been among our longest term vendors in the microcomputer area and good friends to the company."

The TRS-80 was formally introduced at a press conference at the Warwick Hotel in New York on August 3, 1977, to the accompaniment of popping flashbulbs and radio and television coverage. It was greeted in the media as a breakthrough product as far as price was concerned.

One of the most comprehensive articles appeared in *Electronics* magazine.

"The world's largest retailer of electronics, the Radio Shack chain of more than 6,000 stores and outlets, has just entered the consumer-computer market," the article declared. "And it has done so not only with a microcomputer system that it designed itself, but with one that is the market's price leader—$599.95 buys a 12-inch cathode-ray-tube display, keyboard, and cassette tape recorder.

"Called the TRS-80, the microcomputer system is built around Zilog Corp.'s high-performance Z-80 microprocessor and comes with 4,096 bytes each of random-access and read-only memory. It is the easiest to set up and use of any microcomputer system now available. This is because its BASIC assembler is already in ROM and does not need to be loaded into memory. All that is needed is for the separate units to be plugged together. Turned on, the computer system responds by saying 'Ready'. The user then types in simple BASIC language statements either to create programs or to load the blackjack or backgammon programs supplied in the cassette that comes with the system."

The article stressed that the designers of the new computer had concentrated on keeping the machine simple and easy to operate. Another prerequisite was flexibility.

"The TRS-80 is designed with Radio Shack's own 48-line bus that allows peripherals to be daisy-chained together. You don't need an expander to add on peripherals. Each one simply plugs into the back of any other peripheral," the article quoted Don French, who was now the TRS-80 merchandising manager. "We designed our own bus so that each peripheral does its own interfacing, unlike the S-100 (hobbyists') bus, which has the central processing unit doing the work."

The article added:

"Radio Shack will make details of the bus available to enable users to interface peripherals of other makers easily. French also says he chose the Z-80 for its speed; its powerful instructions, which allow the BASIC interpreter to fit into only 4-K bits of ROM; and its single 5-volt supply requirement.

"Radio Shack is also planning to offer its own peripherals. One is a general-purpose expansion box that can be outfitted with additional memory—up to 62 kilobytes of RAM, which, with 12 kilobytes of additional internal ROM, will support extended BASIC and provide such capabilities as graphics, double-precision calculation, and analog interfacing.

"Among other peripheral products to be available are a miniature-floppy disk drive and a dot-matrix impact printer. The drive, which will store 90 kilobytes in a single-sided, single-density format, will be priced below those available on today's market."

An article in the *Fort Worth Star-Telegram* said of the TRS-80, "It appears to be a cassette recorder, a 12-inch television set and a typewriter keyboard flanked by gray cords. The cassette recorder is for program storage. A 300-page manual is offered for those who wish to do their own programming. But for others who have a tough time even using an adding machine, Radio Shack is offering some already prepared programs on cassette tape. These include programs for playing blackjack and backgammon, teaching multiplication and subtraction, and storing menus and conversion tables."

The article concluded: "The TRS-80 may not look like a computer, but it sure is beginning to act like one."

The public relations fallout from the introduction of the TRS-80 exceeded all expectations. Charles Tandy alluded to this in a speech at M.I.T. in 1978.

"We got $50 million worth of free publicity out of it," he reported.

John Roach recalled that the public relations aspects of the TRS-80 figured in Tandy's thinking when he initially approved putting the product into production.

"When he gave us the go-ahead to produce the 1,000 units, he told us, 'It's got to be a good publicity deal,'" Roach said.

No one anticipated the extraordinary success the TRS-80 achieved, Roach declared. He told of a conversation he had with Tandy about a month after the TRS-80's introduction.

"Charles had been invited to make a speech in Dallas and he asked me to go with him," Roach related. "He said, 'You've got to come with me. I don't know anything about computers. I'll make a speech and then you show them the machine and talk about it.'"

On the drive to Dallas, Roach told Tandy, "With the phone calls we're getting, with the publicity we're getting, with the amount of orders coming in, I think we've really got something hot, even if we don't have anything to ship."

Tandy responded, "Well, I'm not sure. I hope you're right."

"He was still, even at that point, not overly confident," Roach went on. "None of us knew that we had something that was going to be as significant as it was or that a new industry was starting that was going to be as important as it turned out to be. We didn't have any great visionary among us who said, 'God, we're fixing to do something that's going to be really significant.' We thought we had a good product that was of interest to the traditional Radio Shack customer, and at $600 we hoped we could sell it."

The TRS-80 was an instantaneous hit, but when the orders starting pouring in there was no way to keep up with the demand.

"Our first team of seven builders and designers had only grown to 15," Lew Kornfeld noted, "and the first off-the-line TRS-80 was a breech delivery on September 15. They came out one-a-day until September 20, when 21 computers got built. The month's grand total was a measly 130. October was better by a factor of three times. Back orders were growing like crazy—a new experience for Radio Shack since its turbulent mail order days. Now, just to get on our waiting list, you had to ante up a 10 percent deposit as a token of your sincere intention to become an owner. By November, we were oversold and flooded with inquiries. Orders were being filled on a first-come, first-served basis, and we were warning people that to give a TRS-80 for Christmas would take fast action."

Although the TRS-80 was an "immediate success," Roach reported, "market awareness was very low. So, in the spring of 1978, we began a series of barnstorming meetings around the country to build awareness. We set up 30 to 50 computers in a hotel and invited the media, the financial community and the public to see and use a microcomputer. This activity played a vital role in the rapid development of the market."

Kornfeld elaborated on the barnstorming project in his book.

"Few people in the entire country had ever seen or touched a computer, much less thought of owning or using one, not at $599.95, not at any price. So we decided to take the TRS-80 and a cadre of handlers and talkers on the road with a series of shows that began in March, 1978. By then, six months after the assembly line had begun to churn in earnest, our computer manufacturing employees had grown from 7 to 385, the factory size from 15,000 to 85,000 square feet, and the back orders from a pile to a mountain.

"These traveling shows, nicknamed 'computer blitzes,' were first planned for the 50 largest domestic SMSA markets. We began with Phoenix which, though only No. 28 in metro ranking, had the advantage of being a good Radio Shack city. It was near enough for an out-of-town rehearsal and blessed with warm weather, so snow couldn't postpone the show. The problem of simultaneously trying to sell TRS-80s in Phoenix while the waiting list was growing in Fort Worth was solved by filling all the Phoenix back orders first and planting enough on the local shelves to fill all new Phoenix orders resulting from the blitz. City by city, we blitzed, filled, stocked and sold on a local basis, while the national program continued on its 'backorderly' way.

"The blitz budget was based on an arbitrary per-store basis: $600 per store in Phoenix-size cities to $1,000 per store in the biggest markets. Phoenix had 36 company stores in March, 1978, so about $21,600 was spent there and in other similar-size cities on media, travel and entertainment.

"Personal invitations were sent to 5,000 customers selected on a basis of recency and frequency, plus a stack of recent mail inquiries.

"Newspaper, TV and radio ads and direct mail literature were created. The kickoff newspaper ad was ¾ of a page.

"A press kit was prepared that included a TRS-80 brochure and catalog, the Tandy annual report and one of Radio Shack's famous free 5-cell flashlights.

"We blitzed once in March, 1978, four times in April, six times in May, seven times in June, eight times in July, seven times in August. By November, we had blitzed 101 times (up from the original plan of 50) which, at two days per blitz, equaled 202 show days."

Hundreds of thousands of people, most of whom had never even seen a computer before, flocked to the shows to take advantage of the opportunity of actually using one of the demonstration machines. Nationwide, the $2.1 million blitz resulted in thousands of TRS-80 sales. Kornfeld estimated that more than 3,100 company-owned Radio Shack stores benefited directly from the blitz by being located in or close to cities where the shows were held.

"Before 1978 was over," Kornfeld reported, "there wasn't a store in our entire system that hadn't sold a TRS-80."

Kornfeld recalled an experience that illustrated the popularity of the TRS-80. He was on a buying trip in Japan in October, 1977, when the phone rang in his room at the Royal Hotel in Okasaka at 7 a.m.

"This is Mr. Z in Florida and I have a complaint about your computer."

"What's your problem?"

"I need one this week."

"We're filling orders on a first-come, first-served basis."

"I know that, but I'm about two months down on your list."

"So you'll get it in two months."

"That's not good enough."

"Look, Mr. Z, I really do appreciate your interest in our merchandise, so I'm going to give you the name and phone number of my executive vice president in Fort Worth. Call him and see if he's a softer touch than I am."

Three days later, Kornfeld was in the Hotel Okura in Tokyo when his phone rang again at 7 o'clock in the morning. It was Mr. Z again.

"Didn't you call that guy in Texas?" Kornfeld asked.

"I did. And he told me the same thing you did...to wait."

"I can't believe you'd phone me here in Japan just to tell me the obvious. Is there more?"

There was, Kornfeld reported. "The guy said he was going to sue us. On what grounds, I couldn't imagine."

Very few products, if any, were ever received with such enthusiasm by the buying public that would-be customers were even threatening lawsuits to move up on the waiting list.

Chapter 27
"The Biggest Name in Little Computers"

The age of the personal computer dawned, and PCs suddenly were a hot new item in the mass media.

Time magazine was one of the first national publications to get into the act with an article on September 5, 1977, under the headline, "Plugging in Everyman." A subhead spoke of "Cheap computers that balance checkbooks and water lawns."

The article told about Michael Mastrangelo, a Manhattan audiovisual consultant, who had a new "servant" in his home, an $11,000 custom-built computer that kept the temperature and humidity at desired levels, put his favorite music on the stereo as he pulled his car into the driveway, phoned him at the office in case of fire or burglary, awakened him in the morning, briefed him on his day's business appointments, reminded him that his car needed an oil change, watered the lawn, and cooked his dinner.

Several other "computer addicts" were featured in the article, including Robert Goodyear, a Framingham, Massachusetts, physicist, who used his machine to type and edit his personal correspondence; Joseph J. Sanger, a Manhattan physician, who cross-indexed his medical journals to provide him with instant, tailor-made refresher courses on any disease he asked for; Irving Osser, a ham radio operator in Beverly Hills, who maintained a log of the people he talked to on his radio; and Robert Phillips of Chicago, who had terminals in every room of his apartment, using them to dim and brighten his lights, tune in his stereo, turn his television on and off, and open and close his drapes.

The article quoted a forecast from Byron Kirkwood, a Dallas microcomputer retailer: "Some day soon every home will have a computer. It will be as standard as a toilet."

On November 21, 1977, a lengthy article on microcomputers in *U.S. News & World Report* was illustrated by a photograph of a man in his shirtsleeves, coffee cup at his side, seated in front of a TRS-80 in the kitchen of his home, while his smiling spouse prepared dinner. The caption underneath the photo read, "Radio Shack's new microcomputer, used here to help manage family finances, is a hot seller at just under $600." The headline over the article asked the rhetorical question, "Soon: A Computer In Every Home?"

U.S. News was as ardent as *Time* over the outlook for the PC. "Computers that can fit on a corner of a desk are showing up in fast-growing numbers of small shops, professional offices, even living rooms," the magazine enthused. "As they do, a major new branch of the electronics industry—microcomputers—is being created almost overnight, with potential markets measured in the billions of dollars per year. Like its big brother in big business, the small computer can keep track of payrolls, inventories and investment portfolios. But the microcomputer version is also compact enough to be used in the home to maintain Christmas card lists, family budgets or collections of favorite recipes.

"Possible applications of the desk-top computer seem almost limitless. New ideas flow in a flood from crowded conferences on personal computing being held around the country. Computer clubs are sprouting all over. A dozen or so magazines on personal computing have been started in the past few months. About 25,000 microcomputers will be sold this year and four times that number next year at prices ranging from $275 to $5,000. Frank J. Burge of Regis McKenna, Inc., a computer public relations firm in Palo Alto, Calif., predicts that by 1985 the market for microcomputers for use in the home will exceed $1.5 billion a year, and the market for microcomputers adaptable for small business applications an additional $800 million.

"The production of microcomputers was dominated by small firms, selling mainly through electronics shops, until the fall of 1977. Now large manufacturers such as RCA, Tandy, and others have moved into the field. The Radio Shack chain began selling a computing system this fall for a little less than $600. Radio Shack says its shops are swamped with orders."

The Albany, Oregon, *Democrat-Herald*, which featured the TRS-80 in an article on PCs, quoted the following forecast from Curtis Cook, the acting chairman of the computer science department at Oregon

State University: "The average American is on the verge of having the computer enter his home. The computer is going to come in just like the calculator did. It won't be as fast, but it will come. The reason is because they can manufacture them so cheap. They can manufacture a whole bunch of small chips—the same thing as your small calculator."

Dick Heiser, who had opened the nation's first retail computer store in Santa Monica, California in 1975, was quoted in *The Los Angeles Herald Examiner* as predicting that in 10 years, "50 million Americans are going to own two computers each—one at home and one at work."

"The lid is off," Theodore Nelson, author of a book on computers, declared. "There is going to be an avalanche in computers as there was with hi-fi, calculators and CB radios."

By the end of October, 1977, only three months after the advent of the TRS-80, more than 37,000 inquiries had been received about the new product, with most of the queries coming from small businesses, Charles Tandy reported. "The orders are flocking in," Tandy enthused to Larry Roquemore, a *Star-Telegram* business writer. "We smell something big here."

The response to the new product was so heavy, Tandy revealed, that one individual placed an order for 10,000 machines. "But we had to quash the deal," he said, "when we found out that the guy dealt in mail-order electronics kits."

Wall Street also appeared appreciative of the long-term benefits that the TRS-80 promised.

On August 29, 1977, the *Wall Street Transcript* published the contents of a report by Thomas H. Mack and Margo N. Alexander of Mitchell, Hutchins, Inc., that claimed the significance of the introduction of the TRS-80 was that Radio Shack, a national retail chain, made the commitment to build and sell an inexpensive home computer. This indicated that the economic feasibility of a $600 simple computer was here.

"Mack and Alexander think Tandy will be another major beneficiary of this potentially explosive home computer market," the *Wall Street Transcript* maintained. "They believe Tandy's extensive in-place distribution network provides cost savings and should allow the company to quickly build up expertise and related product efficiencies. The analysts note that some critics of Tandy have suggested that consumers will not trade up at Radio Shack, because products there are not perceived to be of high quality. Consumer acceptance of this new $600 sophisticated product, they say, will test the validity of this reservation."

Meantime, TRS-80 sales continued to boom, overcoming such setbacks as a severe production backlog that was encountered during the spring of 1978. Lew Kornfeld recalled how the immediate acceptance of the TRS-80 by the buying public reminded him of the beginning of the CB radio boom.

"The memories of the CB were fresh on my mind when Radio Shack entered the PC marketplace," he said. "We were back in the driver's seat again, but there was a glorious difference between the fizzled CB and the emergent PC booms. The TRS-80 and its ilk were serious products, designed not for chit-chat, not for useful short range communications, but as permanent parts of the permanent processes of educational and professional life.

"The PC could handle the storage, retrieval and manipulation of essential data; the performance of repetitive tasks such as payrolls, mailing list labels, processing receipts and invoices. The little computer was faster, cheaper and more accurate than most 'by hand' procedures. But, once built into one's life, it needed to remain 'up and running'; service had to be almost instantaneous; fixes had to stay fixed; bugs had to stay debugged. The utility of a computer was dependent upon the software developed for it, and it was not enough to talk software. It, too, had to be ready to 'up and run.'"

Kornfeld exhibited a prescience in a commentary about the TRS-80 he wrote for the 1977 Tandy Annual Report. "The market we foresee," he opined, "is businesses, schools, services and hobbyists. The market others apparently foresee is 'in-home'—computers used for recipes, income tax, games, etc. We think home use is a later generation happening."

More than a decade later, the "computer in every home" forecast remained, like former President Herbert Hoover's 1932 campaign prediction of "a chicken in every pot," an unfulfilled promise.

The success of the TRS-80 was the number one topic at the annual meeting in Fort Worth on November 11, 1977, attended by the largest number of shareholders in company history who gathered on the still unfinished seventh floor of One Tandy Center. An upbeat Charles Tandy reported that 80 to 100 computers a day were currently being produced. "We have a tremendous backlog," he exulted.

"Last year was the best year ever for the company," Tandy told the shareholders in his opening remarks. "Our cash flow is generating more money than we're spending for expansion." Radio Shack, he said, planned to add 1,000 new stores in fiscal 1978, down slightly from the 1,200 new outlets opened in fiscal 1977. The reason for the decrease, he explained, was the difficulty being experienced in finding suitable and affordable locations.

"But we've got more outlets than any company in the world," he said proudly. "That's a far cry from the 9 outlets we had just 14 years ago."

At the close of the meeting, Tandy called on Jim West for a few words. The peppery vice chairman received an ovation from the audience when he concluded his remarks, "Our stock is the best on the market. Over the years, I've received advice to sell it, but I've never sold a share of my Tandy stock. I've only added to it."

On that high note, a broadly-grinning Tandy adjourned the meeting. It would be the last annual meeting over which Charles Tandy would preside.

* * *

Despite Jim West's optimistic appraisal, Tandy stock was deep in the doldrums, along with the rest of the stock market, at the time of the annual meeting. The Dow-Jones industrial average had dropped almost 20 percent during the first 10 months of 1977, and *New York Times* business columnist Robert Metz took note of what was happening in his column of October 24 about undervalued stocks. The column contained a nice plug for Tandy.

"When stock prices are falling, investors naturally regard the market with apprehension, few having the fortitude to buy for fear of continued selling," Metz wrote. "However, there are those who see down markets as offering an opportunity to buy stocks at relatively low prices. Some believe that there are hundreds of undervalued stocks, now that price multiples of 4 to 5 times anticipated earnings are commonplace.

"Raymond Frankel, president of the Technological Investors Management Corporation, which manages some $20 million, primarily for individual investors, asserts that this year's market weakness means that dozens of growing companies are selling at price-earnings multiples rarely available. Mr. Frankel conceded that many stocks he now favored had fallen on hard times. Some of his current choices are selling at multiples that he says do not reflect their growth potential for the years immediately ahead.

"For example, Mr. Frankel favors the Tandy Corporation, the shares of which fell out of bed in reaction to the collapse in the Citizen's Band radio market. Mr. Frankel said that CB radios represented a maximum of 25 percent of Tandy's volume in the spring of 1976 and had dropped to half that level a year later when the bottom fell out of the CB market.

"Tandy shares, meanwhile, dropped from a peak of 42⅞—when it was obviously overpriced, according to Mr. Frankel—to a low of 21. Meanwhile, Tandy earnings increased from $3.55 in the fiscal year ended June 30, 1976 to $4.34 for the just-completed fiscal year. At last Friday's price of 26¾ then, the stock is selling at less than 5 times anticipated earnings of more than $6 a share in the current fiscal year.

"Tandy's strength lies in its comprehensive monitoring of data on store operations, product lines, market penetration, and incentive pay to store managers, Mr. Frankel said, adding that the company's remarkable growth should continue for some years to come. Obviously, not everyone agrees with Mr. Frankel, and some regard Tandy as vulnerable now that debt has been increased by $100 million in connection with tenders of its own shares."

The Metz column and a subsequent one on November 28 that discussed Tandy's rationale for its stock repurchase program had a salutary effect on the stock price. By early January, Tandy rebounded to 35, helped along by a pivotal announcement that for the first time in company history the billion-dollar barrier in annual sales had been breached. Consolidated sales for the 12 months ended December 31, 1977, had totaled $1.014 billion.

In early March of 1978, Tandy received another boost when it was selected as one of the six best stocks among Fort Worth-based firms by a panel of regional brokerage house representatives. Tandy was the only nonpetroleum company among the analysts' favorites.

"The kicker is Tandy's minicomputer," noted Jim Phillips of Rauscher Pierce. "They are 10 to 12 weeks behind on deliveries and the market seems to be growing fast. Some sources have estimated that in the next five years, 80 percent of the households in the nation will have some sort of minicomputer. If that is only half right, it can be a tremendous new piece of business for Tandy."

Reporting on the survey, Herb Owens, the *Star-Telegram* business editor, wrote: "The respected Value Line Investment Survey reports that Tandy's return on net worth and its return on total capital are a little short of phenomenal. It enjoys a premier position in the burgeoning field of consumer electronics and seems to be doing everything it can to capitalize on that position for the benefit of shareholders."

Financial World chipped in with a tribute to Charles Tandy in an article on March 15 that called him "a born salesman" and "a marketing genius." Tandy Corporation, the magazine declared, "is one of the top growth companies of the decade in sales and profits and an investor's delight."

The article attributed Tandy's success to his ability to keep a tight rein on the company's purse strings. "We started off with no money, so the use of capital was one of the major criteria to measure the ability of our people," it quoted Tandy. "If you turn a decorator loose on a store, you can spend $150,000 easily. That's going to hit your return on capital pretty hard. So we got by for years on $12,000 per store for signs and fixtures. People didn't mind because we weren't selling fixtures."

In early April, Tandy journeyed to Cambridge, Massachusetts, for a talk at the Massachusetts Institute of Technology. In the course of his hour-long presentation, he reminisced about the birth of the TRS-80 and waxed enthusiastic about its early acceptance in the marketplace.

"This past year, in August, we introduced this thing," he said. "We had news conferences and press releases sitting in the Warwick Hotel in New York. We are at one-half the price of the regular market, the closest guy to us. We didn't try to see how far up we could get it. What I wanted to know was, 'Can I get a decent profit?' 'Can I make a sale in here?' We've got a waiting list for these machines. And we're entering a field that absolutely, up till now, there's been no place for us.

"This is where we spend our money—in researching and thinking. And we've got men, a small team. It only took two men to develop that darn computer. Now, that's a little bit of an exaggeration, because we worked with National Semiconductor and Fairchild and Texas Instruments. I don't know how many geniuses. They're the people who knew all the about the chips and all the gut work. We got around to some of the people that make printers. We wanted to talk in terms of three, four, five, six thousand. Well, most of the time, computer companies don't call for that many in a year. We're calling for that many in a month. We're going to make them available to a lot of people. We're going to make them available to businessmen who have never had a chance, that could not afford a computer.

"We think we've got something here that's going to be distributed in a different fashion than our competitors. I say competitors. IBM is our competitor. They don't even know we're in business. (Chuckle). But, in our field, we don't plan to put on all that service that they put on. We don't plan to put on all that programming expense that they put on. They can't put anything out there under about four or five thousand dollars a month. Well, we're gonna put it out there for a total cost of, maybe, $3,500. Total cost. Now, if they came after this kind of business, they're not geared this way.

"We've got 7,000 stores. We're in every village and hamlet all the way from the top of Maine to Nome, Alaska. And they're not going to be running a guy up there. Their custom is sending men out as salesmen, properly attired, making big presentations, because they're after big sales. You can't afford to travel a man all up and down the highways for a $600 transaction. It costs too much money. Having our distribution system gives us the shortest distance between our point of manufacture and the public. And for that reason, we think we'll have a place, a long-time place.

"We're not going to compete with Digital. We're not going to compete with these systems, compete with these big guys. We've got our own little group of small business people who don't want to spend a lot of money, for whom we're prepared to manufacture, and our idea is to fit that size market."

Tandy also made reference in the speech to a Standard & Poor report that had ranked Tandy Corporation number one in five-year growth in earnings among all of the corporations listed on the New York Stock Exchange.

"Our five-year growth rate is 39.7 percent," he reported. "K-Mart, which is a name you know, that last five years has had a 19.5 percent growth rate; Long's Drugs, 19.5; Jack Eckerd, 19; Skaggs, 19; Petrie Stores, 18.9; Melville Shoe Corp., a New England company, Thom McAn Shoes, 16.1. Out of all of them, we're number one.

"Standard & Poor put all those corporations into a computer and brought up all those that had a 10-year record of unbroken growth. Then they put those back into the computer and picked out the companies that had the largest percentage growth in the last five years. Out of all the corporations on the New York Stock Exchange, Tandy Corporation ended up number one. And all this is based on Radio Shack, a company that was broke.

"In pre-tax income per share earnings' growth, Tandy Corporation has had 59.5 percent over the past five years. Skaggs has had 29.7; Edison Brothers, 28.8; Dayton-Hudson, 23.9; K-Mart, 19.7; Standard

Brands, 18.4; Long's Drugs, 17.8. That was not earnings per share; that was pre-tax income. Earnings per share is practically the same. We're at 56.9, K-Mart was at 18, Petrie Stores at 25, Edison Brothers at 25, Dayton-Hudson at 21. These are fine companies we're comparing ourselves with, the best in the business."

The institutional investors who had turned bearish on Tandy after its $100 million stock buyback with borrowed funds in July 1977 were looking at the company more benignly in the spring of 1978. With the price of the stock back up to 37⅛, *Business Week* on April 17, reported that Tandy was back in good favor on Wall Street.

"Tandy has shown that its gross margins are more than adequate to absorb the increased interest expenses that were incurred last summer when the company borrowed to buy back its stock," the magazine declared. "Earnings per share are now expected to climb to around $5.65 or $5.70 for the 1978 fiscal year ending June 30, compared with $4.34 last year. Debt charges on the new debt will come to only 73 cents a share. And several analysts are forecasting that the company may be able to earn as much as $7 or more the following year. What looked like problems to some investors last summer and fall, now look increasingly like intelligent strategic moves."

"What excites analysts is Tandy's apparently firm hold on the consumer electronics business, which has been growing at about twice the GNP rate over the last five years and is expected to continue to outpace the rest of the economy through the next decade as the young adult population swells in size. Radio Shack's share of this $10 billion-a-year business has grown from about 1 percent in 1968 to nearly 10 percent. As a result, Tandy's sales have been rising at a compounded growth rate of about 31 percent per year in the last five years, and its earnings have grown at an even faster pace."

On April 26, the *United States Investor*, a weekly periodical published in Boston, credited the favorable publicity Tandy was receiving with boosting the price of its stock to 39. The publication called it "a remarkable recovery following the adverse news on its Citizen's Band operation."

The following day, came a plug that couldn't have been any stronger had it been written by Charles Tandy himself. The author was A.R. Douglas, an associate in the New York Stock Exchange firm of John Muir & Co. and a syndicated business columnist, who informed his readers:

"We all dream of finding the 'next IBM,' a stock you could have bought in the past decades at any price with a reasonable expectation of future enormous profits. Such a stock and its group may now be in sight. It's the domestic mini-computer stock group. The rate of technical advances taking place in the computer science area generally is on the order of astronomical. A warehouse-sized vacuum tube computer of two decades ago today is reduced to a much more efficient black box on a desk. All largely because of packing informational ability on the order of tens of thousands of bits into a silicon thing the size of a teardrop.

"One immensely promising goal—a mini-computer in your house to help run your house and your life for you, selling for less than a window air-conditioner. To wake you up in the morning, check and anticipate your shopping, your bank account, your health perhaps, your income taxes and on and on, you name it, a new indispensable. It's coming. The investment question is which of perhaps hundreds of stocks to play. Which automobile stock would you have liked back in the early 1920s?

"I opt for Tandy Corporation (NYSE - 38) for the long, long range pull. Over the past decades, it has made fortunes for true believer investors. Tandy manufactures some 40 percent of its electronic product mix, buys the rest at wholesale and retails the lot through its 7,000 Radio Shack outlets. Current sales come to around a billion dollars, up from $117 million in 1968. Sales are worldwide. The stock now sells at a low 7.7 times earnings multiple. Recent earnings history, $4.34 for 1977, an estimated $5.85 for this year ended June and shooting for $7 in 1979 on 11.8 million shares outstanding. Debt is $250 million. Some 92 institutions own 28 percent of the shares. Management is considered excellent. The company is rushing full speed into the microcomputer area. There are 18,000 employees and 16,000 shareholders.

"There is one caveat which helps account for its relatively low P/E multiple. While the company has a long history of stock splits and stock dividends, it has never declared a cash dividend and has averred no intention of doing so."

By the second week of May, Tandy stock was trading at $40 a share, paving the way for another two-for-one stock split, the fourth since April, 1969. The announcement came in a tersely-worded news release on May 12.

"The Board of Directors of Tandy Corporation today declared a two for one stock split-up in the form of a dividend, to be effected by the distribution of one additional share of Tandy Corporation common stock, $1.00 par value, for each share of common stock outstanding. The distribution is expected to be made on June 30, 1978 to stockholders of record on May 31, 1978.

"On March 31, 1978, 11,987,000 shares of common stock were outstanding exclusive of Treasury stock."

Garland P. Asher, Tandy's director of financial planning, gave four reasons for the stock split in a newspaper interview.

1. The company had retired about 10 million shares over the past four years, decreasing the number of shares outstanding to 11.9 million.

2. A stock split would increase the stock's liquidity in that more shares would be traded at the lower price.

3. The split would increase "retail," or individual stock ownership, as opposed to the trading volume generated mainly by institutional investors who usually dealt in higher-priced stocks.

4. The split would foster a "broader ownership," both in number of stockholders and in their geographical location.

At the request of the *Fort Worth Star-Telegram*, Asher made a calculation of the effects of the latest stock split and the three prior ones on a hypothetical investment in Tandy Corporation stock, taking into account the spin-offs of Tandy Brands, Tandycrafts and Stafford-Lowdon.

An owner of 100 shares of Tandy stock before the first stock split in April, 1969 would have, after the latest split, 1,600 shares of Tandy stock, 200 shares of Tandycrafts, 80 shares of Tandy Brands and 50 shares of Stafford-Lowdon, he reported.

During 1968, Tandy stock sold in the $6 to $12 per share price range. Pegging it at a mid-number of $10 per share, a 100-share lot would have had a market value of $1,000.

At the current market, Asher advised, Tandy was selling at $40 per share, Tandycrafts at $17.12, Tandy Brands at $10.75 and Stafford-Lowdon at $11.50. This would give the portfolio a market value of $67,860.

"Buy my stock and I'll make you rich," Charles Tandy had exhorted his people. Those who had followed his advice had reason to rejoice.

The stock split had preceded Charles' 60th birthday by three days, and as he said later, "It was the best birthday present I ever gave myself."

But the extravaganza that Anne Tandy threw for him at their home on Monday night, May 15, qualified as the best birthday party he ever had.

Faced with the problem of what to give a man who has everything, Anne came up with something she could be reasonably certain Charles did not already possess—a real live elephant, replete with a mahout, a couple of shovel-bearing retainers and several buckets.

A delighted Tandy then donned maharajah's garb and clambered aboard the rented elephant for a couple of laps around the courtyard of the Westover Hills mansion, while the several hundred guests cheered. In designing the courtyard, I.M. Pei couldn't have had an elephant in mind, but the space was more than adequate. Later in the evening, as the party progressed, a 4-by-4-foot box was brought into the spacious living room for Tandy to open. When he did, out sprang a bikini-clad beauty who embraced and kissed the honoree. Topping off the festivities were a pair of belly dancers.

Among the multitude of presents stacked up in a corner of the living room, two matching boxes especially caught Tandy's eye. They had been decorated to look like the twin towers of the Tandy Center and were the gifts of Nancy Lee and Perry Bass. Charles wore a beribboned badge on the lapel of his jacket as he cut the birthday cake that contained fondant fruit and flowers, but no candles. On the badge were the letters, "VIP".

It was his moment to savor. And there was so much to celebrate, so much to anticipate.

On August 11, 1978, Tandy Corporation announced 1978 fiscal year sales of $1.059 billion, a 12 percent increase over fiscal 1977, and earnings of $2.75 per share, up 32 percent from the $2.09 reported in the prior year. And on August 23, came an announcement that Tandy planned to open 50 Radio Shack Computer Centers in the nation's top markets during the 1979 fiscal year. Each center combined a store, service facility, schoolroom, and display facility, selling and servicing computers and offering courses in how to run and program them.

"While some of the stores will be located within new or existing Radio Shack stores, most will be separate entities, and within each computer center we expect to see at least one sales manager with extensive computer experience," Lew Kornfeld was quoted in the news release announcing the computer centers.

There were no longer any concerns about having to use the TRS-80s to keep track of store inventories. The TRS-80 was on the way to becoming the hottest-selling PC in the country, with the largest share of the burgeoning personal computer market. Soon, Tandy Corporation would be calling itself "The biggest name in little computers."

Charles Tandy was featured in two glowing magazine articles. In August, *Financial World* published an account of his success in marketing electronics at popular prices. "When you ask Charles Tandy how he turned his Tandy Corporation into such a fabulous growth company (No. 8 this year, No. 9 last)," the article began, "he quips, 'I've been doing it for 30 years. It's a habit.' Then he bursts into happy laughter and qualifies his statement, 'We spend a lot of time on forward planning, and a large percent of our budget goes to advertising.'

"Tandy figured out the right formula for Radio Shack years ago," the article continued. "He puts his stores on known streets and keeps them small. His overhead is also kept in check in terms of both rent and salaries. But the key is in his hiring the most aggressive managers he can find and promising them the chance to make a lot of money. And many of them have. Store managers and other executives are on an extremely complicated bonus plan, which has resulted in 60 of them becoming millionaires. Assisting the stores is a nationwide TV and radio ad campaign that has truly made Radio Shack a household word. Further easing the manager's job is the central computer operation which takes each store's inventory automatically four times a year and ships new supplies as they are needed. Weekly and monthly sales reports are carefully reviewed to spot any potential problems.

"Despite the elaborate use of computers and other advanced management techniques, Tandy Corp. remains a very informal operation. Charles Tandy is known to arrive at headquarters and then wander around the offices talking to executives and secretaries alike for an hour or so before ever entering his office. He does not hesitate to personally call a store manager to congratulate or criticize him. With all of its growth, Tandy has a very clear idea of how he wants every facet of his company run. And rest assured things are done his way. Tandy's philosophy is: 'If things cost less, then more people can afford to buy them.' Accordingly, he keeps the prices in his stores as low as possible. To accomplish this he began importing from the Far East, and more recently started manufacturing some of his product lines.

"Tandy's vision of the future is optimistic. 'We are still looking for places to open stores and ways to refine our product lines.' He pauses. 'Electronics is a fascinating business. We're still getting new technology from the exotic field of space research. Whoever thought we'd see a $600 computer? Well, we have one now.'"

In September, Tandy's beaming countenance graced the cover of *Texas Business*. The accompanying caption stated: "Charles D. Tandy: $816,000 a Year." The magazine named him as the highest-paid chief executive officer of a major publicly-held company in Texas, topping the total compensation of the CEOs of such much larger Texas-based corporations as Tenneco, Halliburton, Dresser Industries, Texas Instruments, and Shell Oil.

"Charles Tandy can't complain about his compensation," the *Texas Business* article declared. "But his shareholders can't complain much either. Return on average shareholders equity has more than quadrupled over the last five years, rising from 8.7 percent in fiscal 1972 to 37.2 percent in fiscal 1977. For the second year in a row, Tandy Corp. was the only retailer in the New York Stock Exchange to record an after-tax return in excess of 30 percent."

In early September, Tandy picked up nationwide press coverage by proposing a constitutional amendment that would put a ceiling on federal spending. In a talk before the Southwest Council of the American Electronics Association, he urged that federal expenditures be limited each year to 20 percent of the gross national product of the previous year.

"There is no doubt that the federal government can operate in peacetime with expenditures of less than 20 percent of the GNP," he declared. "It did so until 1967. Since then, federal expenditures, as a percentage of the gross national product, have generally been above 20 percent. In each of the past four years, federal expenditures have climbed to 22 percent or 23 percent of the gross national product. Applying this proposed limitation to 1979 federal expenditures, and estimating the gross national product at $2 trillion to $3 trillion dollars, the United States would have $460 billion with which to operate in 1979. By the time such a constitutional amendment could be ratified and placed into effect, the GNP would probably be well over $2.5 trillion per year, and the limit on federal expenditures would then be $500 billion. That is as much government as most citizens are willing to pay for."

Passage of such an amendment, besides giving apoplexy to a few free-spending politicians, Tandy maintained, "would do more than anything else I can think of to preserve what's left of our nation's free enterprise system. Why do I say this? Because it would bring excessive federal taxation to a grinding halt. When a nation taxes individuals and corporations at an excessive rate, it discourages investment and expansion. When taxes on profits reach a point where the risk is not worth the reward—and we are approaching that point in this country—our private enterprise system will be well on its way to extinction."

In his own company, however, Tandy had no qualms about going into debt.

On September 7, Tandy Corporation announced it intended to sell at least $75 million of convertible subordinated debentures through underwriters later in the year, with the proceeds being utilized to reduce outstanding long-term bank debt and provide greater flexibility for the future expansion of the business. After meeting with the underwriters in New York, the amount of the offering was increased to $100 million. The 6½ percent debentures, due in the year 2003, were convertible into Tandy Corporation common stock at the rate of $29 a share, which represented a 14.85 percent premium over the closing price of 25¼ of Tandy stock the day before.

The debentures sold out the same day they were offered on October 25, 1978, even though declining stock prices and rising interest rates might have been expected to dampen market enthusiasm for convertible debt issues. The sellout demonstrated anew Charles Tandy's impeccable timing. The issue was planned for sometime during the week, with no specific date set. But after the Dow-Jones industrial index registered a technical uptick of around one point on October 24, following a decline of around 60 points in the prior week, the debentures were priced for offering the next day.

For Charles Tandy, it would be the last convertible debenture offering that he would orchestrate.

He was running out of time.

Chapter 28
"Goodbye, Charlie"

The opening of the new corporate headquarters atop One Tandy Center in January, 1978 had been a nostalgic occasion for Charles Tandy, evoking the memory of Tandy Leather Company's move uptown from 15th and Throckmorton Streets more than a quarter-century earlier. As he had escorted visitors through the premises, he had often mentioned how much he wished Dave Tandy could see the twin towers overlooking the site of the company's former home at 2nd and Throckmorton.

"I bet he'd be proud," Tandy had said. "But I'm glad he doesn't know what it cost."

Janet Lesok, Tandy's secretary, recalled, "He was really proud of the Tandy Center. He really loved it." The weekend before the move, she had hauled boxes of files and supplies to Tandy's new office so that he "could sit down behind his desk on Monday morning." The floors weren't finished and there was dust everywhere, but Tandy was determined he was going to be at his desk among the stacks of boxes.

"He wasn't even able to find his telephone, but he never said a thing, never complained. He was so happy to be sitting at that desk in his new office," she recalled. One incident of that period, what she called "a quiet moment together," remained sharply etched in Mrs. Lesok's memory.

"This was in the winter and it had snowed," she said. "I had walked into his office with something and he was standing at the window just looking out, and he said, 'Come over here, Janet, I want to show you something.' I walked over to the window and he said, 'I want you to study the footprints in the snow and tell me how many people you think are parking on that parking lot down there.' He was trying to figure out how many Tandy people were patronizing the paid parking lot across the street from the Tandy Center or were using the free parking on the other side of the river and riding the subway to the Tandy Center. He was very proud of being able to provide that free parking for our people.

"I'll never forget him standing there counting feet in the snow. His mind just worked like that. 'If these people are parking here, what's the ratio to folks parking on the subway parking lot across the river?'"

She recalled another incident shortly after the move to the Tandy Center, when a cattle truck overturned. "There were a bunch of New Yorkers in the office visiting Charles, and one of them looked out of the window and saw all these cattle roaming around downtown Fort Worth. He began to yell, 'Cows, cows, there are cows in the street.' Charles reacted as if nothing unusual was going on. He said, 'It happens every day, every day about this time.'"

She laughed as she recalled the problem Tandy had coping with the sophisticated new telephone system that had been installed in his new office. "He never got the hang of calling me on my extension. So you know what he did? He'd call the main operator and ask for me by name. Three-quarters of the time when he tried to do something the least bit fancy with the phones, he'd disconnect people with whom he was talking, people in New York and all over the world. Here's a man who could memorize a P&L statement in seven minutes, but couldn't figure out the telephone system."

Tandy loved to drink coffee, and he drank it all day long out of a big thermos that Mrs. Lesok filled in the morning and refilled in the afternoon. He served his guests coffee out of the thermos. But when a group of about 30 Japanese was scheduled to visit him in his office one morning, he told Mrs. Lesok, "Forget about coffee this morning. You'd better make a lot of tea. I mean a whole bunch of tea." Mrs. Lesok not only complied with the request, but also laid in a copious supply of lemons, limes and mint. But when the guests arrived and the translator asked what they would like to drink, they answered, one by one, "Coffee, coffee, coffee." Not one asked for tea.

"The blood just drained out of my face when I saw what was happening," Mrs. Lesok remembered. "They were bound and determined that they would be very Americanized when they got here. No tea. But we found coffee and everybody eventually got coffee. Mr. Tandy kept looking at me with a big grin on his face."

Tandy was still breaking in his new office when he permitted Tina Flori, a TCU journalism student, to spend the better part of a day with him in February for an article she would write for the TCU student magazine entitled, "Twelve Hours with Tandy."

Miss Flori waited in the reception area on the top floor of One Tandy Center, from where she commanded a spectacular view from a 20-foot-high wall of glass. The surrounding walls, she noted, were of smooth, patterned oak, the floor of Italian marble. Sleek wooden coffee tables held Tandy brochures, quarterlies and annual reports. She had been told to be at Tandy's office at 10 a.m. He arrived at 10:55. Punctuality, she would see over the next 12 hours, was not his forte.

Miss Flori described her initial impression of the legendary TCU alumnus:

"Knowing he was nearly 60, had suffered a heart attack several years ago and a gall bladder operation more recently, I had expected a somewhat frail, paunchy older man with typical stooped shoulders, perhaps even a cane. But there he was, large, erect, confident and smiling slightly. His hair was dark, though streaked with gray, distinguished yet slightly unkempt. He wore a conservative blue pin-striped suit, with a large, incongruous belt buckle proudly proclaiming, 'Radio Shack.' He met me in the hall. 'So you're my shadow for the day? Well, let's get started.'"

He led her into his office that occupied a vast corner of the tower and seated himself in a high-backed brown leather chair behind a huge oak desk on which were stacked letters, reports and computer printouts. To his right was a side table with a telephone panel of blinking lights and an intercom system. On the other side of room, opposite his desk, an L-shaped overstuffed couch and chair surrounded a large Oriental coffee table.

Tandy's first appointment of the day was with two men from Baylor University seeking funds for a film they hoped to produce documenting the development of the oral history movement in the United States. Baylor had an oral history department, they informed Tandy. TCU did not. "I don't know how we missed that," Tandy chuckled. "Don't tell them about it or they'll want one."

One of the men mentioned that he believed the University of Texas had interviewed Tandy for its oral history program in business, and Tandy responded, "They don't like profanity."

The Baylor duo failed to impress Tandy. "I'm not exactly sold on the idea. You're just not telling me what I want to hear," he told them. After they left, he turned to Miss Flori and commented, "You know, there's not one university that can't find me to ask for money. I'm annoyed with universities," he added, lighting a cigar. "They haven't taken the time to understand what the political forces are doing to us. What are we selling? What is it we believe in? These are the questions they should be asking. But they don't give a damn. They're only worried about getting federal money. I've always looked up to my teachers. Today, I'm not so sure I would. They're a bunch of damn dreamers in these schools. The students in this country are ignorant about money. But the thinkers will get bad grades. It's the ones who parrot back what their teachers want to hear that get the A's."

When the phone rang on Tandy's desk, he answered it himself. He punched a button and the caller's voice became audible. "I'm Charles Fleer, Mr. Tandy, with the President's Commission on Executive Interchange."

"What was that?" Tandy boomed.

"I'm Charles Fleer, with the President's Commission on Executive Interchange." A short explanation followed and Tandy somewhat reluctantly agreed to a 2 o'clock appointment that afternoon.

Miss Flori then accompanied Tandy to the Century II Club on top of the nearby Fort Worth National Bank Building for a luncheon meeting with a group of top Radio Shack store managers from around the country. "While I double-stepped to keep pace with his long strides," she wrote, "we marched through the shopping area of Tandy Center, along the streets of downtown, into the bank building, up to the 35th floor. Along the way, he would hesitate occasionally, pausing to say a few words to workmen in the process of completing the center, to shopkeepers, to businessmen who greeted him."

When they reached the club, the group was finishing dessert. Tandy took a seat at one end of the room-long table and Miss Flori at the other end. "What do you want to eat?" he called to her. When the waiter said the soup of the day was clam chowder, Tandy said, "Fine, open two cans and bring a couple of salads." The group, she observed, "sat waiting, watching, wondering what the head honcho, whom most had never met before, would have to say to them."

Tandy then rose and cited some recent sales figures, which led to a discussion of the less than satisfactory sales performance of smoke detectors over the past year. He told of a recent experience in a Radio Shack store where a demonstration smoke detector had been set up.

"Hell, I puffed and puffed and blew smoke at that thing and it still wouldn't go off. Well, the store manager didn't have the damn thing hooked up. Then, when it finally did go off, he didn't know how to turn it off."

Tandy spoke for about an hour, Miss Flori reported, pounding the table to emphasize his points, often prodding his captive audience with questions. Then he called for questions or comments from the floor.

"We're a family," he told the group, "and the one thing I don't mind is a bitch or a complaint. It doesn't bother me, because then I know you're thinking." He seemed genuinely concerned about the problems brought to his attention, and several times directed an executive in the room to make a note of what had been said or get off a memo.

It was after 2 p.m. when Tandy headed back to his office and found Charles Fleer waiting to see him. Fleer asked if Tandy did any business with the federal government. "Fortunately," Tandy answered, "we don't do business with the government."

"You're lucky," Fleer responded. "Hell, no, I'm smart," Tandy shot back.

Fleer's mission was to interest Tandy in permitting a government executive to work for a year with Tandy Corporation or for a Tandy executive to go to Washington to work in some governmental agency. "Like the IRS or the SEC?" Tandy asked, laughing. Fleer assured him that those agencies did not participate in the program for obvious reasons. Tandy concluded the interview by subjecting Fleer to a lecture on the faults and failures of government and the shortcomings of politicians.

"Government officials say they're not going to tax the people, they're going to tax business. Well, the only thing business can do is put it back in the price of the product. Hell, there ain't no such thing as a free ride. I just don't see how we can help each other out," he told the representative of the presidential commission.

Tandy's next visitor was Anne Tandy's daughter, Anne, who is now married to John Marion, chairman of the board of Sotheby's, the New York and London auction house. "Little Anne," as she was known, (her mother, of course, was "Big Anne") had dropped by to receive a grand tour of the Tandy Center. She would inherit the vast Burk Burnett estate, valued at $430 million, after her mother's death in 1980.

Tandy excused himself while showing his stepdaughter around the premises, then invited Miss Flori to join them for drinks at Duffy's, a restaurant in the Tandy Center that had opened that day. During the course of an hour, Miss Flori noted, Tandy downed three Jack Daniels Mists to her and Anne's one Chivas Regal and water.

"When he left the table for a few minutes," she wrote, "I took the opportunity to ask Anne how Tandy keeps up the pace that he does. 'He catnaps,' she replied. 'It's amazing. He can fall asleep almost anywhere. Then when he wakes up, he's able to jump right back into the conversation, as if he had heard it all the while he slept. Ten years ago, when he was more involved in the physical work of overseeing the business, you couldn't have kept up with him. He's a dynamic man.'"

That night, Tandy was the featured speaker at the 49th Annual Distinguished Salesman's Award Banquet of the Sales and Marketing Executives of Fort Worth at a downtown hotel. Driving to the hotel with Tandy in his car, Miss Flori picked up a copy of his speech that had been lying on the seat of the car. "No sense in your reading it," Tandy said. "I probably won't stick to it much."

Arriving about 30 minutes late for the 6:15 p.m. affair, he was engulfed by a group of men who had been sweating out his arrival and was escorted to a room behind a curtain where the other head table guests were waiting. He paused to greet his friend, Brad Corbett, chairman of the board of Robintech, Inc., and majority owner of the Texas Rangers, who was the banquet's honoree. When Tandy's name was called, he sauntered casually on stage and took his place at the long head table.

Miss Flori found that Tandy had been right on the mark when he had warned her about not sticking to the text of his speech. He never once referred to the script as he ad-libbed his way through a rambling 30-minute discourse.

"A salesman," he told the audience of sales professionals, "is the guy who persuades you to do it his way. You can't make it in this world without salesmanship. Give me twice as many salesmen and we'll make this economy spin like you've never seen it spin before. I can't live with the fact that the United States government wants us all to live on an equal wage level. You don't want to be treated as equal and neither do I. You're above average—800 percent above average. There's gonna be winners and there's gonna be losers. It's that damn simple.

"The welfare state has run wild. It's destroyed almost all incentive to work. It has destroyed character and self-respect. Competition—not legislation; self-control—not governmental control, are the guideposts." On and on he went, pounding the podium, pointing with his cigar, pushing his glasses up and down, interlacing his remarks with numerous profanities for which he apologized, attacking government controls and bureaucracy, the shortcoming of higher education, the need for stronger, more self-reliant citizens.

"Students and the media have convinced themselves that this country would be better served if our oil industries were nationalized. Fortunately, the liberals can't muster the votes to nationalize our oil industry...Why are we in the United States following our old mother country, England, down the road to destruction?"

When he finished, there was a standing ovation. Several Radio Shack salespeople who had been honored that night stayed behind to shake his hand and introduce him to their wives. Tandy obliged, kissing the ladies, throwing his arms around the shoulders of the men. After the banquet, he played host to the Tandy group for a round of drinks at Duffy's, after which he and several Tandy executives repaired to Tandy's office for a few more libations. By then, Miss Flori was ready to call it a night. Tandy was still going strong. "What? You're leaving? All right, go ahead. If you can't keep up with me..."

* * *

After his 60th birthday party on May 15, it seemed to Janet Lesok that Tandy tired more easily. He often looked haggard at the end of a long day. She found herself worrying about him. It was common knowledge to those close to him that he had a problem climbing stairs and had been depending on nitroglycerin tablets for some time.

Lew Kornfeld had been concerned that day on the parking lot outside of the building on West 7th Street about asking Tandy to walk up a flight of stairs to the second floor conference room for the unveiling of the TRS-80. Luther Henderson had moved the Pier 1 directors' meetings to a site on the ground floor after Tandy had joined the Pier 1 board to keep him from having to trudge up three flights of stairs to the regular boardroom.

Bill Brown, the Boston banker, recalled having Tandy as his guest in Fenway Park to one of the games of the 1975 World Series between the Cincinnati Reds and the Boston Red Sox. "Walking up to our box, Charles had to stop twice and take a nitroglycerin tablet," Brown said. "He was constantly snapping off those nitroglycerine tablets. But he'd stay out until 5 o'clock in the morning drinking champagne, almost like a guy with a death wish."

Despite the urgings of Dr. Bobby Brown and the pleas of Anne Tandy and others for him to slow down a little, ease off on his workload, cut down on the Jack Daniels and Dom Perignon, the endless cigars and late nights, he remained adamant.

"I think Charles made a deliberate decision," Luther Henderson said. "He did not want to be slowed down. He would rather continue to live at the pace he wanted to live at."

"He never spared himself," Bill Collins added. "He drove himself. When he went to national and regional meetings, he'd conduct the meeting himself and then sit with what he called 'his boys,' and he'd fire questions and they'd ask him questions, and he'd stay up till the early hours of the morning. He'd had a pretty hard day and then he'd start the same thing the next day, and he never was in what you might call great physical condition."

Bill Vance recalled dropping in on Tandy in his office one morning and becoming distressed at his appearance. His face seemed drawn and his eyes looked as if they were sinking back in his head. They drank coffee and chatted about old times. Then Vance said to him, "Charles, you should be ashamed of yourself. You're the one who's responsible for your health. You've got a big company here. If something happened to you suddenly, the business could have some problems. Not for long, because you've got enough good people that you've educated in your ways, got them to thinking like you think, that the company will go on. But it could certainly cause some tremors as far as the stock market is concerned. You've got a lot of people depending on you. Many of them have their life's savings invested in this company, and I think you're not taking care of yourself. You haven't lost interest, have you?'"

Tandy was uncharacteristically subdued as he answered.

"I look around me," he said, "and Dad's gone, Gwen's gone, Bill's gone. And most of the people that were nearest and dearest to me, that were really my family, either are gone or have gone off to do something else because they got tired of the battle." He paused for a moment, then continued. "I ask myself, 'What in the hell is the use of getting up in the morning? It just isn't that much fun anymore. All these years, it's been the most fun thing around. I think I've accomplished about all I can accomplish or all I care to accomplish. There's only one other target that I'd like to beat, one goal I'd like to reach. But I don't think I've got that much time."

Vance recalled that he interrupted Tandy at that point and said, "Well, it's got to be the biggest one out there. It's got to be financial. So it's got to be Exxon."

And Tandy said, "Right on, there. We're over a billion now and we're growing fast. But, realistically, I know I'm not going to catch them, and I don't know if I really have any great desire to do it. Probably if I was 30 years old, I would." Then he added, "When I'm here, I don't want to go home. When I go home, I want to go to bed. When I go to bed, I don't want to get up. I've just lost the desire to live."

Vance left Tandy's office shaken. He found himself recalling the dynamic Tandy of earlier times who had once said to him, "Money doesn't mean anything after you know that you've got enough to put bread and butter on the table. You can only wear one suit at a time, one pair of shoes at a time. After that, it's the game that counts, setting your goals, setting your target and hitting that target. That's the fun of it."

Apparently the game was no longer that much fun.

*   *   *

With the announcement of the $100 million debenture offering in September, Tandy took on a back-breaking schedule. Joe A. Tilley, a vice president of Rauscher Pierce Refsnes, Inc. in Fort Worth and a longtime friend and investment advisor of Charles Tandy's, accompanied him to the underwriters' meeting in New York at which the details of the offering were hammered out.

"We had been Tandy's investment bankers since the early 1960s," Tilley pointed out. "We never managed an underwriting, never ran the books, but we were always in for 10 or 15 percent of the management fee and as an underwriter. Charles always remained loyal to us when Tandy grew into a giant company and everybody wanted his business. I went with Charles to New York to look for somebody to manage his first convertible debenture deal. That first deal was run by Blyth Eastman Dillon, E.F. Hutton and us. It was Eastman Dillon then, before they merged with Blyth. Tandy had done business with them out in California. We went to them first and they didn't even want to talk about a deal. We went to Kidder Peabody and to E.F. Hutton. The head of corporate financing at E.F. Hutton was a man named John Shad, who was later the head of the S.E.C. and ambassador to Holland, a good guy. Charles finally made the deal. Eastman Dillon ran the books and we were the co-managers with E.F. Hutton."

Blyth Eastman Dillon, E.F. Hutton and Rauscher Pierce Refsnes were also the principal underwriters for the $100 million convertible subordinated debenture offering that hit the market on October 24, 1978. The meeting to iron out the details of the offering was held in the Blyth Eastman Dillon offices in New York. Afterwards, Tandy and Tilley and several of the investment bankers repaired to the "21" Club to celebrate the closing of the deal. Tilley recalled with a special poignancy an encounter he had with Tandy at the "21" Club after the meeting.

"Charles liked to go where people knew him," Tilley explained. "That's why he liked to go to '21' when he was in New York. One of the Kriendler brothers would always sit down at the table and have a drink with him. Well, when we got there, I knew it was going to be a long evening. So I got up to call home before we started drinking. Charles had the same idea. We both finished our calls at the same time and we ran into each other coming out of the telephone booth. Charles was in a mellow mood and looked at me and said, 'Did you ever dream that a couple of country boys like us from Fort Worth would ever be at '21' in New York after pricing $100 million worth of debentures?' And tears came into his eyes."

In retrospect, Tilley concluded that Tandy's overt display of sentimentality was a signal that he had some sort of premonition of his impending death. "On that last trip, I really think Charles knew he was dying," Tilley said. "At the offices of Blyth Eastman Dillon, they had a million dollar stairway between two or three floors. And Charles was carrying his briefcase and walking up those stairs and gulping heart pills. I jerked that briefcase out of his hand and asked him, 'Why are you doing this? They've got a goddamn elevator.' And he said, 'God, I don't know.' This was maybe a month-and-a-half before he died."

Tilley remained convinced that the arduous schedule of "due diligence" meetings around the country that Tandy scheduled in late October to promote the debenture offering was a major factor in his death. The schedule took him to 11 cities in four days. "That's what really killed Charles," Tilley contended. "It nearly killed me and I was a helluva lot younger and healthier than he was."

Meetings were scheduled with analysts, underwriters, and bankers in major cities from coast to coast. Accompanying Tandy on the round of breakfasts, luncheons, dinners and cocktail parties were Charles Tindall, Phil North and Tilley.

"We flew in the Tandy jet," Tilley reported. "We went to Houston for a breakfast meeting and came back to Fort Worth and had an afternoon meeting at the Century II Club. Then we went to Philadelphia, got there at 10 or 11 o'clock at night, had a breakfast meeting the next morning and went on to New York and Boston for meetings, and came home. Three days after that, we went to Chicago and held four bank meetings and a big luncheon for 250 or 300 people. We left Chicago about 4 o'clock that afternoon and went to Toronto and had an evening meeting there. We left Toronto about 10 o'clock that night and flew to Seattle. Got there about 4 o'clock in the morning, slept till 6:30 and had a breakfast meeting at 7 a.m., followed by a luncheon meeting in San Francisco and a cocktail party late that afternoon in Phoenix. We left Phoenix at about 9 o'clock that night and went to Los Angeles, where we had a series of meetings with banks and financial people, then a luncheon, and came home. This was all within a span of four days. At each meeting, Charles made full-scale presentations, lengthy pitches. It was just murder."

The thing that kept Tandy going, Tilley said, was drinking. "He imbibed a lot of alcohol. When we got to the Ritz-Carlton Hotel in Chicago, Charles thought he had died and gone to heaven because they had 24-hour room service. He stayed up all night drinking Dom Perignon."

On the late night flight from Phoenix to Los Angeles, there was some heavy drinking, Tilley recounted. "It was cocktail party time on the company plane. Tindall got roaring drunk and so did Tandy. I was about half-drunk, but I went to sleep. I woke up to find Tindall and Charles standing nose-to-nose screaming at each other, and then Tindall took a shoe off and hit Charles with it. Tandy walked away disgustedly and said, 'Take care of the sonuvabitch.'

"We stayed at the Beverly Wilshire when we got to L.A. We had dinner there. Tindall sat there saying, 'I guess I'm fired.' I said, 'You oughta be, you dumb sonuvabitch.' The next morning, we were waiting for the limousine to take us to our first meeting of the day. Tindall was by himself, wouldn't talk to anyone, didn't know what to do. I really felt sorry for him. But Charles never woke up with a grudge against anybody. It was forgotten as soon as it happened."

Tilley remembered walking over to the crestfallen Tindall and saying to him loud enough for everyone to hear, "Tindall, you ought to start wearing crepe sole shoes, so you won't hurt anybody."

That broke the ice. Tandy started laughing and soon everyone in the group, including Tindall, was laughing.

Tilley recalled another incident that took place on the flight from Toronto to Seattle. He and Tandy were sitting together, and over a drink Tilley had begun talking about some financial difficulties he had gotten into several years before. It had taken him three years to pay off a note that had been called by his bank, he told Tandy.

"Charles got tears in his eyes," Tilley recounted, "and he said to me, 'Why didn't you tell me? I could have helped you.'

"He'd gotten real sentimental," Tilley went on. "About two weeks before he died, I was seated in his office while he was trying to drum some sense into one of his brother's children. And he told her or him, I can't remember which, 'If you ever get into any trouble in the stock market, you call Joe Tilley.' And he started crying. That wasn't like him at all. It made me nervous as hell. But I feel like he had a pre- monition."

Mary Frank recalled a brief encounter with Tandy in late October. She was doing pilot projects at that time and was managing a telephone store and a home safety devices store called Safe House in the Tandy Center. She had gone up to her office on the 16th floor of One Tandy Tower when she ran into Tandy.

"He loved to prowl," she said fondly. "He was always prowling. He said to me, 'How's your stock? How much do you have? What's your net worth?' I said, 'Charles, I haven't had time to think about it, but I still have everything. I haven't sold a single share.' And he said, 'Good.' And he got into his little private elevator and went upstairs, and a week later he was dead. He was neat..."

Tears filled her eyes.

Janet Lesok recalled the last few weeks of Tandy's life. "He was like a man possessed," she said. "It was like he was getting all of his stuff in order. He was taking care of all kinds of obligations. He was madly go- ing around taking care of business and family matters. I could see him getting tireder and tireder and tireder. But he never stopped. I'd walk into his office and his head would be bobbing tiredly. He had this little lounge and I'd tell him to go in there and lie down for a minute. He'd say, 'I don't have time.'

"The couple of times he did take my advice and go lie down, he'd fall sound asleep with his cigar in his hand, not lit. I thought he was dead. That's how sound asleep he was, that's how tired he was after so many meetings and all that kind of stuff. I think he had this premonition that time was running out and he wasn't through. What was making him so mad was that the computers had just come in and he was so excited about all this computer stuff. He was working overtime on this computer stuff, in addition to all of the other stuff. He never really got to see all that happened with the computers."

Mrs. Lesok entered the hospital to undergo gall bladder surgery five days before Tandy's death. On her last day in the office before checking into the hospital, she recalled admonishing Tandy about missing an 11 o'clock appointment.

"Mr. T, where are you supposed to be right now?" she asked him.

"I don't know, where am I supposed to be?" he answered.

"I'm going into the hospital tomorrow and you're going to have to take care of yourself and see that you get to your appointments," she said.

"If that's the case, then you're not so indispensable," he teased.

"That night he had two parties to go to," Mrs. Lesok remembered. "One was a family affair that the Duemkes (from his mother's side of the family) were giving and the other a Tandy Brands party that the George Kuhnreichs were giving. He tried to make everyone happy and go to each affair. But he was so tired, I could see the bags under his eyes. They were down to here. His coloring wasn't good. The last two times I saw him were at the Kuhnreich party that night and the next morning at the office before I went into the hospital." Kuhnreich, now deceased, was a former Wall Street securities analyst who became a vice president of corporate development for Tandy Corporation.

Ridglea Country Club was the scene of Fort Worth's stellar social event, the Assembly Ball, on Friday night, November 3, 1978. The Assembly is the vehicle for the formal debuts of young women from the city's oldest families. It was an event close to Anne Tandy's heart as the grande dame of Fort Worth society. Although not well herself (she was undergoing treatment for a cancerous condition) she had had a new designer gown created for the occasion and had reminded Charles that morning that he was expected home in ample time to don white tie and tails for the gala festivities.

Charles spent the day at the office, and at noon attended a luncheon of a small group of civic leaders at the Century II Club to discuss the effort he was currently leading to convince American Airlines to move its corporate headquarters from New York to Fort Worth. He had been conferring with American officials about leasing the airline temporary office space in the Leonards and Meacham Buildings and in the Tandy Center while permanent facilities were constructed close to the Dallas-Fort Worth International Airport.

"The luncheon was arranged in typical Tandy style," Bayard H. Friedman, then the chairman of the Fort Worth National Bank, recalled. "Charles called me up and told me I was going to be host at a luncheon so we could talk about this thing. So we met for lunch and talked about it, and just like always, he was willing to give more than anyone else, to make personal concessions, anything to help the city." Tandy was in his usual high spirits, Friedman added, "talking animatedly, waving his arms expansively, looking out over the tops of his half-moon glasses, puffing on his ever-present cigar."

After lunch, Tandy returned to his office and worked until shortly after 5 o'clock. Phil North, who was then officing on the top floor of One Tandy Tower, recalled going down to Charles Tindall's office on the floor below and finding Tandy there.

"I said to him, 'C'mon, Charlie, let's go. You've got to get home to get ready for the Assembly.' So we rode down in the elevator together. He asked, 'Are you gonna be there tonight?' and I told him, 'No, I'm not gonna go.' And he said, 'You're lucky. I'll behave. I'll see you tomorrow.' We got in our cars and left."

It was the last time North saw him alive.

The Tandys joined their close friends, Martha and Elton Hyder, for dinner at Ridglea Country Club before the ball. They then entered the sumptuously-decorated ballroom of the club in time to witness the coterie of debutantes taking their bows. Dancing followed to the music of the Lester Lanin Orchestra.

Anne Tandy left the party around midnight and was driven home by one of her maids, but Charles stayed on. He was having a ball dancing with all of the ladies. Cornelia (Corky) Friedman, Bayard Friedman's wife and a member of the Assembly, was being whirled around the floor by Tandy when he suddenly stopped dancing and said he had felt a pain in his chest. An alarmed Mrs. Friedman suggested that they sit down, but Tandy demurred.

"No," he said. He popped a nitroglycerin tablet and started dancing again. Still concerned, Corky Friedman again urged Tandy to "please sit down."

"Honey," he told her, "I'm not sitting down. When I go, it's gonna be with both guns blazing."

At midnight, as the strains of "Goodnight, Sweetheart" filled the ballroom, Tandy strode up to the bandstand, pulled a wad of $100 bills out of his pocket and arranged for Lanin to keep on playing. The Hyders left the ball around 1:30 a.m. "Charlie was still dancing when we left the club," Hyder said.

Joyce Cantey, whose husband, Emory Cantey, now deceased, was then a partner in Fort Worth's largest law firm, recalled dancing with Tandy just before she and Cantey left the club shortly before midnight because of an after-the-ball party they were giving at their home on Crestline Drive next door to the Elton Hyders.

"He was in high spirits," she said. "He told me he'd be dropping by later. There must have been about 150 people at our house, when along about 2 o'clock or thereabouts, all of a sudden the front door opened and there was Charles. As soon as he came in, we headed straight for the backgammon table, as was our usual custom. We played backgammon all the time. Charles loved to play and was an excellent player. When he was in New York, he played at Doubles, a backgammon club on Park Avenue near the Regency Hotel where he liked to stay.

"Charles was a night person, as am I, and we often played backgammon all night," Mrs. Cantey related. "We had an understanding, however. When we heard the morning paper hit the front door, that was when we quit. On that last occasion, we played until the paper boy arrived at 6:30 in the morning. I walked with Charles to his car. I remember being a little concerned about his driving home, but it was already daylight and he seemed to be fine even though he had been drinking quite a bit. He was drinking bourbon. He always switched to bourbon after champagne. He drank his usual Dom Perignon at the ball. And, of course, he smoked cigars all the while we played.

"I could never beat Charles at backgammon. He was a better player than I am. But I beat him that night for the first and last time. I won $20 from him and I could hardly wait to tell Anne that I had finally beaten Charles at backgammon. I found a $20 bill on the table beside the backgammon board later that morning. I still have the bill. I never framed it or anything, but I've kept it as a memory of Charles. He was a warm, fun man who worked hard and played hard."

Tandy left the Cantey residence at 6:30 a.m. and drove home to the big house in Westover Hills and went to bed in his bedroom adjoining Anne's. At around 10:30 a.m., a maid looked in on him and saw that he was sleeping peacefully.

He never woke up.

At 4 o'clock on Saturday afternoon, November 4, 1978, Martha and Elton Hyder arrived at the Tandy residence to meet Charles and Anne and several other couples for cocktails.

"When we got over there," Hyder said, "a maid opened the door and told us, 'Mr. Tandy died.' I went into his bedroom. He was in bed. I put my arms around him. I wanted to see if he was...he was still warm. I kissed him on the forehead and I said, 'Goodbye, Charlie.'"

Phil North was at his desk in the study of his home in the Ridglea area of west Fort Worth when the phone rang at about 4 p.m. "It was Ruth Carter Johnson's voice," he recalled. "She said, 'Phil?' I said, 'Yes.' She said, 'Charles is dead.' She was crying." Ruth Carter Johnson, the daughter of legendary *Fort Worth Star-Telegram* publisher, Amon G. Carter, Sr., had been married to J. Lee Johnson, III, of Fort Worth. She later married John R. Stevenson of Washington, D.C.

A stunned North drove immediately to the Tandy residence in nearby Westover Hills, where he found Mrs. Johnson, Alice Armer, and Anne Tandy. "They were sitting there crying," he said. "I went in to see Charles. He was very peaceful. He was in his bedroom on the bed, lying on his back, in his pajamas. He had one arm flung back, the right arm, in his normal sleeping position. There was nothing special in his expression, no sign of distress."

Charles David Tandy was dead at the age of 60.

The roller-coaster ride was over.

Chapter 29
A Giant is Laid to Rest

The news of Charles Tandy's death shocked Fort Worth and reverberated nationwide and abroad. Expressions of sympathy poured in from all over the world. Mayor Hugh Parmer of Fort Worth ordered city flags be flown at half-staff beginning Sunday morning, November 5, until after the funeral services at 4 o'clock Monday afternoon. Tandy's death was the lead story on the front pages of newspapers across the country on Sunday morning. Editorial writers and columnists added their paeans of praise.

Under the headline, "A Giant Walked Among Us," the *Star-Telegram* declared in its lead editorial on Monday morning, November 6:

"It is rare when a giant walks among us.

"Charles Tandy was a giant among men.

"His is a story of the American dream, of a man rising as high as his desire and his ability and his enterprise will take him.

"Tandy wanted to succeed and he worked long and hard to achieve success. It was a dizzy, roller-coaster trip that paid off in a billion dollar business.

"Tandy took his beloved Fort Worth along for the ride. He was the city's No. 1 booster. His global enterprises were headquartered here, providing thousands of jobs locally and spreading the name of Fort Worth throughout the world.

"A monument to Tandy's genius is the eight-block Tandy Center still in stages of construction in downtown Fort Worth. Tandy typically overcame seemingly impossible odds, refusing to give up in the face of adversity, to get the project off the ground.

"Many lesser men from the start doubted the possibility of the Tandy Center and eventually stood by to watch the conversion of a decaying section into an exciting, glittering center of business and commerce.

"Tandy's enthusiasm extended to all things that have a potential impact on the quality of life in Fort Worth, whether it be giving a quarter of a million dollars to TCU or supporting the arts.

"Above all else, Tandy was a salesman, and more often than not he was 'selling' his city.

"A friend called him one of the greatest one-on-one conversationalists he had ever met, a man who 'could convince anyone of anything...'

"He was 'the personification of capitalism.' If capitalism means that a man can rise as high as his dream will take him, then Charles David Tandy was a capitalist.

"To Fort Worth he was more. He was a friend.

"He was a giant who walked among us.

"That is the nature of our loss."

Columnist Bob Ray Sanders wrote in the *Fort Worth Observer*, "The Tandy towers are not important to me, although I can appreciate them. I'm most proud of Tandy for his contribution to the arts in Fort Worth. The arts organizations thrived during the past few years largely because of Tandy. I recall that when Jack Butler was heading the Arts Council drive and suddenly found that drive was $40,000 under goal, he called Europe. Charles Tandy was in Europe, you see, and in a three or four-minute transatlantic telephone conversation, the Arts Council made its goal.

"So, when I visit the Fort Worth Art Museum or see a ballet or hear the Texas Boys Choir or attend the Van Cliburn Piano Competition or watch the Fort Worth Symphony or hear an opera, I will think of Charles Tandy. Those will be living memorials to him. As the Christmas season approaches, the Tandy Center will burn four giant candles for the man who built the place and they will remind us of his death. But in the museums and concert halls, I will view the arts at their best and be reminded, not of Tandy's death, but of Charles Tandy's life."

The Daily Skiff, student newspaper at Texas Christian University, said in an editorial, "With his passing, Charles Tandy left behind—among other things—a legacy of support and affection for TCU. Charles Tandy never forgot his origins. After serving in World War II, he returned to his family's 'little country business'—and built it into the billion dollar Tandy Corporation. He encouraged businesses to open branches in his home of Fort Worth and designed the eight-block Tandy Center to stimulate new growth in the downtown area.

"A graduate of TCU's Class of 1940, Tandy remembered his alma mater with characteristic generosity. He devoted his time and talents to serving as a member on the Board of Trustees, but his financial contributions to the University were more widely known. The 'Tandy Challenge,' his offer to match dollar for dollar any pledges over the previous year's total, resulted in nearly $500,000 in funds for the University. TCU loses a benefactor and a friend in Charles Tandy. His influence continues to be felt, however, and we hope that the good he did will live after him."

Tandy employees and their dependents continue to benefit from the Tandy Corporation Educational Scholarship in the TCU School of Business which Charles Tandy established in 1977.

Irwin Lainoff wrote in the Business section of the *New York Post*:

"Charles Tandy used to swing through Wall Street with a warmth that set him apart from most businessmen, who like to fashion themselves in granite. He'd hold court with style, jaunty cigar-holder aloft, and tempt his audience with an outpouring of statistics that he had on his fingertips on how many Radio Shacks he was opening this year and on store sales, margins and advertising outlays. Late at night, though, the man from Texas would sit quietly and explain how Tandy Corporation had filled the vacuum as a retailer of consumer electronic products that had been left by such majors as RCA and General Electric when those companies went the distributor route, rather than through direct retail. He'd draw alternative financial maneuvers for you, some of it so intricate that when he sprung one on Wall Street, the investment community typically was stunned, since many felt his balance sheet was already too leveraged. Before long, you'd realize that here was one of the true marketing giants of our age."

One of the more moving tributes was written by Lew Kornfeld for a memorial issue of *Intercom*, the Radio Shack employee magazine:

"Our gifted and beloved chairman passed away in his sleep on Saturday, November 4, 1978, at age 60. In those six decades he lived 120 years in comparison to ordinary mortals. He thought more thoughts, dreamed more dreams, planned and executed more plans, talked more words to more people, and affected more lives than anyone you and I will ever meet.

"In addition to being a man of extraordinary natural talent, Mr. Tandy was able to convert his talent into success—success not only for himself but for the many thousands who worked with him, who invested in his enterprises, who sold him goods or services. That others shared his success was by design, not by coincidence. It will sound a bit incredible when I say that he wanted his associates to succeed even more than many of them were willing to, meaning simply that some perfectly capable people lacked the drive and ambition to fully capitalize on the golden opportunities Mr. Tandy offered them. Hard to believe? Believe it!

"The chairman was a man whose leadership qualities absolutely dwarf those of any leader, owner or boss I've ever met. He stood tall in any group of distinguished people, radiating intelligence, class, good will, humor. He was always himself. He was always approachable in person or by telephone, a facet of his personality that astounded people who imagine persons of high rank as being unavailable, distant, secluded, too 'important' to make time for strangers or subordinates. He drove his own car. He answered his own phone. He smoked 30 cent cigars. He served coffee from a thermos jug on his desk (and the cups were plastic).

"All but the most recent of our employees have seen Mr. Tandy, so the above comments are mostly directed at our newer folks who now will never have the chance. He believed that everyone's duty was to teach...to teach someone down the line how to be a better business person, how to build an estate, how to communicate and follow up, how to contribute to the corporation and to the community.

"What he expected from us at this particular moment in time—the Christmas selling season—was to break every record in the book. If we don't, it won't be for lack of having been taught how. If we do, it will be a most fitting parting gift to this formidable (but gentle), excellent, eloquent man who considered each of us as 'one of the family' and expected nothing but an honest effort in return."

* * *

On a cold, gray day, under threatening skies from which rain fell intermittently, more than 1,000 mourners overflowed St. Andrews Episcopal Church in downtown Fort Worth on November 6 for the funeral services. The doors to the stately old stone church were opened at 2:30. By the time the muted chimes in the bell tower had rung half past three, the pews of the main cathedral were filled and the overflow was being directed to the chapel and the parish house nearby. Many latecomers were turned away.

Describing the scene in the *Fort Worth News-Tribune*, Ted Stafford wrote:

"The sexton in a black cassock entered the altar area to light the candles. The glow of the burning tapers highlighted the high relief marble carving of 'The Last Supper' that forms the reredos of the Bianco Charra altar. The silence was broken by the full-throated organ. 'A Mighty Fortress' rang against the counterpoint of a Bach fugue. As the volume dropped, the motorcycles of the police escort signaled arrival of the funeral cortege. The pallbearers walked down the north aisle. The family entered by the south door.

"The organ rose to a triumphant pitch and Handel's 'I Know that My Redeemer Liveth' filled the church, echoing from the vaulted roof above the nave. The music ended and there was a brief poignant silence. From the back of the church, the voice of Rev. Louis F. Martin, rector emeritus of St. Andrew's, intoned, 'I am the resurrection and the life...' as he began the traditional Episcopal service of The Order for the Dead. The priest, a friend of the family for many years, had married Charles Tandy and Anne Burnett nine years ago.

"He preceded the solid African mahogany casket with a blanket of 1,000 dark red roses to its place near the chancel. The remainder of the service which followed from the Book of Common Prayer was identical with those that had preceded it for more than 400 years. It was the same Anglican service that had been used for the burial of kings and commoners, princes and paupers since the Reformation. There was no eulogy, and the only mention of the deceased's name was in the prayer. A small choir sang two hymns."

They were "Abide With Me" and "The Old Rugged Cross," hymns Tandy had learned from his mother as a little boy attending Sunday School at the Broadway Baptist Church.

Hundreds of mourners followed the long funeral procession to Greenwood Cemetery, where the casket was borne for entombment in the Tandy family mausoleum by the pallbearers—Perry R. Bass, Dr. Bobby Brown, Coleman Burke, W. W. (Bill) Collins, Robert R. (Bob) Lowdon, Paul W. Mason, Phil R. North, George R. (Bill) Nugent, J. Roby Penn, and John A. Wilson.

Tandy offices closed at 2 p.m. that day to enable employees to attend the services.

* * *

Although shock and grief gripped the entire company as word of Tandy's death was received, there was no panic. "There was no feeling among the employees that the ship was going to sink because Charles was gone," Rachel Barber recalled. "He had coached a number of people to be ready."

Bernie Appel was on his way back from a buying trip to the Orient when he received the news that Tandy died. "I got in from the Orient on Friday and I was going to spend Saturday and part of Sunday in San Francisco to sort of wind down before I came home Sunday late in the day," he remembered. "Carrie Nemser knew where I was going to be and she reached me on Saturday and told me what had happened. I was able to get a Sunday morning flight out and was able to get here in time for a religious ceremony on Sunday.

"That night, I was elected vice president of the synagogue, which was located directly across the street from the Robertson-Mueller-Harper Funeral Home on 8th Avenue where Charles was lying in state. It was a rainy night, really a downpour. I remember during the course of the evening, I went over to the funeral home with some friends, Leon Brachman and Lou Barnett, people who had known Charles well. And we paid our respects.

"I knew the people at Robertson-Mueller-Harper very well. I told them that I just wanted to sit beside Charles for a little while, and they forgot that I was there. And I sat in that room from a quarter of 10 until they chased me out after midnight. Just me alone with the casket. I got everything off my chest...every time he ever yelled at me....He died too young. My objection to his death, and I told him so, I don't know if he heard me, was that he didn't teach enough people enough things. He went out too young.

"Yet we picked up right where he would've. And I think today he'd be very proud of the accomplishments. I'm not sure we did everything the way he would have wanted it. I'm not sure he would have done exactly what we did. But we did do it by the numbers and I think he'd be proud of us. He had built a responsible team of people that could take over. But that was the end of Charles Tandy from our point of view....

"But for years afterwards, whenever my phone rang on a Saturday afternoon or whenever the executive elevator came up on a Saturday and the door opened, I expected Charles Tandy to be on the other end of the line or walk out of the elevator."

Janet Lesok was still in the hospital recovering from her gall bladder surgery when Tandy died. "When I got out of the hospital," she recalled, "I spent at least two months, morning till night, answering all of the thousands of people who had sent flowers, donations in his name to various charities. When I went back to the office after three weeks in the hospital, they had taken everything out of the office, out of his desk, and they had lined it up on tables. They were going to take everything to the Tandy Foundation office. And I saw all those P&L books of his, and I just went to pieces. You see, I hadn't had a chance to get used to this. I hadn't been able to go the funeral. I hadn't had time to learn to deal with it.

"He used to smoke Antony and Cleopatra panatelas. I think, maybe, they cost 25 cents then. When they asked me what I wanted as a keepsake from his office, I chose his cigar box. It's rosewood with a leather top, with his initials tooled into it." The cigar box sits on a desk in the den of Mrs. Lesok's home in southwest Fort Worth. When she opened the box, there was still a handful of cigars inside.

At the time of his death, Tandy's estate was estimated at more than $50 million. But an inventory, appraisement and list of claims filed in the Tarrant County Probate Court in Fort Worth on August 14, 1979 placed a value on the estate of approximately $28.4 million, virtually all of it in Tandy Corporation stock. He personally owned $26.6 million in Tandy stock; a 4.4 percent interest in leases in the Penland Almeda-Genoa Shopping Center in Harris County, Texas, valued at $4,597; a one-sixth interest in half a tract of land in Aransas County, Texas, valued at $22,533, and furniture and furnishings valued at $861. Community property, in which his wife owned a half interest, included Tandy stock valued at $2.7 million; Tandy Brands subordinated debentures valued at $151,056; bank accounts and undeposited checks amounting to $166,997, and miscellaneous personal effects of $72,000.

Anne Tandy, who was named her husband's sole beneficiary, formed the Anne Burnett and Charles D. Tandy Foundation in late 1978 to receive the bulk of his estate. "I've made this gift because of my love and respect for the memory of Charles Tandy and in the belief he intended me to use his legacy for the benefit of others, particularly those who live in Fort Worth," she said in announcing the creation of the foundation.

The settlement of the estate, however, was marred by a bitter court battle between the foundation and Gwen Tandy's eight grandchildren over the disposition of $13.2 million in cash that Charles Tandy had accumulated in two employee savings plans. In 1966, Tandy had established a Charles D. Tandy Grandchildren's Trust at the Fort Worth National Bank to receive the proceeds from the two savings plans in the event of his death. But attorneys for the foundation contended, in a suit filed in state district court in Fort Worth on January 15, 1979, that since Tandy had died "without leaving grandchildren, only stepgrandchildren," there were no true heirs and that the cash in the savings plans should flow with the rest of Tandy's estate to Anne Tandy and from her to the foundation.

On January 22, 1979, Gwen Tandy's two children from her first marriage, Connie Upchurch and Sherwood Johnston, Jr., filed a counter suit in U.S. district court in Fort Worth on behalf of their children, claiming that they were the "grandchildren" Tandy had in mind when he specified that his interest in the employee savings plans should go to the Charles D. Tandy Grandchildren's Trust. Their suit maintained that Tandy regarded his eight stepgrandchildren "as his grandchildren and had treated them as such."

This claim was backed up by Billy R. Roland, the longtime Tandy employee who had handled Tandy's personal affairs. Roland stated in an affidavit that Tandy wanted the funds in the savings plans to go to Connie Upchurch's four children, Kenneth, Jesse, Matthew and Gwendolyn Upchurch, and Sherwood Johnston, Jr.'s four children, Benjamin, Jennifer, Stephanie and Sherwood Johnston III.

"Charles Tandy told me he wanted to leave his benefits to the 'grandchildren's trusts,'" Roland's affidavit said. "I asked, 'Charles, you are referring to those trusts at the Fort Worth National Bank, aren't you?' Charles replied, 'Yes.' I then asked, 'Charles, don't you think we should use the proper name of those trusts?' And he said, 'Just do it the way I said.'"

The acrimonious dispute was finally settled out of court on December 15, 1979. In approving the terms of the settlement, U.S. District Judge

Eldon B. Mahon of Fort Worth ruled that Tandy's designation of his "grandchildren" as his beneficiaries was "ambiguous" and that, therefore, "an equal division should be made to the trusts for the grandchildren of Gwen (Tandy's first wife) as a group, and to a trust for the grandchild of Anne (Tandy's second wife)."

Over the years the trustees of the Anne Burnett and Charles Tandy Foundation have focused its resources primarily on the Fort Worth area in support of nonprofit organizations in the fields of education, health, community affairs, human services, and the arts and humanities. By the end of 1990, the foundation's corpus stood at more than $178 million. That year the foundation made 69 grants totaling $6.5 million, including a gift of $1,250,000 to the Amon Carter Museum in Fort Worth as part of a $10 million communitywide effort to purchase the Thomas Eakins painting, "The Swimming Hole," and keep it on permanent public view in Fort Worth.

Anne Tandy died of cancer on January 1, 1980, at the age of 74. She is survived by her daughter, Anne Windfohr Marion, and a granddaughter, Windie Phillips.

* * *

Shortly after Charles Tandy's death, Billy Roland received a telephone call at his office on a Saturday morning. "It was Little Anne, Anne Tandy's daughter," he said, "asking me to come out to the mansion, that her mother wanted to see me. I told her I was going to the TCU football game that afternoon, but she asked me to come out anyway. When I got there, Big Anne was crying. She told me to go into Charles' bedroom and take any of his clothes that I wanted. I was in a big hurry because my wife was waiting for me to take her to the football game, but I tried on a bunch of clothes. Charles had lost some weight and the pants were tight on a lot of the suits, but I took some suits, a couple of topcoats, and some raincoats. There were racks and racks of ties, but Charles liked gaudy ties. So I didn't take any."

* * *

On November 30, 1978, a memorial fund to receive tax-deductible donations to finance a statue honoring Charles D. Tandy was established by the unanimous vote of the Fort Worth City Council. Harry Tennison, co-chairman of the board of trustees for the memorial fund, appeared before the council to present the plans for the memorial, noting that Mrs. Tandy had requested that it be in the form of a sculpture.

"Charles Tandy was a legend in his own time," Tennison told the council members. "His accomplishments have improved and will continue to improve and enrich the quality of life for this community."

The 9-foot tall bronze statue of Charles Tandy standing atop a 5-foot pedestal was unveiled in ceremonies held in a small park just north of the Tarrant County Courthouse on Wednesday morning, April 15, 1981.

The sculptor, Jim Reno, memorialized Tandy in a typical pose, feet squarely planted, his left hand in his pants pocket and his right hand holding a cigar.

That's how he stands today, looking out with insouciant grace over the city he helped build and in the shadow of the Tandy Center, his real monument. There's the hint of a smile on his face, and standing there looking up at him, you can almost hear him saying:

"Stick with me and I'll make you rich..."

Chapter 30
A Vision, a Dream

On the tenth anniversary of Charles Tandy's death, Tandy Corporation broke ground for a new seven-story Technology Center in downtown Fort Worth. Afterwards, at a civic luncheon attended by a number of Tandy's former associates, John Roach reminisced about his mentor.

"For those who knew Charles Tandy, he can easily be characterized as one of the most unforgettable characters they ever met," Roach told the group. "For those who didn't know him, I can only say you missed one of the most vibrant minds and charismatic personalities that you ever could have met. A man who had no regard for time—his or yours. A man who never had a short meeting. It took four hours of pain and endurance to get a positive answer from him and eight hours of teaching and pain to get a negative answer.

"Stories could be told for hours. While some, on the surface, might not sound too complimentary, they would not be meant in a disparaging way. He had a unique way of making people wonder whether or not they had an intelligence quotient and, at the same time, increase their admiration for him.

"Charles was a financial innovator. The market didn't appreciate his early stock repurchase programs because the market analysts— sometimes referred to by him as those 'dumb bastards'—didn't understand share repurchase. Charles did.

"One of his great attributes was that he was a teacher. He spent long hours explaining concepts. In fact, he explained the concept of gross margin in identical four-hour presentations for 24 consecutive quarters to me when I was leading our data processing activities. The monthly P&L statement was the Bible and many were faced with facts and a learning experience regarding the P&L on a monthly basis.

"Those who knew him, know that the stories about him could go on into the wee hours of the morning, just as he always loved to do. As memories dim, his vision, his dream lives on."

Roach was named board chairman of Tandy Corporation on June 30, 1982, following the retirement of Phil R. North. He had been elected chief executive officer on July 1, 1981, after being named a director in June, 1980, and president and chief operating officer in October, 1980.

Phil North, Charles Tandy's boyhood friend, shepherded the company through the period immediately after Charles' death. At his first annual meeting as chairman and chief executive officer on November 9, 1978, North promised to carry on the business in the same manner it had been operated under Tandy's aegis.

Wall Street had to be convinced.

Tandy stock dropped 2½ points on the first day of trading after Tandy's death, and fell from 25 to a low of 18 over the next six months, indicating investors' concerns over the ability of the management team to keep the company going and growing. Their doubts began to fade, however, in the face of increased earnings that resulted primarily from burgeoning TRS-80 microcomputer sales. Tandy stock began a rebound that found it nearly doubling by the spring of 1980 and continuing to rise.

In his closing remarks at the 1981 annual meeting, North told the assemblage of shareholders:

"If I may, I'd like to take a few moments to reminisce. I don't know how many of you were here on the second Thursday of November three years ago when, to our mutual surprise, I first chaired this meeting. Charles had just died and there was a suspicion that it had been a one-man company.

"But it was not a one-man company. It was a team of talented, dedicated people who continued doing the superlative job they'd always done under his leadership and training. And in the 12 months just ended, sales went up 61 percent. In the last year, John Roach has become chief executive officer. I regard him as a close friend and I'm first in his corner in admiration. We have a directors' meeting immediately following this meeting, and I'm going to ask the board, as of June 30, 1982, to gracefully retire me. And then we'll watch this company proceed onward and upward."

It was a prescient forecast.

Were Charles Tandy to return today, he would find that the company he built has grown to match his vision and eclipse his dream.

Tandy Corporation is the world's largest consumer electronics and personal computer retailer, operating over 7,200 stores and dealer/ franchise outlets, with total 1992 sales of nearly $5 billion and 41,000 employees worldwide. Its Radio Shack chain, with 6,700 company-owned and dealer/franchise stores nationwide, has become the premier marketer of the products of technology, with one out of every three households in the United States buying Radio Shack products every year.

More than 50 percent of the electronics sold in Radio Shack stores are produced in Tandy manufacturing plants in the United States, China, Japan, Taiwan, and South Korea. The plants are supported by research and development teams in Fort Worth and at other locations around the world.

Distribution centers located in Fort Worth; Charleston, South Carolina; Hagerstown, Maryland; Boston, Massachusetts; Columbus, Ohio; and Garden Grove and Woodland, California, ship more than one million cartons per month—more than 38,000 per day—to keep the shelves of the Radio Shack outlets across the country fully stocked.

In a departure from tradition, Tandy Corporation entered the name brand appliance and electronics retailing market in 1985 with the acquisition of the McDuff and VideoConcepts chains. Its Name Brand retailing distribution system has grown to include a chain of boutiques called The Edge in Electronics and a superstore chain known as Computer City.

In the fall of 1992, Tandy unveiled a new concept in electronics and computer retailing with the opening of its first two Incredible Universe "super-superstore" outlets in Arlington, Texas, between Dallas and Fort Worth, and in Wilsonville, Oregon, a suburb of Portland.

In an article about the Incredible Universe, Adam Bryant wrote in *The New York Times* on April 24, 1992, "The two prototype Incredible Universe stores scheduled to open this fall boast specifications that almost match their hyperbolic name: 160,000 square feet; 300 employees; 300 choices of television sets and a vast array of other electronics and appliances, including many non-Radio Shack/Tandy brands; a child-care room, and a restaurant. With plenty of displays to demonstrate products, Tandy wants to create the atmosphere of an adult toy store worthy of a special trip from as far away as 40 miles."

John Roach said he envisioned Radio Shack as the "ultimate convenience store" and the Incredible Universe as the "ultimate destination store."

Tandy Corporation is the nation's largest computer retailer. Its computer operations include two wholly-owned subsidiaries, GRiD Systems and Victor Technologies. GRiD manufactures and markets portable microcomputers chiefly to large corporations and government agencies, while Victor markets desktop and laptop microcomputers through a network of 2,700 dealers and distributors in Europe.

Other Tandy subsidiaries include Memtek Products, makers of audio and video consumer products; O'Sullivan Industries, the largest manufacturer of electronic racks, cabinets and desks; Lika Corporation, manufacturer of multi-layer printed circuit boards; and A&A International, which imports parts and products from overseas sources for Radio Shack, Memtek, GRiD, the Tandy Name Brand Group, and Tandy Electronics Manufacturing. Tandy operates 27 manufacturing plants in the United States and abroad that produce consumer electronics and personal computers for the company's far-flung retail distribution system.

"We have the dream, the organization, and the resources to accept the challenge," Charles Tandy once said. "The opportunities are everywhere."

His dream lives on.

Name Index